THE REGULATION OF NUCLEAR TRADE

NON-PROLIFERATION – SUPPLY – SAFETY

VOLUME II

NATIONAL REGULATIONS

872-8723
1-800-USA Trade
Bureau of Census

Nuclear Legislation Series

NUCLEAR ENERGY AGENCY
ORGANISATION FOR ECONOMIC CO-OPERATION AND DEVELOPMENT

Pursuant to article 1 of the Convention signed in Paris on 14th December, 1960, and which came into force on 30th September, 1961, the Organisation for Economic Co-operation and Development (OECD) shall promote policies designed:

- to achieve the highest sustainable economic growth and employment and a rising standard of living in Member countries, while maintaining financial stability, and thus to contribute to the development of the world economy;
- to contribute to sound economic expansion in Member as well as non-member countries in the process of economic development; and
- to contribute to the expansion of world trade on a multilateral, non-discriminatory basis in accordance with international obligations.

The original Member countries of the OECD are Austria, Belgium, Canada, Denmark, France, the Federal Republic of Germany, Greece, Iceland, Ireland, Italy, Luxembourg, the Netherlands, Norway, Portugal, Spain, Sweden, Switzerland, Turkey, the United Kingdom and the United States. The following countries became Members subsequently through accession at the dates indicated hereafter: Japan (28th April, 1964), Finland (28th January, 1969), Australia (7th June, 1971) and New Zealand (29th May, 1973).

The Socialist Federal Republic of Yugoslavia takes part in some of the work of the OECD (agreement of 28th October, 1961).

The OECD Nuclear Energy Agency (NEA) was established in 1957 under the name of the OEEC European Nuclear Energy Agency. It received its present designation on 20th April, 1972, when Japan became its first non-European full Member. NEA membership today consists of all European Member countries of OECD as well as Australia, Canada, Japan and the United States. The commission of the European Communities takes part in the work of the Agency.

The primary objective of NEA is to promote co-operation between the governments of its participating countries in furthering the development of nuclear power as a safe, environmentally acceptable and economic energy source.

This is achieved by:

- *encouraging harmonisation of national, regulatory policies and practices, with particular reference to the safety of nuclear installations, protection of man against ionising radiation and preservation of the environment, radioactive waste management, and nuclear third party liability and insurance;*
- *assessing the contribution of nuclear power to the overall energy supply by keeping under review the technical and economic aspects of nuclear power growth and forecasting demand and supply for the different phases of the nuclear fuel cycle;*
- *developing exchanges of scientific and technical information particularly through participation in common services;*
- *setting up international research and development programmes and joint undertakings.*

In these and related tasks, NEA works in close collaboration with the International Atomic Energy Agency in Vienna, with which it has concluded a Co-operation Agreement, as well as with other international organisations in the nuclear field.

Publié en français sous le titre:

RÉGLEMENTATION
DU COMMERCE NUCLÉAIRE

VOLUME II
RÉGLEMENTATIONS NATIONALES

ANALYSIS OF NUCLEAR LEGISLATION

Volume I of this study deals with the international aspects of the regulation of nuclear trade, while Volume II deals with national legislation.

This study is part of a series of analytical studies of the major aspects of nuclear energy legislation in force in OECD Member countries. The studies published to date are :

— Regulations Governing Nuclear Installations and Radiation Protection (published in 1972) ;

— Nuclear Third Party Liability (first published in 1967 and published in a new edition in 1976) ;

— Regulations Governing the Transport of Radioactive Materials (published in 1980) ;

— Regulatory and Institutional Framework for Nuclear Activities (Volume I published in 1983 ; Volume II published in 1984). This study brings up to date and expands a study published in 1969.

Also, a Description of Licensing Systems and Inspection of Nuclear Installations in OECD countries was published in 1986.

This study was prepared on the basis of information obtained by the Secretariat up to March 1988. Neither the Secretariat nor the national authorities assume liability therefor.

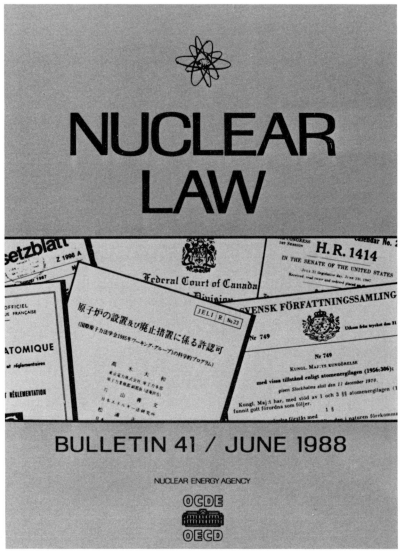

INTRODUCTORY NOTE

This volume of the study on the regulation of nuclear trade deals with the national legislation of OECD countries with significant nuclear programmes and regulations in that field and, in essence, covers two aspects. The first concerns political and administrative controls over imports and exports of "sensitive" products, namely fissile materials and large nuclear equipment as well as technology transfers. In most cases, this description of the provisions applicable is completed with the list of nuclear items whose export is restricted. The second aspect concerns the licensing system governing trade in as well as the import and export of nuclear material to protect users and the public against the hazards created by its radioactive properties.

The reader will also find information on regulations concerning physical protection, industrial property and transport, as well as on multilateral and bilateral agreements involving nuclear trade. To facilitate information retrieval, the descriptions of national legislation follow a plan which is as uniform as possible, given the differences in the legal systems concerned and the material readily available.

The NEA Secretariat takes this opportunity to thank all those in the Member countries whose valuable assistance has helped it to achieve this work.

LIST OF COUNTRIES

AUSTRALIA

TABLE OF CONTENTS

AUSTRALIA

I. INTRODUCTION

The regulation of nuclear trade in Australia cannot be analysed without giving a brief description of the constitutional structure of that country. Australia is governed under a federal system. The Constitution of each of the six States[1] contains general power authorising the Parliament of the State to make laws for the peace, order and good government of the State. The federal Constitution gives power to the federal Parliament to legislate with respect to specified topics (Constitution, e.g. Sections 51, 52) and provides for primacy of federal law over inconsistent State law (Constitution, Section 109). Section 122 of the Constitution gives the federal parliament plenary power to legislate for Australia's six external Territories (Norfolk Island, Australian Antarctic Territory, Ashmore and Cartier Islands, Heard Island and McDonald Islands, the Cocos (Keeling) Islands and Christmas Island) and two internal Territories (the Australian Capital Territory and the Northern Territory). Of the Territories, the Northern Territory is now largely responsible for its own administration, although the federal Parliament retains its plenary powers under Section 122 of the Constitution. The power of the federal Government to control nuclear trade is based primarily on its power to legislate with respect to inter-State and overseas trade and commerce [Constitution, Section 51(i)]; and external affairs [Constitution, Section 51(xxix)]. But other available powers can be, and have been, relied on [e.g. the corporations power in Section 51(xx)].

While Australia has uranium mines and uranium production projects it has on the other hand no nuclear power plants or a developed nuclear industry; since there is no domestic demand for uranium, its production is therefore export-oriented.

The Environment Protection (Nuclear Codes) Act 1978 makes provision for and in relation to the establishment of codes of practice with respect to nuclear activities and other purposes. The development of codes of practice is a consultative process involving the Commonwealth, States and Northern Territory. The Act provides for a public participation phase in the development or revision of codes.

Australia's uranium policy flows from decisions taken by the Government in 1983 following an extensive review of the uranium industry and later by the Government's consideration of the recommendations of the Australian Science and Technology Council (ASTEC) Inquiry into Australia's role in the nuclear fuel cycle. ASTEC was asked by the Prime Minister to undertake this inquiry examining in particular:

- Australia's nuclear safeguards arrangements, giving particular attention to the effectiveness of the bilateral and multilateral agreements and to the scope for strengthening these agreements;
- the opportunities for Australia through the conditions of its involvement in the nuclear fuel cycle to further advance the cause of nuclear non-proliferation having regard to the policies and practices of recipient countries; and
- the adequacy of existing technology for the handling and disposal of waste products by consuming countries, and the ways in which Australia can further contribute to the development of safe disposal methods.

The ASTEC report was received by the Government in May 1984 and most of its recommendations were accepted. In particular, the Government decided that the mining and export of uranium would continue subject to strict safeguards conditions, but only from the Nabarlek, Ranger and Olympic Dam (Roxby Downs) mines. In addition, the Government decided against the development of further stages of the nuclear fuel cycle in Australia resulting in all uranium production being for export only (extracts of the recommendations and the Prime Minister's response of particular reference to nuclear trade are reproduced in *Annex I*).

In addition the Government undertook a review of the Atomic Energy Act 1953 and as a result, new legislation reflecting the Government's policy on nuclear activities has been enacted[2]. This legislation replaced the Australian Atomic Energy Commission (AAEC) with a new Organisation, the Australian Nuclear Science and Technology Organisation (ANSTO), and repeals certain repressive provisions of the Atomic Energy Act 1953 no longer relevant to nuclear activities in Australia, which were drafted when uranium was considered to be a scarce resource of major strategic importance, possibly to be exploited for defence purposes. In addition, other new legislation was passed establishing controls over the possession and transport of nuclear material in Australia and providing a legislative basis for the operations of the Australian Safeguards Office[3].

Three codes of practice are currently in operation (two are relevant to the mining and milling of nuclear material). The Code of Practice on Radiation Protection in the Mining and Milling of Radioactive Ores 1980 and the Code of Practice on the Management of Radioactive Wastes from the Mining and Milling of Radioactive Ores 1982 are applied by the States and the Northern Territory under their respective mining and health legislation.

Laws and regulations which cover nuclear trade are distinguished by two aspects: control and safety. Control is exercised by the Commonwealth through specific nuclear legislation and through general trade legislation regulating imports and exports, namely the *Customs (Prohibited Imports) Regulations as at 31st July 1986* and the *Customs (Prohibited Exports) Regulations as at 31st*

July 1986, both made under the Customs Act 1901. Each of the States and the Northern Territory has enacted legislation relating to safety (radiation protection) aspects and adopted specific regulations under that legislation.

The above laws and regulations will be discussed below when describing the regulation of nuclear trade in Australia, beginning with Government control, its responsibilities and export policy, and continuing with the regulatory structure governing such trade and its different aspects, including transport and physical protection.

While the term "nuclear trade" as a title covers both nuclear and radioactive materials, the distinction between nuclear material (control and non-proliferation) and radioactive materials (radiation protection) reflected in the legislation and federal and state responsibilities is taken into account in the following analysis. Although the legislation governing the possession, use, sale, etc of radioactive materials and radiation-emitting equipment does vary in the States and Territories, due mainly to differences in updatings, it is similar in its principles and, to avoid repetition, it will not be referred to in detail for each State or Territory concerned. Instead, the provisions and procedures will be described generally.

II. TRADE IN NUCLEAR MATERIAL AND EQUIPMENT

As previously mentioned, Australia is a significant producer and exporter of uranium and therefore plays an important role in the international nuclear fuel market. Australia's uranium export policy is based on a framework of bilateral safeguards agreements, non-proliferation objectives and international co-operation in the peaceful uses of nuclear energy. Commonwealth legislation provides for Australian Government control over uranium exports, which are limited to uranium from the mines at Ranger and Nabarlek in the Northern Territory and Olympic Dam in South Australia.

1. Government Control

The Commonwealth Constitution provides [Section 51(i)] that Parliament may make laws concerning interstate and overseas trade. It may also prohibit or permit the export or import of any goods, such permission being subject to any conditions Parliament may decide.

The Australian Government's primary legal authority over uranium and nuclear export matters is the constitutional power over trade and commerce. All uranium projects require Australian Government export approval. As already mentioned, the specific legislation involved is the Customs Act and the Customs (Prohibited Exports) Regulations. A number of other constitutional powers are also relevant, particularly those for Territories (for example, the Commonwealth has retained ownership of uranium in the Northern Territory, where the Ranger and Nabarlek projects are situated) and external affairs, the corporations power and the defence power.

Control vested in the Commonwealth by the Constitution is given effect by the above laws and regulations governing trade in nuclear material and equipment. The pertinent provisions of this legislation will be discussed below as appropriate.

The *Minister for Industry, Technology and Commerce* is the authority responsible for administering the ANSTO Acts, while the *Minister for Primary Industries and Energy* is the appropriate authority for the Nuclear Non-Proliferation (Safeguards) Act, the Atomic Energy Act and for nuclear export controls. The *Director-General of Health* and *ANSTO* are the authorities responsible for nuclear import controls.

2. Export Policy

The principles governing nuclear activities, including trade, have been set out in the Introduction, and they determine Australia's export policy, which may be summarised as follows : the orderly development of national uranium resources making supplies of uranium available only to countries with which Australia has concluded bilateral safeguards agreements for the generation of electricity and other peaceful, non-explosive purposes, ensuring adherence to Australia's nuclear non-proliferation policies and the application of strict safeguards conditions on the use of Australian uranium.

Export controls and procedures

Under Section 112 of the Customs Act 1901, the Governor-General may by regulation prohibit the exportation of goods to a specified place or subject their export to specified conditions and restrictions. The Regulations made pursuant to the Customs Act provide that the exportation of items of nuclear proliferation significance is prohibited unless an approval in writing has been granted by the Minister for Primary Industries and

Energy, or a delegate of the Minister, and is produced to the Collector of Customs.

The trigger lists developed under the Treaty on the Non-Proliferation of Nuclear Weapons — NPT (Zangger Committee List) and the Nuclear Suppliers Group Guidelines (London Club)[4] have provided Australia with the basis for defining *export controls* on nuclear or nuclear-related items.

The Minister for Primary Industries and Energy, in accordance with the Government's uranium export policy, examines each proposed uranium export contract to ensure it meets the Government's requirements, including nuclear safeguards and commercial policy requirements. These requirements must be met before the Minister considers approving any proposed uranium export contracts.

The Minister for Primary Industries and Energy also determines in advance the relevant terms and conditions which must be complied with in any proposed uranium export contract, including :

- compliance with the Australian Government's nuclear safeguards policy ;
- provision for deliveries to be made within a specified period and not to exceed a specified quantity ;
- the method of shipment of the uranium ;
- compliance with the Government's floor price policy ; and
- the use to which the uranium is to be put.

Exports are approved on a shipment-by-shipment basis with shipments typically comprising a number of consignments destined for differing buyers. Some weeks before the proposed date of shipment the uranium producer approaches the Department of Primary Industries and Energy with a formal request for export approval (a Restricted Goods Export Permit) for each consignment. The Department verifies that the proposed deliveries are in performance of an approved contract and that the contract conditions have been adhered to. The Minister's approval for the shipment is then sought on the basis that Restricted Goods Export Permits will only be issued when all the export approval requirements have been satisfied. The Department of Primary Industries and Energy seeks advice on the safeguards aspects of the proposed shipment from the Australian Safeguards Office and the Department of Foreign Affairs and Trade. The Restricted Goods Export Permits are issued and despatched to the port of exit once the export approval requirements have been satisfied.

3. Safeguards

The Commonwealth Government has developed a nuclear safeguards policy which requires the prior conclusion of bilateral and safeguards agreements between Australia and countries wishing to import Australian uranium before any contract is entered into.

This policy was first presented to Parliament on 24th May 1977 by the then Prime Minister and deals with international legal obligations in the bilateral safeguards agreements. The salient points of the statement are that where uranium is to be exported to non-nuclear weapon States such countries should be parties to the NPT ; and all uranium exported from Australia would continue to be covered by IAEA Safeguards ; bilateral agreements should include arrangements ensuring safeguarding of the materials in cases where safeguards under the NPT cease to apply and finally, any transfers to third parties, enrichment to 20 per cent or greater, or reprocessing of nuclear material should be subject to Australia's prior consent. The Government only permits exports of Australian origin nuclear material[5] to countries with which Australia has a bilateral safeguards agreement.

Although the 1977 statement was specific to the export of uranium, some of the bilateral agreements cover nuclear equipment, nuclear technology and material used for nuclear applications (for example, heavy water) as well as nuclear material (for example, uranium) transferred between the parties. The procedure for safeguarding nuclear material exported by Australia is described in a statement in Parliament by the Minister for Foreign Affairs and Trade on 7th May 1985 in reply to a question on this matter (the statement is reproduced in *Annex II*). Some of the agreements also cover co-operation in the development, use and application of nuclear energy for peaceful purposes (see below section VII, Agreements).

a) Nuclear (Non-Proliferation) Safeguards Act 1987

This nuclear safeguards policy has been implemented with the adoption of the above Act (No. 8 of 1987) which gives effect to Australia's international non-proliferation obligations which require domestic legislation. These obligations arise under :

- the Treaty on the Non-Proliferation of Nuclear Weapons ;
- Australia's safeguards agreement of 10th July 1974 with the International Atomic Energy Agency (IAEA) ;
- Australia's bilateral nuclear safeguards agreements with individual countries and EURATOM ;
- the South Pacific Nuclear Free Zone Treaty Act 1986 (No. 140 of 1986) ; and
- the Convention on the Physical Protection of Nuclear Material.

The Act, which is administered by the Minister for Primary Industries and Energy in consultation with the Minister for Foreign Affairs and Trade, provides for physical protection measures in addition to safeguards (see under section V below).

It covers nuclear material, defined to have the same meaning as in the Agreement with the IAEA, as well as associated equipment, associated technology and associated material collectively referred to as "associated items" and lays down a system of permits for purposes of control. The definition of such equipment, technology and materials is reproduced in *Annex III*.

In addition, the Act gives the Australian Safeguards Office a legislative basis (Section 54) from which to administer safeguards[6] and establishes a Director of Safeguards to be appointed by the Governor-General (Section 42).

Safeguards Office

The Australian Safeguards Office administers the national system of accounting and control required under Australia's Nuclear Non-Proliferation Treaty (NPT) safeguards agreement with the IAEA. It is responsible for implementing the "Administrative Arrangements" (See under "Accounting and Control" below) of all Australia's bilateral safeguards agreements and provides technical advice to the Government on safeguards issues.

Director of Safeguards

The tasks of the Director of Safeguards, responsible for the Safeguards Office, are to ensure the effective operation of the Australian safeguards system ; carry out Australia's obligations under the Agreement with IAEA and other international agreements ; monitor other parties' compliance with the provisions of international agreements concluded by Australia ; undertake, co-ordinate and facilitate research and development in relation to safeguards ; and finally, advise the Minister for Primary Industries and Energy on matters relating to operation of the national safeguards system.

The Director, who is appointed for a period not exceeding five years may be re-appointed. In the performance of his tasks he must comply with any directives given by the above Minister and must submit to him a yearly report on safeguards operations. The Minister in turn presents this report to Parliament.

Permits, Authorities and Inspections

The Act applies to nuclear material and associated items (Sections 8 to 10) in Australia or under Australian control.

A system of *permits* has been established to ensure proper control of such material and items. Applications for permits must be lodged with the Director of Safeguards on an approved form (Section 12). Following consideration of the application and related information, the Director sends a written report on the application to the Minister for Primary Industries and Energy.

The Minister does not grant a permit unless the Director has stated in his report

- regarding nuclear material, etc., in a nuclear facility, that he is satisfied, in particular, that appropriate procedures for safeguards and adequate physical security can be applied (Section 14) ;
- regarding nuclear material, etc, to be held outside a nuclear facility that he is satisfied he has been provided with all the information he requires relating to the application (Section 15).

The permit is granted subject to such restrictions and conditions as are contained therein. These concern, in particular, the duration of the permit, specification of the nuclear material etc, use and location, record-keeping and accounting, measures to be taken to ensure the physical security of the material or item and inspections by national and/or IAEA inspectors (Section 13).

When the Minister grants, amends or revokes a permit, a notice to that effect is published in the Commonwealth of Australia Gazette (Section 20).

The Minister may also grant a *special transport permit* for the purpose of transporting nuclear material or associated items from a specified location to another specified location (Section 16).

This permit too is granted subject to certain restrictions and conditions, in particular, its duration, the means and route by which such material and items are to be transported, records, reporting and accounting procedures, etc.

Control over associated technology extends to communication of defined information which must be authorised according to a similar procedure as that for the granting of permits (Sections 17 and 18).

A Register of Permit and Authority Holders is kept by the Director of Safeguards (Section 69).

Inspectors designated to Australia by the International Atomic Energy Agency (IAEA) and declared by the Minister for Primary Industries and Energy (Section 57) to be Agency inspectors for the purposes of the Act carry out safeguards inspections in accordance with the Agency Agreement. Australian domestic inspectors appointed by the Minister carry out inspections for the purposes of the Act and assist the Agency inspectors in their inspections.

The Australian inspectors are empowered, amongst other things, to examine records and documents, take samples and measurements of nuclear material and associated items, and may, in accordance with an agreement between the Director and the owner concerned or pursuant to a warrant, enter premises, vessels, aircraft or vehicles in the discharge of their duties (Section 59). They may also make offence-related searches and seizures (Section 61).

The Agency inspectors have the powers necessary to carry out inspections in accordance with the Agency Agreement (Section 60) (see section VII, Agreements).

Exemptions and Termination

The Minister for Primary Industries and Energy may declare that certain nuclear material is exempted from the scope of the Act provided such material is declared exempt material by the IAEA and if this declaration is not inconsistent with Australia's obligations under an international agreement; this also applies for associated items (Section 11).

Exemption and termination declarations under Section 11 may be made with respect to "associated items" as well as "nuclear material". Such declarations relate only to the application of Part II of the Act, and do not affect the operation of other parts of the legislation. This is of particular importance with respect to exempt nuclear material and associated items.

It should be noted that any person processing or storing exempt nuclear material together with nuclear material within the scope of the Act must notify the Minister in writing of the proposed operation (Section 27).

Sanctions

When a person has possession of nuclear material or an associated item which Australia, under an international agreement, must return or transfer to the country concerned, the Director of Safeguards may seize or give a national inspector authority to seize the material or item to comply with the provisions of the agreement (Section 67).

If a person has possession of nuclear material or an associated item without a permit he is liable to a fine not exceeding 10 000 (Australian) dollars or imprisonment for a term not exceeding five years or both if he is a natural person; a body corporate is liable to a fine not exceeding 50 000 dollars. This also applies for such offences on an Australian ship or aircraft or in the course of a journey to and from Australia (Section 23).

A person breaching the conditions of a permit or authority, or contravening a direction by the Minister is liable to a fine not exceeding 5 000 dollars or imprisonment for a term not exceeding two years or both if he is a natural person; a body corporate is liable to a fine not exceeding 25 000 dollars. This also applies for such offences outside Australia (Section 25).

The Minister may revoke a permit or authority when the holder contravenes a condition of such permit or authority or a direction of the Minister. This also applies to violations outside Australia (Section 19).

As regards unauthorised communication of information of a kind referred to in the definition of associated technology, the offender, if he is a natural person is liable to a fine not exceeding 5 000 dollars or imprisonment for a term not exceeding two years; a body corporate is liable to a fine not exceeding 25 000 dollars (Section 26).

b) Nuclear Non-Proliferation (Safeguards) Regulations

The above Regulations (Statutory Rules 1987 No. 75) of 7th May 1987 were made under the Nuclear Non-Proliferation (Safeguards) Act 1987. They define, in particular, the nuclear material to which Part II of the Act (Control of Nuclear Material and Associated Items) does not apply. Such exemptions concern for example, depleted uranium contained in counterweights installed in aircraft, other than Australian aircraft, in transit through the country; thorium in a finished aircraft part and source material contained in a prescribed chemical mixture, compound or solution in a quantity not exceeding 10 kilograms element weight of uranium or thorium.

c) Accounting and Control

Australia's bilateral agreements contain a provision for the establishment of an "Administrative Arrangement" to ensure fulfilment of the obligations laid down by the agreement. These Arrangements are generally concerned with accounting and reporting procedures and their purpose is to ascertain that Australian origin nuclear material is accounted for from the time it is exported. They are administrative arrangements which do not have treaty status; they are classified as "safeguards-in-confidence" and are not public documents.

The procedures detailed in the Administrative Arrangement are also designed to ensure that the obligations relating to items other than nuclear technology which may be subject to an agreement (material, equipment and technology) are fulfilled. The Administrative Arrangement specifies the extent to which such nuclear items are to be identified by the recipient country's national system of accounting and control. That national system may have to be augmented as necessary to meet the bilateral requirement for identifying the supplier origin of the nuclear material. However, the Administrative Arrangement uses, as far as practicable, the national accounting system introduced to meet IAEA requirements. The procedures are as consistent as is possible with IAEA safeguards procedures to minimise duplication of effort.

As well as detailing the agreed accounting procedures, the Administrative Arrangement specifies both the frequency and the content of the reports to be exchanged by the partners. Regular reports are received from bilateral partners listing the totals of Australian origin nuclear items held in their countries. Corresponding reports are provided to bilateral partners on nuclear material (and nuclear items as required) supplied by them to Australia. Reports include a statement of holdings of nuclear material subject to the particular agreement at the beginning of the reporting period and at the end of the period, and list intervening inventory changes such as exports, operating losses and shipper-receiver differences.

The reporting obligations described above entail an exchange of information between the partners on transfer of items. On the basis of proposals by exporters for transfers of nuclear items that will become or are subject to an agreement, the partners exchange communications designed to ensure that the proposed recipient is authorised to receive the items, and that the items will be accounted for and identified as of Australian origin and safeguarded in accordance with the requirements of the agreement. The Administrative Arrangement sets out the information to be exchanged (e.g. proposed date of shipment, mass and form of nuclear material), and the period within which the communications must take place. Procedures to be followed for communications about transfers to third countries are also outlined.

4. Mining Regime

As already mentioned, mining of uranium is restricted to the Nabarlek and Ranger mines in the Northern Territory and Olympic Dam[7] in South Australia. The following paragraphs will briefly review the legislation applicable to the mining of uranium in the Northern Territory.

a) Atomic Energy Act 1953 as amended

As seen from the preceding section on safeguards, the Nuclear Non-Proliferation (Safeguards) Act 1987 establishes a system of permits and controls for activities involving nuclear materials and equipment, thus replacing the licensing regime previously laid down for different purposes by the Atomic Energy Act 1953.

The areas of the 1953 Act still retained, apart from certain definitions[8] are those covering the Ranger Project and Commonwealth title to uranium in the Territories as well as the requirement to report discoveries of uranium and the production of yellowcake.

The powers in respect of control of material conferred by the Atomic Energy Act 1953 as amended may be exercised only for trade with other countries, between the States and Territories and in relation to substances recovered from or other matters in connection with the Ranger Project Area or a Territory or for other purposes of the Commonwealth (Section 34).

Uranium deposits in the Territories (referred to as prescribed substances in their natural condition) are the property of the Commonwealth (Section 35).

The Minister for Primary Industries and Energy has authorised a person(s) to carry out mining operations in the Ranger Project area on behalf of or in association with the Commonwealth (Section 41). The prescribed substances or minerals recovered then become the property of the Commonwealth [Section 41(3)] ; subject to certain conditions, the Commonwealth may be liable to pay compensation to a person who had a right, title or interest in such substances or minerals, on mutually agreed terms (Section 42). In the case of the Ranger Project, the Commonwealth has agreed to transfer title to the uranium mined back to the Ranger owners.

The Act furthermore provides that, except as specified by regulations, Section 41 is not intended to exclude or limit the operation of any provision of law of a State or Territory that is capable of operating concurrently with them.

b) Other laws concerning the Northern Territory

In addition to the Atomic Energy Act clearly stating the Commonwealth title to uranium deposits in the Northern Territory, the Northern Territory (Self-Government) Act 1978 [Section 69(4)] provides : "All interests of the Commonwealth in respect of minerals in the Territory (*other than prescribed substances* within the meaning of the Atomic Energy Act 1953 ...) are by force of this Section vested in the Territory ...".

In effect, regulations made under the Northern Territory (Self-Government) Act 1978 specify matters in respect of which Territory Ministers may have executive authority, in particular by means of agreements and arrangements between the Territory and the Commonwealth [Sub-regulation 4(5)(f)]. And, as provided by the Atomic Energy Act (see Section 41(4) above), Commonwealth powers with respect to uranium mining operations may be exercised by the Northern Territory acting on the advice of a Commonwealth Minister. Through this mechanism uranium mining in the Northern Territory (apart from Ranger) is authorised under the Northern Territory Mining Act.

Executive authority of the Northern Territory Ministers has been implemented through Regulations 4(5)(b) and (f) of the Northern Territory (Self-government) Regulations, the Mining Act 1980 (NT) and the Agreement dated 8th February 1982 between the Commonwealth and the Northern Territory in relation to the mining of prescribed substances in the Northern Territory. Also relevant are a series of letters between Commonwealth and Northern Territory Governments[9].

Mining Act 1980 (Northern Territory)

The Mining Act 1980 which came into force on 1st July 1982, establishes the mining title system for uranium and other minerals (Part VI). It lays down a three tier title system : exploration licences, exploration retention leases and mineral leases (Parts IV-VI, and Section 35(4) of the Atomic Energy Act). Holders of exploration retention leases may carry out geological, geophysical and geochemical programmes and other works necessary to evaluate the development potential of any mineral ore body of possible economic potential (Section 43). Mineral leases may provide for, in addition to mining of the mineral, the erection of machinery etc, for treatment, processing or refining etc of the mineral involved (Section 60).

Minerals are defined in a way which is broad enough to incorporate uranium [Sub-Section 4(1)]. The Territory Minister is empowered to grant exploration licences without referring to the Commonwealth authorities [Section 175(2)]. Holders of exploration licences are granted various rights (Section 23), including the right to obtain an exploration retention lease, mineral lease and apply for mineral claim, subject to certain provisions of the Act (Sections 60 and 86)[10].

Aboriginal Land Rights (Northern Territory) Act 1976 (Cwlth)

The above Act (Section 41) limits the exercise of any rights under the Atomic Energy Act 1953 authorising mining insofar as entry for exploration to land that is aboriginal land is concerned unless, *inter alia*, the Governor-General declares such entry necessary in the national interest. The Act also contains relevant provisions in relation to the Ranger Project area [Section 41(2)].

Other laws on environmental protection

A number of Commonwealth and Territory laws concerning environmental protection are also relevant in that their provisions must be complied with for the environmental aspects of uranium mining operations[11].

In addition, the Environment Protection (Alligator Rivers Region) Act 1978 (Commonwealth) has provided for the appointment of a Supervising Scientist for the purpose of protecting the environment in that region — the Ranger and Nabarlek Projects are within it — from the effects of uranium mining. His duties include, *inter alia*, supervision and development of programmes on environmental effects and provision of advice on such matters to the Minister for the Arts, Sport, the Environment, Tourism and Territories (Section 5).

5. Import/Export Regulations

As already mentioned, the import and export of nuclear material and equipment in Australia are regulated by Customs law, namely the Customs (Prohibited Imports) Regulations as at 31st July 1986 and the Customs (Prohibited Exports) Regulations as at 31st July 1986, both made under the Customs Act 1901.

a) Imports

Under the Customs Act 1901 the Governor-General may, by regulation, prohibit the importation of goods absolutely, prohibit the importation of goods from a specified place or subject their import to specified conditions or restrictions (Section 50).

The Customs (Prohibited Imports) Regulations define the items subject to import restrictions or which may not be imported. The items concerned are listed in different Schedules to the Regulations, according to the conditions to be complied with in their respect.

At present, nuclear imports into Australia are limited to items falling under the "radioactive" category and are included in the Third Schedule. These items are "radioactive material and substances, including radium and radioactive isotopes, and articles containing radioactive material or substances" (Item 23).

Importers of such items must provide the Collector of Customs with permission in writing from the Director-General of Health or from the ANSTO (formerly from the Australian Atomic Energy Commission).

b) Exports

The Customs Prohibited Exports Regulations were made by the Governor-General under Section 112 of the Customs Act (as to Section 112 see under Export Controls and Procedures above). The Regulations define the items whose export is either prohibited or subject to conditions. The Schedules to the Regulations list the items by category. Regulation 11 provides that the export of goods specified in the Ninth Schedule, which concerns nuclear or nuclear-related materials and equipment, is prohibited without the written approval of the Minister for Primary Industries and Energy or an authorised person (Restricted Goods Export Permit).

It should be noted that the scope of the Ninth Schedule while encompassing the Zangger Committee and London Club trigger lists also includes other items. Extracts from the Ninth Schedule are reproduced in *Annex IV* to this chapter.

III. TRADE IN RADIOACTIVE MATERIALS

As explained in the Introduction, the States — and the Northern Territory — have their own legislation governing the possession and use, etc of radioactive materials and radiation-emitting equipment from the radiation protection viewpoint. In addition, the National Health and Medical Research Council has published radiation protection standards to assist all users of ionizing radiation throughout the Commonwealth. These standards are based on the recommendations of the International Commission on Radiological Protection (ICRP) as amended in 1978 and are entitled : "Recommended Radiation Protection Standards for Individuals exposed to Radiation (1980)".

Some of these radiation protection regulations were made under general State health acts or were enacted on their own and are fairly similar in content. To avoid duplication, the provisions common to all the States and Northern Territory legislation of relevance to trade in radioactive materials will be briefly described below, without specific reference to the regulations proper[12].

Licences are required for the manufacture, storage, transport, sale, etc of radioactive materials and radiation-emitting equipment. Applications must be submitted to the responsible authorities on forms as specified in the regulations.

The application forms must contain, *inter alia*, the following information :

— name and address of applicant ;
— type, quantity and radioactivity of material/type of radiation-emitting device ;
— intended purpose or use.

The period of validity of licences varies according to the State (and Northern Territory), ranging from one to three years.

Holders of radioactive materials or radiation-emitting equipment must keep *records* thereof. The records must state in particular the nature of the materials, their purpose and the manner of storage.

A person engaging in the *sale* of radioactive materials or radiation-emitting equipment must ensure that the purchaser has been granted the appropriate licence.

For purposes of safety and control, duly authorised *inspectors* may inspect premises where such materials or equipment are held and may also examine the materials and equipment as well as any relevant documentation.

Radioactive materials and radiation-emitting equipment whose radioactivity is below levels as specified in the regulations are *exempted* from licensing requirements.

The *penalties* for contravention of the regulations vary according to each State and the Northern Territory. They range from 200 dollars to 10 000 dollars.

At Commonwealth level, the Australian Nuclear Science and Technology Organisation (ANSTO) provides commercial services, in particular, it produces, sells and distributes radioisotopes for medical, scientific, agricultural, etc., uses throughout Australia and abroad (ANSTO Act, Section 5).

IV. TRANSPORT[13]

The transport of radioactive materials by road and rail in Australia is regulated by the States and Northern Territory Governments. Transport by air and sea within the country and for imports and exports is regulated by Commonwealth legislation[14].

The Australia Code of Practice for the Safe Transport of Radioactive Substances 1982[15] provides for activity limits, packaging requirements and safety measures in compliance with those in the IAEA Regulations for the Safe Transport of Radioactive Materials. The Code is applied by the States and the Territories by or through regulations under their respective land transport legislation[16].

V. PHYSICAL PROTECTION

At present, Australia's uranium exports are shipped out in the form of yellowcake[17] which is considered a nuclear source material of low strategic value. In international transport it is protected in accordance with prudent management practice and the physical protection measures are similar to those which apply to valuable cargo (i.e. security barriers as a minimum).

Physical protection measures are applied to Australian shipments of yellowcake under the provisions contained in Australia's bilateral agreements. The agreements oblige the recipient countries in turn to provide adequate physical protection measures on such shipments in compliance with internationally-recommended standards (IAEA INFCIRC/225/Rev. 1).

AUSTRALIA

The Australian Safeguards Office (ASO) is responsible for ensuring that adequate physical protection measures are applied to Australian yellowcake and all other nuclear material within Australia as well as for the export of such products.

Part III of the *Nuclear Non-Proliferation (Safeguards) Act 1987* contains provisions relating to the Convention on the Physical Protection of Nuclear Material which entered into force on 28th October 1987 following Australia's ratification of the Convention. These provisions deal with offences committed in respect of nuclear material.

Any person committing such offences, namely stealing, demanding by threats, threatening to use or using nuclear material and causing personal injury or damage to property is liable to a fine of 20 000 dollars or imprisonment for ten years or both (Sections 33 to 37).

These provisions extend to offences committed outside Australia (Section 38).

VI. INTELLECTUAL PROPERTY IN THE NUCLEAR FIELD

At present, there are no specific regulations on intellectual property or patents in the nuclear field in Australia.

VII. AGREEMENTS

1. Multilateral Agreements

Australia ratified the Treaty on the Non-Proliferation of Nuclear Weapons on 23rd January 1973 and the Convention on the Physical Protection of Nuclear Material on 22nd September 1987.

2. Bilateral Agreements

Australia concluded an agreement with the IAEA on 10th July 1974 in implementation of NPT Safeguards. Under this Agreement all nuclear material within Australia is controlled and accounted for by the Australian Safeguards Office which reports to the IAEA. The IAEA for its part verifies the reports, including by regular inspections of nuclear material held in Australia.

In addition, to date, Australia has concluded twelve agreements on co-operation in the peaceful uses of nuclear energy, setting a framework within which the supply of nuclear material and equipment can take place, with detailed safeguards provisions (see section on Safeguards above). These agreements are termed "safeguards" agreements by Australia to underline its commitment to non-proliferation. They are listed below in chronological order.

— Agreement with ***Finland***, concerning the transfer of nuclear material between Australia and Finland signed on 20th July 1978 and entered into force on 9th February 1980.

— Agreement with the ***Philippines***, on co-operation in peaceful uses of nuclear energy and the transfer of nuclear material signed on 8th August 1978 and entered into force on 11th May 1982.

— Agreement with the ***Republic of Korea***, concerning co-operation in the peaceful uses of nuclear energy and the transfer of nuclear material signed on 2nd May 1979 and entered into force on the same date.

— Agreement with the ***United States***, concerning peaceful uses of nuclear energy signed on 5th July 1979 and entered into force on 16th January 1981. This Agreement was further supplemented by an Exchange of notes constituting an Agreement, detailing each Party's responsibilities regarding safeguards, physical protection, retransfers of nuclear materials, etc. The Agreement entered into force on 2nd August 1985.

— Agreement with the ***United Kingdom***, concerning nuclear transfers between Australia and the United Kingdom signed on 24th July 1979 and entered into force on the same date.

— Agreement with ***France*** relating to the conversion and/or enrichment in France of Australian origin nuclear material supplied to Japan under a sales contract concluded prior to 2nd December 1972, signed on 30th October 1980.

— Agreement with ***France***, concerning nuclear transfers between Australia and France signed on 7th January 1981 and entered into force on 12th September 1981.

— Agreement with ***Canada***, concerning the peaceful uses of nuclear energy signed on 9th March 1981 and entered into force on the same date.

— Agreement with ***Sweden***, on conditions and controls for nuclear transfers for peaceful purposes between Australia and Sweden signed on 18th March 1981 and entered into force on 22nd May 1981. A further Agreement amending this agreement was signed on 12th July 1982.

— Agreement with ***EURATOM***, concerning transfers of nuclear material from Australia to the European Atomic Energy Community signed on 21st September 1981 and entered into force on 15th January 1982.

— Agreement with ***Japan***, for co-operation in the peaceful uses of nuclear energy signed on 5th March 1982 and entered into force on 17th August 1982.

— Agreement with ***Switzerland*** concerning the peaceful uses of nuclear energy, signed on 28th January 1986.

As regards *reprocessing*, agreed conditions in this respect have been incorporated in agreements with France, Sweden, EURATOM, Japan and Switzerland. The agreed conditions include :

— reprocessing of Australian origin nuclear material subject to the agreement may take place under IAEA safeguards in the nuclear fuel cycle programme of the bilateral partner, which has been delineated and recorded by the Parties ;
— reprocessing is to be for the purpose of energy use or for the management of materials contained in spent fuel ;
— the nuclear fuel cycle programme remains as delineated (by reference to commercial scale facilities) and recorded ;
— an undertaking by the partner government to draw any changes to the delineated programme promptly to the attention of the Australian Government ;
— storage and use of plutonium in the programme to be under IAEA safeguards and in accordance with the nuclear fuel cycle programme ;
— transfers of Australian origin nuclear material must be notified in advance to Australia ;
— use of Australian origin plutonium for other peaceful non-explosive purposes, including research (outside the delineated programme) will not necessarily be precluded, but can take place only with Australia's consent.

NOTES AND REFERENCES

1. The States are : New South Wales, South Australia, Western Australia, Queensland, Tasmania and Victoria.
2. The Australian Nuclear Science and Technology Organisation Act 1987 (Act No. 3) and the Australian Nuclear Science and Technology (transitional provisions) Act 1987 (Act No. 4). The purpose of the ANSTO Acts, which entered into force on 26th April 1987, is to establish a successor organisation to the Australian Atomic Energy Commission (AAEC) which was established under the Atomic Energy Act 1953. Act No. 3 provides for :
   — a new Organisation with functions which accord with Government policy. These reflect the realignment of AAEC activities away from work on the nuclear fuel cycle, towards greater emphasis on applications of radioisotopes and radiation in medicine, industry, etc, and for the provision of services and sale of goods in these areas ;
   — a governing Board of Directors of up to seven members including a Chairperson and Deputy Chairperson ;
   — an Advisory Council of up to eleven members, including at least one staff-elected member, to advise the Minister for Industry, Technology and Commerce and the ANSTO Board of Directors on matters relating to the functions of the Organisation.

   (Act No. 3 is reproduced in the OECD/NEA Nuclear Law Bulletin No. 40, December 1987).
   The Atomic Energy Amendment Act 1987, which also entered into force on 26th April 1987, repeals the parts of the Atomic Energy Act 1953 relating to the AAEC and to security provisions.
3. The Nuclear Non-Proliferation (Safeguards) Act 1987 (Act No. 8 of 1987, assented to on 17th March 1987).
4. For further details see Volume I concerning international aspects of nuclear trade.
5. "Australian origin" nuclear material, which is any nuclear material produced or derived from uranium ore mined in Australia, is to be covered by IAEA safeguards while within the jurisdiction of a bilateral partner, whether for use in a reactor or for processing. The IAEA safeguards are implemented through safeguards agreements between the IAEA and the relevant countries. The agreements concluded between the IAEA and countries eligible to receive Australian uranium can be considered in two broad categories. In the case of a non-nuclear weapon State, it is an agreement required by the NPT covering all nuclear material in the country. In the case of a nuclear-weapon State, it is a voluntary agreement whereby safeguards are applied to specific facilities and the nuclear material which passes through them.

There are two levels of fallback or contingency safeguards arrangements which are intended to take effect in the event that existing safeguards should break down. The first level would apply to ensure the continued international safeguarding of all nuclear material present in an importing non-nuclear weapon State, should IAEA safeguards pursuant to the NPT cease to apply in that country. The second level would apply to ensure the continued safeguarding of Australian origin nuclear material, in the case of a non-nuclear weapon State, should the first level of fallback arrangements cease to operate, or, in the case of a nuclear-weapon State, should the IAEA cease to apply safeguards pursuant to that country's agreement with the IAEA.

6. Until adoption of the Act, the Australian Safeguards Office operated a system of accounting for nuclear material and other nuclear items within Australia without direct legislative backing, mainly on the basis of Customs legislation.

7. The Olymic Dam Project (Roxby Downs) is located in South Australia. It should be noted that unlike the situation in the Northern Territory, States have ownership of uranium within their jurisdiction. Western Mining Corporation and the BP Group, a Joint Venture, informed the Government of South Australia that they would proceed with development of the project in December 1985. Full-scale construction commenced in May 1986 following lodgement with the South Australian Government of the formal Notice of Intention to Commit.

8. The Atomic Energy Act 1953 (Section 5) gives the following definitions:
"... "atomic energy" means any form of energy released in the course of nuclear fission, nuclear fusion or other nuclear transmutation;

"Australia" includes the Territories;
... "minerals" includes all substances obtained or obtainable from the earth by underground or surface working;

"prescribed substance" means:

a) uranium, thorium, an element having an atomic number greater than 92 or any other substance declared by the regulations to be capable of being used for the production of atomic energy or for research into matters connected with atomic energy; and
b) any derivative or compound of a substance to which paragraph (a) applies;

"Ranger Project Area" means the land described in Schedule 2 to the Aboriginal Land Rights (Northern Territory) Act 1976 ...".

9. Three examples:

a) exchange of letters (24th/25th May 1978) between the Commonwealth Minister for Trade and Resources and the Chief Minister of the Northern Territory stating that the agencies of the Northern Territory Government should be involved in regular inspection, supervision and monitoring activities applicable to uranium mining projects in the Territory, subject to reimbursement by the Commonwealth of the cost of providing such regulatory services;
b) letter (17th May 1978) from the Prime Minister of the Commonwealth to the Chief Minister of the Territory stating that uranium mining in the Territory should be regulated to the maximum extent possible through the laws of the Northern Territory, and
c) letter (18th December 1979) from the Minister of National Development and Energy to the Northern Territory Minister of Mines and Energy advising that the Commonwealth has no objection to the Territory granting exploration licences for prescribed substances provided the Commonwealth Minister is kept fully informed.

10. See the 1978 Authority issued under Section 41 of the Atomic Energy Act 1953 and the 1979 Ranger Uranium Project Government Agreement as amended between the Commonwealth of Australia and Energy Resources of Australia Ltd. The title to the Nabarlek deposits has been granted to Queensland Mines Limited by way of a special mineral lease under the Mining Act 1939 (NT) now repealed by the Mining Act 1980.

11. Commonwealth legislation:
— Environment Protection (Impact of Proposals) Act 1974;
— National Parks and Wildlife Conservation Act 1975;
— Australian Heritage Commission Act 1975;
— Environment Protection (Alligator Rivers Region) Act 1978, amended by the Environment Protection Alligator Rivers Region) Amendment Act 1987;
— Environment Protection (Northern Territory Supreme Court) Act 1978;
— Environment Protection (Nuclear Codes) Act 1978;
— World Heritage Properties Conservation Act 1983.

Northern Territory legislation:
— Conservation Commission Act 1980;
— Control of Waters Act 1938;
— Soil Conservation and Land Utilisation Act 1970;
— Territory Parks and Wildlife Conservation Act 1976;
— Uranium Mining (Environment Control) Act 1980;
— Mining Act 1980.

12. The legislation and the authorities responsible for its administration are the following:

— *New South Wales*: Radioactive Substances Act 1957. Radioactive Substances Regulations 1959. NSW Radiological Advisory Council. Uranium Mining and Nuclear Facilities (Prohibitions) Act 1986;

— *South Australia*: The Health Act 1935-1982. Radioactive Substances and Irradiating Apparatus Regulations 1962-1979. Radiation Protection and Control Act, 1982. Ionizing Radiation Regulations 1985. South Australia Health Commission;

— *Western Australia*: Radiation Safety Act 1975-1981. Radiation Safety (General) Regulations 1983. Nuclear Activities Regulation 1978. Western Australian Radiological Council;

— *Queensland*: Radioactive Substances Act 1958. Radioactive Substances *Regulations 1961. Queensland Department of Health;*

— *Tasmania*: Radiation Control Act 1977. Radioactive Substances Regulations 1963. Tasmanian Department of Health Services;

— *Victoria*: Health Act 1958 as amended. Health (Radiation Safety) Act 1983. Health (Radiation Safety) Regulations 1983 as amended. Victorian Commission of Public Health. Nuclear Activities (Prohibition) Act 1983;

— *Northern Territory*: Radiation (Safety Control) Ordinance 1978;

— *Capital Territory*: Radiation Ordinance 1983. The responsible authority is the ACT Health Authority.

13. For further details see "Regulations Governing the Transport of Radioactive Materials", OECD/NEA, 1980.

14. The Commonwealth's powers are derived from:

— the Air Navigation Regulations pursuant to Section 26 of the Air Navigation Act 1920-1966. The regulations adopt the provision of the International Civil Aviation Organisation (ICAO) Annex 18 — The Safe Transport of Dangerous Goods by Air; and

— the Commonwealth Navigation Act 1912 which regulates the transport of radioactive materials by sea:

- Marine Orders issued under that Act provide that dangerous goods, which includes radioactive materials, are to be packed, stowed and carried in accordance with the International Maritime Dangerous Goods Code (IMDG Code);
- Administrative procedures exist for the adoption of amendments to the IMDG Code as published by the International Maritime Organisation and take effect in Australia coincidentally with the date of effect set by that Organisation; and
- The IMDG Code includes provisions for dangerous goods of Class 7 — Radioactive Substances — which specify that the International Atomic Energy Agency's (IAEA) Regulations for the Safe Transport of Radioactive Materials, 1973, Revised Edition is the base for the sea transport requirements.

15. This Code is currently being revised and it is expected that recent IAEA amendments will be incorporated in the revision.

16. The following legislation governing the transport of radioactive materials has been enacted since publication of the OECD/NEA Study referred to in Note 13:

— Radioactive Ores and Concentrates (Packaging and Transport) Act 1980 — Northern Territory of Australia;

— Radiation Safety (Transport of Radioactive Substances) Regulations 1982 — Western Australia;

— Radiation Safety (Transport of Radioactive Substances) Regulations 1984 — South Australia.

17. Yellowcake is a mixture of uranium oxides and impurities (about 95 per cent uranium oxides) produced at an uranium mill.

Annex I

GOVERNMENT RESPONSE TO THE ASTEC REPORT EXCERPTS FROM THE PRIME MINISTER'S STATEMENT TO PARLIAMENT

(23rd May 1985)

Recommendation 1

— That exports of Australian uranium should not be limited as a matter of principle but should be permitted subject to stringent conditions of supply designed to strengthen the non-proliferation regime.

Response: ... the Government has decided that the mining and export of uranium will continue subject to strict safeguards conditions, but only from the Nabarlek, Ranger and Olympic Dam (Roxby Downs) mines.

Recommendation 2

— That Australia continue to accord high priority to active and constructive participation in disarmament and arms control negotiations. A principal objective of these negotiations should be the conclusion of a comprehensive nuclear test-ban treaty.

Response: The Government accepts the recommendation which accords with existing policy.

Recommendation 3

— That Australia promote the acceptance by supplier states not to provide nuclear items to non-nuclear weapon states which are not members of the Treaty on the Non-Proliferation of Nuclear Weapons, or a treaty of similar coverage, under which International Atomic Energy Agency safeguards are applied to all those states' nuclear facilities at all times.

Response: The Government accepts this recommendation and will seek the agreement of other supplier countries to this approach.

Recommendation 4

— That Australia continue to support proposals for a nuclear weapons free zone in the South Pacific and for an Indian Ocean Zone of Peace and that Australia examine the feasibility of a regional treaty or treaties involving southern and eastern Asia and Australia, based on non-proliferation concepts contained in the Treaty of Tlatelolco.

Response: The Government accepts the recommendation.

Recommendation 5

— That Australia encourage further development of international guidelines and procedures for the supply of nuclear items with a view to ensuring that countries which are parties to the Non-Proliferation Treaty or a treaty of similar coverage are advantaged; further, that Australia encourage broader participation in forums which are developing lists of items which may form the basis of countries' export control regulations.

Response: The Government accepts the recommendation.

Recommendation 6

— That Australia ratify the Convention on the Physical Protection of Nuclear Material and introduce the necessary enabling legislation. ASTEC also recommends that physical protection standards and measures applied to nuclear material in use, storage and transport within Australia should be incorporated in regulations. The standards and measures should accord as a minimum with those recommended by the International Atomic Energy Agency.

Response: The Government accepts the recommendations ... and will seek to introduce appropriate legislation for domestic physical protection of nuclear material.

Recommendation 7

— That Australia continue to encourage the establishment of a scheme to regulate effectively the storage and use of sensitive nuclear material. Such a scheme should incorporate the concepts of a use statement and verification by the International Atomic Energy Agency of such use.

Response: The Government accepts the recommendation.

Recommendation 10

— That Australia take the necessary action, in consultation with the International Atomic Energy Agency, to provide further resources to the Agency and encourage other Member countries to do the same so that the Agency can improve the efficiency and effectiveness of its safeguards operations.

Response: The Government accepts the recommendation.

Recommendation 13

— That Australia take steps to ensure that nuclear material extracted for nuclear purposes from Australian ores after export would become subject to a safeguards agreement to which Australia is a party.

Response: The Government accepts the recommendation and will take the matter up bilaterally with countries importing relevant Australian mineral ores to ensure that if nuclear material is extracted for nuclear purposes it is subject to bilateral safeguards agreements.

Recommendation 14

— That Australia enter into discussions with governments of countries with which Australia has no bilateral safeguards agreements and within whose jurisdictions Australian origin nuclear material is trans-shipped with a view to concluding government to government arrangements covering the application of physical protection measures to such material.

Response: The Government accepts the recommendation.

Recommendation 15

— That the Australian Government seek agreement with its bilateral partners to make public the texts of the Administrative Arrangements, in such a way as to avoid adverse implications for physical protection and commercial confidentiality.

Response: The Government accepts the recommendation.

Recommendation 16

— That Australia, through its membership of appropriate international organisations, take action to promote the establishment of internationally agreed approaches to the limitation of releases of effluents containing radioactive material that may cross international boundaries.

Response: The Government accepts this recommendation.

AUSTRALIA

Recommendation 17

— That Australia proceed as quickly as possible to complete a code of practice for the disposal of radioactive waste arising from medical, industrial and research use of radionuclides, to identify sites suitable for disposal of low level radioactive waste and to the development of facilities for interim storage and disposal of low and intermediate level radioactive waste.

Response: The Government accepts this recommendation and steps are already under way to have it implemented in co-operation and after consultation with the States.

Recommendations 18 and 19

Recommendation 18

— That the relevant national safety standards for radiation exposure associated with uranium mining and milling continue to be reviewed regularly and incorporated in Federal, State and Territory regulatory procedures, and that the observance of these prescribed standards be appropriately monitored.

Recommendation 19

— That the Australian Government, acting jointly with State and Territory Governments as appropriate, ensure that the safety and environmental monitoring aspects of uranium mining and milling in Australia are soundly established and carried out, including the provision of necessary facilities and staff to the Office of the Supervising Scientist.

Response: The Government accepts the recommendations.

The Commonwealth will seek the continued co-operation of the States and the NT in the review and development of national safety standards, and encourage them to incorporate such standards as soon as possible in appropriate regulatory procedures and to monitor their observance.

To ensure the continued domestic application of best practicable technology to meet safety standards, the Commonwealth will continue to emphasise its international participation in studies relating to uranium mining and milling.

The 1984/85 Budget provides for an increase of 10 in the staffing level of the Office of the Supervising Scientist (from 66 to 76).

Recommendation 20

— That the Australian Government, in association with State and Territory Governments, establish and maintain a national registry of radioactive tailings and waste disposal sites. The administration of the registry should be designed to ensure, as far as is possible, that the records it contains are maintained for as long as the sites to which they refer might constitute a hazard to people or to the environment; the sites themselves should be identified on the ground by long-lasting markers.

Response: The Government accepts the recommendation and will consult the States to seek agreement on implementation of a co-ordinated data registry. The need for legislation will be assessed in the light of these consultations.

Recommendation 21

(i) That Australia ratify the Convention on the Prevention of Marine Pollution by Dumping of Wastes and Other Matter (the London Dumping Convention) and join the OECD Mechanism for Sea Dumping of Radioactive Waste;

(ii) That Australia continue to recognise the concern of island and seaboard countries within the South Pacific region to maintain the oceans as a esource of all mankind and use its influence in international forums to urge other countries, whenever appropriate, to form regional groupings within the framework of the London Dumping Convention to prohibit or severely restrict dumping of radioactive materials in that region;

(iii) That Australia participate actively in scientific assessments of the safety of ocean dumping of radioactive waste; and

(iv) That, pending the outcome of those assessments, Australia support a moratorium on the ocean dumping of radioactive waste.

Response: The Government accepts Recommendations 21(i), 21(ii) and 21(iii) and will move quickly to ratify the Convention on the Prevention of Marine Pollution by Dumping of Wastes and Other Matter (London Dumping Convention) in consultation with the States and will support other aspects of the recommendation in bilateral and multilateral meetings. In respect of Recommendation 21(iv) Australia supports the moratorium and will vigorously oppose ocean dumping of radioactive waste.

Recommendation 22

— That Australia provide support and encouragement for Australian participation in research and development in the disposal of high level radioactive waste and for co-operation with other countries and with international agencies in such research.

Response: The Government accepts the recommendation and will continue to contribute to national and international efforts in R & D on waste management in areas where Australian expertise can be matched with overseas requirements/programs (see also Recommendation 23).

Recommendation 23

— That Australia continue to support research and development on the advanced waste form SYNROC. Provided that the apparent advantages of SYNROC are confirmed by further research, Australia should encourage further international co-operation in SYNROC development with the aim of securing its widest possible use.

Response: The Government accepts the recommendation and will continue to support SYNROC R & D and encourage international co-operation in this area of radioactive waste management technology.

SYNROC properties are being investigated at ANU, AAEC and Griffith University under the NERODC program. In addition the Government has approved an amount of $2.754 million over three years for the construction of a non-radioactive pilot plant at the AAEC to demonstrate the production of SYNROC in full-sized canisters.

Australia has recently entered into bilateral arrangements with both the UK and Japan for co-operation in the R & D of technology for the management of high level wastes beginning with work on SYNROC.

Recommendation 24

— That Australia encourage the development of international guidelines and codes of practice for the storage and disposal of spent fuel and high level wastes, including an agreed basis for assessing the adequacy of waste form and repository performance over long periods.

Response: The Government accepts the recommendation. Although not engaged in long-term spent fuel management or high level waste disposal, Australia can contribute to the discussion of issues in the relevant international forums, and assist in the development of international standards, particularly in areas of direct interest to Australia such as SYNROC.

Recommendation 25

— That Australia not seek to impose particular strategies for radioactive waste management on countries using Australian uranium but rather encourage all countries to adopt the best practicable, rather than merely adequate, waste management strategies.

Response: While the Government accepts that it should encourage all countries to adopt the best practicable waste management strategies, it will vigorously oppose strategies which involve ocean dumping.

Annex II

HOUSE OF REPRESENTATIVES QUESTION

STATEMENT BY THE MINISTER FOR FOREIGN AFFAIRS ON NUCLEAR SAFEGUARDS FOR AUSTRALIAN URANIUM (QUESTION No. 884)

(7th May 1985)

In ensuring that uranium exported by Australia for peaceful purposes is not used in nuclear weapons, the Government relies upon:

a) the operation of its network of bilateral nuclear safeguards treaties, which contain binding international undertakings that:

- Australian uranium will not be diverted to military or nuclear explosive purposes nor used for research thereon;
- Australian uranium and derived generations of nuclear material will be covered by International Atomic Energy Agency (IAEA) safeguards to verify compliance with this;
- Fall-back safeguards will apply if at any stage NPT or IAEA safeguards ceased to operate;
- Prior Australian consent is required to the enrichment of Australian uranium beyond 20 per cent in the isotope U-235, for the reprocessing of spent fuel derived from Australian uranium, and for retransfer of Australian uranium to another country. Although Australia has not received nor consented to any proposal to enrich Australian uranium beyond 20 per cent in the isotope U-235, it has exercised its prior consent rights over reprocessing and retransfer undertaken by certain of our treaty partners on a long-term and specific basis, including within the parameters of clearly defined fuel cycle requirements and a delineated and recorded nuclear fuel cycle programme;
- Adequate physical security to internationally agreed levels to prevent theft of nuclear material will be applied by importing countries;
- Sanctions (enforceable if necessary by compulsory international arbitration) may be invoked by Australia if specified breaches occur; and
- Consultations with bilateral nuclear safeguards treaty partners be held at least annually and more frequently as and when required, particularly in respect of reprocessing and plutonium use questions.

Australia will supply uranium only to countries with which it has concluded nuclear safeguards agreements. Australia has retained the right to be selective as to the countries with which it is prepared to sign nuclear safeguards agreements and to which it is prepared to export uranium. In addition, Australia will not supply uranium to any non-nuclear weapon State not party to the NPT.

Australia has concluded a network of eleven nuclear safeguards agreements (with Finland, the Philippines, the Republic of Korea, the United States of America, the United Kingdom, France, Canada, Sweden, EURATOM, Japan and the IAEA). The operation of this network is constantly monitored by the Government, including through the Australian Safeguards Office (ASO). Where Australian uranium can be and has been exported subject to one or more of the above agreements, ASO maintains a constant check through an elaborate system of notifications and reports on the disposition of all Australian uranium and subsequent generations of produced nuclear material throughout the international nuclear fuel cycle. This monitoring is supplemented by regular consultations. It should be noted that although Australia's nuclear safeguards agreement with the IAEA primarily deals with the application of safeguards in Australia required by the NPT, it also contains obligations for Australia to notify the IAEA when uranium ore concentrate is exported to another non-nuclear weapon State or when other nuclear material under safeguards is exported to another country.

b) International nuclear safeguards applied by the IAEA to verify non-diversion of nuclear material (including Australian uranium) from peaceful purposes within the jurisdiction of Australia's treaty partners.

The Government recognises that the Agency safeguards system is not perfect, although it provides substantial assurance that, in NPT States, the diversion of nuclear material from civil facilities is not occurring. On a technical level, there is continued improvement; both here and on other levels, the Government is committed to and working actively towards the progressive enhancement of the effectiveness of Agency safeguards.

The Government commissioned the Australian Science and Technology Council (ASTEC) to undertake a thorough review of Australia's role in the nuclear fuel cycle, taking into account its commitment to nuclear non-proliferation to an effective NPT and to the application of the most stringent safeguards to future exports of Australian uranium. The Government's response to the ASTEC Report sets out the concrete and methodical programme it has in mind pursuing in this regard.

Annex III

NUCLEAR NON-PROLIFERATION (SAFEGUARDS) ACT 1987

EXTRACT FROM SECTION 4(1)

"'associated equipment' means equipment or plant that:

a) is specially designed, manufactured or built for use, or is specially suited (whether with or without modification or adaptation) for use, in:

i) nuclear activities; or
ii) the production of nuclear weapons or other nuclear explosive devices; and

b) is included in a class of equipment or plant that is declared by the Minister, in writing, to be associated equipment for the purposes of this definition,

and includes a component or part of such equipment or plant;

"associated item" means:

a) associated material;
b) associated equipment; or
c) associated technology;

"associated material" means any material (other than nuclear material, associated equipment or associated technology) that:

a) is of a kind specially suited for use in the construction or operation of a nuclear reactor; and
b) is included in a class of material that is declared by the Minister, in writing, to be associated material for the purposes of this definition;

"associated technology" means any document that contains information (other than information that is lawfully available, whether within Australia or outside Australia and whether for a price or free of charge to the public or a section of the public):

a) that is applicable primarily to the design, production, operation, testing or use of:

i) equipment or plant for:
A) the enrichment of nuclear material;
B) the reprocessing of irradiated nuclear material; or
C) the production of heavy water; or

ii) nuclear weapons or other nuclear explosive devices; or

b) to which a prescribed international agreement applies and that is of a kind declared by the Minister, in writing, to be information to which this definition applies,

and includes any photograph, model or other thing from which such information may be obtained or deduced;".

Annex IV

CUSTOMS (PROHIBITED EXPORTS) REGULATIONS

NINTH SCHEDULE

GOODS THE EXPORTATION OF WHICH IS PROHIBITED UNLESS THE APPROVAL OF THE MINISTER OF STATE FOR PRIMARY INDUSTRIES AND ENERGY OR AN AUTHORISED PERSON IS PRODUCED TO THE COLLECTOR

(as amended on 31st July 1986)

Item No.	Description of Goods
1	(1) Beryllium metal and any goods made wholly of beryllium metal other than beryllium windows for medical X-ray machines (2) Beryllium alloys containing more than 50 per centum of beryllium by weight (3) Beryllium oxide and beryllium compounds
2	Calcium containing both less than one-thousandth (0.001) per centum by weight of boron and less than one-hundredth (0.01) per centum by weight of impurities other than magnesium and boron
3	(1) Balancing machines, fixed or portable, horizontal or vertical: *(a)* suitable for the flexible balancing of centrifuge rotors: *(i)* not less than 75 millimetres, and not more than 410 millimetres, in diameter; and *(ii)* 600 millimetres or more in length; *(b)* having a mass capability of not less than 0.9 kilograms and not more than 23 kilograms; *(c)* capable of balancing to a residual imbalance of 25 millimetre-grams per kilogram per plan or less; and *(d)* capable of the flexible balancing of centrifuge rotors in 3 or more planes (2) Computer equipment specially designed or prepared for use as part of, or in conjunction with, any such balancing machine, and any documents or other materials appurtenant to the operation of such computer equipment
4	Turbo, centrifugal and axial flow compressors and blowers, having a capacity of not less than 1.7 cubic metres per minute and wholly made of, or lined with, aluminium, nickel or an alloy containing not less than 60 per centum of nickel
4A	Equipment (including parts and components) of the following kinds specially designed or prepared for the manufacture or assembly of the rotating components of gas centrifuges for the enrichment of uranium by the use of gaseous uranium hexafluoride, namely: *(a)* filament winding machines specially designed or prepared to fabricate composite rotor tubes from fibrous and filamentary materials, being machines in which the motions for positioning, wrapping and winding of fibres are co-ordinated and programmed in 3 or more axes; *(b)* rotor assembly equipment, including mandrels, clamps and shrink fit machines, being equipment specially designed or prepared for the assembly of rotor tube sections, baffles and end-caps; *(c)* rotor straightening equipment specially designed or prepared for the alignment of rotor tube sections to a common axis, including such equipment that consists of precision measuring probes linked to a computer that subsequently controls the action of components used for aligning the rotor tube sections; *(d)* equipment specially designed or prepared for the manufacture of rings or bellows;
5	(1) Deuterium (2) Compounds, mixtures and solutions containing deuterium in which the ratio of the number of deuterium atoms to hydrogen atoms exceeds 1:5000

Item No.	Description of Goods
6	Dosimeters for personal radiation monitoring capable of measuring: *(a)* in one exposure, a dosage of between 25 and 800 roentgens; or *(b)* dose rates of between one to 80 roentgens per hour, other than film dosimeters and dosimeters designed specifically for use with medical radiation equipment
7	Electrolytic cells specifically designed to produce more than 100 grammes of fluorine per hour
8	Flash discharge X-ray units (including tubes, parts and accessories designed for use in, or in conjunction with, such units) having: *(a)* a peak power greater than 500 megawatts; *(b)* an output voltage greater than 500 kilovolts; and *(c)* a pulse width less than 0.2 microsecond
9	(1) Fluorine (2) The following fluorinated compounds: *(a)* chlorine trifluoride; *(b)* trichlorotrifluoroethane; *(c)* dichlorotetrafluoroethane
10	Fissionable materials, namely: *(a)* plutonium; *(b)* uranium enriched in isotope 235; *(c)* isotope 233 of uranium; *(d)* irradiated uranium containing plutonium; *(e)* irradiated thorium containing uranium 233; and *(f)* compounds, alloys and mixtures of any of the materials specified in this item
11	Graphite (artificial): *(a)* that is in the form of blocks or rods from which a cube of 50 millimetres side or greater can be cut; *(b)* that has a boron content not exceeding 5 parts per million; and *(c)* the density of which is greater than 1.5 grams per cubic centimetre
12	(1) Hafnium metal (2) Alloys and compounds containing more than 15 per centum of hafnium by weight
13	Heat exchanges capable of being used in gaseous diffusion plants, designed to operate at sub-atmospheric pressures, having a leak rate of less than 10^{-4} atmospheres per hour under a pressure differential of one atmosphere, and the clad tubes of which are made of any of the following materials: *(a)* aluminium; *(b)* copper; *(c)* nickel; *(d)* alloy containing more than 60 per centum of nickel; or *(e)* a combination of two or more of the materials specified in this item
14	on separaters that are: *(a)* electro-magnetic; and *(b)* of high sensitivity, including *(c)* mass spectrographs having analyser assemblies capable of handling uranium hexafluoride; *(d)* mass spectrometers having such analyser assemblies; *(e)* solid source mass spectrographs; and *(f)* solid source mass spectrometers
15	(1) Lithium metal (2) Lithium alloys (3) Lithium compounds
15A	Materials of the following kinds specially prepared for the construction of rotating components of gas centrifuges, namely: *(a)* maraging steel, in crude, semi-fabricated or fabricated form, whether or not finally heat-treated, that is capable of an ultimate tensile strength of not less than 2 000 megapascals;

Item No.	Description of Goods
	(*b*) aluminium alloys, in tube form or forgings, that are capable of an ultimate tensile strength of not less than 460 megapascals; (*c*) Filamentary materials suitable for use in composite structures having: (*i*) a specific modulus of not less than 12.3×10^6, being the numerical value derived in accordance with the formula: $\frac{A}{B}$ where: A is the numerical value of Young's modulus, in relation to the material, expressed in megapascals; and B is the numerical value of the density of the material expressed in kilograms per cubic metre; and (*ii*) a specific ultimate tensile strength of not less than 0.3×10^6, being the numerical value derived in accordance with the formula: $\frac{A}{B}$ where: A is the numerical value of the ultimate tensile strength of the material expressed in megapascals; and B is the numerical value of the density of the material expressed in kilograms per cubic metre
15B	Metal-working machines, spin-forming and flow-forming, with double support or 3 rollers, being machines fitted, and designed to be fitted, with a drive motor the maximum continuous power output of which is not less than 18.5 kilowatts
16	Minerals, raw and treated (including residues and tailings), containing more than 0.05 per centum of uranium or thorium, singly or together, including the following materials: (*a*) monazite and monazite sands; (*b*) ores containing thorium (including uranothorianite); and (*c*) ores containing uranium (including pitchblende)
17	Nickel in any of the following forms: (*a*) wire containing not less than 95 per centum of nickel, being wire not exceeding 0.10 millimetres in diameter; (*b*) woven wire mesh composed of wire containing not less than 95 per centum of nickel and containing not less than 60 wires per linear centimetre; and (*c*) nickel powder the particle size of which is less than 200 microns
18	(1) Nuclear reactors capable of operation so as to maintain a controlled self-sustaining fission chain reaction (2) Major components of nuclear reactors including: (*a*) reactor vessels; (*b*) core support structures; (*c*) coolant pumps; (*d*) fuel element handling equipment; (*e*) heat exchangers; and (*f*) control rod drive mechanisms
18A	Plants for: (*a*) the reprocessing of irradiated nuclear reactor fuel elements and equipment especially designed or prepared therefor, including: (*i*) solvent extraction equipment; (*ii*) chemical holding or storage vessels: (*iii*) plutonium nitrate to plutonium oxide conversion systems; and (*iv*) plutonium metal productions systems; and (*b*) the fabrication of nuclear reactor fuel elements
18B	Plants for the production of deuterium and compounds containing deuterium and equipment specially designed or prepared therefor

Item No.	Description of Goods
18C	(1) Plants for: *(a)* the production or purification of uranium hexafluoride; or *(b)* the enrichment or separation of isotopes (2) Equipment specially designed or prepared for use as part of, or in substitution for the whole or any part of, such a plant, including, in particular: *(a)* gaseous diffusion barriers; *(b)* gaseous diffusion housings; *(c)* valves resistant to corrosion by uranium hexafluoride or fluorine; *(d)* gas centrifuge separation units, including auxiliary equipment for use in connection with such units; *(e)* jet-nozzle separation units; *(f)* vortex separation units; *(g)* large axial or centrifugal compressors and special seals for such compressors; *(h)* frequency changers capable of multiphase electrical output of not less than 600 hertz and not more than 2 000 hertz, and parts, components and sub-assemblies for such frequency changers; *(j)* bulging dies; *(k)* pressure gauges capable of measuring pressures to 13.5 kilopascals or less, having sensing elements of nickel, nickel alloy, phosphor bronze, stainless steel, aluminium or aluminium alloy that are resistant to corrosion by uranium hexafluoride or hydrogen fluoride; *(m)* process-control instruments that are resistant to corrosion by uranium hexafluoride or fluorine, whether specially designed or specially suitable for monitoring or controlling the procesing of material in uranium hexafluoride conversion plants or not; *(n)* nuclear-grade viton sealing rings, being rings of the type known as "O" rings, the inside diameter of which is more than 40 millimetres; *(o)* parts and components of any such equipment; and *(p)* any other parts and components of such a plant
19	Positive ion sources suitable for use in mass spectrographs and mass spectrometers and capable of handling uranium hexafluoride
20	(1) Thorium (wrought or unwrought) (2) Compounds containing tritium in which the ratio of tritium to hydrogen by atoms exceeds one part in 1 000 *(a)* alloys containing less than 1.5 per centum of thorium by weight; and *(b)* medicinals
21	(1) Tritium (2) Compounds containing tritium in which the ratio of tritium to hydrogen by atoms exceeds one part in 1 000
22	(1) Uranium, natural or depleted in the isotope 235 (wrought or unwrought) (2) Alloys, mixtures and compounds containing natural uranium or uranium depleted in the isotope 235 with a uranium content exceeding 0.05 per centum, but not including medicinals
23	Valves: *(a)* that are 5 millimetres or greater in diameter with bellows seal; *(b)* that are made of, or lined with, aluminium, nickel or an alloy containing not less than 60 per centum of nickel; *(c)* that are either manually or automatically operated; and *(d)* than have other than metal to metal seats
24	Zirconium, and any goods made of zirconium: *(a)* in which the ratio of hafnium content to zirconium content is less that 1 500 parts by weight; and *(b)* being: *(i)* zirconium metal; *(ii)* alloys containing more than 50 per centum by weight of zirconium; or *(iii)* compounds of zirconium.

AUSTRIA

TABLE OF CONTENTS

AUSTRIA

I. INTRODUCTION

On 15th December 1978 a Federal Act was adopted in Austria, banning the use of nuclear fission for energy purposes (BGBl[1] No. 676/1978). This has, quite naturally, affected the development and the use of nuclear energy in the country without necessarily having an incidence on other nuclear activities.

Austrian laws and regulations governing possession, use etc. and trade in nuclear material and equipment, as well as technology transfers in that field are focused primarily on nuclear security. This general term covers radiation protection, namely the protection of present and future populations against radiation hazards; technical safety of equipment; safeguards, in particular inspections and accounting to prevent nuclear materials from being diverted to unauthorised uses and finally, physical protection of such materials against interference or encroachment by unauthorised third parties.

Dealings with nuclear material and equipment are regulated by the Radiation Protection Act (*Strahlenschutzgesetz*) of 11th June 1969 (BGBl No. 227/1969) and the Safeguards Act (*Sicherheitskontrollegesetz*) of 25th October 1972 (BGBl No. 408/1972) as amended by the Act of 15th June 1978 (BGB1 No. 315/1978) and, to the extent that their carriage is involved, by a number of transport regulations. In addition, the Export Control Regulations of 9th December 1975 (BGBl No. 629/1975) as amended on 6th October 1978 (BGBl No. 518/1978)[2] made under the Safeguards Act, regulate international trade in such material and equipment, together with the Foreign Trade Act (*Aussenhandelgesetz*) of 28th June 1968 (BGBl No. 314/1968).

Responsibility for nuclear trade and its different aspects is not centralised in Austria ; it is shared between the Federal Chancellery and different Federal Ministries.

This Study will describe the regulation of nuclear trade in Austria, reflecting the distinction between the regime for exports of nuclear material and equipment which is characterised by safeguards and physical protection, and that for trade in radioactive materials, governed by radiation protection legislation. In addition, transport will also be discussed, to the extent that it affects nuclear trade.

II. TRADE IN NUCLEAR MATERIAL AND EQUIPMENT

1. Export Regime

a) Nuclear regulations

Under the 1972 Safeguards Act and in fulfilment of Austria's international obligations, the export of nuclear material must be authorised by the *Federal Chancellor* (*Bundeskanzler*)[3]. Therefore, the export of such materials and of nuclear-related equipment is subject to a licence, which is granted when it is established that appropriate safeguards (with reference to the Treaty on the Non-Proliferation of Nuclear Weapons) and physical protection measures are applied in the country of destination.

The *Office of the Federal Chancellor* (*Bundeskanzleramt*), which is responsible for international relations regarding the peaceful uses of nuclear energy, issues the necessary export licences for such items and for related non-nuclear materials (e.g. heavy water). The general rules of the General Administration Procedure Act (*Allgemeines Verwaltungsverfahrensgesetz*) are applicable to the licensing procedure.

The *Export Control Regulations* designate the commodities subject to export licences, in accordance with Article II, Section 4(4) of the Act; these commodities are listed in the *Annex* hereto.

b) General regulations

Under the 1968 Foreign Trade Act the import and export of nuclear material requires in parallel the prior authorisation of the *Federal Ministry for Economy* (formerly the Ministry of Trade and Industry). Most of the items require a licence at Ministerial level; some export licences are granted directly at the Customs Office and a few require no licence under this Act, quite apart from any licence required under the Safeguards Act. This concerns, *inter alia*, fuel charging and discharging machines, nuclear grade graphite, pumps etc.

2. Safeguards

The Safeguards Act was adopted to implement a 1971 Agreement with the International Atomic Energy Agency for the application of safeguards in pursuance of the Treaty on the Non-Proliferation of Nuclear Weapons (see section on Agreements below).

The Act (Article II, Section 2) submits the possession of fissionable materials, enriched uranium, ores and equipment which produces, uses or reprocesses fissionable materials to a system of *safeguards* set up by the Federal Chancellor who is the control authority.

Under the system, holders of radioactive materials must, *inter alia*, draw up an inventory of the materials in their possession, report periodically on the amount they possess, and on any changes in that amount ; reports must also be made regarding modifications in the storage of such materials (Article II, Section 4).

Holders of radioactive materials must allow inspections by the appropriate authorities. When exercising safeguards, disruptions of the normal working order should be avoided and secrecy of technical data ensured ; the economic profit of the nuclear activity should not be taken into account (Article II, Section 6).

Finally, the Act imposes *sanctions* if the required information on radioactive materials is not supplied or if the safeguards provisions are not complied with (Article II, Section 8).

Safeguards inspectors are charged with controlling observance of any conditions imposed and in case of non-compliance with the conditions or of trading without authorisation, a fine is payable where there has been no imposition of a judicial sanction (Article II, Section 7(5), and Section 9).

3. Physical Protection

The *Federal Ministry of the Interior* (*Bundesministerium für Inneres*), after having consulted the Federal Ministry for Health and Environmental Protection (*Bundesministerium für Gesundheit und Umweltschutz*), may impose any measures considered necessary to ensure the protection of nuclear materials at domestic level. His powers in that field also extend to exports of nuclear material and equipment (Safeguards Act, Article II, Section 7). The levels of and physical procedures for physical protection are at least equivalent to the Guidelines in IAEA document INFCIRC/225/Rev.1.

III. TRADE IN RADIOACTIVE MATERIALS

The 1969 *Act on Radiation Protection* provides measures for protecting the life and health of persons and their descendants against radiation injuries (Section 1). As such, it lays down a system of licensing, notification and approval regarding the handling of radioactive materials and the functioning of equipment producing or using radiation.

Originally the Federal Ministry for Health and Environmental Protection was generally responsible for radiation protection matters, and in this connection it was also responsible for administering the Radiation Protection Act and regulations made thereunder (Section 41). However this competence was transferred to the Federal Chancellery on 1st April 1987.

The handling of radioactive materials is defined as "the mining, production, storage, transport, consigning, receiving ... use ... of radioactive materials ..." ; radiation-emitting equipment means "equipment designed to produce ionizing radiations or releasing such radiation while in operation..."[Section 2(e) and (d)].

1. Licensing Procedure

Dealings with radioactive materials and radiation-emitting equipment require to be licensed or approved in accordance with the provisions of the Radiation Protection Act (Sections 5 to 7). It is further specified that an authorisation is required for the handling of radioactive materials which do not need to be licensed under the Act (Section 10).

When filing an application for a *licence* or *approval*, the applicant must submit all documents for appraising the request, including a detailed description of the installation, its plan, a description of the type of operations foreseen and a statement of the radiation protection measures envisaged [Section 5(6)].

Licences for the handling of radioactive materials or the housing of radiation-emitting equipment are generally granted on the basis of the construction of installations containing them [Section 5(1)]. The construction of such installations for use in a branch of activity covered by the Trading and Industrial Code (*Gewerbeordnung*) is subject to approval in accordance with the procedure established by the Code [Section 5(2)]. Such approval may replace the licence.

A licence is also required for dealings with radioactive materials or radiation-emitting equipment which do not require the installations referred to above. The procedure for such licences is similar to that for installations (Section 10).

The possession of radioactive materials or radiation-emitting equipment not subject to licensing under the Act must be *notified* immediately to the authorities.

Models of instruments containing radioactive materials or radiation-emitting equipment must be *approved* by administrative decision and approval will be given only on condition that the radioactive materials remain in a safe containment (Section 19). It is expressly forbidden to distribute such instruments or equipment in Austria before approval is granted [Section 19(6)].

Applications for official approval of models of instruments or radiation-emitting equipment must be accompanied by an expert report from an officially-recognised testing laboratory certifying that the conditions laid down for such approval have been met [Section 19(4)]. The request must also include a detailed description of the instrument or radiation-emitting equipment together with a set of plans and a statement on the use envisaged; where appropriate a description must be given of the radiation protection features it is intended to provide.

Models of radiation sources also require approval. Manufacturers of such sources must seek approval by the authorities, or in the case of foreign manufacturers, through their official agents in Austria (Section 21). Each article of an approved model must have a certificate attached detailing, *inter alia*, the authorised use and the officially imposed conditions (Section 22).

A licence, authorisation or approval as the case may be, is granted if adequate precautions have been taken to protect the life or health of persons and their descendants against radiation injury and the applicant's reliability is established in relation to the branch of activity he plans to engage in [Section 5(3)].

Radioactive materials subject to licensing under the Act can only be sold to authorised persons in accordance with its provisions (Section 24).

Finally, when granting licences, authorisations or approvals, the authorities stipulate the conditions to be observed by the applicant (Sections 7 and 19).

2. Records

All persons trading in radioactive materials must keep a record of their nature and amount as well as of the name and address of the supplier or customer. These records must be accessible at all times to administrative bodies and must be produced to the authorities on request. They must be kept for five years (Section 23).

3. Exemptions

Compulsory licences or authorisations may be waived by regulations by the authorities in respect of materials presenting no danger to life or health or where the radiation sources are of types officially approved in accordance with the Act [Section 13(1) and (2)]. They may also be waived regarding materials in course of transport, when such transport is governed by the regulations applying to the transport of goods by road, rail, waterway, air or parcel post [Section 13(3)].

Also, other exemptions (notifications under the Act) concern radioactive materials which, when handled, do not exceed the radiation values fixed by regulation and instruments, the models of which have received official approval [Section 25(2)].

4. Sanctions

The Radiation Protection Act (Section 39) provides that violation of provisions concerning radioactive materials and radiation-emitting equipment is punishable by a fine of up to 30 000 Austrian schillings or by up to six weeks' imprisonment.

IV. TRANSPORT

The transport of radioactive materials in Austria[4] is strictly controlled for the purpose of ensuring that any such transport is effected as safely as possible. Safety measures of a general nature are embodied in the 1969 Radiation Protection Act.

The international transport of radioactive materials by rail is carried out in accordance with the International Regulations concerning the Carriage of Dangerous Goods by Rail (RID). International transport of such materials by road is subject to the European Agreement concerning the International Carriage of Dangerous Goods by Road (ADR); these provisions also apply to national road transport as provided by the Federal Act concerning the Carriage of Dangerous Goods (*Bundesgesetz über die Beförderung gefährlicher Güter*) of 18th May 1979 (BGBl No. 209/1979).

As regards air transport, the Restricted Articles Regulations of the International Air Transport Association (IATA) are applied in the form of conditions included in the authorisation required for such type of transport. Although Austria has no regulations for the maritime transport of radioactive materials, sea transport operations are effected in accordance with the rules laid down in the International Maritime Organisation's (IMO) Dangerous Goods Code.

The Federal Ministry of Transport is the competent authority for all modes of transport in Austria and as such is normally consulted by the Ministry of the Interior when imposing physical protection measures involving transport operations.

V. INTELLECTUAL PROPERTY IN THE NUCLEAR FIELD

There are no specific provisions concerning intellectual property or patents in the nuclear field.

VI. AGREEMENTS

1. Multilateral Agreements

Austria has concluded the following international agreements:

- Treaty on the Non-Proliferation of Nuclear Weapons, ratified on 27th June 1969;
- Convention on the Physical Protection of Nuclear Material, signed on 3rd March 1980 but not yet ratified.

2. Bilateral Agreements

Austria has concluded the following bilateral agreements :

a) Safeguards Agreements with ***IAEA***

- On 21st September 1971 (BGBl No. 239/1972), Austria concluded an Agreement with the IAEA for the application of safeguards in pursuance of the Treaty on the Non-Proliferation of Nuclear Weapons which came into force on 23rd July 1972.

  Also on 21st September 1971 (BGBl No. 240/1972), a Protocol was concluded to suspend the Agreement of 20th August 1969 between Austria, the United States and the IAEA for the application of safeguards in relation to the leased nuclear material from the United States referred to below.

b) Agreement with the ***United States of America***

- Austria concluded an Agreement for co-operation in the peaceful uses of nuclear energy with the United States on 22nd July 1959. The Agreement provides for exchange of information on research reactors, on health and safety problems related to the use of such reactors and on the use of radioisotopes for research. It also covers the loan of fuels for research reactors built in Austria.
- Pursuant to this framework agreement, Austria entered into a further *Agreement* on the leasing of special nuclear material from the United States. This Agreement, which came into force on 20th January 1970 (BGBl No. 85/1970), lays down the terms and conditions whereby the Austrian Government may lease special nuclear material from the United States it being understood that all leased material is returned to the latter which remains its owner. The Agreement was amended on 14th June 1974 (BGBl No. 708/1974) ; the amendment which came into force on 8th October that same year incorporates other provisions for the supply by the United States of uranium enrichment services and reflects the United States uranium supply policies adopted in 1972. Both Parties agreed that IAEA Safeguards would continue to apply to materials, equipment and facilities transferred under the Agreement.

c) Agreement with the ***French Atomic Energy Commission***

- The Office of the Federal Chancellor concluded an Agreement on co-operation with the French Atomic Energy Commission (CEA) in February 1967. Co-operation covers exchange of documents and scientific information on research and prototype reactors, the use of radioisotopes in industry, agriculture, biology and medicine as well as safety and radiation protection.

NOTES AND REFERENCES

1. BGBl =Bundesgetzblatt =Official Gazette.
2. A further amendment is being prepared.
3. Article II, Section(4)(3) provides as follows: "To the extent that it is necessary for the fulfilment of the obligations undertaken in connection with the Treaty on the Non-Proliferation of Nuclear Weapons, the export of source or special fissionable material and of equipment or material especially designed or prepared for the processing, use or production of special fissionable material requires a licence from the Federal Chancellor. Such licence is to be granted if it is ensured that the source or special fissionable material is subject, in the recipient country, to the safeguards required by Article III of the Treaty on the Non-Proliferation of Nuclear Weapons, and that the nuclear material or nuclear installations concerned are protected against acts and interferences of unauthorised third persons, according to internationally recognised guidelines".
4. For further details see *Regulations Governing the Transport of Radioactive Materials*, OECD/NEA, 1980.

Annex

LIST OF COMMODITIES SUBJECT TO AN EXPORT LICENCE ACCORDING TO THE EXPORT REGULATIONS ISSUED UNDER THE SAFEGUARDS ACT*

1. Nuclear reactors, except zero energy reactors the maximum production plutonium production rate of which does not exceed 100 grammes per year.
2. Equipment for nuclear reactors, i.e.:
   a) reactor pressure vessels and parts thereof;
   b) reactor fuel charging and discharging machines;
   c) reactor control rods;
   d) reactor pressure pipes;
   e) zirconium pipes in quantities exceeding 500 kilogrammes per year;
   f) circulation pumps for the primary coolant.
3. Deuterium and deuterium compounds (e.g. heavy water) where the deuterium/hydrogen ratio exceeds 1:5000, for use in a reactor, if the quantity of deuterium atoms exported to the recipient State exceeds 200 kilogrammes within 12 months.
4. Nuclear graphite, if the total quantity exported to the recipient States exceeds 30 tons within 12 months.
5.** Installations for the reprocessing of irradiated fuel elements and equipment especially designed or prepared for that purpose, i.e.:
   a) fuel element choppers;
   b) dissolvers;
   c) solvent extractors;
   d) holding or storage vessels;
   e) plutonium nitrate to oxide conversion systems;
   f) plutonium metal production systems.
6. Installations for the production of fuel elements.
7.** Equipment specially designed or prepared for the separation of uranium isotopes, except analytical instruments, i.e.:
   A. Gas centrifuges for the separation of uranium isotopes
      Rotating components
      a) complete rotors;
      b) rotor cylinders;
      c) rings or bellows;
      d) baffles;
      e) top and bottom caps;
      f) the materials used for the components described in a) to e) are maraging steel, aluminium alloys, or filamentary materials, each exceeding a given tensile strength.
      Static components
      g) magnetic suspension bearings;
      h) bearings/dampers;
      i) molecular pumps;
      j) motor stators;
      k) feed systems/product and tails withdrawal systems;
      l) machine header piping systems;
      m) UF_6 mass spectrometers/ion sources;
      n) frequency changers (converters or inverters).
   B. Jet nozzle separation units, vortex separation units, gaseous diffusion barriers and gaseous diffuser housings.
8. Source material (natural and depleted uranium, thorium and each of the foregoing substances in the form of metals, alloys, chemical compounds or concentrates) in quantities exceeding 0.5 kilogrammes.
9. Special fissionable material (plutonium 239, uranium 233, uranium enriched in the isotopes 235 or 233, and each material containing one or more of the foregoing substances according to the IAEA Statute) in quantities exceeding 0.5 grammes.
10. Installations for the production of heavy water, deuterium and deuterium compounds and equipment especially designed or prepared therefor.

* Unofficial translation.
** Version of the proposed amendment; see Note 2.

BELGIUM

TABLE OF CONTENTS

BELGIUM

I. INTRODUCTION

Although not among the countries which export nuclear reactors or other large items of equipment relating to the nuclear fuel cycle, Belgium is active in the nuclear equipment and services market and participates in various industrial enterprises in this field. After having, in the past, itself mined mineral resources (Belgian-Congo), it now has to import the raw materials needed for its nuclear power programme.

It may first of all be said that Belgian legislation in the nuclear field reflects the desire of the national authorities to follow closely the provisions of Community law and to take account of the prerogatives attributed to the European Community institutions under the EURATOM Treaty.

There are two aspects to Belgian legislation governing trade, imports and exports in the nuclear field. The first comprises measures by which the government exercises control over trade in and the import and export of "sensitive" raw materials and equipment which can be used to produce nuclear power and which may affect the obligations undertaken by Belgium with regard to the non-proliferation of nuclear weapons or physical protection. Some of these measures, such as the 1955 Act on national security in the field of nuclear energy or the 1981 Act concerning conditions for the export of nuclear material and equipment, are specifically nuclear in nature. To them must be added the general legislation on the regulation of foreign trade.

The second aspect concerns the rules for authorising and controlling trade in radioactive substances and in equipment emitting ionizing radiation, for purposes of radiological safety. The relevant provisions are contained essentially in the General Regulations for the Protection of the Public and Workers against the Hazards of Ionizing Radiation (Royal Decree of 28th February 1963 as amended)[1].

This distinction has served as a basis for the drafting of the present study. The reader will also be given some brief information on the rules regulating intellectual property and on agreements concerning trade in nuclear materials and equipment.

II. IMPORT AND EXPORT OF, AND TRADE IN NUCLEAR MATERIAL AND EQUIPMENT

Regulations in this field consist of provisions relating to national security in the nuclear field, legislation dealing more particularly with the non-proliferation of nuclear weapons and, lastly, general regulations governing foreign trade[2].

1. National Security in the Nuclear Field

The Act of 4th August 1955 concerning national security in the field of nuclear energy empowers the authorities, in the interests of national defence and national security, to subject to the conditions they deem appropriate, research, materials[3], and nuclear production methods carried out or used by physical or legal persons and public establishments which have at their disposal information or materials either supplied by the Government or obtained with its permission.

These measures govern the fitting out, surveillance and conditions of access to premises used for these purposes. Such work is also covered by the rules of secrecy necessary for national security and by the corresponding provisions of the Penal Code (Chapter II, Book I, Title II).

A *Royal Decree of 14th March 1956*[4] (as amended by Royal Decrees of 2nd April 1957 and 18th October 1974) contains provisions relating to the implementation of the Act of 4th August 1955 ; these provisions deal first with the classification of nuclear information and materials needing to be safeguarded and secondly, with the safety measures to be used in respect of documents and materials classified as secret or confidential and of the premises in which such documents and materials are used. In addition, the Decree lays down the conditions which must be met by persons authorised to possess or use such materials and information[5].

Failure to comply with the obligations arising under the Act of 1955 and the Royal Decree of 14th March 1956 is punished by fines and prison sentences (Sections 2 and 3 of the Act and Chapter VI of the Decree).

2. Non-Proliferation of Nuclear Weapons

The production and use, in Belgium, of ores, source materials and special fissile materials[6] are subject to the provisions of the EURATOM Treaty relating to the establishment of a security control and its implementing regulations, which form an integral part of Belgian legislation, and to the inspections provided for in the Treaty on the Non-proliferation of Nuclear Weapons on the basis of the 1973 IAEA-EURATOM so-called Verification Agreement (Acts of 2nd December 1957 and 20th July 1978).

More specifically, an Act concerning conditions for the export of nuclear material, equipment and technological data was adopted on *9th February 1981*. The material, equipment and technological data covered by this Act are to be defined by Royal Decree, in the light of the international nuclear agreements to which Belgium is Party (the Decree has not yet been published).

As stated in its Section 1, the purpose of the Act is to ensure that the international agreements on the non-proliferation of nuclear weapons signed by Belgium are implemented. With this in view, it is prohibited to export to non-nuclear weapon states, within the meaning of the NPT, nuclear material and equipment or nuclear technological data and consequential information, except for peaceful uses and subject to the required controls.

To secure compliance with these conditions, each export operation is subject to prior authorisation by the Minister responsible for energy (the Minister of Economic Affairs), following the opinion of an *Advisory Committee*.

The members of the Advisory Committee are appointed by the King; members include, in particular, representatives of the Ministries responsible for Economic Affairs, Foreign Relations, Foreign Trade, Justice, Public Health, the Environment and Scientific Policy (Section 1).

The precise composition of the Committee as well as the conditions for granting the above-mentioned authorisation and the procedure to be followed in this respect are to be laid down by Royal Decree, as yet unpublished (Section 3). Should the need arise, the Committee will be able to call upon scientific experts to deal with questions submitted to it.

The Ministry responsible for energy has the task of ensuring compliance with the Act, without prejudice to action taken by the police. Provision is made under the Act for *penal sanctions* for breaches or attempted breaches of its provisions or those of its implementing decrees (Section 6).

The introduction *(exposé des motifs)* of the Act states that it does not affect the application of the legislation in force with regard to the import, export and transit of goods (see the following section), or transport, third party liability and health protection as concerns nuclear materials. Nor are the provisions of the Act intended to contravene the principle of the free movement of materials and equipment within the European Community.

3. Control of Nuclear Imports and Exports (General Regulations)

The law in this field is based on the *Act of 11th September 1962* (as amended by an Act of 6th July 1978), an Act of general application relating to the import, export and transit of goods. It delegates power to the King, the Head of the Executive, to regulate, by Decree discussed in the Council of Ministers, the import, export and transit of goods, in particular by a system of licensing, the levying of special duties or by formalities such as certificates of origin, in order either to:

— safeguard the vital interests of an economic sector or those of the national economy taken as a whole;
— safeguard the country's internal or external security;
— ensure implementation of treaties, agreements or arrangements with economic objectives or dealing with safety, and of the decisions or recommendations of international or supra-national organisations;
— help ensure compliance with the general principles of law and humanity recognised by civilised nations.

Under the Act of 11th September 1962, the competent Ministers may, when granting licences, lay down special conditions for the granting and use of licences.

Moreover, the Act provides that, when justified by special circumstances, the competent Ministers, acting together, may, by a reasoned decision, suspend the validity or order the withdrawal of licences.

The Act also provides for penal sanctions in the event of breaches or attempted breaches of its provisions. In implementing this Act, a Royal Decree of 24th October 1962 specified the general conditions for granting, and the validity and use of import, export and transit licences.

This implementing Decree stipulates that the following shall be null and void:

1. Licences obtained on the basis of applications containing inaccurate or intentionally incomplete statements.
2. Licences used to cover operations other than those for which they were granted.
3. Licences whose holders do not comply with the conditions imposed when the licence was granted.

Licences are issued in the name of the natural or legal persons to whom they are granted, and it is forbidden to assign licences or accept assignment of them.

a) Exports

Products requiring an export licence are listed in the annexes to a *Ministerial Order of 7th April 1988 — No. 935* (Moniteur belge of 11th May 1988) promulgated jointly by the Ministers of Economic Affairs, of Foreign Affairs, of Foreign Trade and Co-operation on

Development, and of Agriculture ; this Ministerial Order repeals previous Orders dealing with the same subject (those of 24th September 1985 and 19th October 1987). The Order of 7th April 1988 is supplemented by a Notice published in the Moniteur belge also on 11th May 1988.

The nuclear items for which an export licence is required are indicated in List II annexed to the Ministerial Order entitled "Products requiring an export licence" ; included in this List, under the heading "Energie atomique — supports de technologie", are nuclear material and nuclear installations as well as the other nuclear-related items of equipment subject to the licensing regime. The revised list is reproduced in the *Annex* to this Chapter. The Notice supplementing this list is also reproduced in the Annex.

No licence is required for export to the other BENELUX Economic Union countries.

b) Imports

At present, items requiring an import licence are listed in a *Ministerial Order of 24th September 1985* and its annexes (Moniteur belge of 29th October 1985) ; this Ministerial Order repeals previous orders dealing with the same subject.

A licence is required :

1. To import *all* goods originating in certain named countries.
2. To import certain goods, whatever the country of origin ; it should be noted, however, that nuclear items and equipment do not fall into this category.

c) Transit

Current regulations governing transit operations are to be found in a *Ministerial Order also of 7th April 1988* (Moniteur belge of 11th May 1988).

The goods requiring a transit licence are identical to those contained in List II of the Ministerial Order of 7th April 1988 requiring a licence for the export of certain goods and therefore include nuclear items and equipment.

It should be noted that a licence is required for transit only inasmuch as the goods come from certain specific countries or are destined for other specific countries and inasmuch as unloading and reloading is to be carried out in Belgium.

III. TRADE IN RADIOACTIVE SUBSTANCES

Belgian legislation in this field is essentially contained in a single text, namely the *General Regulations concerning the Protection of the Public and Workers against the Hazards of Ionizing Radiation*. This text was first promulgated by means of a Royal Decree dated 28th February 1963, adopted in pursuance of the Act of 29th March 1958 relating to the protection of the population against the hazards arising from ionizing radiation (as amended by the Acts of 29th May 1963, 3rd December 1969 and 14th July 1983) ; the 1963 Decree has been amended many times[7].

The General Regulations of 1963 are designed to ensure nuclear security and radiological safety with respect to all nuclear activities[8], subjecting them to a licensing or prior declaration procedure and to controls, the strictness of which depends on the degree of danger represented by these activities. The Regulations govern, in particular, the supervision of classified establishments, lay down radiation protection standards on the basis of the Directives of the Commission of the European Communities, specify the conditions for the processing and disposal of radioactive waste and the measures to be taken in the event of a radiation accident, and deal with the transport of radioactive substances[9].

The provisions relating to the import, carriage in transit and distribution of radioactive substances are also found in the General Regulations (Chapter IV).

1. Authorisation and Control

Radioactive substances and equipment containing such substances may be imported into or carried in transit through Belgium only by persons or enterprises licensed for this purpose by the Minister of Public Health (Section 38)[10].

Applications must include information concerning the identity (or business name) of the applicant, the licence he may hold under the rules regulating classified establishments, the purposes for which the substances are to be used, the characteristics of the substances in question and the third party liability insurance policy.

Licences may be granted subject to conditions other than those provided for in these Regulations and, in particular, limits may be imposed on the quantities, activity level and nature of the substances imported. Licences may be either general or specific, are granted for a limited period of time and may be revoked.

Radioactive substances or equipment containing them may be *imported* only via the customs offices designated for the purpose by the Minister of Public Health, with the agreement of the Minister of Finance (Section 39).

Beforc making any delivery, the firm distributing the imported substances must first obtain a declaration from the consignee in which the latter certifies that he possesses the operating licence required under the provisions of these Regulations governing classified establishments (Section 40).

Special accounting procedures are used with regard to the delivery of radioactive substances. Moreover, importers and distributors are required to supply the Minister of Public Health with monthly information about imports and deliveries effected and the consignees (Section 41 of the Regulations).

Licences for *transit* operations are subject to special conditions; a licence will be granted only if a person resident in Belgium and authorised for this purpose undertakes to compensate fully the victims of any accident. However, this requirement does not apply when the transport operation is covered by the special regime of nuclear third party liablity under the Paris Convention and the Brussels Supplementary Convention (Section 43).

Belgian legislation provides for the mutual recognition between the BENELUX countries of licences for the import, transport, carriage in transit and distribution of radioactive substances (Royal Decree of 27th July 1966).

The *conditioning* of radioactive substances being imported or in transit must comply with all the requirements under the General Regulations. There are particular provisions designed to prevent the theft or loss of such substances (Section 44).

2. Penal Sanctions and Prohibitions

Importing radioactive substances whose use is not authorised under the Regulations is prohibited. A ban may also be imposed, where necessary, on the distribution of certain radioactive substances designated by the Minister of Public Health (Section 64 of the General Regulations). The importation and marketing of certain articles and items of equipment such as pedoscopes or radioactive lightning conductors is prohibited. It is also forbidden to add radioactive substances to beauty products, cosmetics, toys and household products and items.

Breaches of these Regulations are punished by prison sentences and fines in accordance with the provisions of the Act of 29th March 1958, as amended, concerning protection of the public against the hazards of ionizing radiation (Sections 5 to 8 of the Act and Section 80 of the General Regulations of 1963).

3. Medical and Other Uses

Under the General Regulations (Chapter V), the importation, distribution, offering for sale and sale (as well as the preparation) of radioisotopes (or preparations containing them) used in an unsealed form in human or veterinary medecine are subject to the granting of a licence by the Minister responsible for Public Health.

The licence application, sent to the Minister, must provide detailed information about the substances concerned, the conditions of use, the distributor or importer and the protection measures envisaged (Section 45) and must also give reasons justifying the intended use. The licence specifies the substances and preparations to which it applies and the place where the operations involved must be carried out.

These licences are granted for a specific period of time not exceeding ten years; special conditions may be attached to them.

When the radioisotopes come from a foreign country, the application for an import licence must contain proof that the product is marketed in the country of origin with the approval of the competent authorities. Details must also be supplied with regard to the activity level and half-life of the isotope and the useful life of the product, its packaging and the sphere in which it is used (Section 45).

Manufacturers and importers of unsealed radioactive substances must deliver them directly to the doctors or veterinary surgeons authorised to use them. Suppliers must ask an authorised chemist to verify that radioisotopes and preparations containing them comply with the regulations (Section 49).

Manufacturers or importers of apparatus emitting ionizing radiation intended for use in diagnosis or therapy, must first request approval from the Public Health Department.

The provisions applicable to apparatus emitting ionizing radiation used for medical purposes also apply to the sources of radiation contained in such apparatus.

By way of derogation from the general ban imposed by the General Regulations (Section 64), the Minister responsible for Public Health may, following a favourable opinion from the Higher Council for Public Health, allow produce intended for human or animal consumption to be treated by ionizing radiation, subject to appropriate conditions including, in particular, approval of the apparatus used and the methods of treatment (Section 65).

The importation of irradiated foodstuffs is also subject to the authorisation of, and conditions laid down by the Minister responsible for Public Health.

All produce processed in this way must indicate, on

its packaging, that it has been preserved by ionizing radiation, the nature, method and date of the irradiation and the dose administered.

These general provisions have been supplemented by more detailed regulations designed to allow the marketing of various irradiated foodstuffs[11].

IV. TRANSPORT[12]

In addition to the internal security measures required for the transport of radioactive substances and the transport licence which must be obtained in advance from the Minister responsible for Public Health, in compliance with the provisions of the General Regulations of 1963, when a consignment originates from abroad, the applicant must deliver a certificate from the competent authorities of the country of origin, certifying that the information communicated is accurate.

V. PHYSICAL PROTECTION

As a Member State of EURATOM, Belgium has signed the 1980 International Convention on the Physical Protection of Nuclear Material. Furthermore, it bases its regulations on the IAEA Recommendations in this sphere (INFCIRC/225).

Since 15th October 1975, the internal provisions regulating the physical protection of nuclear materials during their use, storage and transport are contained in the Recommendations issued by the Nuclear Security Service.

Furthermore, in addition to the provisions of the General Regulations concerning the Protection of the Public and Workers against the Hazards of Ionizing Radiation (Chapter X), which require persons in possession of nuclear substances to take the necessary measures to prevent their theft, loss or misuse and, in such an event, to notify the competent public authorities without delay, an Act was passed recently to implement Articles 7 and 8 of the International Convention on the Physical Protection of Nuclear Material.

The purpose of this *Act of 17th April 1986* (Moniteur belge of 16th June 1986) is to introduce new Articles in the Penal Code and the Code of Criminal Procedure specifying the penalties applying to persons guilty of theft, extortion, violence or other crimes involving nuclear material (Articles 331 bis and 477 to 477 sexies).

A new Article 487 bis defines nuclear material as: plutonium other than that whose isotopic concentration in plutonium 238 exceeds 80 per cent, uranium 233, uranium enriched in uranium 235 or 233, uranium containing the mixture of isotopes occurring naturally other than in ores or their residues, and any material containing one or more of the above elements or isotopes.

A new Chapter 1 bis is added to Book II, Title IX of the Penal Code, entitled "Physical Protection of Nuclear Material". Any person who intentionally, without the appropriate authorisation or approval, receives, obtains, possesses, uses, alters, assigns, abandons, transports or disperses nuclear material is punishable by imprisonment. Sentences are more severe when such offences have caused personal injury or damage to property.

The amendment to the Code of Criminal Procedure (Article 12 bis) allows Belgian courts to deal with offences committed in other countries Party to the 1980 Convention when the person committing the offence is physically present in Belgium and has not been extradited by the Belgian Government.

VI. INTELLECTUAL PROPERTY IN THE NUCLEAR FIELD

There is no national legislation dealing specifically with patents and inventions in the nuclear field. It is therefore the ordinary law which applies in this case, subject to the relevant international agreements to which Belgium is Party.

It should however be pointed out that, without prejudice to the provisions of the above-mentioned Act of 4th August 1955 on National Security in the Field of Nuclear Energy (safeguarding sensitive information), the Minister responsible for industrial property rights may issue a joint statement with the Minister of Defence that the making public of an invention or trade secret is contrary to the national interest and, consequently, prohibited for a specified period of time. Similarly, they have the power to determine and control temporarily the conditions for exploiting inventions and trade secrets or to reserve the benefits derived from them to the State (*Act of 10th January 1955* concerning the making public and exploitation of inventions and trade secrets affecting national defence or security, published in Moniteur belge of 26th January 1955).

Under this procedure, which is implemented upon application for a patent, the owner of the invention is given the right to compensation. The owner may request the total or partial withdrawal of the prohibitions. Provision is made for the punishment of breaches of the provisions of the Act (Penal Code, Article 309).

VII. AGREEMENTS

1. Multilateral Agreements

On 2nd May 1975, Belgium ratified the Treaty on the Non-Proliferation of Nuclear Weapons.

Belgium is also Party to the Agreement between the European Atomic Energy Community, the IAEA and the Community Member States Party to the NPT (signed on 5th April 1973), implementing Article III of this Treaty (so-called Verification Agreement).

Belgium has also undertaken to comply with the Nuclear Suppliers Group Guidelines (London Club[13]).

2. Bilateral Agreements

Belgium is Party to many agreements covering scientific, technical and economic co-operation, as widely defined, in the field of nuclear energy.

Only those agreements which, directly or indirectly, generally or specifically, deal with trade in nuclear material, equipment and, where applicable, technology have been listed in this section.

a) Nuclear co-operation framework agreements

- Exchange of letters dated 14th May and 13th June 1963 between the Atomic Energy Commissions of Belgium and ***Pakistan*** for the exchange of personnel, information and equipment.
- Nuclear Co-operation Agreement, signed on 7th December 1963, between the ***Polish*** and Belgian Governments.
- Exchange of letters on 30th January 1965 between the ***Indian*** and Belgian Governments providing for the exchange of information, equipment and personnel.
- Agreement, signed on 8th March 1965 in Moscow, between the Belgian Atomic Energy Commission, the ***Netherlands*** Stichting Reactor Centrum and the ***USSR*** State Commissariat, for the exchange of information and experts in the nuclear field.
- Agreement, concluded on 29th January 1974, between the Belgian and ***Romanian*** Governments on co-operation in the field of the peaceful uses of nuclear energy and providing for the exchange of information, research workers, experts and technicians. The Agreement entered into force on 15th June 1974.
- Agreement, concluded on 3rd March 1981, between the Belgian and ***South-Korean*** Governments on collaboration in the field of the peaceful uses of nuclear energy.
- Agreement, signed in Brussels on 8th November 1984, between the Belgian and ***Egyptian*** Governments on co-operation in the field of the peaceful uses of nuclear energy (the text is reproduced in Nuclear Law Bulletin No. 37).
- Agreement, signed in Peking on 18th April 1985, between the Belgian Government and the Government of the ***People's Republic of China*** on co-operation in the field of peaceful uses of nuclear energy.

b) Agreements for the supply of nuclear materials

In this field, Belgium is covered also by the various co-operation agreements concluded by EURATOM with the United States, Canada and Australia regulating, in particular, the conditions of non-proliferation linked to the supply of nuclear material, equipment and technology. Supply contracts are negotiated and concluded by the Belgian firms concerned in agreement with the EURATOM Supply Agency.

c) Industrial co-operation agreements

— Memorandum of Understanding, concluded in January 1967, between the Belgian Government and the Government of the ***Federal Republic of Germany*** on collaboration between these two countries in the field of the development and marketing of fast breeder reactors.

Following this Agreement, Belgian electricity producers (Electronucléaire) acquired shares in the SBK Company (Schnell-Bruter-Kernkraftgesellschaft), the owner of the 300 MWe FBR power plant at Kalkar, built by the international INB consortium (International Natrium-Brutreaktor Baugesellschaft) in which the Belgian nuclear construction industry is represented.

— Société électronucléaire des Ardennes (SENA) : this is a Franco-Belgian enterprise set up under the auspices of EURATOM to construct and operate the Chooz I nuclear power plant (310 MWe). An Agreement on Radiation Protection relating to this plant was concluded in September 1966.

— Société belgo-française d'énergie nucléaire mosane (SEMO) : this Franco-Belgian joint enterprise was set up under the auspices of EURATOM to construct and operate the Tihange nuclear power plant (870 MWe) in May 1971.

— Euro-HKG (Europaïsche Gesellschaft zur Auswertung von Erfahrungen bei Planung, Bau und Betrieb von Hochtemperatuureaktoren) : created in 1974, this research association brings together certain European electricity producers interested in the development of high temperature reactors, and undertakes studies and comparisons of the various techniques available. Belgium is represented in this association by Electronucléaire.

— Memorandum of Understanding, concluded on 10th January 1984, between Belgium, the Federal Republic of Germany, France, Italy and the United Kingdom, on co-operation in the field of fast breeder reactors.

— Convention, signed on 20th March 1980, between Belgium, France and Spain, relating to the Eurodif Company. Adhesion of Italy on 11th August 1984.

NOTES AND REFERENCES

1. Regulations concerning radiation protection and the safety of nuclear installations do not fall within the scope of this study. As regards nuclear safety, reference should be made in particular to "Licensing Systems and Inspection of Nuclear Installations", OECD/NEA, 1986.
2. Cases involving nuclear foreign trade are dealt with essentially by the *Ministry of Foreign Affairs* (Scientific Affairs Office of the Political Affairs Directorate) and by the *Ministry of Foreign Trade* and the *Ministry of Economic Affairs* (Nuclear Applications Service and Atomic Energy Commission, "Office central des contingents et licences"), without prejudice to the supervisory powers entrusted to the Ministry of Justice. Belgian Government policy with regard to nuclear exports is contained in particular in the "Declaration of Common Policy" adopted by Belgium as by the other Member States of the European Community on 20th November 1984 (cf. Volume I of the study).
3. "Materials" must here be understood in the physical sense of the term and has, essentially, the same meaning as the term "nuclear substances" (cf. Note 7 below).
4. This Decree also provides that the implementation of these measures will be entrusted to a *Nuclear Security Service*, responsible, within Belgium, for identifying breaches of the regulations in this field. The duties of this Service, which is placed under the authority of the Ministry of Justice, have been extended to the application of the EURATOM safeguards (Royal Decree of 30th May 1960) and of the regulations on the physical protection of nuclear material (Royal Decree of 28th February 1963, as amended). The Service is headed by the Director of Nuclear Security, assisted by a Security Officer (*Royal Decree of 2nd April 1957* on the duties of certain persons responsible for supervising safety measures and for tracking down and reporting on infringements in the field of nuclear energy).(For further details, see : "Regulatory and Institutional Framework for Nuclear Activities", Vol. I, OECD/NEA, 1983).
5. The Decree specifies in particular the conditions which (natural) persons must satisfy in order to be authorised to have possession of classified documents or materials, to conduct an activity in premises in which such documents or materials are held, and lastly, to have access to the information arising from these documents or materials (Section 21 of the Decree). The decision whether or not to grant such authorisation is taken by the Director of Nuclear Security, after enquiry by the Service (Section 22). The person thus authorised to be in possession of classified documents or materials must keep a register for each class of documents or materials in which a note is made of the chronological order in which they were received or transmitted, together with a file in which the data contained in the registers are copied and numbered. This information is to be communicated without delay to the Security Officer (of the Nuclear Security Service) (Sections 7 to 11). The Security Officer also keeps a

register and a file in which this information is recorded. He must also, at least once a year, carry out a check of documents and materials and, every six months, make a complete inventory of documents and materials classified as top secret ("très secret" — Section 12). "Top secret" or "secret" documents and materials may be kept and used only in premises protected by a security system installed in compliance with the instructions of the Director of Nuclear Security (Section 15).

6. Within the meaning of Article 197 of the EURATOM Treaty.

7. The text used as a basis for this study is the consolidated text of the Regulations, dated January 1987.
The various uses of radioactive substances for purposes of national defence are regulated by general military Regulations concerning protection against the hazards of ionizing radiation (Royal Decree of 11th May 1971, as amended by Royal Decree dated 5th December 1975).

8. These Regulations have an extremely wide scope since they apply, in particular, to the following:
   1. importation, production, manufacture, possession, transport and use for commercial, industrial, scientific, medical or other purposes, of apparatus, facilities or substances capable of emitting ionizing radiation;
   2. offer for sale, sale and assignment for a consideration or free of charge of substances capable of emitting ionizing radiation or of apparatus or facilities containing such substances;
   3. processing, handling, storage, removal and disposal of radioactive substances and waste.

   Radioactive substances are defined in the Regulations as "substances constituted by any element emitting ionizing radiation or containing such an element", i.e. all substances presenting the phenomenon of radioactivity [Section 2(a)].

9. For further details on these points, see the relevant studies published by the OECD/NEA.

10. Within the Ministry responsible for Public Health, the *Public Health Department* is responsible for ensuring the protection of the public against the hazards of ionizing radiation. Within this Department, the *Radiation Protection Service* has the task of enforcing the General Regulations for the protection of the public and workers against the hazards of ionizing radiation, in particular as concerns the importation and marketing of radioactive substances and equipment capable of emitting ionizing radiation. This Service also acts as Secretariat for the *Interministerial Commission for Nuclear Safety and National Security in the Field of Nuclear Energy*, which is responsible for finding ways to guarantee the protection of workers and the public against the hazards which all activities involving radioactive substances may present. For this purpose, it co-ordinates the activities of the various Ministerial departments concerned (Labour and Employment, Justice, Public Health, Foreign Affairs, the Interior, and Defence).
The Minister responsible for Public Health is also the supervisory authority of the *Higher Council for Public Health* which is consulted, in particular, with regard to the drafting of regulations concerning ionizing radiation.

11. For further details, see NEA Nuclear Law Bulletin No. 35.

12. The regulations governing safety during transport are described in the study "Regulations Governing the Transport of Radioactive Materials", OECD/NEA, 1980.

13. See, on these points, Volume I of the study.

Annex

EXTRACTS FROM LIST II ANNEXED TO THE ORDER OF 7TH APRIL 1988 REQUIRING AN EXPORT LICENCE FOR CERTAIN PRODUCTS*

(Replaces List II annexed to the Order of 24th September 1985)

ATOMIC ENERGY — TECHNOLOGICAL AIDS (see definition in Section 1 000)**

A. NUCLEAR MATERIAL

A.1 Special fissionable products and other fissionable products except:

i) consignments of up to one effective gramme;
ii) consignments of up to three effective grammes provided they are contained in a sensing component of instruments.

Technical notes:

1. special fissionable product means plutonium 239, uranium 233, uranium enriched with uranium 235 or 233 and any product containing the above-mentioned elements.
2. Uranium enriched with uranium 235 or 233 means uranium containing the isotopes 235 and/or 233, the ratio of the aggregate content of these isotopes to that of uranium 238 exceeding the ratio of uranium 235 to uranium 238 in the natural state.
3. Other fissionable products means americium 242m, curium 245 and 247, californium 249 and 251, plutonium isotopes other than plutonium 238 and 239, "previously separated" and any product containing the above-mentioned elements.
4. Effective grammes of special fissionable products or other fissionable products means:
   a) for plutonium and uranium 233, the weight of the elements in grammes;
   b) for enriched uranium with a content of at least 1 per cent uranium 235, the weight of the elements in grammes multiplied by the squared enrichment ratio expressed as a decimal weight fraction;
   c) for enriched uranium with a content of less than 1 per cent uranium 235, the weight of the elements in grammes multiplied by 0.0001;
   d) for americium 242m, curium 245 and 247 and californium 249 and 251, the weight of the isotopes in grammes multiplied by 10.
5. Here, "previously separated" means the result of any process to increase the concentration of the isotope concerned.

A.2 Natural or depleted uranium in any form whatsoever or incorporated in any substance where the uranium concentration is more than 0.05 per cent by weight, excluding:

i) consignments with a natural uranium content of:
   1. 10 kg or more for any application, or
   2. up to 100 kg for civilian non-nuclear applications;

ii) uranium depleted in U-235 where the U-235 content is below 0.35 per cent;

iii) depleted uranium specially manufactured for civilian applications as follows:
   1. safety shields
   2. packaging
   3. ballast
   4. counterweights.

* Unofficial translation.
** Section 1 000, *Technological aids*: printed books and other publications, and any products intended or designed for the transfer of knowledge, inasumuch as they include technological information relating to the design, manufacture and use of the products covered by this list.

A.3 Deuterium, heavy water, deuterium paraffins and other inorganic and organic compounds, mixtures and solutions containing deuterium in which the ratio of deuterium to hydrogen exceeds 1:5000, excluding consignments of the above products with a deuterium content of up to 10 kg.

A.4 Zirconium metal: alloys containing over 50 per cent zirconium by weight; compounds in which the ratio of hafnium to zirconium is less than 1:500 by weight; products entirely manufactured from these products, excluding:

i) consignments of up to 5 kg of zirconium metal or zirconium alloy

ii) zirconium sheets or strips up to 0.025 mm (0.00095 inches) thick, specially manufactured for use in photographic flash bulbs and intended for this use, in consignments of up to 200 kg.
(see explanatory note at the end of the list)

A.5 Nickel powder and porous nickel metal as follows:

a) powder with a nickel content of at least 99 per cent and a particle size of less than 100 micrometres.

b) porous nickel metal manufactured with material described in paragraph a) above, excluding separate porous nickel metal sheets of not more than 930 cm^2 to be used in storage batteries for civilian purposes.

Note: Paragraph b) of this Section concerns porous nickel metal obtained from nickel powder as defined in paragraph a) after compacting and sintering in order to obtain a metal material with fine pores interlinked throughout the structure.
(see explanatory note at the end of the list)

A.6 Nuclear grade graphite, with a purity level of less than 1 ppm boron equivalent and a density of over 1.5 g/cm^3, excluding individual consignments of at least 100 kg.
(see also Section 1673)

A.7 Lithium as follows:

a) metal, hydrides or alloys containing lithium 6-enriched lithium up to a concentration higher than that occurring in nature (7.5 per cent in numbers of atoms);

b) any other material containing lithium 6-enriched lithium (including compounds, mixtures and concentrates), excluding lithium 6-enriched lithium contained in thermoluminescent dosimeters.

NB: For natural lithium deuteride and lithium 7-enriched lithium deuteride see Section A.3.
(see explanatory note at the end of the list)

A.8 Hafnium as follows: metal, alloys and hafnium compounds containing over 60 per cent hafnium by weight and their manufactured products, excluding consignments of the above-listed products containing not more than 1 kg of hafnium.
(see explanatory note at the end of the list)

A.9 Beryllium as follows: metal, alloys containing over 50 per cent beryllium by weight, beryllium-containing compounds and their manufactured products, excluding:

i) metal windows for X-ray equipment;

ii) finished or semi-finished oxides specially designed for electric components as supports for electronic circuits;

iii) consignments of up to 500 g of beryllium with a purity level of up to 99 per cent, or up to 100 g of beryllium with a purity level of over 99 per cent, provided that the consignments do not contain monocrystals;

iv) consignments of up to 5 kg of beryllium contained in compounds with a purity level of less than 99 per cent.
(See explanatory note at the end of the list)

A.12 Tritium, compounds and mixtures containing tritium with a ratio of tritium to hydrogen of over 1: 1000 in numbers of atoms, and products containing one or several of the above mentioned substances, excluding:

i) consignments of tritium, compounds, mixtures and individual products containing one or more of the above-mentioned substances not exceeding 100 curies;

ii) tritium contained in phosphorescent paint, phosphorescent products, gas and aerosol detectors, electronic tubes, anti-lightning or static electricity devices, ion generating tubes, detector cells in gas chromatography devices and calibration equipment;

iii) tritium compounds and mixtures the separation of whose components cannot lead to changes in the hydrogen isotope mix where the ratio of tritium to hydrogen is more than 1:1000 in numbers of atoms.

A.13 Materials for nuclear heat sources, as follows:

a) plutonium in any form whatsoever with a Pu-238 content exceeding 50 per cent, excluding:

i) consignments of up to 1 gramme of plutonium;
ii) consigments of up to 3 effective grammes when they are contained in sensitive instrumentation;
iii) Pu-238 contained in cardiac pacemakers;

b) "previously separated" neptunium 237 in any form whatsoever, excluding consigments of up to 1 gramme of neptunium 237.

Technical note: Here, "previously separated" means the result of any process to increase the concentration of the isotope concerned.

A.14 Materials specially designed or prepared for the separation of isotopes of natural uranium, depleted uranium, special fissionable materials and other fissionable materials, in particular resins specially designed for chemical exchanges. (For facilities for the separation of isotopes see Section B.1)

B. NUCLEAR INSTALLATIONS

B.1 Facilities for the separation of isotopes of natural uranium, special fissionable products and other fissionable products, and their specially designed or prepared equipment and components, including:

a) Units specially designed for separating isotopes from natural uranium, depleted uranium, special fissionable products and other fissionable products, such as:

1. Gas centrifuge assemblies;
2. Jet nozzle separation units;
3. Vortex separation units;
4. Laser isotopic separation units;
5. Chemical exchange separation units;
6. Electromagnetic separation units;
7. Plasma separation units;
8. Gaseous diffusion separation units.

b) Components specially designed for these units, in particular:

1. Valves entirely formed of or coated with aluminium, aluminium nickel alloys or an alloy containing at least 60 per cent nickel, with a diameter of at least 0.5 cm, closed by a system of bellows, excluding valves not meeting this definition.
2. Compressors and blowers (turbo-compressor, centrifugal and axle types) entirely composed of or coated with aluminium, aluminium nickel alloys or an alloy containing at least 60 per cent nickel, with a capacity of at least 1 700 litres (1.7 m^3) per minute, including compressor seals, excluding blowers and compressors not meeting this definition.
3. Gaseous diffusion barriers.
4. Gaseous diffuser housings.
5. Heat exchangers made of aluminium, copper, nickel or alloys containing over 60 per cent nickel, or combinations of these metals in the form of clad tubing, designed to operate at a pressure below atmospheric pressure, with a leakage rate of less than 10 pascal (0.1 millibar) per hour with a pressure differential of 10^5 pascal (1 bar), excluding heat exchangers not meeting this definition.

(For equipment specially designed or prepared for separating isotopes see Section A.14)

B.2 Facilities for reprocessing spent fuel assemblies from nuclear reactors, and especially designed or prepared equipment and components therein, including:

a) Fuel element chopping units, in other words remote-controlled equipment for cutting, chopping or shearing spent fuel assemblies, bundles or rods from nuclear reactors.

b) Anti-criticality safety containers (e.g. small diameter, ring-shaped or flat containers) specially designed or prepared for dissolving spent fuel from nuclear reactors and capable of withstanding highly radioactive and corrosive liquid, suitable for remote-controlled loading and maintenance.

c) Countercurrent solvent extractors and equipment for processing by ion exchange, specially designed and prepared for use in a facility for reprocessing natural and depleted uranium or special fissionable products and other irradiated fissionable products.

d) Control instrumentation specially designed or prepared for driving and controlling equipment for reprocessing source materials and special fissionable products and other irradiated fissionable products.

Note: A plant for reprocessing spent fuel assemblies from nuclear reactors contains items of equipment and components which normally enter into direct contact with and directly control the spent fuel and the reprocessing flows of main source materials and fission products.

B.3 Nuclear reactors, namely reactors capable of operation so as to maintain a controlled self-sustaining fission chain reaction, and specially designed or prepared items of equipment and components for use in connection with a nuclear reactor, including the following:

a) Pressure vessels, namely metal vessels as complete units or as major shop-fabricated parts therefor, which are especially designed or prepared to contain the core of a nuclear reactor and capable of withstanding the operating pressure of the primary coolant, including the lid of the reactor pressure vessel.

b) Fuel handling equipment, including reactor fuel loading and unloading machines.

c) Control rods, namely rods specially designed or prepared for the control of the reaction rate in a nuclear reactor, including the neutron absorber element, support or suspension systems and control rod guide tubes.

d) Electronic instrumentation for controlling the power levels of nuclear reactors, including systems for setting the reactor control rods and radiation measuring and detection instruments for determining neutron flux levels.

e) Pressure tubes, namely especially designed or prepared tubes for containing fuel elements and the primary coolant in a nuclear reactor above an operating pressure in excess of 50 atmospheres.

f) Primary coolant pumps, namely pumps especially designed or prepared for circulating primary coolant in nuclear reactors.

g) Internals, especially designed or prepared for operating a nuclear reactor, in particular core support systems, thermal shields, deflectors, core grid plates and diffuser plates.

h) Heat exchangers.

Note: A "nuclear reactor" includes the equipment located inside the reactor vessel or directly attached to it, equipment for regulating core power and the components normally containing primary coolant and entering in direct contact with the coolant or controlling it.

B.4 Facilities and equipment specially designed for fabricating nuclear reactor fuel elements and equipment specially designed for those facilities.

Note: A plant for the fabrication of fuel elements includes equipment which:

1. normally comes into direct contact with, directly processes, or controls, the production flow of nuclear material;
2. seals the nuclear material within the cladding;
3. checks cladding integrity or leak tightness;
4. checks final solid fuel quality.

B.5 Facilities for producing heavy water, deuterium or deuterium compounds and their specially designed or prepared equipment and components.

B.6 Facilities for producing uranium hexafluoride (UF_6), specially designed and prepared equipment (including that for purifying UF_6) and their specially designed or prepared components.

C. OTHER NUCLEAR-RELATED EQUIPMENT

C.1 Neutron-generating systems, including tubes, designed so as to operate without external vacuum system and using electrostatic acceleration to induce a tritium-deuterium reaction.

C.2 Energy-generating and/or propulsion equipment specially designed with a view to use with military spatial, maritime or mobile nuclear reactors.

Note: This Section does not apply to conventional energy-generating equipment which, although designed with a view to use in a specific nuclear power plant, might in principle be used in conjunction with conventional systems.

C.3 Electrolytic cells for fluorine production, with a production capacity of over 250 g of fluorine per hour.

C.4 Especially designed equipment for separating lithium isotopes.

C.5 Especially designed equipment for producing tritium or recovering tritium.

BELGIUM

EXPLANATORY NOTE

(Sections 1301, 1631, 1635, 1648, 1649, 1658, 1661, 1670, 1671, 1715)

Atomic energy list : A4, A5, A7, A8 and A9

1. *Source materials*

Where a definition covers source materials, it includes all materials from which the metal may be extracted, in other words ores, concentrates, coarse metal, white metal, residues and slag (ash).

2. *Metals and alloys*

Unless otherwise specified, metals and alloys cover all unworked forms and semi-finished products listed below:

Unworked forms: sinter, anodes, wire, bar (including notched bar and bolt rod), balls, billets, blocks, bloom, cathodes, crystals, cubes, dice, sponge, grains, granules, shot, pig, ingot, billet, powder, washers, lumps.

Semi-finished products (whether or not coated, plated, drilled or punched):

i) Refined or worked materials, manufactured by flattening, drawing, forging, extruding, impact pressing, deep drawing, shot blasting, grinding and milling, in other words: rings, hoops, angle-bar, disks, U- and T-shaped iron and special iron, thin and extra thin sheets, bands, drawn or extruded wire, wire (including uncoated welding strip, bolt rod and rolled wire), flakes, pressings or drop forgings, forgings, powder, sections, strip, thin, medium and thick plate, tubes and pipes (including round and square section tubes and hollow rods).

ii) Parts cast in sand, dies, metal moulds, plaster and other types of moulds, including pressure castings, fritted parts and others forms obtained through powder metallurgy.

NOTICE CONCERNING THE ORDER OF 7TH APRIL 1988 REQUIRING AN EXPORT LICENCE FOR CERTAIN PRODUCTS

(Extracts)

ATOMIC ENERGY LIST

Consignments of limited quantities may be authorised under certain conditions and exceptionally for certain items under A1, A2, A3, A4, A5, B3 and C1 of the Atomic Energy List

CANADA

TABLE OF CONTENTS

CANADA

I. INTRODUCTION

Canada is an exporter in the nuclear field of uranium[1], and of heavy water reactor and other nuclear technology, equipment and facilities for the agricultural, medical and industrial use of radionuclides. Its laws with respect to nuclear trade in general and nuclear export in particular are designed and implemented to reflect its policy which is supportive of the use of nuclear material, equipment and technology for peaceful purposes only, and is prohibitive of the use of that material, equipment and technology for or in connection with the proliferation of nuclear weapons.

All activities concerning the development, application and use of atomic energy are governed principally by the *Atomic Energy Control Act* and the regulations made pursuant to that act. Other legislation having a direct bearing on these matters are the *Export and Import Permits Act*, the *Customs Act*, the *Radiation Emitting Devices Act* and the *Transportation of Dangerous Goods Act*. The Canadian Government's current and longstanding nuclear export policy is to be found in two ministerial statements of 1974 and 1976. The provisions of these acts, regulations and policy statements and their interaction, as well as the authorities responsible for their implementation in the context of Canada's nuclear trade regulatory regime are the central subjects of this study. The impact of the *Criminal Code*, laws regarding physical security, transport and intellectual property will also be examined. Finally, Canada's international non-proliferation obligations and commitments under nuclear co-operation agreements will be briefly described.

II. NUCLEAR EXPORT POLICY

Canada's nuclear export policy has been articulated in two ministerial statements made in the House of Commons in 1974 and in 1976. The first of these statements was made in the House of Commons on 20th December 1974 by the Minister of Energy, Mines and Resources; the second ministerial statement was made on 22nd December 1976 in the House of Commons by the Secretary of State for External Affairs. (The statements are reproduced in *Annex I* and *Annex II* respectively.) The combination of these two statements make exports of nuclear technology, equipment and material from Canada subject to stringent safeguards requirements.

Exports are authorised only after a formal commitment by the importing country that nuclear technology, equipment and material of Canadian origin or their derivatives will be used for peaceful purposes only. As a result of the 1976 statement, exports are in effect limited to those countries which have signed the Treaty on the Non-Proliferation of Nuclear Weapons or which agree to equivalent controls.

It will be observed from the ministerial statements referred to above that certain principles have been established as a result of which the regulatory regime provides for certain pre-conditions with respect to exports. Those pre-conditions are :

1. that the items supplied or produced with supplied material (including subsequent generations thereof) will not be diverted to any explosive purpose ;
2. that safeguards obligations undertaken by importing countries will be verified through inspection mechanisms of the IAEA ;
3. that the retransfer of items supplied and produced with the material (including subsequent generations thereof) will be accomplished only with the consent of the Canadian government ;
4. that the high enrichment (to more than 20 per cent) and reprocessing of material supplied or produced with that supplied will be accomplished only with the consent of the Canadian government ;
5. that IAEA safeguards or mechanisms of bilateral verification or guarantees will be in place for the life of the supplied items and material ; and
6. that adequate measures of physical security exist in the importing country to protect the items and material supplied from the threat of diversion.

An export will be authorised only after an intergovernmental commitment by the importing country that the items and material will be subject to the foregoing conditions. It should also be noted that Canada was one of the original participants in the Nuclear Suppliers' Group (known as the London Club) and that it has adopted the guidelines of that group setting out conditions under which nuclear materials, equipment or technology will be transferred.

III. LEGISLATION — NUCLEAR AND TRADE-RELATED

The preamble of the *Atomic Energy Control Act*[2] (hereinafter the Act), provides a succinct description of its purpose and reads as follows :

"Whereas it is essential in the national interest to make provision for the control and supervision of the development, application and use of atomic energy, and to enable Canada to participate effectively in measures of international control of atomic energy which may hereafter be agreed upon ; therefore, His Majesty by and with the advice and consent of The Senate and House of Commons of Canada, enacts as follows:".

From the reference to the "national interest" in the preamble just quoted, it can be seen that the Federal government claimed legislative jurisdiction over the development, application and use of atomic energy on that basis. Federal legislative jurisdiction has been judicially upheld in the case of *Denison Mines Ltd. v. Attorney General of Canada*[3] among others. In order to accomplish its purpose, Parliament established a corporation known as the Atomic Energy Control Board[4] (hereinafter the Board), and by section 9 of the Act empowered the Board to make regulations, with the approval of the Governor in Council, for the purposes set out in that section. Relevant to this study is paragraph 9(d) of the Act which reads as follows :

"9. The Board may with the approval of the Governor in Council make regulations

.....

(d) regulating the production, *import*, *export*, transportation, refining, possession, ownership, use or *sale* of prescribed substances and any other things that in the opinion of the Board may be used for the production, use or application of atomic energy".

It is by this paragraph of section 9, in particular, that the Board has been empowered by Parliament to regulate nuclear trade. Other paragraphs of section 9 empower the Board to make regulations concerning other aspects of the development, application and use of atomic energy. In the exercise of the power granted to it by section 9, the Board made the *Atomic Energy Control Regulations*[5] (hereinafter the Regulations).

Apart from the radiological health and safety, inspection and enforcement provisions of the Regulations, their principal function is to establish a comprehensive licensing scheme with respect to every aspect of the development, application and use of atomic energy. Like all licensing schemes, the Regulations proceed from the basis of a prohibition except in accordance with a licence issued pursuant to the Regulations. Sections 3, 4, 5 and 8 of the Regulations are the principal licensing sections. For clarity and ease of reference, they read as follows :

"3. Subject to section 6, no person shall, unless exempted in writing by the Board, produce, mine, prospect for, refine, use, *sell* or possess for any purpose any prescribed substance except in accordance with a licence issued pursuant to section 7.

4. Subject to section 6, no person shall, unless exempted in writing by the Board, use, *sell* or possess any device or equipment containing radioactive prescribed substances except in accordance with a licence issued pursuant to section 7.

5.(1) No person shall

(a) import any prescribed substance,
(b) export any prescribed substance, or,
(c) export any prescribed item,

except in accordance with a licence issued pursuant to section 7.

(2) A licence referred to in subsection (1) shall be produced by or on behalf of the licensee to a collector of customs at the port of entry into or exit from Canada of the prescribed substance or the prescribed item, as the case may be, or at such other place as is designated by the Deputy Minister of National Revenue for Customs and Excise, before the prescribed substance or the prescribed item is released for *import* or *export*.

8. Unless exempted in writing by the Board, no person shall operate a nuclear facility *except* in accordance with a licence issued pursuant to section 9." (emphasis added).

It will be observed that the sections of the Regulations just quoted use the terms "prescribed substance" and "prescribed item". The term "prescibed substance" is defined by section 2 of the Act as follows:

"'Prescribed substances' means uranium, thorium, plutonium, neptunium, deuterium, their respective derivatives and compounds and any other substances that the Board may by regulation designate as being capable of releasing atomic energy, or as being requisite for the production, use or application of atomic energy ;".

Pursuant to the power granted to the Board to designate prescribed substances in the foregoing definition, the Board has designated other prescribed substances in subsection 2(2) of the Regulations as follows :

"(2) For the purposes of the definition "prescribed substances" in section 2 of the Act, radioactive isotopes of all elements and any substances containing such isotopes are designated as being capable of releasing atomic energy, or as being requisite for the production, use or application of atomic energy".

The term "prescribed item" is defined in subsection 2(1) of the Regulations in the following terms :

> "Prescribed item" means an item, other than items 8001, 8005 and 8050, included in Group 8 of the Export Control List made pursuant to the Export and Import Permits Act or an item included in item 10003 of that list that relates to equipment and materials described in Group 8 ;". (This list is reproduced in *Annex III.*)

The combination of the definitions of "prescribed substances", "prescribed item" and the prohibition against import or export contained in section 5 of the Regulations are the principal linch pins between the Act and the Export and Import Permits Act[6] and the Customs Act[7]. These latter acts form the administrative and one of the enforcement frameworks with regard to the import and export of prescribed substances and items. The Export and Import Permits Act is the responsibility of the Secretary of State for External Affairs and the Customs Act is that of the Minister of National Revenue. Beginning with the prohibitions contained in the Regulations and in the Export Control List made under the Export and Import Permits Act, we come to section 101 of the Customs Act which reads as follows:

> "101. Goods that have been imported or are about to be exported may be detained by an officer until he is satisfied that the goods have been dealt with in accordance with this Act, and any other Act of Parliament that prohibits, controls or regulates the importation or exportation of goods, and any regulations made thereunder."

It should be noted here that the "officer" referred to in section 101 just quoted is the collector of customs referred to in subsection 5(2) of the Regulations.

The import and sale in Canada of equipment capable of producing and emitting radiation but not intended for the production of atomic energy within the meaning of the Act are regulated pursuant to the *Radiation Emitting Devices Act*[8]. That act is the responsibility of the Minister of National Health and Welfare, and it prohibits the sale or lease in Canada and the import into Canada of such equipment unless it meets the conditions set out in section 4 or is authorised to be imported, sold or leased by a regulation made under paragraph 11(1)(c).

The *Transportation of Dangerous Goods Act*[9] is the responsibility of the Minister of Transport and applies to the transportation of dangerous goods by all modes of transportation. The schedule to the Transportation of Dangerous Goods Act lists as Class 7, radioactive materials and prescribed substances within the meaning of the Act. These materials and substances are therefore subject to the Transportation of Dangerous Goods Act insofar as their transportation is concerned. It is important here to note that regulations made pursuant to the Transportation of Dangerous Goods Act make reference to regulations made by the Board pursuant to section 9 of the Act concerning the packaging and labelling for transport of radioactive prescribed substances. These latter regulations are entitled the Transport Packaging of Radioactive Materials Regulations[10] and the interrelationship between the Transport Packaging of Radioactive Materials Regulations and regulations made pursuant to the Transportation of Dangerous Goods Act is such that there is no duplication and no conflict between them. Basically, the Transport Packaging of Radioactive Materials Regulations deal with the packaging for transport of certain prescribed substances whereas the Transportation of Dangerous Goods Act and the regulations made pursuant to that act deal specifically with the actual transportation of those substances.

With regard to domestic security for facilities and certain prescribed substances, the Board has made the *Physical Security Regulations*[11] pursuant to section 9 of the Act which make provision for the security requirements and systems, and the implementation of international safeguards, at certain nuclear installations in Canada.

Finally, the *Criminal Code* provides the enforcement mechanism with respect to all regulations made by the Board pursuant to the Act in particular and the application, development and use of atomic energy in Canada in general. The *Criminal Law Amendment Act, 1985*[12] sets out specific criminal offences relating to or involving nuclear material. Nuclear material is defined for purposes of that act in subsection 5(1) as follows :

> "For the purposes of this section, 'nuclear material' means
>
> *a)* plutonium, except plutonium with an isotopic concentration of plutonium 238 exceeding 80 per cent,
> *b)* uranium 233,
> *c)* uranium containing uranium 233 or uranium 235 or both in such an amount that the abundance ratio of the sum of those isotopes to the isotope uranium 238 is greater than 0.72 per cent,
> *d)* uranium with an isotopic concentration equal to that occurring in nature, and
> *e)* any substance containing anything described in paragraphs *a)* to *d)*,
>
> but does not include uranium in the form of ore or ore residue".

The foregoing constitutes the general legal framework under which the regulation of trade in nuclear materials and items is administered.

IV. IMPLEMENTATION OF LEGISLATION

1. Atomic Energy Control Board

As previously indicated, the Act created a "corporation"[13] composed of five persons. The President of the National Research Council of Canada is the ex-officio member appointed by Parliament, and four other members are appointed by the Governor in Council. One of the five members thus appointed is also appointed as President of the Board[14]. The Board is an agent of the constitutional head of the Government[15] and is also a departmental corporation within the meaning and for the purposes of the *Financial Administration Act*[16]. Decisions of the Board are made by a majority vote of the members thereof and the Board reports to Parliament through a designated Minister[17]. Further, the Board is legally obliged to comply with any general or special direction given by the designated Minister with reference to the carrying out of its purposes[18]. The powers conferred by Parliament on the Board under the Act are to be found principally in sections 8 and 9. In particular, section 9 has empowered the Board to make regulations with the approval of the Governor in Council. The power conferred on the Board by that section is very broad and all-encompassing. The most extreme example of the scope of the Board's regulation-making power is to be found in paragraph 9(g) which reads as follows :

"9. The Board may with the approval of the Governor in Council make regulations

g) generally as the Board may deem necessary for carrying out any of the provisions or purposes of this Act".

2. Licensing Regime

In exercising its power to make regulations pursuant to section 9 of the Act, the Board decided that it would be actively involved in the regulation of atomic energy in Canada and that it would reserve unto itself, inter alia, the power to decide whether or not to grant certain licences. Basically, two kinds of licence exist under the Regulations. The first kind is issued pursuant to section 7 of the Regulations which reads in part as follows :

"7(1) The Board or a designated officer may issue a licence for any purpose referred to in section 3 or in respect of any device or equipment referred to in section 4 upon receipt of a written application from the person requiring such licence".

To repeat what has been said earlier, these licences generally relate to the production, mining, prospecting for, refining, using, selling or possessing of prescribed substances and equipment containing prescribed substances as well as the export and import of such substances and equipment.

The second kind of licence is issued pursuant to section 9 of the Regulations which reads in part as follows :

"9(1) Subject to section 10, the Board may issue a licence to operate a nuclear facility upon receipt by the Board of a written application setting out such of the following matters as the Board may require ...".

For both kinds of licence, applications are considered on the basis of information supplied by the applicant for the licence. The Board or designated officer will require to know, in the case of a section 7 licence, the nature and quantity of the prescribed substance ; the purpose for which that substance is required ; the maximum quantity likely to be required at any one time ; a full description of the premises in which the substance is to be located, and details of any equipment in connection with which it is to be used ; a description of the measures to be taken to prevent theft, loss or any unauthorised use of the substance ; a description of the measures to be taken to prevent persons being exposed to ionizing radiation in excess of limits set out in the Regulations ; a description of the method of disposing of the substance ; a description of the qualifications, training and experience of any person who is to use the substance and any other information necessary to evaluate the application. Following consideration of the information provided, the Board or designated officer may decide to refuse to issue a licence at all, or may grant a licence, subject to conditions imposed upon the licensee. Finally, section 27 of the Regulations authorises the Board or a designated officer to revoke, suspend or amend a licence issued pursuant to the Regulations.

Licences are always issued for a fixed term. Certain licences regarding prescribed substances and equipment are issued only for a one-year term. Generally speaking, the length of the term is a function of the Board's perception of the need for supervision and control of the licensee. A licence whose term has or is about to expire may be re-issued if the Board or a designated officer is satisfied at that time that the continuation of the activity is warranted and that the licensee has previously conducted himself in an appropriate manner, having regard to the nature of the operation, with respect to health, safety, security and the environment.

Following the issue of a licence, supervision and enforcement of the conditions of that licence and with the Regulations is generally performed by the Board's inspector staff. Section 12 of the Regulations reads as follows :

"12(1) The Board or a designated officer may appoint as an inspector any person who, in its or his opinion, is qualified to be so appointed

(a) to inspect any premises on which a prescribed substance is located or a nuclear facility is being constructed or operated;
(b) to inspect records in respect of any prescribed substance or nuclear facility that are required to be kept by these Regulations in order to establish whether the health and safety requirements of these Regulations are or have been complied with;
(c) for the purpose of complying with the terms of any international agreement to which Canada is a party; or
(d) for any other purpose relating to the enforcement of these Regulations.

(2) An inspector shall be furnished with a certificate of his appointment setting out
(a) the purpose for which he has been appointed and the place or area in respect of which he has been appointed, and
(b) the period for which he has been appointed to act as an inspector,

and may at all reasonable times enter any place to which his certificate relates for the purpose of carrying out any inspections specified in the certificate and shall, if so required, produce the certificate to the person in charge thereof.

(3) Where
(a) any loss or theft of any prescribed substance,
(b) any occurrence described in section 21, or
(c) any breach of these Regulations or a condition of any licence has occurred, an inspector appointed for the purpose described in paragraph (1)(a) and for the place or area for which the loss, theft, occurrence or breach has taken place may direct
(d) the person holding the appropriate licence to submit a report respecting
i) the circumstances of the loss or theft of the prescribed substance or of the occurrence or the breach of these Regulations or the condition of the licence, as the case may be, and
ii) any remedial action to be taken in respect thereof; and
(e) such action to be taken as he deems necessary to remedy the breach of these Regulations or the condition of the licence, as the case may be, and to minimise the consequences, if any, of the occurrence".

It will be seen from the foregoing that the Board's inspector staff have considerable power in connection with the supervision and enforcement of compliance. In addition to these provisions, an inspector has available to him the provisions of the Criminal Code relating to search and seizure[19]. The reason that this is so is that a breach of the Act or any regulation made pursuant to the Act is a criminal offence punishable either on summary conviction or by indictment. Section 19 of the Act reads as follows:

"19(1) Any person who contravenes or fails to observe the provisions of this Act or of any regulations made thereunder is guilty of an offence and is liable on summary conviction to a fine not exceeding five thousand dollars or to imprisonment for a term not exceeding two years or to both, but such person may, at the election of the Attorney General of Canada or of the province in which the offence is alleged to have been committed, be prosecuted upon indictment, and if found guilty is liable to a fine not exceeding ten thousand dollars or to imprisonment for a term not exceeding five years or to both.

(2) Where an offence described in subsection (1) has been committed by a company or corporation, every person who at the time of the commission of the offence was a director or officer of the company or corporation is guilty of the like offence if he assented to or acquiesed in the commission of the offence or if he knew that the offence was about to be committed and made no attempt to prevent its commission, and in the prosecution of a director or officer for such like offence, it is not necessary to allege or prove a prior prosecution or conviction of the company or corporation for the offence".

While it can be seen that there is no reference in section 19 to the Criminal Code, subsections 27(1) and (2) of the *Interpretation Act*[20] read as follows:

"27(1) Where an enactment creates an offence,
(a) the offence shall be deemed to be an indictable offence if the enactment provides that the offender may be prosecuted for the offence by indictment;
(b) the offence shall be deemed to be one for which the offender is punishable on summary conviction if there is nothing in the context to indicate that the offence is an indictable offence; and
(c) if the offence is one for which the offender may be prosecuted by indictment or for which he is punishable on summary conviction, no person shall be considered to have been convicted of an indictable offence by reason only of having been convicted of the offence on summary conviction.

(2) All provisions of the Criminal Code relating to indictable offences apply to indictable offences created by an enactment, and all the provisions of the Criminal Code relating to summary conviction offences apply to all other offences created by an enactment, except to the extent that the enactment otherwise provides.

As a result of the foregoing, it can be seen that all of the mechanisms and procedures of the Canadian criminal justice system are linked to the administration and enforcement of the law with regard to nuclear energy matters. Finally, it is important here to point out that the breach of a condition of a licence is as much a criminal offence as is a breach of the Act or the Regulations. The reason this is so is to be found in the prohibition sections already referred to. Section 3 for example reads in part as follows :

"3. ... No person shall ... possess for any purpose any prescribed substance except in accordance with a licence issued pursuant to section 7".

The link between the Criminal Code and the breach of a licence condition is that when a licensee who is authorised to possess a prescribed substance breaches a condition of his licence with respect to that possession, he no longer possesses "in accordance with a licence" to use the language of section 3 just quoted, and is therefore in breach of section 3 of the Regulations which is a breach of section 19 of the Act and thus prosecutable under the Criminal Code by virtue of subsection 27(2) of the Interpretation Act quoted above.

3. Import and Export

Section 5 of the Regulations prohibits the import or export of a prescribed substance or the export of a prescribed item except in accordance with a licence issued pursuant to section 7 of the Regulations. Subsections 7(4) and (5) of the Regulations relate to the matter of licences for import or export. These two subsections together require an application for a licence to import or export and, in the case of the export of a prescribed substance, the Board must be satisfied that the price and quantity of the substance meet any criteria respecting price and quantity that may be specified by the designated Minister as being in the public interest. There are currently no criteria respecting price and quantity that have been specified by the Minister.

In addition to the Regulations, trade in nuclear commodities is also subject to the conditions established by the *Export and Import Permits Act*. The purpose of that act is basically to establish a list of commodities and items the export or import of which is controlled. As indicated earlier in this study, certain nuclear materials and items are on the list and therefore a potential exporter must obtain an export permit from the Secretary of State for External Affairs. Section 3 of the Export and Import Permits Act authorises the Governor in Council to establish the Export Control List for any of the following purposes :

a) ensure that arms, ammunition, implements or munitions of war, naval, army or air stores or any articles deemed capable of being converted thereinto or made useful in the production thereof or otherwise having a strategic nature or value will not be made available to any destination wherein their use might be detrimental to the security of Canada ;

b) to implement an intergovernmental arrangement or commitment ;

c) to ensure that any action taken to promote the further processing in Canada of a natural resource that is produced in Canada is not rendered ineffective by reason of the unrestricted export of that natural resource ; and

d) to limit or keep under surveillance the export of any raw or processed material that is produced in Canada in circumstances of surplus supply and depressed prices and that is not a produce of agriculture.

Section 4 of the Export and Import Permits Act empowers the Governor in Council to establish an Area Control List which contains countries to which he deems it necessary to control the export of any goods. (This list is reproduced in *Annex IV*.)

Section 5 of the Export and Import Permits Act allows for the establishment of an Import Control List controlling the import of any item in order to take account of supply and distribution conditions in Canada of an article that is scarce or subject to governmental controls in the country of origin ; to implement actions taken under certain Canadian legislation ; and to implement intergovernmental arrangements or commitments.

As stated earlier the Export and Import Permits Act is the responsibility of the Secretary of State for External Affairs whose department issues export and import permits for goods contained either in the Export or the Import Control Lists. Such permits must specify the quantity and quality of the item exported or imported, the name of the exporter or importer and the destination and place of origin of the item. The permits may be made subject to any other terms or conditions as are described in the permit or provided for in the regulations made pursuant to the Export and Import Permits Act. It should be emphasized here that in order to avoid duplication, arrangements have been made that the Board's licence is endorsed upon the import or export permit itself.

The Secretary of State for External Affairs is also empowered to provide an import certificate to facilitate certain imports which are time limited[21].

The Export and Import Permits Act itself contains provisions which establish offences and penalties for exporting or importing without a permit[22]. At this point it will be seen that in the context of the import or export of prescribed substances and items, there is a prosecutorial discretion to be exercised by the Attorney General with respect to the institution of a prosecution under section 19 of the Act or under the Export and Import Permits Act. Finally, all of the powers of a customs officer under the Customs Act respecting search, detention, seizure, forfeiture and so forth apply mutatis mutandis to any goods that are presented for export or import pursuant to the Export and Import Permits Act.

4. Radiation Emitting Devices

The sale, lease and import into Canada of radiation emitting devices which do not comply with standards established pursuant to the *Radiation Emitting Devices Act* are prohibited. It should be noted that that act does not apply to any radiation emitting device that is designed primarily for the production of atomic energy within the meaning of the Act and that therefore the two acts complement rather than conflict with each other. Generally speaking, radiation emitting devices are divided into classes, and regulations are made by the Govenor in Council pursuant to the Radiation Emitting Devices Act prescribing standards with respect to the design, construction and functioning of each class of device. Those regulations also authorise, under certain circumstances and under certain conditions, the import, sale or lease of devices and their components notwithstanding the standards established. This act also has provision for the appointment of inspectors for its enforcement and the prosecution of offences as well as extensive provisions concerning search and seizure.

5. Mining

Canadian uranium mining policy is organised to meet two areas of concern. The first is the maintenance of adequate reserves of uranium to supply domestic needs and the second is to ensure the export of surplus uranium only to countries which agree to the regime of safeguards established by Canada.

In 1974, the Minister of Energy, Mines and Resources, created the Uranium Resources Appraisal Group of the Department of Energy, Mines and Resources which is charged with the responsibility of making annual estimates of Canada's uranium resources for the purpose of preparing directives to govern exports from Canada. At the moment, uranium mines are nuclear facilities within the meaning of the Regulations and must be licensed pursuant to section 9 of the Regulations subject to a minimum limit of 10 kg of uranium or thorium per year from any deposit thereof[23], or of a concentration of less than 0.05 per cent by weight[24].

The administrative experience of the Regulations with respect to uranium mines has suggested several differences between uranium mines and other nuclear facilities, as a result of which, the Board is presently making a separate regulation applicable to uranium mines.

V. TRANSPORT

Because prescribed substances are only one type of dangerous commodity whose transport requires regulation, the Board has followed the policy of leaving the regulation of transport to those agencies which possess the necessary expertise and which are vested with the necessary powers either under the *Transportation of Dangerous Goods Act* or other legislation regarding transportation. Thus the Board avoids duplication and the prospect of conflicting laws. The Board has reserved unto itself however the power to regulate the packaging of prescribed substances for transport. To return to the Transportation of Dangerous Goods Act, the Canadian Transport Commission pursuant to that act is responsible for regulating shipments by rail, while the Department of Transport is responsible for regulating shipments by other means of transport. Road transportation is jointly regulated and administered by the federal Department of Transport and its provincial and territorial counterparts. The Transportation of Dangerous Goods Act provides that the handling, offering for transport and transporting of dangerous goods by any means of transport, whether or not the goods originate from or are destined for any place in Canada must comply with all applicable prescribed safety requirements. Furthermore, all containers, packaging and means of transport must comply with all applicable prescribed safety standards and must display all applicable prescribed safety marks. Section 21 of the Transportation of Dangerous Goods Act provides that regulations may be made by the Governor in Council in order to carry out the purposes and provisions of that act.

There is also provision for the Minister of the Transport, who is responsible for the Transportation of Dangerous Goods Act, to issue a permit for the exemption from application of that act as well as for authorising the handling, offering for transport or transporting of dangerous goods in a manner that does not comply therewith, if he is satisfied that the manner actually employed provides a level of safety equivalent to that provided by the Transportation of Dangerous Goods Act or the regulations made under it.

Generally, the transport rules are based on international standards. The specific regulatory regimes applicable are contained in the *Transportation of Dangerous Goods Regulations*, the *Regulations for the Transportation of Dangerous Commodities by Rail*, the *International Maritime Dangerous Goods Code* of the International Maritime Organisation, and the *Technical Instructions for the Safe Transport of Dangerous Goods by Air* of the International Civil Aviation Organisation.

Packaging of certain material, is controlled pursuant to the *Transport Packaging of Radioactive Materials Regulations*[25], made under section 9 of the Act. Under these regulations, the Board is responsible for issuing package design approval certificates attesting that the design of a package meets the requirements of those regulations. In issuing such certificates the Board may also impose limitations or conditions on the use or method of transport of the package in the interest of health, safety or security. The certificate issued by the Board is void if any limitation or condition is not complied with.

VI. PHYSICAL SECURITY

The requirements for the maintenance of security systems, equipment and procedures at certain nuclear installations (physical protection) are prescribed by the *Physical Security Regulations*[26]. These regulations define the different areas of a nuclear facility and establish the requirements for entry to each area. Licensees are required to keep facilities for which they hold a licence under surveillance by security guards. Licensees are further required to make arrangements for a response force to provide assistance at a facility when required.

The Physical Security Regulations prohibit the entry of any person into any area of the facility unless that person has the written authorisation of the licensee. Furthermore, entry to an inner area of a facility requires the written authorisation of the Board. Special authorisations are issued to inspectors appointed pursuant to the Regulations and to inspectors designated under any agreement between the Government of Canada and the IAEA. The purpose of special authorisations is to facilitate the discharge of the IAEA inspectors' duties for safeguards purposes.

VII. INTELLECTUAL PROPERTY IN THE NUCLEAR FIELD

The *Patent Act*[27] is the responsibility of the Minister of Consumer and Corporate Affairs.

Section 22 of the Patent Act reads as follows :

> "22. Any application for a patent for an invention that, in the opinion of the Commissioner, relates to the production, application or use of atomic energy shall, before it is dealt with by an examiner appointed pursuant to section 6 or is open to inspection by the public under section 10, be communicated by the Commissioner to the Atomic Energy Control Board".

The reason for section 22 is to afford the Board and the Minister responsible for the Act the opportunity to consider whether or not such a patent should be appropriated by the government. In this respect paragraphs 10(1)(c) and (d) of the Act are relevant. They read as follows :

> "10(1) The Minister may,
>
> *c)* with the approval of the Governor in Council, acquire or cause to be acquired by purchase, lease, requisition or expropriation, prescribed substances and any mines, deposits or claims of prescribed substances and patent rights relating to atomic energy and any works or property for production or preparation for production of, or for research or investigation with respect to, atomic energy ; and

d) with the approval of the Governor in Council, license or otherwise make available or sell or otherwise dispose of discoveries, inventions and improvements in processes, apparatus or machines, and patent rights acquired under this Act and collect royalties and fees therefrom and payments therefor".

What is noteworthy about the interrelation between the two sections quoted above is that the Board is not acting as regulator in this area but rather as a technical adviser to the Commissioner of Patents and to the Minister.

VIII. AGREEMENTS

1. Multilateral Agreements

Canada is a Party to the 1968 Treaty on the Non-Proliferation of Nuclear Weapons, having ratified the Treaty on 8th January 1969.

Canada also signed the 1980 Convention on the Physical Protection of Nuclear Material on 23rd September 1980.

2. Bilateral Agreements

Canada has entered into several bilateral agreements under which co-operation in nuclear matters is presently taking place or can take place between Canada and other countries. In general, all of these agreements emphasize the insistence by Canada on the development and application of atomic energy for peaceful purposes. These agreements are listed in *Annex V*.

NOTES AND REFERENCES

1. Canadian uranium resources (reasonably assured) have been estimated at approximately 232 000 tonnes with industrial production in 1984 of 11 170 tonnes U in concentrate. See "Uranium, Resources, Production and Demand, Statistical Update 1986", OECD/NEA, December 1986.
2. Revised Statutes of Canada (R.S.C. 1970) c.A-19, Amended (Am.) Statutes of Canada (S.C.) 1974-75-76 c.33, S.C. 1978-79 c.9, S.C. 1984 c.31.
3. (1972) 32 D.L.R. (3rd) 419.
4. Section 3 of the Act.
5. Consolidated Regulations of Canada c.365
Am. SOR/78-58 Canada Gazette Part II — 25/1/78, p. 406
SOR/79-422 Canada Gazette Part II — 13/3/79, p. 2211
SOR/83-459 Canada Gazette Part II — 8/6/83, p. 2313
SOR/83-739 Canada Gazette Part II — 12/10/83, p. 3552
SOR/85-335 Canada Gazette Part II — 1/5/85, p. 1884
SOR/85-1039 Canada Gazette Part II — 13/11/85, p. 4587
SOR/86-252 Canada Gazette part II — 19/3/86, p. 1022
SOR/88-144 Canada Gazette Part II — 16/3/88, p. 1395.
6. R.S.C. 1970 c.E-17
Am. — c.29 (2nd Supp)
Am. — C.32 (2nd Supp)
— S.C 1974 c.9
— S.C. 1980-81-82-83 c.167
— S.C. 1984 c.25
— S.C. 1986 c.1
— S.C. 1987 c.16.
7. S.C. 1986 c.1
Am. — S.C. 1986 c.9
— S.C. 1987 c.32.
8. C.34 (1st Supp)
Am. — S.C. 1984 c.23.
9. C. 1980-81-82-83 c.36 and 165
Am. — 1984 c.40
— 1985 c.26
— 1987 c.34.
10. SOR/83-740 Canada Gazette Part II, 12/10/83, p. 3553
Am. — SOR/83-740 Canada Gazette Part II, 12/10/83, p. 3984
— SOR/83-740 Canada Gazette Part II, 21/3/84, p. 1095.
11. SOR/83-77 Canada Gazette Part II, 26/1/83, p. 411
Am. — SOR/84-81 Canada Gazette Part II, 25/1/84, p. 343
— SOR/85-1016 Canada Gazette Part II, 13/11/85, p. 4516.
12. C. 1985 c.19
13. Section 3 of the Act.
14. Section 5 of the Act.
15. Section 3 of the Act.
16. R.S.C. 1970 c.F-10.
17. Section 20 of the Act.
18. Section 7 of the Act.
19. Criminal Code section 433 et seq.
20. R.S.C. 1970 c.I-23
Am. — C.10 and 29 (2nd supp)
— S.C. 1972 c.17
— S.C. 1974-75-76 c.s 16 and 19
— S.C. 1977-78 c.22
— S.C. 1978-79 c.11
— S.C. 1984 c.41
— S.C. 1986 c.35.
21. Section 9.
22. Sections 13, 14 and 19.
23. Paragraph 6(1)(b) of the regulations.
24. Paragraph 6(2)(a) of the regulations.
25. SOR/83-740 Canada Gazette Part II, 12/10/83, p. 3553
Am. — SOR/83-740 Canada Gazette Part II, 26/10/83, p. 3984
— SOR/83-740 Canada Gazette Part II, 21/3/84, p. 1095.
26. SOR/83-77 Canada Gazette Part II, 26/1/83, p. 411
Am. — SOR/84-81 Canada Gazette Part II, 25/1/84, p. 343
— SOR/85-1016 Canada Gazette Part II, 13/11/85, p. 4516.
27. R.S.C. 1970 c.P-4
Am. — C.10 (2nd Supp)
— S.C. 1984 c.40
— S.C. 1987 c.41.

Annex I

HOUSE OF COMMONS DEBATES — ENERGY

Announcement of Safeguards in Respect of Export of Nuclear Material, Facilities and Technology by the Minister of Energy, Mines and Resources on 20th December 1974

"I am announcing today the decision of the government to require more stringent safeguards in respect of the sale abroad of Canadian nuclear technology, facilities and material. I will in this statement set forth some of the important elements of that decision including the safeguards that must be met by any country seeking to purchase a nuclear facility, technology, or material from Canada. Not only will these binding safeguards apply to all future sales, but the government has decided to negotiate additional safeguards in respect of uranium supply contracts already approved. Existing contracts and contracts pending will be allowed to proceed during the course of the next calendar year while new safeguards are being negotiated.

The events that led to the review by the government of nuclear safeguards are well known....

Canada's commitment to nuclear power as a peaceful energy source extends back almost thirty years. As a result of intensive research and development over that period, Canada is now in the fortunate position of possessing, in addition to a large uranium resource, one of the most successful of the world's nuclear reactor systems CANDU.

The spread of international acceptance of CANDU has coincided lately with a radical alteration in the international energy situation. Reliance on imported oil to satisfy the bulk of their energy needs has become, for most countries, especially those of the developing world a particularly onerous burden on their economies.

It has become demonstrably clear that additional energy sources are needed urgently, nuclear power is the single most important other new source that is now commercially feasible and many countries are making the decision to use it. Canada has already made a decision to rely for part of its energy requirements on nuclear power and a number of countries have turned to us to supply fuel, technology or equipment. With uranium resources in excess of our requirements and a competitive Canadian reactor, we are in the position to make an important contribution to the pressing energy needs of the world and are willing to make it.

At the same time, the government is more than ever conscious of its responsibility to ensure that Canadian nuclear resources do not contribute to nuclear proliferation. This requires that Canada should apply the maximum "safeguards" or restraints attainable to inhibit importing states from using nuclear supplies to further the production of nuclear explosive devices.

The export of certain nuclear equipment, including reactors, fuel fabrication and reprocessing plants, heavy water plants and their major components, and related technologies, will require safeguards.

I would like now to outline the provisions that will be required in every safeguards arrangement. The provisions, to be administered by the International Atomic Energy Agency, or through appropriate alternative procedures meeting the requirements of the Treaty on the Non-Proliferation of Nuclear Weapons, will cover all nuclear facilities and equipment supplied by Canada for the life of those facilities and equipment. They will cover all nuclear facilities and equipment using Canadian-supplied technology. They will cover all nuclear material — uranium, thorium, plutonium, heavy water — supplied by Canada, and future generations of fissile material produced from or with these materials. They will cover all nuclear materials, whatever their origin, produced or processed in facilities supplied by Canada.

Most importantly, all safeguards arrangements will contain binding assurance that Canadian-supplied nuclear material, equipment and technology will not be used to produce a nuclear explosives device, whether the development of such a device be stated to be for peaceful purposes or not.

All potential Canadian exporters of nuclear material, equipment or technology are advised that prior to making offers of supply, they must ascertain from the Department of Industry, Trade and Commerce and the Atomic Energy Control Board that there are no safeguards impediments.

While adopting these safeguards Canada will of course continue to work with other exporting nations to strengthen the international safeguards structure.

Future exports of the CANDU reactor, along with the major programme of construction already underway and planned domestically, will bring significant benefits to employment in the high technology nuclear industry of Canada.

To ensure that Canadians enjoy the economic gains from sales abroad, the government will encourage the supply from Canada of major high technology components and services. In regard to domestic nuclear power programmes, the Department of Industry, Trade and Commerce, in co-operation with my department and with Atomic Energy of Canada Limited will consult with the provinces to establish a co-operative approach of preference for Canadian material, equipment and services.

The Canadian nuclear equipment industry at present has the capacity to produce the components for the nuclear steam supply system for at least three nuclear reactors a year. Domestic requirements will average four units every year over the remainder of this decade, while exports could add at least one additional unit every year. Nearly $100 million in capital investment has already been committed or planned by the private sector of the industry to expand capacity. Future domestic and export demands will stimulate a further expansion involving perhaps another $100 million industrial investment.

The Department of Industry, Trade and Commerce will examine the advisability of providing selective assistance through its incentive programmes to help the industry upgrade its capability.

Contingent on compliance with the new safeguard structures required for nuclear exports, the government has authorised Atomic Energy of Canada Limited to negotiate the following sales:

— With Argentina, the supply of goods and services for the nuclear part of a second 600 megawatt CANDU nuclear power station. Subject to escalation, these goods and services are estimated at $90 million, and the heavy water at a further $60 million.

— With Iran, the supply of goods and services for two 600 megawatt CANDU nuclear power units, and possibly two additional.

— With the Republic of Korea, the supply of goods and services for one complete nuclear reactor power unit.

Once again subject to full compliance with the safeguard requirements, and in so far as Canadian capacity permits, the government has further authorised AECL to negotiate the following:

— With Denmark, the supply of goods and services for the nuclear part of a CANDU nuclear power station.

— With Romania, agreements covering CANDU-PHW (Pressurised Heavy Water) licensing, AECL consultancy, fuel design, development and manufacturing, heavy water production and plant construction, and a scientific and technical exchange.

— With the United Kingdom, agreements covering CANDU/SGHWR (PTHWR) technological exchange, and supply of heavy water. (SGHWR: Steam Generating Heavy Water Reactor; PTHWR: Pressure Tube Heavy Water Reactor).

— With the Italian company, Pregettazioni Meccaniche Nucleari, a licensing agreement to supply CANDU reactor units in Italy.

The government has reaffirmed the policy guidelines on uranium enrichment as announced on 1st August 1973. Canadian involvement in uranium enrichment will be determined within those guidelines.

Canada has made the decisions on safeguards that I have just outlined in the spirit of the Treaty on the Non-Proliferation of Nuclear Weapons which is designed not only to stop the proliferation of nuclear weapons but to ensure the benefits of lower cost energy are shared by all nations."

CANADA

Annex II

HOUSE OF COMMONS DEBATES — ENERGY

Change in Nuclear Export Policy

Statement by the Secretary of State for External Affairs on 22nd December 1976

"I wish to announce a change in Canada's nuclear export policy, a matter of central concern to the people and Government of Canada, raising as it does fundamental issues affecting world economic growth and world peace.

... It is a challenge to the Government of Canada to respond to the demand of Canadian public opinion that this country exercise its influence toward the betterment of the global society in which we and our descendants must live. In the area of nuclear policy there is no simple answer or it would have long since been adopted. It is rather the need to balance energy requirements, the advance of technology which regardless of what we do will make nuclear capability within the reach of a wider and wider group of countries, and the need to establish a sound international framework which will curb the spread of nuclear weapons and yet take into account the legitimate economic aspirations of sovereign states. I wish to make quite clear, however, that the first priority, indeed the overriding priority, is to prevent the spread of instruments of destruction.

In this context I am pleased to announce that the Canadian government has decided upon a further strengthening of the safeguards requirements which apply to the export of Canadian reactors and uranium. Shipments to non-nuclear weapon states under future contracts will be restricted to those which ratify the Non-Proliferation Treaty or otherwise accept international safeguards on their entire nuclear programme. It follows from this policy that Canada will terminate nuclear shipments to any non-nuclear weapon state which explodes a nuclear device.

This requirement is in addition to those outlined in December 1974. The purpose of the Canadian safeguards policy is simple and straightforward. We wish to avoid contributing to the proliferation of nuclear weapons while at the same time satisfying the legitimate requirements for uranium and technology of countries which demonstrate the intention of restricting Canadian assistance only to peaceful non-explosive uses. Nuclear export policy already requires binding assurances that what Canada provides will not be used for explosive purposes. Existing policy, however, does not cover what a country receives from other suppliers or what it might do on its own. The new policy will close this gap. We will have, therefore, assurance by treaty that Canada's nuclear customers will have been selected from those countries which have made a clear and unequivocal commitment to the non-proliferation of nuclear weapons.

The development of the CANDU reactor has been one of Canada's great technological achievements. This technology is needed to reduce the world's dependence on oil. Moreover, our industrialised trading partners look to Canada as a source of uranium to fuel the nuclear reactor programmes which they, like ourselves, have undertaken to meet a growing share of energy needs. In the absence of alternative technologies, developing countries will also look to nuclear power once they have exploited other conventional energy resources and have built up the national power grids necessary for large present reactors. While research into conservation and renewable energy technologies should be intensified, energy planning in Canada and elsewhere must look to energy resources presently available.

While the Canadian government recognises the legitimate energy requirements of its trading partners, it is determined to do everything within its power to avoid contributing to nuclear weapons proliferation. It is for this reason that the Government of Canada has unilaterally decided to strengthen further Canada's safeguards requirements. As in the past we are prepared to accept the commercial consequences of being clearly ahead of other suppliers. This is the price we are prepared to pay to curb the threat to mankind of nuclear proliferation.

We recognise that for this policy to be fully effective we must persuade other nuclear suppliers to adopt similar export policies. In discussions amongst suppliers we have urged that a collective decision be taken to restrict their nuclear exports to non-nuclear weapon states to those which have ratified the Non-Proliferation Treaty or otherwise accept full scope safeguards. We regret that to date it has not been possible to reach a collective decision to this effect. Canada, however, is determined to assume responsibility where it has the power to act, that is, with regard to Canada's own exports of nuclear equipment, technology and uranium. We are charting a course which we hope will serve as a compelling example for other nuclear suppliers.

With this announcement I am calling on other nuclear exporters to review their own export policies, not in the light of commercial gain but in the interests of maintaining a safe and secure world."

Annex III

EXTRACTS FROM THE EXPORT CONTROL LIST ESTABLISHED UNDER THE EXPORT AND IMPORT PERMITS ACT 1970 (AS LAST AMENDED IN 1984)

Group 8 — Atomic Energy Materials and Equipment

Materials

8001 Source (fertile) and fissionable materials, including but not limited to the following:

1) minerals, raw and treated (including residues and tailings) that contain either uranium or thorium or any combination thereof, exceeding 0.05 per cent by weight, as follows:
   a) ores containing uranium including pitchblende,
   b) monazite and monazite sands,
   c) ores containing thorium including urano-thorianite;
2) natural uranium, unwrought or wrought including alloys and compounds of natural uranium, having an uranium content exceeding 0.05 per cent, excepting medicinals;
3) uranium 233, alloys containing uranium 233 and compounds of uranium 233;
4) uranium enriched in the isotope 235, alloys containing uranium enriched in the isotope 235, and compounds of uranium enriched in the isotope 235;
5) irradiated uranium containing plutonium;
6) plutonium, alloys containing plutonium and compounds containing plutonium;
7) thorium, unwrought or wrought, and alloys and compounds containing thorium, excluding alloys containing less than 1.5 per cent of thorium by weight, and excluding medicinals;
8) irradiated thorium containing uranium 233.

(All destinations, including the United States.)

8005 Deuterium and compounds, mixtures and solutions containing deuterium, including heavy water and heavy parafins, in which ratio of deuterium atoms to hydrogen atoms exceeds 1:5000 by number.

(All destinations, including the United States.)

8008 Zirconium metal, alloys containing more than 50 per cent zirconium by weight, and compounds, in which the ratio of hafnium content to zirconium content is less than one part to 500 parts by weight, and products manufactured wholly thereof.

8011 Nickel, as follows:

1) powder with a nickel content of 99 per cent or more, and a particle size of less than 100 microns;
2) porous metal with a mean pore size of 25 microns or less, and a nickel purity content of 99 per cent or more, except single porous nickel metal sheets not exceeding 930 square centimetres (144 square inches) in size, intended for use in batteries with civil applications. (See also item 5635.)

Note: Subitem (2) refers to porous nickel metal manufactured from nickel powder, described in subitem (1) that has been compacted and sintered to form a metal material with fine pores interconnected throughout the structure.

8012 Beryllium metal and manufactures wholly thereof, except beryllium windows for medical X-ray machines; alloys containing more than 50 per cent of beryllium by weight; oxides and other compounds.

8104 Fluorine.

8015 Chlorine trifluoride.

8034 Artificial graphite having a boron content of less than, or equal to, 1 part in 1 000 000 parts, the total thermal neutron absorption cross section being less than, or equal to, 5 millibarns per atom. (*See* item 5673).

8035 Lithium, as follows:

1) metal;
2) hybrides, in which lithium, whether normal, depleted or enriched in the 6 isotope, is compounded with hydrogen or its isotopes or complexed with other metals or aluminium hybride;
3) alloys, as follows:
   a) magnesium-based alloys containing 10 per cent or more lithium;
   b) containing 50 per cent or more lithium either norma or depleted in the 6 isotope; or
   c) containing any quantity of lithium enriched in the 6 isotope; and
4) any other material containing lithium enriched in the 6 isotope, including compounds, mixtures, and concentrates.

8037 Hafnium metal, and alloys and compounds of hafnium containing more than 60 per cent hafnium by weight.

8038 Calcium containing both less than one hundreth (0.01) per cent by weight of impurities other than magnesium and less than 10 parts in 1 000 000 of boron.

8039 Tritium, its compounds and their mixtures in which the ratio of tritium to hydrogen by atoms exceeds 1 part in 1 000. (*All destinations, including the United States*)

8050 Radioactive materials, non-fissionable, including but not limited to radium, radioactive carbon, radioactive cobalt and radioactive phosphorus.
(*All destinations, including the United States*)

Equipment

8100 Parts for specially designed equipment described in items 8101 to 8141 inclusive of this List.

8101 Plant and equipment specially designed for the fabrication of fuel elements containing source (fertile) or fissionable materials. (*See* item 8001)

8105 Plant and equipment specially designed for the production or concentration of deuterium or deuterium oxide. (*See* item 8005)

8118 Equipment specially designed for the separation of isotopes of uranium or lithium.

8119 Machines, materials or equipment specially designed for use in the processing or irradiated nuclear materials in order to isolate or recover fissionable materials, such as nuclear reactor fuel chopping machines, countercurrent solvent extractors, and specially designed pats and accessories therefor.

8123 Equipment specially designed for the processing of source (fertile) or fissionable material including plants specially designed for the production of uranium hexafluoride (UF_6).

8127 Valves, 3 centimetres or greater in diameter, with bellows seals, wholly made of or lined with aluminium, nickel, or alloy containing 60 per cent or more nickel, either manually or automatically operated.

8129 Gas centrifuges capable of the enrichment or separation of isotopes and specially designed parts and equipment for gas centrifuges and gas centrifuges installations.

8130 Blowers and compressors (turbo, centrifugal, and axial flow types), wholly made of or lined with aluminium, nickel, or alloy containing 60 per cent or more nickel, and having a capacity of 1 700 litres per minutes (60 cubic feet per minute) or greater.

8131 Electrolytic cells for the production of fluorine, with a production capacity greater than 250 grams of fluorine per hour.

8133 Heat exchangers, suitable for use in gaseous diffusion plants (i.e. heat exchanger made of aluminium, copper, nickel, or alloys containing more than 60 per cent nickel or combinations of these metals as clad tubes), designed to operate at subatmospheric pressure, with a leak rate of less than 10^{-4} atmospheres per hour under a pressure differential of 1 atmosphere.

8136 Nuclear reactors, i.e. reactors capable of operation so as to maintain a controlled, self-sustaining fission chain reaction and equipment specially designed therefor. (*See* item 8100) (*All destinations, including the United States*)

8140 Neutron generator tubes designed for operation without an external vacuum system, and utilising electrostatic acceleration to induce a tritium/deuterium nuclear reaction.

8141 Process control instrumentation, specially designed or modified for monitoring or controlling the processing of irradiated fissionable or fertile materials and lithium.

Group 10 — Miscellaneous Goods and Materials

....

10003 Technical data in material form, including but not limited to technical drawings, photographic negatives and prints, recordings, design data and technical and operating manuals, that can be used in the design, production, operation or testing of equipment and materials described in Groups 3 to 9, inclusive, of the List, *except* data available to the public, i.e. in published books and periodicals.

Annex IV

EXPORT AND IMPORT PERMITS ACT

Area Control List

(Effective 3rd July 1981)

His Excellency the Governor General in Council, on the recommendation of the Minister of Industry, Trade and Commerce, pursuant to sections 4 and 6 of the Export and Import Permits Act, is pleased hereby to revoke the Area Control List established by Order in Council P.C. 1970-1999 of 17th November 1970 as amended, and to establish the annexed Area Control List in substitution therefor.

Albania
Bulgaria
Czechoslovakia
German Democratic Republic and East Berlin
Hungary
Libya (Effective 10/1/86)
Mongolia
Democratic People's Republic of Korea
Socialist Republic of Vietnam
Poland
Romania
Union of Soviet Socialist Republics

Annex V

A. Canadian Bilateral Agreements for Nuclear Co-operation that satisfy 1974 and 1976 policies*: 1st May 1987

Country	Title	Date in Force	Comment
Australia	Agreement between the Government of Canada and the Government of Australia concerning the peaceful uses of Nuclear Energy	October 1959	Subsequently Amended March 1981
Colombia	Agreement between the Government of Canada and the Government of the Republic of Colombia for co-operation in the peaceful uses of Nuclear Energy		Signed but not yet ratified
Egypt	Agreement between the Government of Canada and the Government of the Arab Republic of Egypt for co-operation in the peaceful uses of Nuclear Energy	November 1982	
EURATOM	Agreement between the Government of Canada and the European Atomic Energy Community (EURATOM) for co-operation in the peaceful uses of Atomic Energy	November 1959	Subsequently Amended January 1978 December 1981
Finland	Agreement between the Government of Canada and the Government of the Republic of Finland concerning the uses of nuclear material, equipment, facilities and information transferred between Canada and Finland	August 1976	Subsequently Amended May 1984
Indonesia	Agreement between the Government of Canada and the Government of the Republic of Indonesia concerning the peaceful uses of Nuclear Energy	July 1983	
Japan	Agreement between the Government of Canada and the Government of Japan for co-operation in the peaceful uses of Atomic Energy	July 1960	Subsequently Amended August 1978 April 1983
Korea	Agreement between the Government of Canada and the Government of the Republic of Korea for co-operation in the development and application of Atomic Energy for peaceful purposes	January 1976	
Philippines	Agreement between the Government of Canada and the Government of the Republic of the Philippines concerning the peaceful uses of nuclear material, equipment, facilities and information transferred between Canada and the Republic of the Philippines	April 1983	
Romania	Agreement between the Government of Canada and the Government of the Socialist Republic of Romania for co-operation in the development and application of Atomic Energy for peaceful purposes	June 1978	

* See Annexes I and II.

Country	Title	Date in Force	Comment
Sweden	Agreement between the Government of Canada and the Government of Sweden concerning the uses of nuclear material equipment, facilities and information transferred between Canada and Sweden	November 1978	Subsequently Amended December 1981
Turkey	Agreement between the Government of Canada and the Government of the Republic of Turkey for co-operation in the peaceful uses of Nuclear Energy	July 1985	
United States of America	Agreement for co-operation concerning civil uses of Atomic Energy between the Government of Canada and the Government of the United States of America	July 1955	Subsequently Amended June 1956 June 1960 May 1962 July 1980

B. Canadian Bilateral Agreements for Nuclear Co-operation that satisfy 1974 policy only*

Country	Title	Date in Force	Comment
Argentina	Agreement between the Government of Canada and the Government of the Argentine Republic for co-operation in the development and application of Atomic Energy for peaceful purposes	January 1976	
Spain	Agreement between the Government of Canada and the Government of Spain for co-operation in the development and application of Atomic Energy for peaceful purposes	April 1976	

* See Annex I.

FINLAND

TABLE OF CONTENTS

FINLAND

I. INTRODUCTION

In Finland, the legal system governing activities in the nuclear field consists of a body of laws, decrees as well as government decisions which also cover trade in nuclear[1] and radioactive materials and related equipment. These texts reflect three considerations, namely, nuclear safety, radiation protection and the non-proliferation of nuclear weapons, particularly in the context of imports and exports.

This system makes a distinction between "nuclear energy legislation" which covers material and equipment suited for the generation of nuclear energy and "radiation protection legislation" which encompasses all radioactive materials and sets permissible limits for protection of workers and the general public.

The Atomic Energy Act of 1957 and Decree of 1958, made under the Act, originally governed nuclear activities in Finland. They were cancelled by a Nuclear Energy Act adopted on 11th December 1987 (No. 990/87). This new Act entered into force on 1st March 1988 and replaces the 1957 Act, covering all uses of nuclear energy. In particular, the Act applies to the possession, fabrication, production, transfer, handling, use, transport, *export* and *import* of nuclear material, ores and concentrates containing uranium or thorium as well as to equipment, devices and nuclear information [Section 2(3) and (4)] (see Nuclear Law Bulletin No. 41).

The Nuclear Energy Decree (No. 161/1988) made in implementation of the Act, entered into force on the same date, and *inter alia* specifies the scope of the Act; the Decree defines the licensing procedure under the Act, namely regarding export and import licences for uranium and thorium bearing ores, nuclear material and equipment (Chapters 6 and 7) as well as for transport, mining and enrichment (Chapters 8 and 9). It also deals with licences concerning nuclear information.

The above 1987 Act and 1988 Decree, together with general trade legislation regulate nuclear trade in Finland. As regards the safe conduct of nuclear activities, the Radiation Protection Act of 26th April 1957 as amended (No. 174/57) and the Radiation Protection Decree of 27th September 1957 (No. 328/57), made under the Act, set up a system of 'safety permits" for the use of radioactive materials.

This study will discuss the above-mentioned legislation as well as transport of nuclear and radioactive materials in the context of imports and exports. In addition, a description is provided of the agreements concluded by Finland in the field of peaceful nuclear co-operation.

II. NUCLEAR EXPORT POLICY

In connection with export permits, one basic constraint affects the considerations of the licensing authorities, namely, that the export operation concerned shall not conflict with the obligations of international agreements binding on Finland. These obligations include:

— the requirement that IAEA Safeguards shall be applied in the receiving state in accordance with Article III.2 of the Treaty on the Non-Proliferation of Nuclear Weapons (NPT) (as set out in IAEA document INFCIRC/209, as amended);
— the requirement that, for transfers or retransfers of items subject to the provisions of certain bilateral agreements, in certain cases the prior consent of the other party must be obtained.

Some of the bilateral agreements as well as the NPT also contain provisions concerning measures to facilitate nuclear co-operation between the States parties. These provisions must also be taken into account.

In addition, Finland has stated that it will base its nuclear export policy on the criteria set out in the Nuclear Suppliers Group Guidelines (so-called London Club)[2]. Implementation of this decision means that the receiving state, if a non-nuclear weapon state must, in respect of the items to be exported, have given the Government of Finland guarantees of:

— non-explosive use;
— adequate physical protection;
— IAEA safeguards with adequate duration and coverage;
— passing on, in the case of retransfer, similar requirements to the third state.

Furthermore, the receiving states' general attitude towards non-proliferation is also an important consideration.

Finally, in the context of non-proliferation, the requirement that Finland's commitments under international treaties be observed is clearly stated in the nuclear energy legislation.

Nuclear trade is based on a system of special permits issued under the relevant regulations and in compliance with Government Decisions. Such permits are granted by the regulatory authority, the *Ministry of Trade and Industry* or the Finnish *Centre for Radiation and Nuclear Safety*, the competent authority for all questions concerning the safe use of ionizing radiation and nuclear energy as well as the physical protection and safeguards of nuclear material and related matters. The Centre grants export and import licences in cases where considerations concerning non-proliferation policy have been defined through appropriate bilateral agreements Finland has concluded. In other cases the licences are granted by the Ministry of Trade and Industry after having consulted the Centre. In addition, permits for activities not covered by the Nuclear Energy Act (safety permits, see under section IV) are issued by the Centre which also ascertains that all licensed activities are carried out in compliance with the approved conditions.

The opinion of the Ministry for Foreign Affairs is occasionally sought informally when uncertainty has prevailed about the general lines of export policy. The same applies regarding the Standing Committee for Foreign Affairs of the Council of State. The members of this Committee are Cabinet Members.

III. TRADE IN NUCLEAR MATERIAL AND EQUIPMENT

The Nuclear Energy Act (No. 990/87) provides that a special permit is required for the possession, transport, use, import and export of nuclear material. Nuclear material is defined in the Act as "special nuclear materials and source materials, such as uranium, thorium and plutonium".

1. General Licensing Regime for Imports and Exports

This regime is based on the 1974 Act on Protection of Foreign Trade and Economic Growth of the Land (No. 157/74) and a 1974 Decree of the same title (No. 162/74). The regime provides for the means to regulate, ie restrict and monitor, both import and export through import/export permits and import/export declarations.

A "restriction list" has been issued in Section 1 of the above Act and Section 2 of the above Decree. Since the list does not include any nuclear items, only a declaration is needed. This must provide the following information :

— classification
— tariff title
— amount of goods
— value
— country of origin/purchase.

The system is administered by the Export and Import Permits Office, which is assisted by the Customs authorities for control purposes.

The Customs procedures and duties are defined within the general regime provided by the Customs Act of 14th July 1978 (No. 573/78) and the Customs Decree of the same date (No. 574/78).

2. Nuclear Licensing Regime for Imports and Exports

The Nuclear Energy Act stipulates that a special permit is required for the export and import of the following items :

— nuclear material and nuclear waste, uranium and thorium ores and their concentrates ;
— other materials than nuclear material which are especially suitable for the generation of nuclear energy ;
— equipment and devices which are intended for or otherwise especially suitable for use in nuclear facilities ;
— equipment and devices which are intended for or otherwise especially suitable for the production of nuclear material or materials suitable for the generation of nuclear energy ;
— special equipment necessary for the manufacture of such equipment and devices ;
— nuclear information in written or similar physical form but not publicly available.

The constraints for export permits have been described under section II. The main concerns regarding import permits are the possible adverse safety and waste management consequences of the use of the imported item. Also, possible bilateral obligations restricting the use or retransfer of the imported item and material produced by using it are an important consideration.

IV. TRADE IN RADIOACTIVE MATERIALS

All radioactive materials are subject to radiation protection legislation[3] and the following description of licensing procedures in this connection also apply to "nuclear material" and equipment referred to in section III above.

The following paragraphs will describe the licensing procedure laid down by the Radiation Protection Act (No. 174/57) and Decree (No. 328/59) for the export and import of radioactive materials generally.

1. Licensing Regime

A permit in accordance with the Radiation Protection Act (Section 2), a "safety permit", is needed for import, export and transport of, as well as trade in, radioactive materials if the activity exceeds certain limits.

The exemption limits referred to above vary according to the isotope in question from 0.1 to 100 μCi. Even all materials with specific activity less than 0002 μCi/g are exempted; for solid materials occurring in nature the specific activity limit is 50 times higher.

The issuance of a safety permit is subject to the preconditions stated in the Radiation Protection Decree, namely that:

— the radiation protection regulations are complied with; and
— there is no reason to reject the application.

The safety permits for trade cover import, export, commerce and transport of radioactive materials if not explicitly restricted to only some of these functions. The Annexes to the permit specify the details of the activities covered, e.g. the intended use of materials, the types of radiation sources, the manufacturers and the suppliers. If essential changes are going to take place in the activities, they must be accepted by the permit authority, namely the Finnish Centre for Radiation and Nuclear Safety to which such authority was delegated by Decree of the Ministry of Social Affairs and Health.

A safety permit for an import or export not connected with trade is issued for well specified operations only, such as the import of a radiation source and its transportation to the place of use.

As regards nuclear material, the permit under the Radiation Protection Act is incorporated in the permit under the Nuclear Energy Act.

2. Administrative Procedures

In accordance with the requirements that radioactive materials may only be offered for sale, imported or exported by a person holding a permit to do so (Radiation Protection Decree, Section 21), Customs authorities may deliver such materials only to a person entitled to import them. The Customs authorities must also notify the Finnish Centre for Radiation and Nuclear Safety of the nature and quantity of radioactive materials imported or exported and the name and address of the importer or exporter concerned.

V. TRANSPORT

Under the Nuclear Energy Act (Section 2), both domestic and transboundary transport[4] of materials suitable for the generation of atomic energy also requires a special permit. This transport permit is normally applied for and issued together with the safety permit and the export or import permit.

A foreign association or authority may on special grounds be granted a permit for:

— transportation of nuclear material or nuclear waste on Finnish territory;
— import or export in connection with transit or transport of nuclear material, nuclear waste or ores or concentrates containing uranium or thorium; and
— occasional use of a nuclear reactor in a means of transport.

In connection with control purposes such permits can be granted to an international agency or a foreign authority which is assigned to undertake such control work as is required by an international treaty concerning nuclear energy to which Finland is a Contracting Party.

Safety is not normally a question connected with export. However, as regards a transport permit for the export operation, consideration of the application is based mostly on a general assessment of the possibilities of effecting the international transfer and related transport in accordance with the requirements concerning:

— safety (here the IAEA Regulations on Safe Transport of Radioactive Materials, as well as the corresponding regulations issued by international organisations for different modes of transport, form the basis of assessment);

- safeguards notifications (as specified in IAEA document INFCIRC/153);
- bilateral notifications, if required;
- physical protection (here IAEA documents INFCIRC/225 and INFCIRC/254 as well as certain Nordic recommendations provide the basis for the assessment)[5];
- insurance coverage for nuclear third party liability.

It should be noted that the provisions of the Radiation Protection Act and Decree contain conditions which only cover the radiation protection aspects in connection with export or import. These are then incorporated in the corresponding permit issued under the Nuclear Energy Act and Decree.

Finally, before any actual transfer of materials, the permit holder is required to submit a detailed transport plan for acceptance by the Centre for Radiation and Nuclear Safety. In this connection, the Centre checks that the transfer and the related transport operation will be carried out in accordance with domestic and international regulations, licensing conditions and treaty obligations relevant from the point of view of the Centre's competence. The Centre also controls by means of inspections that no unlicensed exports have taken place. The actual transfer of items across the borders of the country is controlled by the Customs authorities.

VI. PHYSICAL PROTECTION

The Nuclear Energy Act refers to physical protection. In particular, it provides that sufficient physical protection measures must be taken to prevent illegal uses of nuclear energy (Section 7) and that the Council of State may issue general regulations regarding physical protection (Section 81).

In addition, Finland has signed the IAEA Convention on the Physical Protection of Nuclear Material and it will eventually be enacted into law. Also, account is taken of the IAEA recommendations in this respect (INFCIRC/225), and provisions aiming at physical protection are included in the permits.

VII. INTELLECTUAL PROPERTY IN THE NUCLEAR FIELD

The Nuclear Energy Act (Section 78) and the Radiation Protection Act (Section 10) prohibit the control authorities from making use of any business or professional secrets they may discover during inspection or verification of nuclear or radioactive materials and equipment.

It should be noted that the general regime in the field of intellectual property and patents legislation applies in the nuclear sector.

VIII. AGREEMENTS

Finland has entered into agreements, both multilateral and bilateral which have a direct or indirect bearing on nuclear trade. However, only those concerning this subject directly are mentioned below. No reference is made to international agreements concerning general trade (e.g. free trade) or to those which, while mentioning nuclear material, deal exclusively with transport arrangements.

1. Multilateral Agreements

The following are the two Agreements providing for international control measures regarding nuclear trade:

- The 1968 Treaty on the Non-Proliferation of Nuclear Weapons, which entered into force for Finland on 5th March 1970; and

— The 1980 Convention on the Physical Protection of Nuclear Material, signed by Finland on 25th June 1981; to be ratified in 1988.

2. Bilateral Agreements

The following refer to general nuclear co-operation and safeguards, and deal explicitly with nuclear material, equipment and technological information (but not with specific deliveries and related guarantees of peaceful use). All the agreements contain specific clauses requiring the prior consent of the supplier country in case of retransfer of the materials supplied as well as safeguards and physical protection provisions.

a) Framework agreements for nuclear co-operation

— Agreement between the Government of Finland and the Government of ***Sweden*** on the peaceful uses of atomic energy, signed on 15th October 1968 and entered into force on 5th September 1970.
The various forms of co-operation in the Agreement include:

- exchange of data and information in the nuclear field;
- prospecting and producing uranium or other raw material essential in the use of nuclear energy;
- potential acquisition and supply of equipment, facilities, source material, special fissionable material or fuel;
- acquisition of patent rights;
- acquisition of assistance and services;
- promoting industrial co-operation.

These so-called "commercial" provisions remain in force for a period of thirty years unless their validity is extended by the Parties. All other provisions, including those containing safeguards rights, were concluded to remain in force until the Parties ruled otherwise.

— Agreement between the Government of the Republic of Finland and the Government of the ***United Kingdom*** for co-operation in the peaceful uses of atomic energy, signed on 24th May 1968 and entered into force on 20th February 1969 for a period of thirty years.

This Agreement concerns in particular, the supply by the United Kingdom to Finland of nuclear reactors, equipment and materials as well as provision of related assistance. A further Agreement was concluded on the same date by an exchange of notes between both countries concerning consultations and negotiations due to certain new treaty obligations arising from the United Kingdom's subsequent accession to the Treaty establishing the European Atomic Energy Community.

— Agreement between the Government of the Republic of Finland and the Government of the ***Union of Soviet Socialist Republics*** for co-operation in the peaceful uses of nuclear energy, signed on 14th May 1969 and entered into force on 28th September 1969. This Agreement concerns, in particular, the following forms of co-operation:

- co-operation between the competent authorities;
- supply of reactors, equipment or materials to Finland;
- assistance in designing, constructing and using the above-mentioned items;
- delivery of nuclear fuels, source material or special fissionable material for the above-mentioned reactors and dealing with these fuels etc after they are spent;
- assistance in designing and constructing a nuclear fuel production plant;
- supply of equipment and materials, nuclear material notwithstanding, to the Soviet Union;
- sale of uranium enrichment services to Finland.

The "commercial" provisions remain in force for a period of thirty years unless their validity is extended by the Parties. The provisions containing safeguards rights were concluded to remain in force until the Parties rule otherwise.

— Agreement between the Government of the Republic of Finland and the Government of the ***United States of America*** for co-operation concerning the civil uses of atomic energy, signed on 8th April 1970 and entered into force on 7th July 1970 for a period of thirty years.

This Agreement concerns in particular exchange of information on the peaceful applications of atomic energy, and the supply by the United States of nuclear fuels to Finland. It will be superseded by the following Agreement.

— Agreement between both the above countries for co-operation concerning the peaceful uses of nuclear energy, signed on 2nd May 1985, which will enter into force for a period of thirty years by an exchange of notes between the Parties.

This new Agreement deals with essentially the same questions as the previous one, but lays a greater emphasis on safeguards and physical protection requirements, also specifying that no transfer of sensitive nuclear facility or technology[6] or major critical components shall take place.

b) Safeguards

— Agreement between the Government of the Republic of Finland and the *International Atomic Energy Agency **(IAEA)*** on Safeguards (INFCIRC/155), signed on 11th June 1971 and entered into force on 2nd September 1972.

c) Agreements on transfers of nuclear reactors, equipment and technology

— Agreement between the Government of the Republic of Finland and the Government of ***Sweden*** concerning the guidelines to be followed for exports of nuclear materials, equipment or technology concluded by an exchange of notes of 4th March 1983 and entered into force on the same date. It will remain in force until denounced by either Party.

This Agreement was made in pursuance of the framework Agreement between both countries and deals in particular with safeguards aspects, namely, the Parties assume the following commitments :

- not to use material or equipment that is referred to in IAEA document INFCIRC/254 Annex A and acquired from the other State Party in a way that may lead to production of any kind of nuclear explosive device ;
- IAEA safeguards measures applied to the possession and use of the above-mentioned material or equipment must, as to their extent and duration, correspond to the provisions in IAEA document GOV/1621[7] ;
- the Parties apply physical protection to nuclear material acquired from the other State Party to the minimum extent required in IAEA document INFCIRC/254 Annex B ;
- any above-mentioned material or equipment, or material or equipment produced using them, shall not be exported unless the recipient state has certified that they shall not be used in a way that may lead to production of any kind of nuclear explosive device.

— Agreement between the Government of the Republic of Finland and the Government of ***Canada*** concerning the uses of nuclear material, equipment, facilities and information between Finland and Canada, signed on 5th March 1976 and entered into force on 15th August 1976 for a period of thirty years.

The Agreement lays down the procedures to be followed, in particular regarding the application of safeguards, notifications, and prior consent in respect of the equipment, nuclear material, facilities and information transferred between the Parties. It was followed by an Agreement concerning its implementation (interpretation and guidelines) through an exchange of notes, signed on 8th June 1984 which entered into force on the same date.

— Agreement between the Government of Finland and the Government of ***Australia*** concerning the transfer of nuclear material between Finland and Australia, signed on 20th July 1978 and entered into force on 9th February 1980 for a period of thirty years.

The Agreement regulates in particular, the transfer of nuclear material transferred between the two Parties as well as quantities of derived nuclear material directly proportional to the transferred nuclear material used for its production.

NOTES AND REFERENCES

1. The term "nuclear" is used here in the strict sense: it covers only material, equipment and technology of special significance for the production of fission energy and does not concern radioisotopes.
2. Issued as IAEA document INFCIRC/254, the Guidelines specify the guarantees which an exporter country shall require from an importer country in connection with the transfer of certain types of nuclear material, equipment and technology to non-nuclear weapon states. In addition to requiring international safeguards on what is being exported — in accordance with, but in some cases over and above the NPT — the Guidelines state that nuclear material and equipment involved in the field of nuclear energy may only be exported if the material or equipment is subject to satisfactory physical protection. The same shall apply in the event of re-exports. For a detailed analysis of these matters see Volume I of this study dealing with international aspects.
3. A Decision of the Ministry of Social Affairs and Health of 5th November 1968 on radiation protection (No. 594/68 as amended by Decisions No. 872/76 and 775/78) also forms part of the radiation protection legislation. This Decision covers, *inter alia*, definitions and concepts for ionizing radiation, permissible radiation doses, exemptions from safety permits as well as general provisions on radioactive materials and waste, in particular regarding storage and transport.
4. For further details, see *Regulations Governing the Transport of Radioactive Materials*, OECD/NEA, 1980.
5. INFCIRC/225 contains IAEA recommendations on the physical protection of nuclear material for facilities as well as transports. The Nordic recommendations are contained in an informal document (NKA/NT 4 — 1981) on physical protection of transport of nuclear material in and between Nordic countries, based on INFCIRC/225 but adjusted to individual practices and experience in the respective Nordic countries. The recommendations can be said to represent a sharpened version of the IAEA regime. For INFCIRC/254 see Note 2 *supra*.
6. This Agreement gives the following definitions:

   "sensitive nuclear facility" means any facility designed or used primarily for uranium enrichment, reprocessing of nuclear fuel, heavy water production, or fabrication of nuclear fuel containing plutonium;

   "sensitive nuclear technology" means any information (including information incorporated in equipment or an important component) which is not in the public domain and which is important to the design, construction, fabrication, operation or maintenance of any sensitive nuclear facility, or other such information which may be designated by agreement of the parties.
7. See Volume I of this study.

FRANCE

TABLE OF CONTENTS

FRANCE

I. INTRODUCTION

In recent years, the need for efficient control of trade in sensitive nuclear material and equipment, especially from the viewpoint of the non-proliferation of nuclear weapons and France's international commitments, has led the authorities to strengthen the regulations in this field. The purpose of these regulations is, on the one hand, to monitor closely the movements of nuclear material and ensure that the material itself and the premises where it is held are protected, and, on the other, to control exports and imports.

Various bodies have been set up at government level to take general policy decisions in this field, draft the necessary regulations and ensure their implementation.

Alongside these aspects relating essentially to foreign trade, there remains the obligation to protect users, the public and the environment against the hazards of ionizing radiation presented by radioactive products and equipment emitting such radiation. There is thus a need to make a distinction, in the context of the regulation of trade, between, on the one hand, the security questions raised by nuclear material of strategic importance and large items of nuclear equipment and, on the other, radiation protection questions raised by radioisotopes. This distinction is reflected in the present study. To facilitate comprehension, an explanation of a number of terms is given in *Appendix I*.

II. IMPORT AND EXPORT OF NUCLEAR MATERIAL AND EQUIPMENT

The French system for controlling foreign trade in sensitive nuclear material and equipment is rather complex. It is based on a series of regulations with varying objectives, and involves the intervention of several bodies at both governmental and administrative level.

A description will first be given of the role of the bodies set up by the Government to determine the policy to be followed as regards the export of "sensitive" materials from the non-proliferation of nuclear weapons' viewpoint, and to take decisions with regard to major projects for the export of equipment.

Next, the system set up by the Act of 25th July 1980 on the protection and control of nuclear material will be studied. Lastly, consideration will be given to the regulations, especially fiscal and customs regulations, by which the import and export of nuclear material and large items of equipment are controlled (control of the final destination and export licences).

In practice, such control is exercised both at government level for the most important cases, and at administrative level by virtue of regulations which are either specifically nuclear or form part of the general regulation of foreign trade.

A. CONTROLS OF A POLITICAL NATURE

The fact that the export of nuclear material and equipment can have implications for national security and France's international commitments explains why general policy decisions in this field are taken at the highest level, i.e. the President of the Republic, acting in his capacity as guarantor of national independence and territorial integrity.

The need to ensure that such exports do not result in the proliferation of nuclear weapons led the Head of State to set up, in 1976, under his Chairmanship, a specialised Committee : the *Council for Foreign Nuclear Policy*.

The task of the Council[1] is to define the major principles of French foreign nuclear policy, especially with regard to the export of sensitive nuclear technology, equipment and products.

On 11th October 1976, the Council determined foreign trade policy with regard to nuclear material from the viewpoint of preventing the proliferation of nuclear weapons[2].

These orientations allow the Administration to consider applications for exports according to the following procedure. For large nuclear plants, some two months before an export contract is signed, the exporter must make contact with the Ministerial Department(s) concerned (Notice to exporters, dated 21st January 1986 — see below : Control of the export of sensitive materials and equipment from the non-proliferation of nuclear weapons' viewpoint).

For other nuclear items, the exporter must contact the Ministry responsible for Industry, which then proceeds with interministerial consultations.

Among bodies which may influence Government policy in this field, the *Atomic Energy Committee* may also be cited. This Committee was originally created within the Atomic Energy Commission (CEA), as a public body with powers over all applications of nuclear energy, chaired by the Prime Minister or a Minister delegated by him, failing which by the Administrator-General of the CEA.

Since the changes made to the CEA by the Decree of 24th August 1982, the Atomic Energy Committee plays the role of a restricted interministerial committee in the field of atomic energy[3]. Apart from its CEA duties (deciding CEA programmes, adopting the CEA budget, and approving share acquisitions and sales etc.), the Committee may be asked to look into general nuclear policy matters.

Note should also be taken, in another field, of the Central Office for the Prevention of Illicit Trading in Weapons, Ammunition, Explosives and Nuclear, Biological and Chemical Materials, set up under the Decree of 13th December 1982. This Office, set up under the Minister of the Interior, has jurisdiction in the field of offences relating to the manufacture, possession, trade and unlawful use etc. of nuclear material in cases where those committing the offence intended to engage in illicit trading or to use the material to endanger the State's authority or public safety.

B. CONTROLS OF AN ADMINISTRATIVE NATURE

Among radioactive products, so-called "nuclear" material is given special treatment, being either fissile, fusible (easy to melt) or fertile[4].

Such material is subject to a threefold system of control. First, it is subject to a protection and control scheme designed essentially to prevent its loss, theft or misuse. Secondly, it is subject to "final destination" control by the customs authorities. Finally, an intensified control is applied with regard to the export of nuclear material and equipment requiring special checking measures from the non-proliferation of nuclear weapons' viewpoint.

1. Protection and Control of Nuclear Material

a) Scope

The basic item of legislation in this field is the *Act of 25th July 1980 on the protection and control of nuclear material* which submits the import, export, preparation, possession, transfer, use and transport of nuclear material to prior authorisation and control.

As concerns the particular case of exports, it will be noted that the Act of 1980 (Section 2) requires exporters to specify to purchasers and sub-purchasers the conditions as to the subsequent use of the nuclear material which may be imposed under an export licence. This provision means that the future user of the material may find that various restrictions have been imposed as a condition for export.

The Act is supplemented by an *implementing Decree of 12th May 1981* on the protection and control of nuclear material[5]. The fusible, fissile and fertile materials included under the Decree are as follows : plutonium, uranium, thorium, deuterium, tritium and lithium 6, as well as materials, other than ores, containing such elements or their compounds. However, the Decree (Section 8) fixes thresholds below which the materials are exempt from the licensing regime[6]. Below these thresholds, a simple declaration to the Minister of the Interior is all that is required. An Order of 14th March 1984 lays down the protection and control measures applicable to nuclear material for which a simple declaration has been made.

The *licence* is granted by the Minister responsible for Industry after consultation with the Minister of the Interior. In the case of import and export licences, the Minister of Foreign Affairs is also consulted. He must give his opinion within a period of fifteen days. Licences may also be granted by the Minister of Defence, whether or not jointly with the Minister of Industry, in the case of nuclear material in the field of defence.

Each licence is given for one or more of the materials referred to in the Decree, and for one or more of the activities covered by the regulations.

If the applicant carries on his activites in several premises, a separate licence must be granted for each of them. Moreover, if premises include more than one separate installation, the Minister responsible for Industry may grant a specific licence for each installation.

The licence application must provide detailed information about the applicant, his competence to carry on the activities described, the nature of these activities, including a description of the installations in which the materials in question will be held, and, where appropriate, the means of transport used, the nature and maximum quantities or flux of the materials concerned, and the various measures taken to ensure adequate control (Section 4 of the 1981 Decree).

Detailed rules as to the application for and form of licences may, if necessary, be decided by joint order of the Ministers of Industry, the Interior, Finance and Transport.

Licences may be issued subject to conditions and limits relating to their duration and to quantities of materials held, and may be suspended or revoked, primarily in cases where an offence has been committed.

The Minister of Industry must be given prior notice of any changes in the circumstances under which the licensed activities are carried out, and a fresh application is required for any changes deemed important by the Minister.

b) Protection and control regime

Licence holders are required to perform obligations which constitute the second part of this legislation and are covered by the general term of control or inspection. Under the Act of 25th July 1980, this is interpreted in a very broad sense : the aim is to prevent losses, theft or misappropriation of nuclear material.

A distinction has to be made between inspection and control which is the responsibility of the licence holder, and the duty laid on government authorities to check that such measures are being applied.

As regards the obligations of the licence holder, the Decree of 12th May 1981 distinguishes between :

- measures to follow up and account for materials ;
- measures for the containment and surveillance of materials and for the physical protection of the premises where they are held ;
- measures for physical protection in the course of carriage.

i) Follow-up and accounting

The follow-up of and accounting for nuclear material must enable the licence holder at any time to know the quantities of materials in his possession, how they are being used, and any processing to which they are subject, so as to reveal any anomalies.

Provision is made for verification by stocktaking at regular intervals. The licence holder must inform the Minister of Industry of any anomaly and immediately notify the police and gendarmerie of any disappearance of nuclear material, whether due to theft, loss or misappropriation. An Order of 24th June 1982 lays down detailed arrangements for follow-up and accounting procedures for nuclear material.

ii) Measures for the containment and surveillance of materials and for physical protection

The Decree of 12th May 1981 distinguishes between :

- measures for the containment of materials within establishments or installations which are designed to prevent unauthorised or unjustified movements of materials ;
- surveillance measures to ensure that containment is complete, that there is no abnormal departure of materials and that there is no tampering with the accounting or surveillance systems ;
- physical protection measures, properly so-called, concerning premises, facilities and installations where materials are held and designed to protect them against misappropriation or unlawful acts.

For the purpose of physical protection measures, nuclear material is divided into three categories set out in a table annexed to the Decree and corresponding to protection measures of increasing importance (storage conditions, physical barriers, presence of guards, etc.).

These levels of physical protection and the classification of nuclear material correspond in the main to the criteria set out in the table annexed to the International Convention on the Physical Protection of Nuclear Material (see Volume I of this study).

iii) Protection of nuclear material in the course of transport

For the physical protection of nuclear material in the course of transport, the Decree of 12th May 1981 provides that protection measures also depend on the category to which the material belongs :

- for all nuclear material (except, however, for natural uranium, depleted uranium and thorium), prior notice of a transport operation must be given to the Minister of Industry and the Minister of the Interior ;
- for material in Categories I and II, prior approval of the transport arrangements must be obtained from the Minister of Industry ;
- for material in Category I, provision is made for special protection by an escort provided by the carrier with the assistance, where necessary, of the police.

The rules governing the protection and control of nuclear material were laid down by joint Order dated 26th March 1982 of the Ministers of Industry, the Interior, and Transport, after obtaining the opinion of a special committee responsible to the Minister of Industry, namely, the *Committee for Protection of the Transport of Nuclear Material.*

This Order of 26th March 1982 (amended by an Order of 12th June 1986) on the protection and control of nuclear material in the course of carriage makes the *Institute for Protection and Nuclear Safety* (created within the CEA by the Order of 2nd November 1976), responsible, under the authority of the Minister of Industry, from the operational viewpoint for the management and follow-up of the transport of nuclear material. French and foreign carriers holding a licence must give the Institute and the Minister of the Interior at least fifteen-days advance warning of any transport operation. No such operation may be carried out without the prior approval of the Institute. The 1982 Order also contains detailed provisions on the organisation of the transport of materials depending on the mode of transport used.

An Order of 31st July 1987 concerns protection and control of nuclear material carried by aircraft and prescribes the measures the carrier must take to this effect. The latter must, in particular, submit in advance to the Minister responsible for Industry a transport plan for Category I and II material.

c) Offences, criminal penalties and liability

The Act of 25th July 1980 provides for criminal penalties in three cases :

- unlawful appropriation of nuclear material, covering cases of theft and misappropriation ;
- the unauthorised exercise of activities within the scope of the Act or the provision of deliberately misleading information for the purpose of obtaining a licence ;
- failure to declare a loss or a theft of materials is punishable by imprisonment of between fifteen days and two years and a fine (Section 8).

A sentence of imprisonment may or may not be accompanied by a fine.

This criminal liability applies particularly to the licence holder, the head of the establishment where the nuclear material is held and the employees who have "legal" custody of such material, since they are directly responsible for the statutory inspection and control measures.

Where the licence holder is an incorporated body, as is nearly always the case, the directors are responsible for compliance with the law. They must designate a representative for each establishment containing nuclear material, with particular responsibility for ensuring the regular application of controls over such material. This representative, normally the head of the establishment, must, in turn, inform the employees directly responsible for the control and custody of the nuclear material of the penalties to which they may be liable if an offence is committed. Employees must acknowledge in writing that they have been informed of the penalties they may incur should they fail to declare a loss or theft.

Breaches of the legislation on the protection of nuclear material may be formally reported by officers or agents of the judicial police, in line with the normal rule of French criminal law. Offences may also be reported by officials in the inspection service or any other service specially concerned with such matters by reason of their work : e.g. customs officers in the case of imports and exports, fraud prevention officers, and, as regards nuclear installations, inspectors of large nuclear installations and inspectors from the Central Service for Protection against Ionizing Radiation (SCPRI).

Moreover, the enforcement of measures relating to nuclear materials under the Act of 25th July 1980 and the Decree of 12th May 1981 is a particular responsibility of the Minister of Industry who appoints the officials to carry out this work. These officials are bound by a duty to respect the confidential nature of their work.

Lastly, special mention must be made of the co-ordinating role played by the *Interministerial Committee for Nuclear Safety* which the Decree of 4th August 1975, as amended, entrusts, *inter alia*, with the task of co-ordinating action relating to the inspection and safety of nuclear material.

2. Control of Imports and Exports (Final Destination)

In addition to the nuclear legislation considered in the preceding paragraphs, the regulations in this field provide, on the one hand, for restrictions dealing with control of the final destination of strategic interest products[7] and, on the other, for a system of administrative control, the specific purpose of which is the prevention of the proliferation of nuclear weapons.

The dual nature of this control stems from the fact that French regulations take into account both the COCOM Atomic Energy List and the London Club Guidelines Trigger List. A Decree-Law of 18th April 1939 organising the control of exports of war and similar equipment and a Decree of 30th November 1944 establishing a general control over imports and exports in war time are the texts which had originally set controls. Since then, the prohibition principle was replaced by freedom to export and import goods, except for forbidden products listed in Notices published in the Official Journal.

At present conditions for importing and exporting goods subject to final destination control are prescribed in an *Order of 30th January 1967*, amended by an Order of 13th January 1986 ; the latter Order fixes, subject to certain derogations[8], the general rules in this field as well as the procedures to be followed according to the customs systems applicable. Section 37 of the 1967 Order provides that *imports* of products subject to final destination control are carried out according to procedures defined therein, subject to special arrangements which are laid down in Notices to importers. The same applies for exports (Section 39). The General Directorate for Customs and Indirect Duties (*Direction générale des douanes et droits indirects*) is the competent administration.

The import and export of products subject to final destination control are governed by a special regime (Sections 36, 79 and 80 of the Order of 30th January 1967 as amended), consisting of Notices to importers and exporters which specify their obligations and list the products concerned. The most recent is the *Notice of 5th March 1988.*

According to this Notice, imports, exports and re-exports of the products listed in its Annex, as well as commercial transactions with foreign countries involving purchase or sale of any such products without their import into French territory are subject to final destination control. Technology exports involving products subject to final destination control are also subject to a licence when their final destination is a country referred to in COCOM controls. The reference number of the product with a position corresponding to that on the COCOM list (COCOM section number) must be set down following its commercial designation on import, export and re-export certificates, as well as on any application for a licence for purchase or sale without import into French territory.

According to the products, different documents may be required : for *exports* of items referred to in the Annex to the above Notice, barrying an exceptional derogation, an international nominative certificate for import issued to the foreign buyer by his country's competent authorities must be submitted. A certificate checking the delivery, stamped by the authorities of the buyer country is also needed. As regards *imports* of such products, it is provided that an international import certificate and a delivery verification certificate must be issued by the General Directorate for Customs and Indirect Duties.

Principles applicable to technology transfers

By "technology" is meant technological documents, other than documents generally available to the public, containing information to do with the design, production, testing or use of goods or processes. The export of technology subject to final destination control, in accordance with the COCOM list of nuclear items, must be covered by a model 02 export licence granted in advance by the customs authorities.

Principles applicable to products

The products subject to final destination control are those contained in the list published by way of Notice to importers and exporters, whatever the origin or country of manufacture (see list in *Appendix II*).

— All importers of products on the list must obtain for the foreign buyer, who will request it, an international import certificate (*certificat international d'importation* — CII) and/or a delivery verification certificate (*certificat de vérification de livraison* — CVL) when use is made of such documents in dealings between the seller's country and that of the importer.
— All exports of products on the list must be covered by an 02 model export licence or an authorisation for the export of war equipment in the case of products falling into this category, delivered in advance by the authorities. When the manufacture or delivery of the products requiring an export licence take longer than the period the licence remains valid (twelve months), it is possible to conclude a prior agreement with regard to the exports planned.
— All international trade transactions require prior official authorisation by the Administration. The final destination control of the products on the list does not involve merely obligations with regard to the arrival of the products at their destination (including travel arrangements) but also includes, in trade with a number of countries, the need either to obtain or to provide, or both, certain documents. The nature of these documents depends on the country with which trading is taking place (countries are divided into three groups). No. 02 licences, authorisations and documents involving the customs services are granted by the Financial and Commercial Authorisations Service (SAFICO), which is also responsible for receiving any documents which must be presented.

3. Control of the Export of Sensitive Materials and Equipment from the Viewpoint of the Non-Proliferation of Nuclear Weapons

This special control procedure, relating to nuclear material and equipment, and large nuclear units was established by letter of the Prime Minister of 29th May 1975 (large nuclear units — not published) and by two directives of the Prime Minister of 10th December 1979 (nuclear material and equipment — not published). It is described in a *Notice to exporters published in the Official Journal of 21st January 1986* concerning products which it is forbidden to export (cancelling and replacing the previous Notice dated 17th May 1981).

Under this Notice, exporters are informed that, for the purposes of preventing the proliferation of nuclear weapons, a stricter control than those described above is applied to the export of the products, materials and equipment described in the lists attached to the Notice (Annexes I to III). The list of products subject to control is in fact longer than the COCOM Atomic Energy List (final destination control).

These provisions apply to the export, even temporarily, of the products in question. They apply even if the products processed in France remain the property of a natural or legal person based abroad.

The procedures for exporting to all countries are laid down in the above-mentioned Order of 30th January 1967 (Title II, Chapter II, Section II) which makes such exports conditional upon the granting of an *export licence* (final destination control).

Applications for export licences, accompanied by *pro forma* invoices, are sent to the General Directorate for Customs and Indirect Duties which decides whether or not a licence should be issued. When a product is included both in the list in the Notice of 21st January 1986 and in that of final destination control, only one application for a licence is filed by the exporter.

For the export to any country of large nuclear plants[9], an *application for prior approval* must first be made, following the procedure laid down by the Order of 30th January 1967 ; prior approval is granted by the General Directorate for Customs and Indirect Duties, on the recommendation of the Ministries concerned.

Each application must be accompanied by :

1. a copy of the draft commercial contract ;
2. an information sheet containing :

- the planned delivery dates;
- a summary list of all the equipment it is prohibited to export and which is required for the construction and starting up of the nuclear plant in question;
- a provisional descriptive list of the materials or equipment to be incorporated in the nuclear plant and having the special features of articles included in the product lists in Annex I — materials, and in Annex II — equipment. It should be noted that when a given product is both on these lists and on that of products subject to final destination control (see above), a single export licence application is sufficient.

Any subsequent technical change in the materials or equipment in question must be detailed in an application to rectify the prior authorisation.

For the purposes of the interministerial consultation procedure, mentioned at the beginning of this study, the Notice of 21st January 1986[10] recommends firms intending to export a large nuclear plant first to contact one or more of the following ministerial departments:

- the Ministry of Industry (*Direction générale de l'énergie et des matières premières, Délégation à l'action extérieure*);
- the Ministry of Foreign Affairs (*Direction des affaires politiques, Sous-direction des questions atomiques*);
- the Ministry of Defence (*Délégation générale pour l'armement, Mission atome*);
- the Ministry responsible for Foreign Trade (*Direction des relations économiques extérieures*).

It is only on the basis of the prior authorisation from the General Directorate for Customs and having obtained approval from the ministerial departments concerned (eventually by decision of the Prime Minister after the advice of a restricted interministerial group) that the export licence application may formally be lodged. The General Directorate for Customs considers the applications, accompanied by pro forma invoices, and reaches a decision with regard to them. Licences are granted for a period of twelve months.

The text of Annexes I and II to this Notice, containing, respectively, the list of materials and of equipment the export of which is subject to this control, is reproduced as *Appendix III* (Notice to exporters published in the Official Journal of 21st January 1986).

III. TRADE IN RADIOISOTOPES — SECURITY MEASURES

This section deals with the legislation governing, amongst other things, the sale, import and export of radioisotopes and apparatus emitting ionizing radiation, with a view to protecting workers, the public and the environment from the hazards of such radiation.

1. General Provisions

French regulations concerning radioisotopes are at present fairly dispersed and are in the process of being put together. Only the general regulations governing the use of radioisotopes and products containing them will be dealt with here, and not provisions relating to radiation protection or the regime applicable to major nuclear installations and installations classified for environmental protection purposes[11]. The regulations on radioisotopes are to be found in the Public Health Code. Radioisotopes are governed by the rules on poisonous substances.

Orders dated 15th November 1951 and 21st January 1957 included radioisotopes, respectively, in the category of poisonous substances in Section I, Table A[12] of the Public Health Code dealing with substances to be used for the purposes of trade, industry and agriculture, and in Section II, Table A of the same Code which lists substances to be used for medical purposes ("natural or artificial radioisotopes and their salts").

Moreover, radioisotopes are included in Table A (Toxic substances) of Title III "Restrictions on trade in certain substances and objects" of Book V "Pharmacy" of the Public Health Code (Part II). As such, they are covered by the regulations governing poisonous substances which lay down the penalties incurred under Article L.626 for breaches of the provisions on production, transport, import, export, possession, offer, transfer, acquisition and use of substances classified in the regulations as poisonous.

Article R.5168 of the Public Health Code further provides that the use of or trade in such substances "may, for reasons of hygiene and public health, be prohibited or made subject to special conditions (see below) by joint Order of the Minister of Public Health and the other Ministers concerned, after hearing the opinion of the French *Conseil supérieur d'hygiène publique*" (Public Health Board).

Radioisotopes are subject to rules governing their use, and the Public Health Code deals separately with natural radioisotopes and artificial ones.

2. Natural Radioisotopes

Chapter V-I, entitled "Ionizing radiation" of Title I, Book I of the Public Health Code (Part I) provides (Article L.44.1) that "the sale, purchase, use and possession of natural radioactive elements (radioisotopes) are subject to conditions laid down by administrative regulation". No general regulations have yet been passed. A draft Decree, providing that natural radioisotopes used in similar circumstances to artificial ones should be subject to the same authorisation procedure as that laid down for artificial radioisotopes, is currently being studied.

3. Artificial Radioisotopes

Given the importance and diversity of the uses of *artificial* radioisotopes, a special regime has been laid down for them in Chapter II of Title III "Restrictions on trade in certain substances and objects" of Book V — Pharmacy — of the Public Health Code (Part I). Article L.632 provides that the preparation, import, and export of artificial radioisotopes, in whatever form, can be carried out only by the Atomic Energy Commission (CEA) or the natural or legal persons specially authorised for this purpose having regard to the opinion of the *Interministerial Committee for Artificial Radioisotopes* (CIREA)[13].

Persons in possession of artificial radioisotopes or products containing such radioisotopes may use them only on the conditions laid down at the time of their being obtained (Article L. 634).

Furthermore, under Article L.640, provisions applying to the possession, sale, and marketing, in whatever form, of artificial radioisotopes and products containing them will be laid down by administrative regulation.

A Decree of 26th November 1956 detailed the licensing regime applying to artificial radioisotopes in Articles R.5230 to R.5238 of the Public Health Code (Part II). Article R.5235 (as amended by a Decree of 13th January 1986), which deals with radioisotope applications other than for medical or human biology purposes, provides that "*the authorisation*, without which, in terms of Article L.632 (of the Public Health Code) no physical or legal person other than the Atomic Energy Commission may prepare, import or export artificial radioisotopes, shall be granted by the Chairman of the Interministerial Committee provided for under Article L.633" (CIREA).

The possession with a view to distributing, transfer and use of artificial radioisotopes (particularly of radioactive sources or products or apparatus containing them) is also subject to this licensing regime.

Licences, granted for a maximum period of five years which may, after hearing the opinion of the CIREA's second section, be renewed, must indicate the identity or business name of the licence holder, and the premises in which the operations in question will be carried out.

These licences are issued on a personal basis and are non-transferable. They may be suspended or revoked for security reasons, without prejudice to the penalties to which offenders are liable (Article R.5237).

In the case of *import*, *export* or possession prior to *distribution*, the licence application must be accompanied by a file containing, in particular, detailed information on the radioisotopes, radioactive sources or apparatus concerned, the field of application, quality controls, instructions for use and, in the case of imports, the relevant authorisations obtained in the country of origin (Article R.5235.3).

A declaration must be made by the licence holder in respect of any imports, using a form to be presented to the customs authorities after being stamped by the standing Secretariat of the CIREA. In the case of exports, the same procedure applies except that it is the exporter and not the consignee who must submit the form (Article R.5237.1).

A record must be kept in the establishment concerned of the *acquisition* or *transfer* of radioisotopes, and in particular radioactive sources, with a view to monitoring the movements of such products. This obligation applies also to establishments engaged in importing and exporting (Article R.5237.2).

The licensing system for artificial radioisotopes which has just been described does not apply to :

- fusible, fissile or fertile artificial radioisotopes used in major nuclear installations (which fall under the licensing regimes described previously for such installations) ;
- radionuclides with a low specific activity or substances containing artificial radioisotopes with a low specific or total activity, as defined in the technical norms laid down jointly by the Ministers responsible for Public Health and Industry.

The CIREA, in plenary sitting, has the task of formulating opinions and proposals concerning regulations on artificial radioisotopes, particularly with regard to imports and the general conditions of sale, and the distribution of, and trade in such products (Article R.5233). In certain circumstances, the CIREA may have to lay down rules for the use of radioisotopes entitled "Particular conditions for use", equivalent to administrative instructions.

Originally, the CEA, as the most important national producer of artificial radioisotopes, also effected the import of products which it had not itself prepared. Nowadays, a large number of orders are placed with foreign suppliers, thus giving rise to imports made directly by authorised bodies within the meaning of Article L.632.

Licence holders must submit to controls concerning the conditions of manufacture and use of radioisotopes, and existing stocks (Article R.5238). These controls are carried out by the CEA and the SCPRI (Decree of 17th October 1984).

In the case of radioisotopes to be used for medical purposes, authorisations specific to each product are required in addition to the general import licence. Thus, since 1975, before any new radiopharmaceutical product can be marketed, it must obtain a marketing licence identical to those required for special pharmaceutical items. Similarly, a Notice of 19th July 1978 of the Minister of Health introduces, for products to be used for medical analyses and involving artificial radioisotopes, a licensing regime specific to each product.

4. Prohibitions and Special Regulations

Over and above these general provisions, French regulations on radioisotopes contain a number of specific prohibitions.

Article L.44.2 provides that, without prejudice to the provisions of the Labour Code and those referred to in Article L.44.3 (Decree of 24th April 1959 on the medical applications of ionizing radiation), ionizing radiation may be used on the human body for purposes of medical diagnosis and therapy only, the main objective being to exclude the use of pedoscopes (this Article deals with all radioisotopes).

Article L.635 of the Public Health Code prohibits all advertising relating to the use of artificial radioisotopes or products containing them in human or veterinary medicine, except that aimed at the medical profession and chemists.

Similarly, it is prohibited to add them to foodstuffs, health products or so-called beauty products as defined in an Order of the Minister of Health (Article L.636). Article L.639 lays down the penalties for breaches of the regulations. This provision is to be set alongside Article R.5163, which prohibits the addition of radioisotopes (natural and artificial) or products containing them to foodstuffs or health and beauty products[14].

Mention may also be made of the general provision in Article R.168 governing poisonous substances, which provides that the use of or trade in the substances listed in Table A of the Public Health Code (see above) may be prohibited or made subject to special conditions.

More recently, an Order of 11th October 1983 prohibits the use of radioisotopes in the fabrication of lightning conductors as well as the marketing and import of such articles.

Apart from these various prohibitions, mention should be made of the existence of special regulations relating to radioisotopes and apparatus emitting ionizing radiation in the field of the irradiation of foodstuffs and of trade in irradiated merchandise[15] and in the field of medical applications. This latter sector, which has given rise to numerous regulations, like the former, is not dealt with in this study.

Suffice it to say that a similar system of prior authorisation was introduced by Article R.5234 (as amended by a Decree of 13th January 1986). This Article provides that the authorisation without which, under Article L.632 of this Code, no natural or legal person other than the Atomic Energy Commission may prepare, import or export, in whatever form, artificial radioisotopes shall be granted by the Minister responsible for Public Health, having regard to the opinion of the first section of the Interministerial Committee for Artificial Radioisotopes provided for in Article L.633 (CIREA).

The following activities require this authorisation :

- the possession, with a view to the distribution or transfer of artificial radioisotopes, particularly of radioactive sources and products or apparatus containing them ;
- the marketing of all types of radioactive sources and products or apparatus containing them ;
- the possession with a view to using, and the actual use of artificial radioisotopes.

The licences thus granted (for an initial period of five years) must specify the licence holder and the establishment in which the operations in question will be carried out.

IV. TRANSPORT

Apart from the provisions on physical protection of nuclear material during its carriage (see Section II.B.1 above), the transport of radioactive materials in France is regulated by a general set of laws controlling all transport of dangerous substances. Consequently the entire legislation concerning dangerous substances is directly applicable to radioactive materials, although in the case of certain modes of transport, e.g. rail, road, inland waterway and sea, special provisions do exist. Thus, transport of radioactive materials is governed both by general requirements for dangerous substances and by rules covering more specifically radioactive materials, the two sets of regulations being cumulative rather than exclusive.

Act No. 263 of 5th February 1942 is the basic law governing the carriage of dangerous substances by rail, road or inland waterway. It also covers the handling of dangerous substances in seaports. It is in fact an outline law giving the Minister of Transport full powers to issue orders stating all requirements and standards concerning the loading, unloading, packaging, supervision and handling of dangerous substances.

To this effect, on 15th April 1945, an Order was issued by the Minister of Transport approving the *Regulations on the carriage of dangerous substances by rail, road and inland waterway*. This Order has been amended many times to take into account developments in technical standards[16].

Special provisions concerning radioactive materials were added to this basic Order and published in the form of a Ministerial Order on 24th June 1974 under the title "Transport and Handling of Dangerous Substances : Transport of Radioactive Materials, Class IV(b)" (special section No. 74.68 bis).

The French regulations are based almost entirely on the Recommendations of the International Atomic Energy Agency (IAEA), Vienna, as set out in the 1973 Revised Edition of the Regulations for the Safe Transport of Radioactive Materials.

The 1974 Order (revised by an Order of 5th November 1986) applies to any and all transport of radioactive materials by road, rail or inland waterway within French territory. As far as international transport is concerned, France has adopted the following :

- the International Regulations concerning the Carriage of Dangerous Goods by Rail (RID) (the edition currently used in France is dated 1st July 1977) ;
- the European Agreement concerning the International Carriage of Dangerous Goods by Road (ADR) (the edition currently used in France is dated 21st April 1976) ;
- Regulations for the Transport of Dangerous Goods on the River Rhine (ADNR) (the edition currently used in France is dated 1st January 1977).

Although the 1945 Order only concerns overland transport (by rail, road and inland waterways) it is used as a reference for other modes such as sea and air transport, as it provides full technical details regarding definitions and classifications of dangerous substances.

Sea transport is governed by an Order dated 12th March 1980 setting out the safety rules for the carriage of dangerous goods by sea.

The Order of 22nd August 1957, on the transport of dangerous substances by air, as amended by the Order of 10th December 1963, constitutes the French regulations on the transport of radioactive materials by air. By provisionally introducing the Restricted Articles Regulations of the International Air Transport Association (IATA) into French law, the Order of 22nd August 1957, gives them official and normative status. For the time being the IATA rules form the bulk of French law on the subject, as there is no distinction between domestic and international arrangements concerning the carriage of radioactive materials by air.

These national and international laws and regulations constitute the legal framework within which all activities concerning the transport of dangerous substances in general, and of radioactive materials in particular, are organised. For further details see the study published by OECD/NEA in 1980 on "Regulations Governing the Transport of Radioactive Materials".

V. INTELLECTUAL PROPERTY IN THE NUCLEAR FIELD

No specific legislation to regulate industrial property in the field of nuclear energy has yet been passed, and this topic is therefore governed by the ordinary law (Act of 2nd January 1968, as amended in 1978).

Certain provisions do, however, exist which could affect nuclear inventions and which were adopted with regard to inventions in the field of national defence or affecting economic development. The State can thus, by Decree, expropriate certain patents, paying compensation to the inventor, or, on its own initiative, grant a licence to certain bodies with regard to a patent for an invention in the field of national defence.

The only specific regulations deal with the Atomic Energy Commission's (CEA) activities, and are contained in the Decree of 14th December 1972, adopted in implementation of the Decree of 29th September 1970 relating to CEA. Section 7 of which provides that "invention patents arising from Commission activities shall be filed in its name. Inventors may receive an award, details of which shall be determined by the Administrator-General, having regard to the opinion of the (Atomic Energy) Committee or in accordance with rules approved by him". This provision is aimed essentially at inventions affecting the CEA's fundamental tasks in the scientific and technical fields.

Given the absence of special regulations, the need to make arrangements for the protection of industrial property in the nuclear field has made itself felt, and such protection has been organised on a contractual basis in the form of the French Nuclear Patents Management Company *(Société française pour la gestion des brevets d'application nucléaire — BREVATOME)*, an institution covering all nuclear processes so as to enable them to be protected and developed rationally and to ensure that the rights arising from the results of research contracts are shared between public bodies and private companies.

This company, created in 1958, brings together the main parties concerned : CEA, Electricité de France (EDF) and industry. It is responsible for settling industrial property rights arising from research contracts concluded between the CEA and industry and financed by the latter, and for bringing together French nuclear patents.

The members of BREVATOME retain ownership of the patents belonging to them, but they entrust the management of their nuclear patents to the company. It is up to BREVATOME and the industrial inventor to agree in each case whether an invention may or may not have nuclear applications. For inventions which are not patentable (manufacturing processes, know-how, computer codes, etc.), BREVATOME has formulated contractual clauses for the transfer of information by means of research contracts and collaboration contracts which take the form of "systems" agreements (involving the overall design of an installation) and "components" agreements ("accords systèmes" and "accords composants"). Industrial secrets are protected by the insertion in these contracts of confidentiality clauses (in the nuclear domain, a given technical field may be made up for the most part of non-patented techniques) and so-called "succession" clauses which prohibit the transfer of rights arising from the contract without the prior agreement of the parties.

VI. BILATERAL AGREEMENTS CONCERNING TRADE IN NUCLEAR MATERIAL AND EQUIPMENT

France is Party to a large number of bilateral (or multilateral) agreements covering, in broad terms, scientific, technical and economic co-operation in the field of nuclear energy.

Mention is made in this section only of agreements which, directly or indirectly, generally or specifically, relate to trade in nuclear material, equipment and, where appropriate, technology.

1. Framework Nuclear Co-operation Agreements

— Agreement between the Government of the French Republic and the Government of the ***USSR*** on co-operation in the field of energy, signed on 17th October 1975.

  This is a framework agreement on co-operation in the energy field. It covers, in particular, nuclear power production.

— Co-operative Agreement between the Government of the French Republic and the Government of the ***People's Republic of China***, signed on 21st January 1978.

  This scientific and technical co-operation agreement was followed by Agreements concluded by the French Atomic Energy Commission (CEA) with the Chinese Science Academy on 15th January 1979 and the Ministry of Industry on 22nd November 1982 respectively (the latter Agreement was extended in 1984).

— Co-operation Agreement in the nuclear field between the Government of the French Republic and the Government of the ***United Arab Emirates***, signed on 6th March 1980.

  This Agreement deals with scientific co-operation between the two countries. It provides for research concerning nuclear equipment in the Emirates.

— Co-operation Agreement between the Government of the French Republic and the Government of ***Bangladesh*** on the use of nuclear energy for peaceful purposes, signed on 29th August 1980.

  This framework Agreement provides for the conclusion of more specific co-operation agreements, particularly for the supply of materials and equipment. It includes a reference to the application of the IAEA safeguards.

FRANCE

— Co-operation Agreement between the Government of the French Republic and the Government of the ***Arab Republic of Egypt*** relating to the peaceful uses of nuclear energy, signed on 27th March 1981.

The provisions of this Agreement are, on the whole, identical to the preceding one.

— Agreement between the Government of the French Republic and the ***Republic of Korea*** relating to the peaceful uses of nuclear energy, signed on 4th April 1981.

This Agreement is essentially identical to the two preceding ones. It has been supplemented by an Exchange of Letters relating to the application of nuclear non-proliferation safeguards in the field of the transfer of sensitive materials, equipment and information.

— Agreement between the Government of the French Republic and the Government of the ***Hungarian People's Republic*** on scientific and economic co-operation in the field of energy and raw materials, dated 11th July 1983.

This Agreement provides for the setting up of co-operation with regard to the application of nuclear energy to heating.

2. Agreements Relating to the Supply of Materials, Equipment and Services

— Co-operation Agreement between the Government of the French Republic and the ***Swiss Federal Council*** on the use of atomic energy for peaceful purposes, signed on 14th May 1970.

Under this Agreement, the Parties undertake to co-operate in the fields of the processing of spent fuel, and the mutual supply and import of nuclear materials and equipment; it also promotes co-operation between the nuclear industry in each country.

— Co-operation Agreement between the Government of the French Republic and the Government of ***Japan*** on the use of nuclear energy for peaceful purposes, signed on 26th February 1972.

This Agreement provides for the mutual supply of source materials, special fissile materials and nuclear equipment and installations; it also covers the supply of services and the exchange of industrial information in the nuclear field.

This Agreement refers to the application of IAEA Safeguards. It is, moreover, supplemented by an Agreement concluded on 22nd September 1972 between France, Japan and the IAEA on the application of these safeguards.

— Co-operation Agreement between the Government of the French Republic and the Government of the ***Republic of Iraq*** on the use of nuclear energy for peaceful purposes, signed on 18th November 1975.

This Agreement also provides for the supply of materials and equipment and the provision of services in the nuclear field; moreover, it refers to the application of IAEA Safeguards.

The Agreement was supplemented by an Exchange of Letters on 11th September 1976 with regard to the application of IAEA safeguards to the trade operations dealt with in the preceding Agreement.

— Memorandum of Understanding between France and the ***People's Republic of China***, signed on 5th May 1983.

This Agreement, relating to the supply of nuclear power plants, was followed by the signature of a letter of intent on 12th March 1986 concerning the delivery of two reactors.

3. Agreements Involving the Non-Proliferation of Nuclear Weapons

— Agreement between the IAEA, the Government of the French Republic and the Government of the ***Islamic Republic of Pakistan***, signed on 18th March 1976.

The purpose of this Agreement is to apply the IAEA safeguards to the co-operation between France and Pakistan for the construction of a spent fuel reprocessing plant.

— Agreement between the IAEA, the Government of the French Republic and the Government of the ***South African Republic***, signed on 16th December 1976 and 5th January 1977, for the application of IAEA safeguards to the Koeberg nuclear power plant.

— Reference should also be made to the Agreements on IAEA safeguards concluded with the Republic of *Korea*, *Japan* and *Iraq*, respectively (see above).

— Agreement concluded on 20th and 27th July 1978 between France, ***EURATOM*** and the ***IAEA*** on the application of IAEA safeguards to materials and installations on French territory.

4. Supply Agreements

— Agreement between the Government of the French Republic and the Government of ***Australia*** concerning nuclear transfers between France and Australia, signed on 7th January 1981.

— This Agreement applies to nuclear materials, equipment and technology transferred between Australia and France for peaceful purposes; it refers to the application of IAEA safeguards, and is supplemented by various technical annexes.

A large number of co-operation and defence agreements have also been concluded between the French Government and various countries in French-speaking Africa, covering the export by such countries of nuclear raw materials. Included among these agreements are the following:

— Agreement of 22nd June 1960 with the ***Republic of Mali*** on source materials and strategic products;

— Agreement of 27th June 1960 with the ***Democratic Republic of Madagascar*** on source materials and strategic products;

— Annex III to the particular Agreements concluded on 11th, 13th and 15th August 1960 with the ***Central African Republic***, the ***Republic of the Congo*** and the ***Republic of Chad***;

— Agreement of 17th August 1960 with the ***Gabonese Republic*** on source materials and strategic products;

— Annex II to the Defence Agreement of 24th April 1961 with the ***Republic of Dahomey (Benin)***, and the ***Republic of Niger***;

— Annex II to the Defence Agreement of 19th June 1961 with the ***Islamic Republic of Mauritania***;

5. Industrial Co-operation Agreements

— Agreement concluded on 26th May 1978 between the French Atomic Energy Commission (CEA), the ***Kernforschungszentrum Karlsruhe*** — KFK (Federal Republic of Germany) and the ***Power Reactor and Nuclear Fuel Development Corporation*** — PNC (Japan), relating to co-operation in the field of fast neutron reactors;

— Memorandum of Understanding concluded on 10th January 1984 between France, the ***Federal Republic of Germany***, ***Belgium***, ***Italy*** and the ***United Kingdom***, relating to co-operation in the field of fast breeder reactors;

— Agreement, signed on 20th March 1980, between France, ***Belgium*** and ***Spain***, relating to the EURODIF Company. Adhesion of Italy on 11th August 1984.

— Agreement concluded on 30th April 1987 between the ***Société générale pour les techniques nouvelles (SGN)*** and the ***Japan Nuclear Fuel Society (JNFS)*** (transfer of reprocessing technology).

NOTES AND REFERENCES

1. Set up under the Decree of 1st September 1976 as amended by the Decree of 4th September 1981, the Council is chaired by the President of the Republic. It comprises, in addition to the Prime Minister, the Minister responsible for Foreign Trade, the Minister for Industry and Research, the Minister of Foreign Affairs, the Minister of Defence, the Minister for Economic Affairs and Finance, the State Secretary attached to the Minister for Industry and Research, responsible for Energy, and the Administrator-General of the Atomic Energy Commission. Other Ministers and certain senior civilian or military officials may be invited to participate in the Council's work on matters falling within their province. The General Secretary of the Office of the President of the Republic handles secretarial duties for the Council.
2. The communiqué published by the Council on 11th October 1976 reads as follows: "France remains willing to contribute towards the applications of nuclear energy for peaceful purposes; she intends to retain control over her nuclear export policy while complying with her international commitments; she will not promote the proliferation of nuclear weapons; she will guarantee the safe supply of nuclear fuel for the nuclear power plants she has provided and will respond to legitimate needs for access to the relevant technology; the French Government believes it is essential for all suppliers in the nuclear field to avoid facilitating the proliferation of nuclear weapons through commercial competition; it is ready to discuss these problems with supplier and non-supplier countries".
3. The Committee is chaired by the Prime Minister or by a Minister delegated by him for that purpose, failing which by the Administrator-General of the CEA. It consists of the Administrator-General, the General Policy Director at the Ministry of Research, the Budget Director, the Chairman of the National Scientific Research Centre (CNRS), a person of standing selected by the Prime Minister, three persons selected by the Minister of Defence, and five experts in science and industry, one of whom acts as High Commissioner.

4. The right to prospect for and mine radioactive ores is not dealt with in this study. See, on this topic: "Regulatory and Institutional Framework for Nuclear Activities", Vol. I, OECD/NEA, 1983.
5. A second Implementation Decree, of 15th May 1981, deals specifically with the protection and control of nuclear materials in the field of defence.
6. Plutonium or U-233: 3 grammes;
Uranium enriched to 20 per cent U-235 or more: 15 g of contained U-235; Uranium enriched to less than 20 per cent U-235: 250 g of contained U-235;
Natural uranium or uranium with a lower U-235 content than natural uranium;
Thorium: 500 g;
Deuterium: 200 kg;
Tritium: 2 g;
Li-6 enriched lithium: 1 kg of contained Li-6.
7. Among Community measures designed to eliminate various customs duties and taxes as well as quantitative restrictions on the movement of goods, two texts dealing with products covered by the Treaty establishing the European Atomic Energy Community (EURATOM) should be mentioned: the Notice of 23rd December 1958 to importers and exporters, relating to the import and export of the products referred to in Annex IV of the Treaty (use of a document accompanying such products and called "EURATOM free movement certificate", for use by the customs authorities); the Notice of 9th January 1959 to importers of products from Member countries of the European Atomic Energy Community, aiming at the elimination of quantitative restrictions affecting certain products.
8. A Notice, published in the Official Journal on 6th September 1970, of concern to importers of products from various countries that are free from all quantitative restrictions on imports. This Notice, which deals with the liberalisation of trade and provides for the liberalisation of all quantitative restrictions on imports, based on exporting areas, gives, in its Annex I, a list of the products (in particular, U-235 depleted uranium and thorium and nuclear reactors) for which, by way of exception, an import quota has been retained. Annex II contains a list of products, the import of which is subject to the granting of an administrative visa (uranium and thorium ores, U-235 depleted uranium and thorium, X-ray apparatus). The following tables give a list of those products.

TABLES (annexed to Notice published in the Official Journal of 6th September 1970)

Annex I

LIST OF PRODUCTS REMAINING SUBJECT TO AN IMPORT QUOTA

Tariff numbers	Designation of products	Zones I	II	III	East Germany
1	2	3	4	5	6
....					
Ex.81-04	Other base metals, unwrought or wrought; wrought or unwrought cermets:				
....					
	— M. U-235 depleted uranium			X	X
	— N. Thorium			X	X
....					
Ex.84-59	Machinery, equipment and mechanical machines, not mentioned or included elsewhere in Chapter 84.				
	— A. For production of products referred to in 28-51 A				X
	— B. Nuclear reactors ..				X
	— C. Specially designed for recycling irradiated nuclear fuel (sintered radioactive metal oxides, cladding, etc.)				X
....					

Annex II

LIST OF PRODUCTS WHOSE IMPORT IS SUBJECT TO ADMINISTRATIVE CLEARANCE

Tariff numbers	Designation of products	Zones I	II	III	East Germany	Competent administrative services
1	2	3	4	5	6	7
26-01 C	Uranium ores	X	X			C.E.A.
26-01 D	Thorium ores	X	X	X	X	C.E.A.
....						
81-04 M	U-235 depleted uranium	X	X			C.E.A.
81-04 N	Thorium	X	X			C.E.A.
....						
84-45 A	Machine-tools specially designed for use in recyling of irradiated nuclear fuel			X	X	DIMME
....						
90-20	X-ray appliances			X	X	DCMEE
....						

9. The list of large nuclear plants (Annex III of the Notice of 17th May 1981) is as follows:
   - nuclear research centres;
   - research, power and propulsion reactors;
   - enrichment plants;
   - uranium fluoration plants;
   - spent fuel reprocessing plants;
   - plants for the manufacture of fuel elements;
   - plants for the production of heavy water or deuterium;
   - plants for the production of tritium.

10. The provisions of this Notice do not apply to war equipment or equipment treated as equivalent thereto governed by the Decree-Law of 18th April 1939 (as amended by the Order of 2nd April 1971), which, in particular, includes explosive nuclear devices in the list of equipment the export of which is, unless otherwise provided, prohibited. The preparation, possession, transfer etc. of nuclear materials for defence purposes and their transport in this context are subject to authorisation and control by the Minister of Defence. The Decree of 15th May 1981 fixing the conditions for protection and control of nuclear materials in the field of defence is supplemented by an Order of the same date on the assignment of nuclear materials in the field of defence.

11. It may simply be pointed out that the radiation protection rules applying to the use of radioactive substances were mainly contained in the Decree of 20th June 1966 relating to the general radiation protection principles (for the implementation of the EURATOM basic standards) and in the Decree of 15th March 1967 on the protection of workers against the hazards of ionizing radiation.
    These Decrees have recently been revised in the light of the amendments made to the EURATOM basic standards.
    Furthermore, radioisotopes are taken into account in determining whether the Act of 1976 on installations classified for environmental protection purposes (and the Decree of 24th October 1967 on the classification of radioisotopes) applies to a given installation. They are also dealt with in regulations on mines (Decree of 27th January 1959), atmospheric pollution (Act of 2nd August 1967) and water (Act of 16th December 1964).
    For further details, see *Regulatory and Institutional Framework for Nuclear Activities*, Vol. I, OECD/NEA, 1983; see also Nuclear Law Bulletin.

12. Table A covers radioisotopes:
    - from the uranium and radium series;
    - from the actinium series;
    - from the thorium series and their salts except for naturally radioactive water and mud;
    - radioactive intermediates or residues from the production of such salts;
    - artificial radioisotopes;
    - preparations of all kinds made radioactive by the incorporation of radioisotopes, naturally radioactive water or mud or by any other process.

13. The creation of the Interministerial Committee for Artificial Radioisotopes (CIREA) was provided for under Article L.633 of the Public Health Code (Decree of 3rd May 1954). The Committee, as composed in accordance with the provisions of the Decree of 26th February 1979, includes, under the chairmanship of a Counsellor of State, representatives from the various ministries concerned, and from the CEA and other specialised public bodies such as the Central Service for Protection against Ionizing Radiation (SCPRI). It comprises two sections, one for medical applications and the other for non-medical ones. For further details, see *Regulatory and Institutional Framework for Nuclear Activities*, Vol. I, OECD/NEA, 1983.

14. This prohibition is expressed in wider terms in the abovementioned Decree of 20th June 1966 (Section 3): "It is forbidden to add radioactive substances in the manufacture of foodstuffs, cosmetics and household products, and to use radioactive substances in the manufacture of toys". See also the Decree of 18th December 1967 which adds natural and artificial radioisotopes to the list of substances which it is forbidden to use in the manufacture of toys or playthings.

15. Cf. Nuclear Law Bulletin, in particular No. 35, OECD/NEA, June 1985.

16. See in this respect, the Nuclear Law Bulletin.

*
**

Droit nucléaire, CEA collection, Synthèses Series, Eyrolles, 1979.

Législation et réglementation des activités nucléaires — Compilation of texts published by the Atomic Energy Commission, Legal Affairs Department, Editions Conseils, with periodic updatings.

La réglementation française des contrôles à l'exportation à des fins de sécurité, by Philippe Deslandes in Le contrôle des exportations de haute technologie vers les pays de l'Est, B. Chantebout and B. Warusfel, Collection Droit-Sciences Economiques, Paris, 1987.

Appendix I

DEFINITIONS

The fact that French regulations in this field have not been standardized means that the technical terms used to describe the different categories of radioactive products vary widely. Some clarifications may, therefore, be useful.

A distinction is made in the regulations between natural radioelements — radioelements the existence of which owes nothing to human intervention (Decree of 20th June 1966 and non-approved French standard M 60.001 "Nuclear Energy"), and artificial radioelements — those whose existence arises from human intervention (same source)*. Further, the expression "radioactive substances", used in the system applicable to installations classified for environmental protection purposes (Act of 19th July 1976), is defined by the Decree of 20th June 1966 as: "all substances constituted by one or more natural or artificial radioelements or containing such elements". This definition is to be compared with that in the European Community basic standards for radiation protection (Council Directive of 15th June 1980, amended on 3rd September 1984), in terms of which a radioactive substance is: "any substance that contains one or more radionuclides, the activity or the concentration of which cannot be disregarded as far as radiation protection is concerned".

As for nuclear materials whose fissile or fertile properties mean that different regulations are required than those governing radioelements, there is no standard definition either, and it seems preferable to use as a basis EURATOM Regulation No. 3227 of 19th October 1976 which divides nuclear materials into "special fissile materials", "uranium enriched in U-235 or U-233", "source materials" and "ores".

* Article L.631 of the Public Health Code also contains the following definition: "All radioelements obtained by synthesis or nuclear fusion shall be considered as artificial radioelements".

Appendix II

NOTICE TO IMPORTERS AND EXPORTERS CONCERNING PRODUCTS AND TECHNOLOGIES SUBJECT TO FINAL DESTINATION CONTROL*

(5th March 1988)

This notice classifies the products and technologies subject to final destination control (CDF) and replaces all previous notices relating to such control which are therefore cancelled.

Annex

LIST OF PRODUCTS AND TECHNOLOGIES SUBJECT TO FINAL DESTINATION CONTROL

(EXTRACTS)

Item	Designation of products

A. Nuclear materials

A.1 Special fissile products and other fissile products, except:

i) Consignments of up to one effective gramme;
ii) Consignments of up to three effective grammes when contained in the sensing component of an instrument;
iii) Special fissile products or other fissile products contained in cardiac pacemakers.

Technical Notes:

1. "Special fissile product" means plutonium 239, uranium 233, uranium 235- or 233-enriched uranium and any product containing the above-mentioned elements.
2. "Uranium 235- or 233-enriched uranium" means uranium containing the isotopes 235 or 233, or both, the ratio of the aggregate content of these isotopes to that of uranium 238 being higher than the ratio of uranium 235 to uranium 238 in the natural state (isotopic ratio 0.72 per 100).
3. "Other fissile products" means americium 242m, curium 245 and 247, californium 249 and 251, plutonium isotopes other than "previously separated" plutonium 238 and 239 and any product containing the above-mentioned elements.
4. "Effective gramme" of special fissile products or other fissile products means:
   a) For plutonium isotopes and uranium 233, the weight of the isotopes in grammes;
   b) For uranium enriched to 1 per cent or more U-235, the weight of the elements in grammes, multiplied by the squared enrichment expressed as a decimal weight fraction; and
   c) For uranium enriched to less than 1 per cent U-235, the weight of the elements in grammes multiplied by 0.0001;
   d) For americium 242m, curium 245 and 247 and californium 249 and 251, the weight of the isotopes in grammes multiplied by 10.
5. For this item "previously separated" means the result of any process to increase the concentration of the controlled isotopes.

Administrative simplification note: Consignments of enriched uranium in which the U-235 content is below 20 per cent, in the form of previously supplied fuel for use in exported reactors which meet all the requirements set out in the Administrative simplification note under item B.3.

* Unofficial translation.

FRANCE

Item	Designation of products
A.2	Natural uranium and depleted uranium in any form or incorporated into any substance where the uranium concentration exceeds 0.05 per cent by weight, except: *i)* Consignments with a natural uranium content of: 1) up to 10 kg for any application, or 2) up to 100 kg for civilian non-nuclear applications; *ii)* Uranium 235-depleted uranium, where the uranium 235 content is less than 0.35 per cent; *iii)* Depleted uranium specially fabricated for civilian applications as follows: 1) Safety shields; 2) Packaging; 3) Ballast; 4) Counterweights. *Administrative simplification note*: 1. Uranium with a view to uranium 235-enrichment (contract enrichment) provided that: *a)* Any uranium 235-enriched uranium is reimported following enrichment; and *b)* Any depleted uranium (tailings) resulting from the enrichment process is reimported, unless the uranium 235 content in the depleted uranium is not more than 0.25 per cent. *Administrative simplification note*: 2. Consignments of uranium in the form of previously supplied fuel for use in exported reactors which meet all the requirements set out in the Administrative simplification note under item B.3.
A.3	Deuterium, heavy water, deuterium paraffins and other inorganic and organic compounds containing deuterium in which the isotopic ratio of deuterium to hydrogen is more than 1:5000, excluding consignments of the above products with a deuterium content of up to 10 kg. *Administrative simplification note*: Consignments of deuterium oxide (D_2O) for use in exported reactors which meet all the requirements set out in the Administrative simplification note under item B.3.
A.4	Zirconium metal; alloys containing over 50 per cent zirconium by weight; compounds in which the hafnium/zirconium ratio is less than 1:500 by weight; and products entirely fabricated with these elements, excluding: *i)* Zirconium metal and zirconium alloy in consignments of up to 5 kg; *ii)* Zirconium in the form of sheets or plates with a maximum thickness of 0.025 mm (0.00095 inch), specially manufactured for use in photographic flash bulbs and intended for this use, in consignments of up to 200 kg (See explanatory note to item 1631).
A.5	Nickel powder and porous nickel metal as follows: *a)* Powder with a nickel content of 99 per cent or more and an average particle size of less than 10 micrometres measured according to the ASTM B 330 standard. *b)* Porous nickel metal obtained from material defined in *a)* above, excluding porous nickel metal sheets whose size is below 930 cm^2 for batteries for civilian applications. *Note*: Paragraph b) refers to porous metal nickel obtained from nickel powder as defined in paragraph a) of this item, after compacting and fritting with a view to forming a metal material with fine pores interlinked throughout the structure. *Administrative simplification note*: Nickel powder in uncompacted form in consignments of up to 4 000 kg for civilian non-nuclear applications.
A.6	Nuclear-grade graphite, i.e. having a purity level of less than 1 ppm boron equivalent and a density of more than 1.6 g/cm^3, excluding separate consignments of up to 100 kg (see also note 2 to item 104).
A.7	Lithium as follows: *a)* Metal, hydrides or alloys containing lithium 6-enriched lithium up to a concentration higher than that occurring in nature (7.6 per cent in numbers of atoms); *b)* Any other material containing lithium 6-enriched lithium (including compounds, mixtures and concentrates), excluding lithium 6-enriched lithium contained in thermoluminescent dosimeters. (For natural lithium deuteride or lithium 7-enriched lithium, see item A 3) (see explanatory note to item 1631).

Item	Designation of products
A.8	Hafnium as follows: metal, alloys and compounds containing over 60 per cent hafnium by weight, and their manufactured products, excluding consignments of the above products not containing more than 1 kg hafnium. (See explanatory note to item 1631.)
A.9	Beryllium as follows: metal, alloys containing over 50 per cent beryllium by weight, beryllium-containing compounds and their manufactured products. *Administrative simplification note*: *i)* Metal windows for X-ray equipment; *ii)* Finished or semi-finished oxide forms specially designed for electronic component parts or as supports for electronic circuits. (See explanatory note to item 1631.)
A.12	Tritium, compounds and mixtures in which the ratio of tritium to hydrogen is over 1:1000 in atoms and products containing one or more of the above-mentioned substances. *Note*: This item does not concern tritium contained in luminescent paint, luminescent products, gas and aerosol detectors, electronic tubes, lightning or static electricity devices, ion-generating tubes, detector cells for gas chromatography and calibration devices. *Administrative simplification note*: 1. Consignments of tritium, compounds, mixtures and separate products containing one or more of the above-mentioned substances not exceeding 100 curies. *Administrative simplification note*: 2. Tritium compounds and mixtures the components of which, when separated, cannot lead to the development of an isotopic hydrogen mixture where the ratio of tritium to hydrogen is higher than 1:1000 in atoms.
A.13	Materials for nuclear heat sources, as follows: *a)* Plutonium in any form with a plutonium isotopic assay of plutonium 238 of more than 50 per cent, excluding: *i)* Consignments of up to one gramme of plutonium; *ii)* Consignments of up to 3 effective grammes when contained in a sensing component in instruments; *iii)* Plutonium 238 contained in cardiac pacemakers; *b)* "Previously separated" neptunium 237 in any form except consignments of up to one gramme of neptunium 237. *Technical note*: For this item "previously separated" means the result of any process to increase the concentration of the controlled isotopes.
A.14	Materials specially designed or prepared for the separation of isotopes of natural uranium, depleted uranium, special fissile products or other fissile products, in particular, resins specially designed for chemical exchanges. (For isotopic separation plants see item B.1.)

B. Nuclear installations

Item	Designation of products
B.1	Installations for the separation of isotopes from source materials, special fissile products and other fissile products, and their specially designed or prepared equipment and components, including: *a)* Units specially designed for separating isotopes from source materials, special fissile products and other fissile products, such as: 1) Gas centrifuge assemblies; 2) Jet nozzle separation units; 3) Vortex separation units; 4) Laser separation units; 5) Chemical exchange separation units; 6) Electromagnetic separation units; 7) Plasma separation units; 8) Gaseous diffusion units;

Item	Designation of products

b) Components specially designed for such units, including:

1) Valves consisting entirely of aluminium or coated with aluminium, aluminium alloys, nickel or an alloy containing at least 60 per cent nickel, with a diameter of at least 0.5 cm, closed by bellows, excluding valves not meeting this definition;
2) Compressors and blowers (turbo-compressor, centrifuge and axial types) entirely consisting of or coated with aluminium, aluminium, nickel alloys or an alloy containing at least 60 per cent nickel, with a capacity of 1 700 litres (1.7 m^3) per minute or more, including compressor seals, excluding blowers and compressors not meeting this definition;
3) Gaseous diffusion barriers;
4) Gaseous diffuser housings;
5) Heat exchangers consisting of aluminium, copper, nickel or alloys containing over 60 per cent nickel, or combinations of these metals in clad tubing, designed to operate at a pressure below atmospheric pressure with a leakage rate of less than 10 Pa (0.1 millibar) per hour with a pressure differential of 1 bar, excluding heat exchangers not meeting this definition.

Note: For materials specially designed or prepared for isotope separation see item A.14.

B.2 Installations for the reprocessing of irradiated fuel assemblies from nuclear reactors, and their specially designed or prepared equipment and components, including:

a) Fuel element chopping and shearing equipment, namely remote controlled equipment designed to cut, chop or shear spent fuel assemblies, bundles or rods from nuclear reactors;
b) Anti-criticality safety vessels (small diameter, annular or slab tanks) specially designed or prepared for dissolving spent nuclear fuel and capable of withstanding a highly radioactive and corrosive liquid, which can be loaded and handled by remote processes;
c) Countercurrent solvent extractors, and equipment for ion exchange processing specially designed and prepared for use in a plant for reprocessing natural uranium, depleted uranium or special fissile and other spent fissile products;
d) Control instrumentation specially designed or prepared for controlling and monitoring the reprocessing of source materials and special fissile products and other irradiated fissile products.

Note: A spent nuclear fuel reprocessing facility includes equipment and components normally entering into direct contact with and directly controlling the spent fuel and the process flows of major source materials and fission products.

B.3 Nuclear reactors capable of operation so as to maintain a controlled self-sustaining fission chain reaction and specially designed or prepared equipment and components for use in connection with a nuclear reactor including:

a) Pressure vessels, namely metal vessels as complete units or as major shop-fabricated parts therefor, specially designed or prepared to contain the core of a nuclear reactor and capable of withstanding the operating pressure of the primary coolant, including the vessel lid;
b) Fuel handling equipment, including reactor fuel loading and unloading equipment;
c) Control rods, namely rods specially designed or prepared for the control of the reaction rate in a nuclear reactor, including the neutron absorber rod and the support and suspension systems and control rod guide tubes;
d) Electronic devices for controlling the power levels of nuclear reactors, including the reactor control rod regulating mechanisms and radiation measuring and detecting devices for determining neutron flux levels;
e) Pressure tubes, namely tubes specially designed or prepared to contain fuel elements and the primary coolant in a reactor at an operating pressure in excess of 50 atmospheres;
f) Primary coolant pumps, namely pumps specially designed or prepared for circulating liquid metal as primary coolant for nuclear reactors;
g) Internals, specially designed or prepared for operating a nuclear reactor, including core support systems, thermal shields, deflectors, core grid plates and diffuser plates;
h) Heat exchangers.

Note: A "nuclear reactor" includes the equipment located inside the reactor vessel or directly attached to it, equipment for controlling power inside the core, and components normally containing the primary coolant, entering into direct contact with the coolant or controlling its flow.

Administrative simplification note: Civilian electronuclear reactors and water-cooled and moderated reactors, including their major components and first fuel loads and moderators, provided that:

Item	Designation of products
	a) The reactor is designed to use uranium enriched to up to 20 per cent; *b)* The fuel supplied is uranium enriched to up to 20 per cent; *c)* The reactor is not designed for use in nuclear ships.
B.4	Installations specially designed for fabricating fuel elements for nuclear reactors and specially designed equipment for such installations. *Note*: A fuel fabrication installation includes the equipment (1) normally entering into direct contact with the nuclear material flow and processing it or directly controlling it, (2) sealing the nuclear material in the cladding, (3) checking cladding integrity and leak tightness (4) checking the final quality of the solid fuel.
B.5	Heavy water, deuterium or deuterium compound production installations, and their specially designed or prepared equipment and components.
B.6	Installations for producing uranium hexafluoride (UF_6), and their specially designed and prepared equipment (including the UF_6 purification equipment) and their specially designed or prepared components.
	C. Other equipment relating to the nuclear field
C.1	Neutron generating systems, including tubes, designed to operate without external vacuum system and using electrostatic acceleration to induce a tritium-deuterium nuclear reaction.
C.2	Power-generating or propulsion equipment specially designed with a view to use with military, marine or mobile nuclear reactors.
C.3	Electrolytic cells for fluorine production, with a production capacity of more than 250 g of fluorine per hour.
C.4	Equipment specially designed for separating lithium isotopes.
C.5	Equipment specially designed for tritium production and recovery.
C.6	Frequency changers (converters or inverters) specially designed or prepared for supplying motor stators for gas centrifuge enrichment, presenting all the following characteristics, and their specially designed components: *a)* Multiphase output of 600 Hz to 2 kHz; *b)* Frequency control better than 0.1 per cent; *c)* Harmonic distortion of less than 2 per cent; *d)* Efficiency of more than 80 per cent. (See also item B.1 in the list.)

FRANCE

Appendix III

NOTICE TO EXPORTERS PUBLISHED IN THE OFFICIAL JOURNAL ON 21ST JANUARY 1986

Annex 1

LIST OF MATERIALS WHOSE EXPORT IS THE SUBJECT OF NUCLEAR NON-PROLIFERATION CONTROL

Note: Where a product is included both in this list and in that of products subject to final destination control, a single licence application is submitted by the exporter.

Item	Designation of products
A.1	Special fissile products and other fissile products: *a)* Uranium 235-enriched uranium in all chemical and physical forms *b)* Uranium 233 in all chemical and physical forms or uranium 233-enriched uranium *c)* Plutonium in all chemical and physical forms *d)* New fuel and fertile elements for nuclear reactors *e)* Irradiated fuel and fertile elements for nuclear reactors Under this item, the products must be identified by stating the physical and chemical forms and isotope composition of the uranium or plutonium. Quantities must be expressed in the usual unit plus the metal equivalent values of the uranium or plutonium atomic elements.
A.2	Source materials, in any form or incorporated in any substance where the source material concentration exceeds 0.05 per cent by weight: *a)* Unprocessed or processed uranium or thorium ores, including tailings, containing over 0.05 per cent by weight of uranium, thorium or combinations of these products as follows: 1. Ores containing uranium, including pitchblende 2. Monazite and monazite sands 3. Ores containing thorium, including uranothorianite 4. Tailings containing uranium and/or thorium *b)* Uranium 235-depleted uranium, natural uranium, thorium in all chemical and physical forms, including alloys and compounds with a uranium content of more than 0.05 per cent and thorium content of more than 1.5 per cent, excluding medical products. In this item, the products must be identified by stating the physical and chemical forms and isotopic composition of the uranium or thorium. In addition to the usual unit, quantities must include the metal equivalent values of the uranium or thorium atomic elements.
A.3	Deuterium and compounds, mixtures and solutions containing deuterium, including heavy water and heavy paraffins, in which the ratio of deuterium atoms to hydrogen atoms exceeds 1:5000 in numbers. In addition to the usual unit, the quantities must also be expressed as the atom equivalent value of the deuterium.
A.4	Zirconium in all chemical and physical forms where the ratio of the hafnium weight to zirconium weight is less than 1:500, except alloys containing less than 50 per cent zirconium. The main dimensions of the products must be supplied in addition to the zirconium content by weight.
A.6	Artificial graphite with a boron content of up to 1 ppm and a total microscopic effective thermal neutron absorption section of up to 5 millibarns per atom.

Item	Designation of products
A.7	Lithium in all chemical and physical forms. The products must be identified by stating the chemical and physical forms and isotopic composition of the lithium. In addition to the usual unit, the quantities must be expressed as the metal equivalent value of the lithium atomic element.
A.12	Tritium, tritium compounds and mixtures where the ratio of tritium to hydrogen is over 1:1000 in atoms. *Notes*: 1. The only tritium compounds and mixtures excluded from the above definition are those where the separation of tritium from its compounds would not induce the development of a hydrogen isotopic mixture where the ratio of tritium to hydrogen would exceed 1:1000 in atoms. 2. The tritium quantities specified above and contained in the product categories mentioned below are excluded from this definition: *a)* Labelled compounds not containing more than 100 curies per consignment *b)* Luminescent products, gas and aerosol detectors, electronic tubes, devices for measuring the intensity of lightning or static electricity variations, ionization devices, including devices for removing static electricity, ion-generator tubes, detector cells for gas chromatography equipment and calibration standards. Provided each product or device does not contain more than 40 curies of tritium in any chemical or physical form whatsoever. In addition to the usual unit, tritium quantities must include the value in curies.

Annex 2

LIST OF EQUIPMENT WHOSE EXPORT IS SUBJECT TO NUCLEAR NON-PROLIFERATION CONTROL

Note: Where a product is included both in this list and in that of products subject to final destination control, a single licence application shall be submitted by the exporter.

Item	Designation of products
B.1	Installations for separating isotopes from source materials, special fissile and other fissile products, and their specially designed or prepared equipment and components, including: *a)* 1. Valves with a diameter of at least 3 cm, closed by means of bellows, entirely made of or coated with aluminium, nickel or an alloy containing at least 60 per cent nickel, operated manually or automatically; 2. Automatic or manual valves and fittings and their parts with a diameter of over 0.5 cm, entirely made or coated with aluminium, nickel or alloy containing at least 60 per cent nickel. 3. Headers specially designed or prepared for incorporation in a cascade of centrifuges, entirely made of or coated with stainless steel, aluminium, nickel or alloys containing at least 60 per cent nickel. 4. Specially designed or prepared transfer stations for handling UF_6, entirely made of or coated with stainless steel, aluminium, nickel or alloys containing at least 60 per cent nickel. *b)* Uranium isotope separation plant 1. Gas centrifuges for enriching or separating isotopes and specially designed parts and equipment for gas centrifuges and gas centrifuge plant. 2. Separation jet nozzles or slots, with a collar curve of less than 1 mm and bundle of nozzles of this type. 3. Static vortex generators including inlets and exits. *c)* Compressors and blowers, of the turbo compressor, centrifuge and axial flow types, entirely made of or coated with aluminium, nickel or an alloy containing at least 60 per cent nickel and with a capacity of at least 1 700 litres per minute (60 cubic feet per minute). *d)* Heat exchangers for use in installations processing uranium hexafluoride, i.e. heat exchangers made of aluminium, copper, nickel or alloys containing over 60 per cent nickel or combinations of these metals in clad tubing designed to operate at a pressure below atmospheric pressure, with a leakage rate of less than 10 Pa (0.1 millibar) per hour with an atmospheric pressure variation of 10^5 Pa (1 bar). *e)* Gaseous diffusion barriers and gaseous diffuser housings.

Item	Designation of products
	g) Molecular pumps with an internal diameter ranging from 7.5 to 40 cm and similar height, made of or coated with stainless steel, nickel or alloy containing at least 60 per cent nickel.
	h) Ring-shaped motors and stators, with a frequency range of 400 to 2 000 Hz.
	i) Frequency changers and generators with a frequency range of 400 to 2 000 Hz and an output of over 200 kW
	j) Magnetic bearings, centering or suspending devices with a maximum flux diameter of 200 mm.
	k) 1. Martensite steel cylindrical tubes with structural hardening, made of aluminium alloys or composite materials and having the characteristics mentioned at the end of the section[1]. 2. Sampling scoops specially designed for use in centrifuges, entirely made of or coated with stainless steel, aluminium or nickel alloys or alloys containing over 60 per cent nickel.
	l) Rings and cylindrical bellows with a wall thickness of not more than 3 mm, a diameter ranging from 7.5 to 40 cm, a length of not more than 30 cm, made of martensite steel with structural hardening, aluminium alloy or composite materials with the characteristics mentioned at the end of the section[1].
	m) Unworked, semi-finished or finished cylindrical disks with a thickness of not more than 3 cm and a diameter ranging from 7.5 to 40 cm, made of martensite steel with structural hardening, aluminium alloy or composite materials with the characteristics mentioned at the end of the section[1].
	n) Mass spectrometers for UF_6.
	o) Specially designed or modified control instrumentation for controlling or monitoring uranium enrichment such as thermal flowmeters.
	p) Device for analysing the UF_6 content of hydrogen.
	q) Technical documentation relating to uranium isotopes separation plant and including: 1. general design plans and the specification tables for the plant 2. detailed plans, "as fitted" plans, manufacturing ranges of specific equipment used in the plant.
	(1) Special characteristics of the materials for constructing the rotating components of centrifuges. 1. Martensite steel with structural hardening: ultimate tensile strength at least $2.05.10^9$ Pa. 2. Aluminium alloy: ultimate tensile strength of at least $0.46.10^9$ Pa. 3. Composite materials: with a specific modulus of at least $12.3.10^6$ and specific ultimate tensile strength of at least $0.3.10^4$.
	Note: "Specific modulus" is the Young's modulus in Pa divided by the density in kg/m^3. "Specific ultimate tensile strength" is the ultimate tensile strength in Pa divided by the density expressed in kg/m^3.
B.2	Plants for the reprocessing of irradiated fuel elements from nuclear reactors, and their specially designed or prepared equipment and components, including:
	a) Machines for chopping, cutting or shearing spent fuel
	b) Dissolvers, evaporators, containers and storage vessels capable of withstanding nitric acid or oxidising nitrates, which may be loaded or handled by remote control and presenting at least one of the following characteristics: 1. Walls or internals containing at least 2 per cent boron or boron equivalent. 2. A maximum internal diameter of 17.8 cm if the shape is cylindrical. 3. A distance of 7.6 cm between walls for a slab tank or annular container.
	c) Counterflow solvent extractors for a flow rate of less than 5 m^3/h, capable of withstanding nitric acid or oxidising nitrates and including: 1. Mixers-decanters 2. Pulse columns 3. Centrifugal extractors
	d) Specially designed or modified control instrumentation for use in spent fuel reprocessing plants, such as: 1. Liquid-phase alpha counting channel 2. Shielded liquid sampling benches (remote control sampling device) 3. Shielded analysis channel.
	e) Heavy remote control handling machines of more than 0.25kN
	f) Complete systems for converting plutonium nitrate to plutonium oxide

Item	Designation of products
	g) Complete systems for converting plutonium oxide to plutonium metal *h)* Technical documentation relating to a reprocessing plant, unit or laboratory and including: 1. General design plans and specification tables for the plant 2. Detailed plans, "as fitted" plans, manufacturing ranges for specific equipment to be installed in the plant.
B.3	Nuclear reactors, namely reactors capable of operation so as to maintain a controlled self-sustaining fission chain reaction and specially designed or prepared equipment and components to be used in connection with a nuclear reactor including: *a)* Reactor pressure vessels *b)* Fuel handling equipment, including fuel loading and unloading machines *c)* Reactor control rods and their mechanisms *d)* Reactor core instrumentation 1. Device controlling the power levels of reactors 2. Neutron measurement channels *e)* Reactor pressure tubes *f)* 1. Cooling pumps for nuclear reactors 2. Liquid metal pumps *g)* Internals specially designed or prepared for operating a nuclear reactor, namely the core support system, thermal shields, deflectors, core grid plates and diffuser plates. *h)* Steam generators, sodium heat exchangers and their specialised accessory equipment *i)* Pressurisers and specialised accessory equipment.
B.5	Plants for the production of heavy water, deuterium and deuterium compounds and specially designed or prepared equipment and components, including: *a)* Mass spectrometers for deuterium analysis *b)* Dry pumps specially designed for handling hydrogen and its isotopes *c)* Hydrogen compressors operating at a pressure of more than 100 bars *d)* Hydrogen isotope separation column *e)* Technical documentation relating to a heavy water production plant and including: — The general design plans and specification tables for the plant. — Detailed plans, "as fitted" plans, manufacturing ranges of specific equipment to be fitted in the plant.
B.6	Plants for the production of uranium hexafluoride, their specially designed and prepared and components, including: *a)* Heat exchangers capable of withstanding uranium hexafluoride *b)* Flame reactors *c)* Technical documentation relating to a uranium fluoridation plant and including: 1. General design plans and specification tables or the plant 2. Detailed plans, "as fitted" plans, manufacturing ranges of specific equipment to be fitted in the plant.
C.1	Neutron-generating systems.
C.3	Electrolytic cells for fluorine production with a capacity of more than 250 g of fluorine per hour.
F.1	Machines for producing electron beams or ion beams with a capacity of at least 0.1 TW (impedance less than 1 ohm).
F.2	Oscillators capable of supplying a reproducible pulse of up to 3.10^{-9} second.
F.3	*a)* Lasers capable of supplying a mean capacity of more than 1 W and with a wave length ranging between 1.55 and 1.6 micrometre. *b)* Lasers capable of supplying pulsed energy of more than 20 joules and with a mean capacity of more than 20 GW. *c)* Optical equipment specially designed for operating with the above-mentioned lasers, including: 1. Pockels cells with a diameter of more than 5 cm. 2. Faraday rotors with a diameter of more than 10 cm. 3. Space filtering systems using secondary vacuum.

Annex 3

LIST OF LARGE NUCLEAR UNITS

Large nuclear units include the following:

- Nuclear research centres
- Research, power and propulsion reactors
- Isotope separation plants
- Uranium fluoridation plants
- Spent fuel reprocessing plants
- Fuel fabrication plants
- Heavy water or deuterium production plants
- Tritium production plants.

FEDERAL REPUBLIC OF GERMANY

TABLE OF CONTENTS

FEDERAL REPUBLIC OF GERMANY

I. INTRODUCTION

In the Federal Republic of Germany, nuclear trade is, first of all, placed in the general context of the aims of the basic nuclear legislation, the Act on the peaceful use of atomic energy and protection against its hazards (Atomic Energy Act)[1]. The Act is intended to:

— promote research into and the development and use of nuclear energy for peaceful purposes;
— protect lives, health and property from hazards associated with nuclear energy and from the harmful effects of ionizing radiation;
— provide compensation for damage caused by nuclear energy or ionizing radiation;
— prevent the domestic or external security of the Federal Republic of Germany from being endangered by reason of the use or release of nuclear energy;
— ensure fulfilment of the international obligations of the Federal Republic of Germany in the field of nuclear energy and radiation protection.

To achieve these objectives, the Federal Government, with the consent of the Federal Council[2] may issue ordinances, the most important of which in the context of the present study is the Radiation Protection Ordinance[3]. Nuclear trade in general (domestic and foreign trade) is therefore subject to the provisions of the Atomic Energy Act and its implementing ordinances. Thus, the applicable norms concerning radiation protection and financial security (second and third objective) as well as physical protection (fourth objective) must be observed. Non-observance constitutes an offence (Atomic Energy Act, Section 46) or even a crime (Penal Code, Section 328).

In addition, the international obligations of the Federal Republic of Germany (fifth objective) must be respected, i.e. notably the acts emanating from the European Communities (EURATOM directives and regulations), the international transport agreements, the nuclear third party liability conventions, and the Treaty on the Non-Proliferation of Nuclear Weapons.

While the above principles apply to both domestic and foreign trade in nuclear material, the latter is subject also to the general foreign trade legislation contained in the Foreign Trade Act[4] as implemented by the Foreign Trade Ordinance[5]. The Foreign Trade Act (Section 1) stipulates the principle that all economic transactions between the Federal Republic of Germany (including West Berlin) and foreign States are unrestricted, subject to the limitations provided for by the Act itself, other laws and international agreements. The Foreign Trade Act allows restrictions to be prescribed by ordinance, and the Foreign Trade Ordinance specifies such restrictions in relation to trade in nuclear material, installations and equipment.

This general legislative framework will be discussed in further detail below. However, it is useful to note already at this stage, that the legislation of the Federal Republic of Germany distinguishes between:

a) "nuclear fuel", the handling, possession, custody, transport, export, and import of which is regulated by the Atomic Energy Act itself;
b) "other radioactive substances", which are covered by the Radiation Protection Ordinance;
c) nuclear material, installations and equipment whose international trade is governed by the Foreign Trade Ordinance.

The definitions of "nuclear fuel" and "other radioactive substances" are given below under "Trade in nuclear material".

II. TRADE IN NUCLEAR MATERIAL

The Atomic Energy Act (Section 2) employs the generic term "radioactive substances" which comprises "nuclear fuel" and "other radioactive substances". Nuclear fuel is defined as meaning special fissionable material in the form of plutonium 239, plutonium 241, uranium 233, uranium enriched in the isotopes 233 or 235, any substance containing one or more of the aforesaid substances, uranium and substances containing uranium of the natural isotopic mixture of such purity as to enable a continuous self-sustaining chain reaction to be maintained in a suitable installation (reactor). Other radioactive substances mean substances other than nuclear fuel which spontaneously emit ionizing radiation.

The import and export of radioactive substances require a licence or a declaration; exemptions from these requirements are provided for in certain cases.

1. Import and Export Requiring a Licence

a) Nuclear fuel

The import and export of nuclear fuel requires a licence (Atomic Energy Act, Section 3), subject to the exemptions mentioned below. Import and export are defined as any form of shipment into or out of the realm of the Act. An import licence is granted if the importer is reliable and it is ensured that the nuclear fuel to be imported will be used in conformity with the provisions of the Atomic Energy Act, the ordinances made thereunder, and the international obligations of the Federal Republic of Germany in the field of nuclear energy. The latter conditions refer in particular to the obligations resulting from the EURATOM Treaty and the Treaty on the Non-Proliferation of Nuclear Weapons (see the section on safeguards below). A licence for the export of nuclear fuel is granted if the exporter is reliable and it is ensured that the fuel to be exported will not be used in such a way as to jeopardise the international obligations of the Federal Republic of Germany in the field of nuclear energy, or its internal or external security. The above requirements do not affect any other legal provisions on import or export. This means that the provisions of the Foreign Trade Act and of the Foreign Trade Ordinance (see below) and the applicable customs regulations must be observed. Any person who, without having obtained the required licence, imports, exports or otherwise conveys nuclear fuel into or out of the realm of the Act, shall be liable to imprisonment for a term of up to five years or a fine[6].

The Federal Office of Economics[7] is competent for licensing the import and export of nuclear fuel (Atomic Energy Act, Section 22). In granting such licences, the Office is bound by the technical instructions issued by the Federal Minister responsible for nuclear safety and radiation protection[8].

The import and export of nuclear fuel is controlled by the Federal Minister of Finance or the customs authorities designated by him; in the Free Port of Hamburg, this function is exercised by the Free Port Authority of that city. Also, for nuclear exports to and from Berlin (West), special regulations are in force which provide for participation by the Allies.

b) Other radioactive substances

In principle, the import and export of other radioactive substances requires a licence, unless they are already covered by a licence for the import or export of nuclear fuel (Radiation Protection Ordinance, Section 11). Import and export are defined as in the Atomic Energy Act, except that the transit does not fall under this definition so that the transit of other radioactive substances is exempt from export or import licensing (other licences must of course be obtained, e.g. a transport licence).

As in the case of nuclear fuel, the licensing authority is the Federal Office of Economics. An import licence is issued if the importer is reliable and if he has ensured that such substances will be acquired for the first time after import by persons holding the necessary handling licence. Similarly, an export licence is issued if the exporter is reliable and if he has ensured that the radioactive substances to be exported will not be used so as to endanger the internal or external security of the Federal Republic of Germany or its international obligations (Radiation Protection Ordinance, Section 14).

2. Import and Export Requiring a Declaration

a) Radioactive substances

The import of radioactive substances requires no licence, only a declaration to the customs authorities and the Federal Office of Economics, if the importer is able to certify that the substances are to be acquired, immediately after being imported, by persons holding licences for the storage of nuclear fuel, for nuclear installations, for treatment, processing or other uses of nuclear fuel outside nuclear installations, for handling other radioactive substances exempted in special cases from holding a handling licence [Radiation Protection Ordinance, Section 12(1) and Annex V].

A declaration to the customs authorities and the Federal Office of Economics is also required in case of import, for commercial or industrial purposes, of [Section 12(2) and Annex VI]:

- devices equipped with gauges or indicators containing firmly bonded radioactive paints which do not exceed certain limits;
- certain uraniferous ceramic articles or glassware;
- optical or electronic components or electrical and gas devices intended for lighting, containing radioactive materials of low activity and radiotoxicity.

b) Other radioactive substances

The export of other radioactive substances requires only a declaration, if the activity per consignment does not exceed certain activity levels [Section 12(3) and Annex VII].

3. Exemptions

No licence or declaration is required for the import and export of:

- radioactive substances which are exempted from a handling licence, such as radioactive substances with low specific activity and devices of approved design containing radioactive substances (Section 13);
- other radioactive substances by the Federal Armed Forces [Section 11(3)].

III. TRADE IN "SENSITIVE" NUCLEAR MATERIAL, INSTALLATIONS AND EQUIPMENT

1. General Rules

The Atomic Energy Act and the Radiation Protection Ordinance expressly stipulate that other legal provisions on import and export remain unaffected. In this context, the Foreign Trade Act and the Foreign Trade Ordinance issued thereunder are of particular relevance. To the extent that the Foreign Trade Act allows limitations, an ordinance may prescribe that transactions — generally or under certain circumstances — must be licensed or are prohibited (Section 2). Legal transactions and acts in the field of foreign trade may be restricted so that obligations resulting from internatioal agreements ratified by the legislature in the form of a federal act may be fulfilled (Section 5). Section 7 of the Act permits the restriction of foreign transactions in order to assure the security of the Federal Republic of Germany, to avoid a disturbance of the peaceful community of the people, or to avoid a significant disturbance of the Federal Republic's foreign relations.

Annexed to the Foreign Trade Act is the Import List (Einfuhrliste), Part III of which contains a list of commodities (Warenliste) and Part II two country lists (Länderlisten)[9] (see *Annex II* to this chapter). Country List A/B contains those countries with which trade has largely been liberalised by the Federal Republic of Germany, while a number of restrictions apply to trade with the countries enumerated in Country List C.

The Foreign Trade Ordinance is accompanied by the Export List[10], Part I B of which forms the Nuclear Energy List (Kernenergieliste, — see Annex I to the present chapter). A number of country lists[11] are annexed to this Ordinance. Country List D enumerates those countries whose authorities issue International Import Certificates, and Country List E mentions the countries whose authorities issue transit permits (see Annex II to this chapter).

All these lists have a significance in trade in "sensitive" nuclear material, installations and equipment, as will be explained below.

2. Export

The above provisions of the Foreign Trade Act are implemented by Section 5 of the Foreign Trade Ordinance which prescribes that the export of goods listed in the Nuclear Energy List requires a licence ; the same applies to documents related to the manufacturing of such goods. A licence is also required for the export of documents concerning the technologies, technical data and technical processes referred to in that Section, if they are addressed to non-residents residing in a country appearing on Country List C (technology transfer independent of commodities). The Nuclear Energy List distinguishes between materials, installations and equipment for nuclear technological purposes. The first-mentioned term comprises not only nuclear fuel within the meaning of the Atomic Energy Act but also a number of other nuclear and non-nuclear material. This list implements the Guidelines for Nuclear Transfers of the Nuclear Suppliers Group (so-called London Club) and the "Common Policy Statement" of the European Community countries[12].

The term "resident" means natural and legal persons having their domicile or habitual residence in the realm of the Foreign Trade Act. Subsidiaries and establishments of non-residents are considered as residents under certain conditions [Section 4(1) Nr. 3 of the Foreign Trade Act]. Consequently "non-residents" are persons not meeting those requirements.

The Federal Office of Economics is competent for granting export licences for items on the Nuclear Energy List as well as related documents and technologies whenever such licences concern commercial transactions[13]. The Länder authorities are responsible for granting such licences if they concern other transactions (e.g. for scientific purposes). Licences concerning countries appearing in Country List C are issued only after international consultation, except for commodities subject to a simplified licensing procedure (see *Annex I* to the present chapter).

The Federal Office of Economics thus ensures co-ordination of all commercial export licences required under the Atomic Energy Act and the Radiation Protection Ordinance (see above) as well as under the foreign trade legislation.

Only exporters are entitled to apply for an export licence using a prescribed form (Section 17 and Annex 5 of the Foreign Trade Ordinance). The application must be accompanied by certain documents according to whether or not the purchasing country[14] or the country of consumption[15] appears on Country List D. thus, the following documents are required:

- an International Import Certificate from the purchasing country, if this country is listed on Country List D, or
- an International Import Certificate from the country of consumption, if the purchasing country is not listed on Country List D but the country of consumption is so listed, or
- other documents showing that the goods will remain in the country of consumption named in the application, if neither the purchasing country nor the country of consumption is listed on Country List D.

The licensing authorities may, in special cases, waive the requirement to attach the above documents, provided that this does not jeopardise the interests specified in Section 7 of the Foreign Trade Act, particularly international co-operation in the field of common export control. The export licence and the export certificate (Ausfuhrerklärung) must be presented to the customs agency which handles the exportation. A copy of the export licence must be submitted to the customs agency.

3. Import

Residents, to which residents of the European Communities are assimilated, may import commodities in accordance with the Import List annexed to the Foreign Trade Act, without having to obtain a licence (Sections 10 and 10a of the Foreign Trade Act). In all other cases, an import licence is required, i.e. in case of import by non-residents and in cases specified by the Import List. The Import List indicates for each commodity whether or not an import licence is required. Contrary to the Export List, it does not contain a Nuclear Energy List or special provisions for "sensitive" nuclear material, installations and equipment so that the general rules apply. The latter provide for a licence-free import by residents. A licence is only required if the country where the commodities originated or were bought does not appear on the Country Lists A/B or C or is subject to restrictions imposed by the European Communities.

The general customs clearance formalities must be observed. In certain cases, an import control declaration and/or a certificate of origin must be presented (Sections 27 to 29 of the Foreign Trade Ordinance). In the framework of international co-operation in the field of export control, the Federal Office of Economics issues, upon application, international import certificates and delivery verification certificates. The resident importer is entitled to apply for such certificates and has to notify the import to the Federal Office of Economics (Section 29b of the Foreign Trade Ordinance).

4. Transit

The transit of the commodities listed in the Nuclear Energy List is prohibited (Section 38 of the Foreign Trade Ordinance) if such commodities:

a) are not to be shipped into a country of consumption appearing on Country List A/B;
b) are not shipped from a country appearing on Country List E or on account of a person residing in one of these countries; and
c) are not accompanied by
  i) an export certificate from the country of despatch (transit permit), or
  ii) in case of despatch from Sweden or Switzerland, by a certified copy of the export permit of the country of despatch.

The Customs Office examines whether the transit is permitted when the goods leave the territory of the Federal Republic of Germany. Transit permits may be issued only by the authorities appearing on Country List E.

5. Transit Trade Transactions

Transactions are restricted by virtue of Section 7(1) of the Foreign Trade Act (Section 40 of the Foreign Trade Ordinance). Transit trade transactions are defined as transactions by which goods which are outside the realm of the Foreign Trade Act or have been brought inside the realm but not yet been cleared by customs, are acquired by residents from non-residents and sold to non-residents; the same definition applies to legal transactions by which such goods are sold to other residents before being sold to non-residents.

Sale of the commodities mentioned in the Nuclear Energy List in the framework of a transit trade transaction is subject to a licence, if the countries of sale or consumption are the Republic of South Africa and Namibia or appear on Country List C. No such licence is required if the commodity is exported in the framework of a transit trade transaction and the export must be licensed.

Sale of those commodities within the framework of a transit trade transaction must be licensed if such commodities are shipped into the realm of the Foreign Trade Act. No such transit licence is required if in case of export the country of purchase or consumption is a Member State of the European Communities.

6. Sanctions

Section 70 of the Foreign Trade Ordinance (which implements Section 33 of the Foreign Trade Act) lists a number of administrative offences.

In particular, any person who intentionally or negligently, without having obtained a licence, exports the goods appearing on the Nuclear Energy List or documents related thereto or sells such goods in the framework of a transit trade transaction, or who organises any prohibited transit of such goods, is liable to a fine of up to DM 500 000.

Such intentional acts constitute criminal offences, punishable by imprisonment of up to three years or a fine, if they endanger the safety of the Federal Republic of Germany, disturb the peaceful community of the people, or disturb significantly the foreign relations of the Federal Republic of Germany (Section 34 of the Foreign Trade Act). The attempt is punishable. In case of negligence, the punishment is imprisonment of up to one year or a fine.

IV. TRANSPORT[16]

The transport of radioactive substances (i.e. nuclear fuel and other radioactive substances) is governed by the Atomic Energy Act and the Radiation Protection Ordinance, as well as by the legal provisions applicable to each mode of transport; these are based on the Act on the Transport of Dangerous Goods[17]. The Federal Republic of Germany is a party to a number of international agreements concerning the transport of dangerous goods.

The transport of nuclear fuel must be licensed by the Federal Institute of Physics and Technology[18] while the Länder authorities grant licences for the transport of other radioactive substances. The latter, acting as Agents of the Bund, are responsible for controlling the transport of radioactive substances; they have to ensure compliance with all applicable transport provisions, in particular those relating to physical protection and safety measures.

V. SAFEGUARDS

As a Member State of the European Atomic Energy Community (EURATOM), the Federal Republic of Germany is bound by the safeguards provisions of the EURATOM Treaty (Articles 77 to 85) and Regulation No. 3227/1976 (EURATOM) of 19th October 1976 of the Commission of the European Communities concerning the application of the provisions on EURATOM Safeguards.

By Acts of 4th June 1974[19] the Federal Republic of Germany adopted the Treaty on the Non-Proliferation of Nuclear Weapons and the Agreement of 5th April 1973 between Belgium, Denmark, the Federal Republic of Germany, Ireland, Italy, Luxembourg, the Netherlands, EURATOM and the IAEA in implementation of Article III(1)(4) of the Treaty on the Non-Proliferation of Nuclear Weapons (Verification Agreement).

The Agreement of 5th April 1973 was given effect by an Act containing detailed provisions regarding the safeguarding of fissionable materials[20].

The Federal Republic of Germany applies the Guidelines for Nuclear Transfers (IAEA INFCIRC/254) of the so-called London Club and has participated in the Declaration of Common Policy by the Member States of the European Community of 20th November 1984 (IAEA INFCIRC/322).

VI. PHYSICAL PROTECTION

The Federal Republic of Germany has signed, as a Member State of EURATOM, the Convention on the Physical Protection of Nuclear Material.

The licensing requirements for the transport of nuclear material provide, *inter alia*, that necessary protection must be provided against disturbance or other interference by third parties [Section 4(2) No. 5 of the Atomic Energy Act, Section 10(1) No. 5 of the Radiation Protection Ordinance]. The Federal Minister responsible for nuclear safety and radiation protection has determined such protection measures in the form of "safety catalogues" (not published). The physical protection measures imposed by the licensing and control authorities are based on the IAEA recommendations (INFCIRC/225, Rev.1, INFCIRC/254, Annex B).

VII. INTELLECTUAL PROPERTY IN THE NUCLEAR FIELD

Neither the Atomic Energy Act nor the Patent Act (Patentgesetz) contain special provisions on inventions and patents in the field of nuclear energy.

There exists however the possibility of so-called secret patents (Sections 50 to 55 of the Patent Act). Whenever a patent is applied for inventions which constitute a state secret, i.e. facts, objects or discoveries which are accessible to a limited number of persons only and must be kept secret from a foreign power in order to prevent a grave detriment to the external security of the Federal Republic of Germany (Section 93 of the Penal Code), the Patent Office prohibits publication after having heard the Minister of Defence. The continued necessity of this prohibition is controlled *ex officio* and upon application by the Minister of Defence, the applicant or patent owner. The latter may claim compensation under certain conditions specified by the Patent Act.

The Federal Republic is Party to the (NATO) Agreement for the mutual safeguarding of secrecy inventions relating to defence and for which applications for patents have been made, signed in Paris on 21st September 1960[21].

A number of nuclear collaboration agreements concluded by the Federal Republic of Germany contain provisions on the use and protection of intellectual property.

Particularly comprehensive provisions on this subject are to be found in the Treaty of Almelo on collaboration in the development and exploitation of the gas centrifuge process for producing enriched uranium, concluded on 4th March 1970 between the Federal Republic of Germany, the Netherlands and the United Kingdom (Article IV and Annexes I and II).

VIII. AGREEMENTS

1. Multilateral Agreements

The Federal Republic of Germany has concluded the following:

— Treaty of 1st July 1968 on the Non-Proliferation of Nuclear Weapons (BGBl. 1974 II, p. 786);
— Agreement of 5th April 1973 between Belgium, Denmark, the Federal Republic of Germany, Ireland, Italy, Luxembourg, the Netherlands, EURATOM and IAEA in implementation of Article III(1) and (4) of the Treaty on the Non-Proliferation of Nuclear Weapons (Verification Agreement — BGBl, 1974 II, p. 795);
— Convention of 3rd March 1980 on the Physical Protection of Nuclear Material (not yet ratified).

2. General Bilateral Co-operation Agreements in the Peaceful Uses of Nuclear Energy

Agreements with the following countries are still in force:

— Canada, 11th December 1957 (BAnz 1958 no. 46, p. 1);
— India, 5th October 1971 (BGBl. 1972 II, p. 1014);
— Romania, 29th June 1973 (BGBl. II, p. 1485);
— Brazil, 27th June 1975 (BGBl. 1976 II, p. 335);
— Indonesia, 14th June 1976 (BGBl. 1977 II, p. 362);
— Iran, 4th July 1976 (BGBl. 1978 II, p. 285);
— Spain, 5th December 1978 (BGB1. 1979 II, p. 134)
— Egypt, 26th October 1981 (BGBl. 1982 II, p. 568);
— People's Republic of China, 9th May 1984 (BGBl. II, p. 555);
— Republic of Korea, 11th April 1986 (BGBl. II, p. 727);
— USSR, 22nd April 1987 (BGBl. 1988 II, p. 394).

3. Bilateral Co-operation Agreements in Special Fields

— Agreement of 8th June 1976 with the ***United States of America*** in the field of liquid metal-cooled fast breeder reactors (BGB1. II, p. 1449); extended by Agreement of 26th August and 7th October 1986 (notice in US Department of State Bulletin, vol. 86, No. 2119, p. 86);

— Agreement of 10th March 1978 with ***Brazil*** on exchange of technical information and co-operation in the safety of nuclear installations (BGBl. II, p. 951), extended by Agreement of 30th May and 27th July 1983 (BGBl. II, p. 685);

— Agreement of 29th August 1978 with ***France*** on exchange of information and co-operation in the field of safety research on light water reactors (BGBl. II, p. 1301) amended and extended by an Additional Agreement of 28th September 1983 (BGBl. 1984 II, p. 945);

— Agreement of 4th September 1978 with the ***United Kingdom*** concerning the application of safeguards to the proposed exports to Brazil of uranium enriched in the United Kingdom by URENCO (United Kingdom Treaty Series 1979, No. 68);

— Agreement of 14th March and 4th April 1979 with the ***United Kingdom*** on the exchange of information on important questions concerning the safety of nuclear installations and on co-operation in the preparation of safety standards (BGBl. II, p. 435);

— Technical Exchange and Co-operative Arrangement of 30th April 1981 with the ***United States of America*** in the field of reactor safety research and development (notice in Department of State Bulletin, Vol. 81, No. 2053, p.89);

— Arrangement of 6th July 1981 with the ***United States of America*** for the exchange of technical information and co-operation in nuclear safety matters (BGB1. II, p. 658), extended by Arrangement of 17th July 1986 (BGB1. 1987 II, p. 197);

— Agreement of 8th October 1981 with ***Argentina*** on exchange of technical information and co-operation in the safety of nuclear installations (BGBl. II, p. 959);

— Agreement of 4th July 1986 with ***Sweden*** following a contract on exchange of spent nuclear fuel (Sveriges Överenskommelser 1986, No. 48).

— Agreement of 11th February 1977 with the ***United States of America*** in the field of gas-cooled reactor concepts and technology (BGB1. II, p. 345 and TIAS 9046) and Addendum of 30th September 1977 (accession of France and Switzerland — TIAS 9047) ; both extended by Agreements of 20th January and 7th April 1987 (BGBl. II, p. 728);

— Memorandum of Understanding of 10th January 1984 for co-operation in the field of liquid metal fast breeder reactors with ***Belgium***, ***France***, ***Italy*** and the ***United Kingdom*** (BGBl. II, p. 517).

4. Multilateral Industrial and Scientific Co-operation Agreements

— Convention of 19th January 1967 with ***France*** and the ***United Kingdom*** on the construction and operation of a very high flux reactor (BGBl. II, p. 2431) and 19th July 1974 (accession of the United Kingdom — BBGBl. 1976 II, p. 245), last amended by the Additional Protocol of 9th December 1981 (BGBl. 1982 II, p. 264);

— Agreement of 4th March 1970 with the ***Netherlands*** and the ***United Kingdom*** on collaboration in the development and exploitation of the gas centrifuge process for producing enriched uranium (Almelo Treaty, BGBl. 1971 II, p. 930);

5. Safeguards Agreements

— Agreement of 24th February, 12th and 13th March 1970 with the IAEA and ***Argentina*** for the transfer of a training reactor and enriched uranium therefor (UNTS Vol. 795, p. 3);

— Agreement of 26th February 1976 with the IAEA and ***Brazil*** for the application of safeguards (UNTS Vol. 1022, p. 299);

— Agreement of 9th June 1982 with the IAEA and ***Spain*** for the application of safeguards in connection with the Agreement between the Federal Republic of Germany and Spain of 5th December 1978 in the field of the utilisation of nuclear energy for peaceful purposes (IAEA-DOC. INFCIRC/305).

NOTES AND REFERENCES

1. Gesetz über die friedliche Verwendung der Kernenergie und den Schutz gegen ihre Gefahren (Atomgesetz), as revised and newly published on 15th July 1985, Federal Gazette (Bundesgesetzblatt — BGBl.) 1985 I, p. 1565. A minor amendment to Section 9(b) was made by the Act of 18th February 1986 (BGBl. 1986 I, p. 265).
2. The Federal Council (Bundesrat) is composed of Government representatives of the Länder, i.e. the federal States.
3. Verordnung über den Schutz vor Schäden durch ionisierende Strahlen (Strahlenschutzverordnung) of 13th October 1976, BGBl. I, p. 2905, last amended on 22nd May 1981, BGBl. I, p. 445. The Ordinance is currently being revised.
4. Aussenwirtschaftsgesetz of 28th April 1961 (BGBl. I, p. 481) last amended on 24th April 1986 (BGBl. I, p. 560).
5. Verordnung zur Durchführung des Aussenwirtschaftsgesetzes (Aussenwirtschaftsverordnung) of 18th December 1986 (BGBl. I, p. 2671).
6. Section 328 of the Criminal Code (Strafgesetzbuch).
7. Bundesamt für Wirtschaft.
8. At present the Minister of Environmental Affairs, Nature Conservation and Reactor Safety (Bundesminister für Umwelt, Naturschutz und Reaktorsicherheit), BGBl. 1986 I, p. 864.
9. Last version published in the Federal Bulletin (Bundesanzeiger — BAnz) No. 241 of 31st December 1986.
10. Anlage AL zur Aussenwirtschaftsverordnung, last amended on 25th March 1988 (BAnz No. 68a).
11. Anlage L zur Aussenwirtschaftsverordnung, Annex to BGBl. I, No. 70 of 31st December 1986.
12. INFCIRC/254 and INFCIRC/322, see Volume I of this study dealing with international aspects of nuclear trade.
13. Section 28 of the Foreign Trade Act and Ordinance determining competence in the field of foreign transactions (Verordnung zur Regelung um Zuständigkeiten im Aussenwirtschaftsverkehr — AZV) of 18th July 1977 (BGBl. I, p. 1308), last amended on 4th May 1983 (BGBl. I, p. 556).
14. The purchasing country is the country where the non-resident resides who acquires the goods from the resident. Otherwise the country of consumption is considered as a purchasing country [Section 8(4) of the Foreign Trade Ordinance].
15. This is the country in which the goods are supposed to be used, consumed, treated or processed; if that country is not known, it is the latest known country to which the goods will be shipped [Section 8(5) of the Foreign Trade Ordinance].
16. For further details see analytical study in the same series: *Regulations Governing the Transport of Radioactive Materials*, OECD/NEA, 1980.
17. Gesetz über die Beförderung gefährlicher Güter.
18. Physikalisch-Technische Bundesanstalt.
19. BGBl. II, pp. 785, 794.
20. Ausführungsgesetz zum Verifikationsabkommen of 7th January 1980, BGBl. I, p. 17.
21. BGBl. 1964 II, p. 772.

Annex I

NUCLEAR ENERGY LIST*

(Annex AL, Part I B, to the Foreign Trade Ordinance — 25th March 1988)

01 Materials for nuclear technological purposes

0101 Special and other fissionable material, except:

i) consignments of up to one effective gramme,
ii) consignments of up to three effective grammes if contained in a sensing component of instruments.

Technical Notes:

1. "Special fissionable material" means plutonium 239, uranium 233, uranium enriched in the isotopes 235 or 233, and any other material containing the aforesaid substances.
2. "Uranium enriched in the isotopes 235 or 233" means uranium containing the isotopes 235 or 233 or both in a quantity exceeding that of natural uranium (isotopic relation in natural uranium 0.72 per cent).
3. "Other fissionable material" means pre-separated americium 242m, curium 245 and 247, californium 249 and 251, all plutonium isotopes except plutonium 238 and 239, as well as any other material containing the aforesaid substances.
4. Effective gramme of "special or other fissionable material" means
   a) plutonium and uranium 233, the mass in grammes,
   b) for uranium enriched in the isotope 235 to one per cent or more, the mass in grammes multiplied by the square of its enrichment (expressed in decimals),
   c) for uranium enriched in the isotope 235 to less than one per cent, the mass multiplied by 0.0001,
   d) for americium 242m, curium 245 and 247, californium 249 and 251, the mass in grammes multiplied by 10.
5. Material is pre-separated within the meaning of note 3 above which, after separation, is manufactured by a process leading to a higher concentration of the isotope concerned.

Note:

Simplified licensing procedure for the following commodities: uranium enriched to less than 20 per cent in the isotope 235, in the form of nuclear fuel to be used as further supply for nuclear reactors already exported which meet all the conditions of note 2 to Section 0203.

0102 Natural and depleted uranium, in any form or contained in any material in which the concentration of uranium exceeds 0.05 per cent, except

i) consignments containing 110 kg or less natural uranium, for all purposes, or 2 100 kg or less for civil non-nuclear purposes,
ii) depleted uranium containing less than 0.35 per cent uranium 235, in consignments containing 1 000 kg or less uranium, for non-nuclear purposes,
iii) depleted uranium especially manufactured for the following civil purposes:
   1. shielding
   2. packaging
   3. ballasts
   4. counterweights.

Note:

Simplified licensing procedure for the following commodities:

1. Natural uranium for enrichment in the isotope 235, under the following conditions:
   a) enriched uranium is returned after completion of the enrichment process, and
   b) all depleted uranium (tailings) originating from the enrichment process is returned if it contains more than 0.35 per cent uranium 235.

* Unofficial translation.

2. Uranium in the form of reactor fuel to be used as further supply for nuclear reactors already exported which meet all the conditions of note 2 to Section 0203.

0103 Deuterium, heavy water, deuterated paraffins as well as other compounds, mixtures and solutions containing deuterium containing more than 0.02 per cent of deuterium, except consignments of the above substances containing up to 10 kg deuterium.

Note:

Simplified licensing procedure for the following commodities: deuterium oxide (D_20) to be used as further supply for nuclear reactors already exported which meet the conditions of note 2 to Section 0203.

0104 Zirconium metal, alloys containing more than 50 per cent of zirconium and zirconium compounds if the hafnium content of the zirconium is below 0.2 per cent, as well as goods entirely produced from such materials, except:

i) zirconium metal and alloys in consignments of up to 5 kg.

Note:

This exception does not apply to zirconium tubes.

ii) zirconium in the form of foils or stripes, up to 0.025 mm thick, especially produced and designed for flash bulbs, in consignments of up to 200 kg.

Note:

Simplified licensing procedure for the following commodities: if they are used
in already exported civil power reactors which meet all the conditions of note 2 to Section 0203, or
in recognised civil research reactors:

a) parts consisting of zirconium metal as alloys especially designed for these reactors, such as cladding tubes and caps as well as their separating elements, lining tubes, heat insulation tubes, pressure and heating tubes, on condition that none of these parts contain fissionable materials,

b) zirconium metal or alloys in consignments of up to 100 kg, for planned use in, or planned support of, these reactors.

0105 Nickel powder and porous nickel metal as follows:

a) nickel powder of a purity of 99 per cent or more and a mean particle size below 10 micrometers according to ASTM Standard B330;
b) porous nickel metal produced from the material under a) by means of pressing or sintering, except single porous nickel metal sheets up to a size of 930 cm^2 for use in batteries for civil purposes.

Note:

Simplified licensing procedure for the following commodities: nickel in the form of uncompacted powder for non-nuclear civil purposes, in consignments of up to 4 000 kg.

0106 Nuclear grade graphite (boron content less than 5 ppm and density greater than 1.5 g/cm^3), except consignments of up to 100 kg.

0107 Lithium as follows (as to deuterides containing natural lithium or lithium enriched in the isotope 7, see Section 0103):

a) metal, hydrides and alloys containing lithium enriched in the isotope 6 in a higher concentration than natural lithium (more than 7.5 per cent lithium 6);

b) other material containing lithium enriched in the isotope 6, including compounds, mixtures and concentrates, but excluding lithium enriched in the isotope 6 contained in thermoluminescent dosimeters.

0108 Hafnium as follows: metal, alloys and compounds containing more than 60 per cent of hafnium, and products made therefrom, except consignments of the aforesaid substances containing up to 1 kg hafnium.

0109 Beryllium as follows: metal, alloys containing more than 50 per cent of beryllium, beryllium compounds and products made therefrom, except

i) metal windows for X-ray machines,
ii) oxide shapes, in fabricated or semi-fabricated form especially designed for electronic parts or as substrates for electronic circuits,
iii) consignments of up to 500 grammes beryllium having a purity of 99 per cent or less, or consignments of up to 100 grammes beryllium having a purity of more than 99 per cent if containing no single crystals,
iv) consignments of beryllium compounds containing up to 5 kg beryllium with a purity of less than 99 per cent.

0112 Tritium and compounds, mixtures and products containing more than 0.1 per cent tritium as well as products containing one or more of the aforesaid substances except:

i) consignments with an activity below 37 Giga becquerel (100 Ci),

ii) tritium contained in luminous paints, self-luminous products, gas and aerosol detectors, electron tubes, lightning or static elimination devices, ion-generating tubes, detector cells of gas chromotography devices, and calibration standards,

iii) compounds and mixtures of tritium where the separation of the constituents cannot result in the evolution of an isotopic mixture of hydrogen in which the tritium portion exceeds 0.1 per cent.

0113 Materials for nuclear heat sources as follows:

a) plutonium in any form whose isotopic content of plutonium 238 exceeds 50 per cent, except:

i) consignments of up to one effective gramme,

ii) consignments of up to three effective grammes if contained in sensing components of instruments,

iii) plutonium 238 in cardiac pacemakers;

b) pre-separated neptunium 237 in any form, except consignments of up to one effective gramme of neptunium 237.

Technical Note:

"Pre-separated" within the meaning of b) above means material which after separation is manufactured by a process leading to a higher concentration of the isotope concerned.

0114 Materials especially designed or prepared for the isotopic separation of natural and depleted uranium as well as of special and other fissionable material, including especially designed chemical exchange resins (for isotopic separation installations see Section 0201).

02 Installations for nuclear technological purposes

0201 Installations for the isotopic separation of natural and depleted uranium and of special and other fissionable material; control and surveillance devices as well as equipment, apparatus and parts especially designed or prepared for that purpose, in particular:

a) equipment especially designed for the isotopic separation of natural and depleted uranium, of special and other fissionable material, according to processes such as:

1. gaseous diffusion
2. centrifuge
3. jet nozzle
4. vortex separation
5. chemical exchange
6. electromagnetic separation
7. plasma separation
8. laser.

b) components especially designed for the above equipment such as:

1. valves consisting entirely of UF_6 resistant material or coated entirely with such material having a rated width of 5 mm or more and equipped with bellows;
2. blowers and compressors (turbo, centrifugal and axial flow types) which consist completely of, or are lined completely with UF_6 resistant material and have a suction volume of 1.7 m^3/min, including gaskets therefor;
3. heat exchangers consisting of UF_6 resistant material or of copper, or a combination of these materials if plated tubes are used, constructed for operation with pressures below 1 bar and a leakage rate of less than 0.1 mbar/h at a pressure difference of 1 bar;
4. gaseous diffusion barriers;
5. gaseous diffuser housings;
6. pressure gauges and sensors consisting of UF_6 resistant material, including phosphorous bronze, having the following qualities:

   i) measuring range up to 1 300 N/m^2, and

   ii) measuring accuracy better than 1 per cent;
7. UF_6 mass spectrometers equipped with magnetic or quadrupole systems, prepared for on-line operation, having the following specifications:

   i) unit resolution for mass greater than 320,

   ii) ion sources made from, or lined with nichrome, monel, or nickel plated,

   iii) electron bombardment ionization source,

   iv) collector system for isotopic analysis.

Technical Notes:

1. Equipment for isotopic separation installations according to the gas centrifuge process comprise for example:

a) rotating gas centrifuge components made from high strength materials as follows:

1. complete rotor assemblies,
2. rotor tubes with the following properties:
   i) maximum wall thickness 12 mm,
   ii) diameter between 75 mm and 400 mm;
3. rings or bellows designed to support or join together rotor tubes and having the following properties:
   i) maximum wall thickness 3 mm,
   ii) diameter between 75 mm and 400 mm;
4. baffles:
   disc-shaped components of between 75 mm and 400 mm diameter to be mounted inside the centrifuge rotor tube;
5. top and bottom caps:
   disc-shaped top or bottom rotor caps of between 75 mm and 400 mm diameter;

b) static gas centrifuge components made from UF_6 resistant materials as follows:

1. rotor housings having the following properties:
   i) inner diameter of between 75 mm and 400 mm,
   ii) wall thickness of between 6 mm and 30 mm, and
   iii) plane-parallel caps manufactured with high precision;
2. liquid cooled magnetic suspension bearings, the magnets having the following properties:
   i) annular magnets with a relation between outer and inner diameter smaller or equal to 1.6:1,
   ii) initial permeability of 0.15 H/m or more,
   iii) remanence of 98.5 per cent or more,
   iv) ienergy product of 80 000 J/m^3 (10^7 gauss-oersteds) or more, and
   v) deviation of the magnetic axe from the geometric axe lower than 0.1 mm;
3. bearings and dampers:
   rotating bearings of the pivot/cap type mounted on a damper;
4. molecular pumps:
   cylinders having internally machined or extruded helical grooves of rectangular cross-section and a minimum depth of 2 mm; further typical properties are:
   i) wall thickness of minimum 10 mm,
   ii) diameter of between 75 mm and 400 mm, and
   iii) 1:1 length to diameter ratio;
5. motor stators:
   multi-phase AC hysteresis motors for synchronous operation within a vacuum, having the following properties:
   i) frequency range of 600-2000 Hz,
   ii) power range of 50-1000 VA, and
   iii) laminated low loss iron core with layers 2 mm thick or less;
6. withdrawal hooks, consisting of tubes with a diameter of up to 5 mm, for the withdrawal of UF_6 gas from the rotor chamber;

c) UF_6 resistant components for gas centrifuge plants as follows:

1. feed systems, product and tails withdrawal systems, including feed autoclaves used to produce the UF_6 gas stream for the centrifuge cascades having the following properties:
   i) pressure resistance of up to 100 N/m^2,
   ii) throughput of 1 kg/h or more,
2. desublimers (cold traps) with the following properties:
   i) pressure resistance of up to 3 N/m^2,
   ii) operating range from 203 K (—70 °C) to 343 K (+ 70 °C);
3. stations for trapping enriched and depleted UF_6 into containers;
4. especially designed and prepared piping and header systems for handling UF_6 within the centrifuge cascades.

d) Equipment for the manufacture of gas centrifuges:

1. devices for rotor mounting and balancing:
   i) devices for the mounting of rotor segments, chamber discs and bottom caps, in particular precision plugs, precision cramps and assembling machines,
   ii) devices for the alignment of rotor segments around a common axe, in particular computer-controlled precision sounds for the control of pneumatic bending devices:

A. devices for balancing in 3 or more axes in vacuum test chambers,

B. tangential speed of 300 m/s or higher;

2. devices for the manufacture of rings and bellows having the following properties:
   i) diameter between 75 mm and 400 mm,
   ii) length of 12 mm or more, and
   iii) bellow depth of 2 mm or more.

2. High strength materials for rotors and rotor components are:
a) maraging steel capable of an ultimate tensile strength of 1.7 x 10^9 N/m^2 or more,
b) aluminium alloys capable of an ultimate tensile strength of 0.46 x 10^9 N/m^2 or more,
c) filamentary materials suitable for use in composite structures and having a specific modulus of 12.3 x 10^6 or greater and a specific ultimate tensile strength of 0.3 x 10^6 or greater ("Specific Modulus" is the Young's Modulus in N/m^2 divided by the density in Nkg/m^3: "Specific Ultimate Tensile Strength" is the ultimate tensile strength in N/m^2 divided by the density in Nkg/m^3).

3. UF_6 resistant materials are:
a) stainless steel,
b) aluminium and aluminium alloys,
c) nickel or alloys containing more than 60 per cent nickel,
d) fluorine/carbon compounds.

0202 Plants for the reprocessing of irradiated fuel elements and equipment especially designed or prepared therefor, in particular:

a) Irradiated fuel element chopping machines, i.e. remotely operated equipment especially designed or prepared for cutting, chopping, shredding or shearing irradiated fuel assemblies, bundles or rods;

b) Critically safe tanks (e.g. small diameter, annular or slab tanks) especially designed or prepared for dissolution of irradiated nuclear fuel, resistant to hot, highly corrosive liquids and suitable for remote filling and maintenance;

Note:

Sub-item b) comprises tanks which:

1. withstand hot highly corrosive nitric acid,
2. are made from stainless steel, titanium, zirconium or other materials of high quality, and
3. have the following characteristics for the control of radioactive criticality:
   walls or inner structures having a boron equivalent of at least 2 per cent and a maximum diameter of 17.8 cm (7 inches) in case of cylindric tanks or a maximum width of 7.6 cm (3 inches) in case of disc-shaped or annular tanks,

c) countercurrent solvent extractors and ion exchangers especially designed and prepared for use in a plant for the reprocessing of irradiated natural and depleted uranium or of irradiated special and other fissionable material;

Note:

Sub-item c) comprises liquid extractors which withstand hot highly corrosive nitric acid and are manufactured, according to especially high quality standards (special welding processes, controls and quality assurances), from stainless steel, titanium, zirconium or materials of comparable high quality;

d) process control equipment especially designed or prepared for monitoring and controlling the reprocessing of irradiated natural and depleted uranium, or irradiated special and other fissionable material;

1. A plant for the reprocessing of irradiated fuel elements includes the equipment and components which normally come in direct contact with and directly control the irradiated fuel and the major nuclear material and fission product processing streams.

2. Plants for the reprocessing of irradiated fuels within the meaning of this Section also comprise:

a) complete conversion systems for the conversion of plutonium nitrate to plutonium oxide, especially designed or prepared for the conversion and especially adapted to avoid criticality and radiation effects and to minimise toxicity risks,
b) complete production systems especially designed or prepared for the production of plutonium metal and especially adapted to avoid criticality and radiation effects and to minimise toxicity risks.

0203 Nuclear reactors, i.e. reactors capable of maintaining a controlled self-sustaining fission chain reaction, as well as equipment and components especially designed or prepared for use in connection with a nuclear reactor, in particular:

a) reactor pressure vessels, i.e. metal vessels, as complete units or as major shop-fabricated parts therefor, which are especially designed or prepared to contain the core of a nuclear reactor and are capable of withstanding the operating pressure of the primary coolant, including the top plate for a reactor pressure vessel,

b) handling equipment for reactor fuel elements, including charging and discharging machines,

c) control rods, i.e. rods especially designed or prepared for the control of the reaction rate in a nuclear reactor, including the neutron absorbing part and its support or suspension structure as well as the rod guide tubes, *d)* electronic equipment for the regulation and control of the power level in nuclear reactors, including control rod drive mechanisms, radiation detectors and neutron flux measuring devices,

e) reactor pressure tubes, i.e. tubes which are especially designed or prepared to contain fuel elements and the primary coolant in a reactor at an operating pressure in excess of 50 atmospheres,

f) primary coolant pumps, i.e. pumps especially designed or prepared for circulating the primary coolant in nuclear reactors,

g) internals especially designed or prepared for the operation of a nuclear reactor, e.g. support structures for the reactor core, thermal shields, cold traps, core grid plates and diffuser plates,

h) heat exchangers.

Notes:

1. A "nuclear reactor" comprises all the components inside the reactor vessel or those directly connected to it, the equipment for the control of the power level as well as the components normally containing the primary coolant of the reactor core and come into direct contact with or control the coolant.
2. Simplified licensing procedure for the following commodities: water-cooled and water-moderated civil power reactors including their main components as well as first loadings of fuel elements and moderators, under the following conditions:

   a) the reactor is constructed for operation with uranium having an enrichment to 20 per cent or less,

   b) uranium with an enrichment to 20 per cent is used as fuel,

   c) the reactor is not constructed for ship propulsion.

0204 Installations and equipment especially designed for the fabrication of nuclear reactor fuel elements.

Note:

A plant for the fabrication of fuel elements includes equipment which:
1. normally comes in direct contact with, or directly processes, or controls, the production flow of nuclear material,
2. seals the nuclear material within the cladding,
3. controls the integrity of the cladding or the sealing,
4. controls the final treatment of the solid fuel.

0205 Plants for the production of heavy water, deuterium and deuterium compounds and equipment especially designed or prepared therefor.

0206 Plants for the production of uranium hexafluoride (UF_6) and equipment or components especially designed or prepared therefor (including UF_6 purification equipment).

03 Equipment for nuclear technological purposes

0301 Neutron generating systems, including neutron generator tubes, designed for operation without external vacuum system and using electrostatic acceleration to trigger a deuterium/tritium nuclear reaction.

0302 Power generation or propulsion equipment, especially designed for use in military nuclear reactors, space reactors, ship reactors or mobile reactors.

Note:

This item does not comprise conventional power generation equipment which can be used in conventional systems even if such equipment was designed for use in a nuclear power plant.

0303 Electrolytic cells for the production of fluorine with a production capacity exceeding 250 g fluorine/h.

0304 Equipment especially designed for separation of lithium isotopes.

0305 Equipment especially designed for tritium production or recovery.

0306 Frequency changers (converters or inverters) especially designed or prepared for the control of motor stators for gas centrifuge enrichment having all the following characteristics, as well as especially designed parts therefor (see also Section 0201):
a) multiphase output of 600 to 2000 Hz,
b) frequency stability better than 0.1 per cent,
c) harmonic distortion less than 2 per cent, and
d) efficiency greater than 80 per cent.

Annex II

COUNTRY LISTS

(Annexes to the Foreign Trade Act and the Foreign Trade Ordinance)

Country	A/B	C	D	E
Afghanistan	+			
Albania		+		
Algeria	+			
American Virgin Islands	+			
American Oceania	+			
Andorra	+			
Angola	+			
Anguilla	+			
Antigua and Barbuda	+			
Argentina	+			
Aruba	+			
Australia	+			+
Australian Oceania	+			
Austria	+		+	
Azores	+			
Bahamas	+			
Bahrein	+			
Bangladesh	+			
Barbados	+			
Belgium	+		+	+
Belize	+			
Benin	+			
Bermudas	+			
Bhutan	+			
Bolivia	+			
Botswana	+			
Brazil	+			
British territories in the Indian Ocean	+			
British Virgin Islands	+			
Brunei	+			
Bulgaria		+		
Burkina Faso	+			
Burma	+			
Burundi	+			
Caiman Islands	+			
Cambodia	+			
Cameroon	+			
Canada	+		+	+
Canary Islands	+			
Cape Verde	+			
Central African Republic	+			
Ceuta and Melilla	+			
Chad	+			
Chile	+			
China, People's Republic of		+		
Colombia	+			
Comoros	+			
Congo	+			
Cook Islands	+			
Costa Rica	+			
Cuba		+		
Curaçao	+			
Cyprus	+			
Czechoslovakia		+		
Denmark	+		+	+
Djibouti	+			
Dominica	+			
Dominican Republic	+			
Ecuador	+			
Egypt	+			
El Salvador	+			
Equatorial Guinea	+			
Ethiopia	+			
Faroe Islands	+			
Falkland Islands	+			
Fiji	+			
Finland	+			
France	+		+	+
French Guyana	+			
French Polynesia	+			
Gabon	+			
Gambia	+			
Germany, Federal Republic of	+			
Ghana	+			
Gibraltar	+			+
Grenada	+			
Greece	+		+	+
Greenland	+			
Guadeloupe	+			
Guatemala	+			
Guinea	+			
Guinea-Bissau	+			
Guyana	+			
Haiti	+			
Honduras	+			
Hong Kong	+			+
Hungary		+		
Iceland	+			
India	+			

Country	A/B	C	D	E
Indonesia	+			
Iran	+			
Iraq	+			
Ireland	+		+	
Israel	+			
Italy	+		+	+
Ivory Coast	+			
Jamaica	+			
Japan	+		+	+
Jordan	+			
Kenya	+			
Kiribati	+			
Kuwait	+			
Laos	+			
Lesotho	+			
Lebanon	+			
Liberia	+			
Libya	+			
Liechtenstein	+			
Luxembourg	+		+	+
Macao	+			
Madagascar	+			
Madeira	+			
Malawi	+			
Malaysia	+			
Maldives	+			
Mali	+			
Malta	+			
Martinique	+			
Mauritania	+			
Mauritius	+			
Mayotte	+			
Mexico	+			
Monaco	+			
Mongolia		+		
Montserrat	+			
Morocco	+			+
Mozambique	+			
Namibia	+			+
Nauru	+			
Nepal	+			
New Caledonia	+			
New Zealandic Oceania	+			
New Zealand	+			+
Nicaragua	+			
Netherlands	+		+	+
Netherlands Antilles	+			
Niger	+			
Nigeria	+			
Niue	+			
North Korea		+		
North Yemen	+			
Norway	+		+	+
Oman	+			
Pakistan	+			
Panama	+			
Papua-New Guinea	+			
Paraguay	+			
Peru	+			
Philippines	+			+
Pitcairn Islands	+			
Polar areas	+			
Poland		+		
Portugal	+		+	+
Puerto Rico	+		+	
Qatar	+			
Reunion	+			
Romania		+		
Rwanda	+			
San Marino	+			
Sâo Tomé and Principe	+			
Saudi Arabia	+			
Senegal	+			
Seychelles	+			
Sierra Leone	+			
Sikkim	+			
Singapore	+			
Solomon Islands	+			
Somalia	+			
South Africa	+			+
South Korea	+			
South Yemen	+			
Spain	+		+	
Sri Lanka	+			
St. Christopher and Nevis	+			
St. Helena	+			
St. Lucia	+			
St. Pierre and Miquelon	+			
St. Vincent	+			
Sudan	+			
Suriname	+			
Svalbard	+			
Swaziland	+			
Sweden	+		+	
Switzerland	+		+	+
Syria	+			
Taiwan	+			
Tanzania	+			
Thailand	+			
Togo	+			
Tokelau Islands	+			
Tunisia	+			+
Turkey	+		+	
Turks and Caicos Islands	+			
Tuvalu	+			
Uganda	+			
Union of Soviet Socialist Republics		+		
United Arab Emirates	+			
United Kingdom	+		+	+
United States of America	+		+	+
Uruguay	+			
Vanuatu	+			
Vatican City	+			
Venezuela	+			
Vietnam		+		

ITALY

TABLE OF CONTENTS

ITALY

I. INTRODUCTION

Although Italy is not a country which exports nuclear power reactors, it is nevertheless an active supplier of equipment and services in the nuclear field. It also imports nuclear raw materials in order to satisfy the needs of its energy programme, and for this purpose follows the provisions of the EURATOM Treaty. Furthermore, Italy is an active partner in international nuclear co-operation.

Some general remarks are required before undertaking the study of the regulation of trade in nuclear material and equipment in Italy. First, the legislation applicable in this field stems essentially from two sources: Act No. 1860 of 31st December 1962 on the peaceful uses of nuclear energy (revised by Presidential Decree No. 519 of 10th May 1975) (*Act No. 1860*), this basic text being supplemented by the provisions of the Decree of the President of the Republic No. 185 of 13th February 1964 on the safety of nuclear installations and the protection of workers and the public against the hazards of ionizing radiation (amended and supplemented several times by implementing decrees) (*DPR No. 185*); this Decree is the fundamental text for everything involving in particular radiation protection and nuclear safety.

Another characteristic of the Italian regulations on nuclear trade lies in the close interaction between the relevant Community legislation (the Treaty establishing the European Atomic Energy Community — EURATOM, and its implementing regulations and directives) and the provisions of domestic law (the EURATOM Treaty was brought into force in Italy by Act No. 1203 of 14th October 1957).

In Italy, responsibility for the technical development and control of nuclear activities is largely concentrated in a body governed by public law, the National Commission for Research and Development of Nuclear and Alternative Energy Sources (*Comitato Nazionale per la Ricerca e per lo Sviluppo dell'Energia Nucleare e delle Energie Alternative — ENEA*)[1]. This body has extensive responsibilities with regard to controls over nuclear raw materials, physical protection and the implementation of safeguards. In practice, responsibilities are divided, tasks of a regulatory and administrative nature in the field covered by this study being entrusted principally to the *Ministry of Industry, Commerce and Crafts*, while those of a technical nature are performed by the ENEA.

The *Ministries for Foreign Affairs, and Foreign Trade*, together with the Ministry of Industry, Commerce and Crafts are, in consultation with ENEA for technical questions, responsible for negotiating agreements relating to international trade in nuclear material and equipment and are, more particularly, the competent authorities with regard to the restrictions and controls resulting from such agreements. Although there is no legislation or declaration of general policy on the approach and objectives of the Italian Government with regard to the export of "sensitive" nuclear material and equipment, it should be noted that Italy has adhered to the Declaration of Common Policy adopted in November 1984 by the Member States of the European Atomic Energy Community (see Volume I of this study).

A special feature of the basic Italian legislation (Act No. 1860 and DPR No. 185) is that the licensing and control of the use of, trade in and import and export of nuclear raw materials (ores, source and fissile materials) and other radioactive materials (see the section on terminology below) are all dealt with together.

However, for ease of analysis and for purposes of harmonization with the plan followed in the other descriptions of national legislation in this volume, the rules relating to nuclear raw materials (which are "sensitive" from the viewpoint of the risk of the proliferation of nuclear weapons) will be dealt with separately from those regarding radioactive materials, the regulation of which is essentially carried out with a view to ensuring radiation protection. In a separate section from those dealing with specifically nuclear regulations, a description will be given of provisions concerning the import and export of nuclear material and equipment in the framework of the general regulation of international trade. The competent regulatory authority in this field is the *Ministry for Foreign Trade*.

Furthermore, the rules concerning transport, physical protection and nuclear patents will be dealt with separately[2] as will the bilateral agreements concluded by Italy.

II. TRADE IN NUCLEAR MATERIAL

1. Terminology

One of the difficulties encountered in analysing Italian legislation on nuclear trade stems from the wide variety of terms used to describe the different sorts of nuclear material. Thus, Section 1 of Act No. 1860 refers directly to the definitions of special fissile materials, enriched uranium, source materials and ores contained in

Article 197 of the EURATOM Treaty[3]. However, this same Act and DPR No. 185 also refer in many provisions to (other) "radioactive materials" over and above the materials already mentioned, without giving any formal definition thereof. Furthermore, Section 5 of DPR No. 185 defines "radioactive substances" as all substances presenting the phenomenon of radioactivity, but this very broad term is not used in the context of the regime for licensing and controlling nuclear activities. It may be pointed out in passing that Act No. 1860 does contain a definition of "nuclear material", but one which refers exclusively to the provisions of the Act dealing with nuclear third party liability, and is therefore not applicable in the framework of this study.

For convenience, it is therefore proposed, in the rest of this study, to interpret the expression "radioactive materials" in such a way as to cover materials other than those expressly defined in the EURATOM Treaty, which latter are nuclear raw materials which may be used to produce energy[4].

2. Radioactive Ores (Special Provisions)

Section 2 of Act No. 1860 provides, in the light of the definition of ores in the EURATOM Treaty, that concessions for prospecting for and mining radioactive ores shall be regulated by the provisions of Royal Decree No. 1443 of 29th July 1927 on mines. Such concessions are awarded by the Minister of Industry, Commerce and Crafts (General Directorate for Mines, Section 2 of the Act), after consultation with the *Higher Council for Mines*. Members of the Council include a representative from ENEA.

In practice, deposits of uranium and thorium belong, in compliance with the 1927 Decree, to the State. It should be mentioned that there are special rules regulating the prospecting for and mining of ores in the Autonomous Region of Sicily (Act of 1st October 1956).

Subject to the prerogatives of the European Atomic Energy Community (see below), *trade* in radioactive ores requires the prior authorisation of the Minister of Industry, Commerce and Crafts (Act No. 1860, Section 4). The *import* and *export* of radioactive ores is subject to the prior authorisation of the Minister for Foreign Trade, granted with the approval of the Minister of Industry, Commerce and Crafts (Section 4 of Act No. 1860).

Lastly, the Act establishing ENEA provides that this body is responsible for applying safeguards within the meaning of EURATOM Regulation No. 3227/76 (Section 2 of the 1971 Act amended by the 1982 Act establishing ENEA and Section 3 of Act No. 1860) in respect of activities related to radioactives ores. Furthermore, DPR No. 185 (Chapter IV) lays down requirements for the radiation protection of persons employed in mines, which fall outside the scope of the present study.

Anyone who, without a licence, trades in the ores referred to in Article 197 of the EURATOM Treaty (see above), is punishable by criminal sanctions (Act No. 1860, as amended by Decree No. 1704 of 30th December 1965, Section 29).

Trading in radioactive ores is subject to the provisions of Chapter VI of DPR No. 185, supplemented by the provisions of the Ministerial Decree of 26th October 1966 and the Decree of 13th November 1964 creating a register of trading transactions, which deal with trade in ores, source materials and radioactive materials. Since the rules applicable to ores are not, on this point, different from those applying to the other categories of materials, they will be described in the following section.

3. Nuclear Material (Fissile and Source Materials)

Since the Italian regulations provide for separate provisions and procedures with regard to, on the one hand, the possession of, and on the other, trade in nuclear material (unless this involves commercial dealings only, without there being any possession of materials), this distinction will be reflected in the following description.

a) Possession

The basic principle, laid down by Act No. 1860 (Section 3, as amended by DPR No. 1704 of 30th December 1965), is that all persons who "possess special fissile materials or other source materials in any quantity", must *report* them within five days (*obbligo di denuncia*) to the Ministry of Industry, Commerce and Crafts. DPR No. 185 (Sections 30 and 31) specifies in addition that the possessor of such materials must comply with this formality and keep accounts of the materials in accordance with the regulations passed by the Ministry of Industry, Commerce and Crafts in consultation with ENEA and the Interministerial Council for Consultation and Co-ordination[5].

However, a possibility of *exemption* from the obligation to report such materials was introduced by Act No. 1008 of 19th December 1969 amending Act No. 1860[6]. Its single Section allows the Minister of Industry, Commerce and Crafts, in agreement with the Minister of Health and after consultation with the ENEA, to grant such exemptions, by way of decree, in the case of materials presenting a limited hazard only. A Ministerial Decree of 15th December 1970 (amended on 7th March 1973) gives the list and quantities of materials which are thus exempted from the declaration procedure[7] (see *Annex I* to this chapter).

A Decree of the Minister of Industry, Commerce and Crafts, dated *4th November 1982*, then defined the procedures relating to the declaration of possession and the keeping of accounts of special fissile materials, source materials and ores, and of registers. These requirements are based on the provisions of EURATOM Regulation No. 3227 of 19th October 1976 on safeguards.

Under this same Decree, those in possession of fissile materials and nuclear raw materials (source materials and ores), in whatever quantity and physical form, are obliged to notify them in accordance with the model annexed to the Decree (Section 1). Declarations must be sent, within five days of entering into possession, to the Ministry's General Directorate for Energy Sources and Basic Industries; a copy of each declaration must also be sent to ENEA (Directorate for Nuclear Safety and Health Protection) which is responsible for carrying out the necessary inspections and security controls with regard to these materials (Section 2; see also Section 3(2) of Act No. 1860). The model forms which must be filled in by those possessing such materials and sent to the competent authorities are reproduced in *Annex II* to this chapter.

Each declaration must be followed, within fifteen days after the end of the month in which possession of the materials was taken, by the sending of a form prepared on the basis of the model laid down in the above-mentioned EURATOM Regulation. Those in possession of materials must also supply information as to their type and chemical composition (Section 4).

Declarations must be updated annually at 31st December by persons in possession of materials, using forms indicating the situation of the materials at that date (physical inventory).

The above-mentioned Decree of 1982 also specifies (in Chapter III) the conditions applying to the keeping of records and accounts for materials, there being an obligation to keep such accounts constantly up to date and to include balance sheets of materials by area, with an indication of the source of supply.

Registers of materials must, in particular, include:

- physical inventories;
- accounting inventories;
- movements of materials on entry into and exit from each balance-sheet area;
- any differences between consignors and consignees;
- accounting corrections;
- the various origins of the loss and consumption of materials.

All the information relating to these declarations and accounting must be kept for five years by the person possessing the materials and made available on request to ENEA inspectors (Section 13 of the 1982 Decree; see also Section 13 of DPR No. 185 on the general powers of inspection enjoyed by ENEA).

The information which those in possession of materials are required to send to the Community authorities under the EURATOM Treaty (Chapter VII), must also be sent to ENEA.

Failure to declare materials or to comply with the provisions on registration is punishable by penal sanctions under Act No. 1860 (Section 28) and DPR No. 185 (Chapter XI).

b) Trade

Trade in fissile materials and raw materials (source materials and ores) is regulated in the first instance by the provisions of the EURATOM Treaty. It is also, in subsidiary fashion, covered by the same legislation as is applicable to the possession of such materials, namely Act No. 1860 and DPR No. 185. This explains why Act No. 1860 and DPR No. 185 (Section 4) do not expressly mention trade in "fissile materials". As a general rule, such trade is subject to control by the Minister of Industry, Commerce and Crafts.

In this connection, Italian legislation emphasizes the field of competence enjoyed by the Community and the pre-eminence of the EURATOM Treaty over domestic legislation, by providing (Section 4 of Act No. 1860) that trade in ores and source materials (and radioactive materials) is subject, when the European Atomic Energy Community has not exercised its right of option under Article 57 of the EURATOM Treaty and taking into account the Treaty's rules on the supply of fissile materials, to a *licence* from the Ministry of Industry, Commerce and Crafts. The Community prerogatives thus, in a way, take precedence over the jurisdiction of the Italian authorities. For its part, the State has a *right of option* over source materials. This right must be exercised within thirty days of the application for a licence (Section 4 of Act No. 1860).

The procedure itself is very simple since authorisation is deemed to have been granted thirty days after the lodging of the application if the competent Administration has raised no objections during this period.

As is the case for ores, a licence for the *import* and *export* of other nuclear raw materials, to the extent that such import and export are allowed under the economic and monetary regulations in force (see section IV, below), is granted by the Minister for Foreign Trade with the assent of the Ministry of Industry, Commerce and Crafts (Act No. 1860, Section 4).

DPR No. 185 (Chapter VI) also contains provisions relating to trade in ores, source materials and other radioactive materials. All persons engaging in trade in such materials (including radioactive materials) must keep a special register containing records of all commercial operations involving such materials and information concerning the contracting parties (Section 36). Commercial operations involving such materials are classified in two categories called A and B. *Category A* includes operations involving a limited hazard only, restricted to the immediate surroundings of the location in which the operations are carried out. This category covers radioactive substances in sealed containers, on condition that the activity level of these substances is inferior to limits laid down by Decree of the Minister of Industry, Commerce and Crafts, in agreement with the Ministers of the Interior, of Labour and Social Security, and of Health, on the advice of ENEA and the Interministerial Council for Consultation and Co-ordination[8]. All category A commercial operations, require a clearance certificate (*nulla osta* procedure) issued by the Prefect after consultation with the Provincial Medical Officer of Health (now the local health authorities) and the Provincial Labour Inspector, guaranteeing that the location and equipment involved are appropriate (Sections 32 and 33 of the said Decree).

Commercial operations in *category B* include those with materials involving a hazard for the neighbourhood populations beyond the site where they are performed. This category includes the storage of substances with an activity level equal to or higher than those in category A or in whatever quantity when the operation involves the handling and opening of transport containers. These operations require a certificate guaranteeing that the location chosen is appropriate and that the equipment used and the training of the staff are satisfactory. The clearance certificate is issued by the Minister of Industry, Commerce and Crafts, in agreement with the Ministers of the Interior, of Labour and Social Security, and of Health, after consultation with ENEA. The procedure for issuing the certificate as well as the formalities to be complied with by the applicant are laid down by Decree of the Minister of Industry, Commerce and Crafts, adopted in agreement with the Ministers mentioned above after consultation with ENEA and the Interministerial Council for Consultation and Co-ordination (Sections 34 and 35 of DPR 185). The relevant provisions are contained in a Ministerial Decree of 26th October 1966 which provides in particular that the Minister of Industry, Commerce and Crafts is responsible for verifying the correctness of the application and the accuracy of the information provided, and that it shall consult ENEA before forwarding the application to the other Ministries concerned. These latter have sixty days in which to give their opinion on whether the authorisation should be granted and whether it should be made subject to any conditions.

c) Exceptions to the general regime and sanctions

The Minister of Industry, Commerce and Crafts is empowered, in agreement with the Minister of Health and after consultation with ENEA, to determine exceptions to the declaration and licensing system provided for under Act No. 1860 for the possession, trade in and transport of small quantities of special fissile materials, raw materials and other radioactive materials, on condition that precautions are taken to protect workers and the public against the hazards of ionizing radiations (Act No. 1008 of 19th December 1969 and Ministerial Decree of 15th December 1970, Section 3 — see Annex I).

Any person engaging in trade in raw materials or other radioactive materials without the necessary licence is punishable by penal sanctions (Act No. 1860, Section 29 and DPR No. 185, Chapter XI).

III. TRADE IN RADIOACTIVE MATERIALS

Since certain of the provisions relevant here have already been analysed in the previous section, a brief mention only will be made of them whereas texts specifically relating to radioactive materials will be dealt with in greater detail.

1. Possession and Use

Without prejudice to provisions regulating trade properly so-called, Section 3 of Act No. 1860 requires all persons in possession of radioactive materials (other than fissile or raw materials) to declare them within five days when the quantities of the materials in question are such that their total radioactivity at the time the declaration is made exceeds the limits laid down by regulations in pursuance of Sections 30 and 31 of DPR No. 185. *The declaration procedure* and obligations connected therewith are the same as for "nuclear material".

A Decree by the Minister of Industry, Commerce and Crafts, dated 27th July 1966 and published on 14th November 1966 (not to be confused with the Ministerial Decree also dated 27th July 1966 dealing with transport), provides in this respect that persons in possession of natural or artificial radioactive materials in whatever form and whether or not they are contained in an apparatus or other product, are obliged to make a declaration when the the total radioactivity level of these materials exceeds the values laid down by this same Decree (one-tenth of a millicurie for the most toxic radionuclides).

These values, based on Community Directives on radiation protection, were modified by a Ministerial Decree of 19th July 1967.

Under the Decree of 27th July 1966, the declaration of possession must be sent within five days of receiving the materials to the General Directorate of Energy Sources and Basic Industries of the Ministry of Industry,

Commerce and Crafts, and contain, in particular, information as to the identity of the person in possession and the supplier, the place where the materials are held, their physical and chemical specifications, and the mode of transport used. A copy of this declaration is also sent to ENEA. Those in possession of radioactive materials must update their inventory every year (Section 9). The Decree of 27th July 1966 was amended by a Decree of the Minister of Industy, Commerce and Crafts dated 25th September 1982 as regards the special forms to be filled in for the declaration of possession of other radioactive materials (Sections 5 and 9, and Annexes).

Section 6 specifies that in addition to the mandatory declaration, *accounts* must be kept of these same materials in accordance with conditions laid down by the Minister of Industry, Commerce and Crafts, in consultation with ENEA and the Interministerial Council for Consultation and Co-ordination. This second obligation applies when the total radioactivity of the materials in question exceeds the limits laid down in the Decree. A special register must be kept for this purpose.

In addition, all persons in possession of natural or artificial radioactive substances, in whatever form, apparatus containing such substances or apparatus emitting ionizing radiation, whether fixed or mobile, must report the fact to the Provincial Public Health Officer within ten days and, where appropriate, to the Labour Inspectorate or port authorities, indicating the protection measures adopted. The person in possession of these substances or apparatus must, in addition, obtain an *approval certificate* from the Provincial Public Health Officer, issued after consultation with the Provincial Commission responsible for protecting the public against the hazards of ionizing radiation (Sections 92 and 93 of DPR No. 185).

The use in industry of radioisotopes whose total radioactivity or weight is equal to or exceeds the limits determined by the Ministerial Decree of 27th July 1966, amended by the Ministerial Decree of 19th July 1967 pursuant to Section 30 of DPR No. 185, is subject to a joint licence from the Minister of Industry, Commerce and Crafts and the Minister responsible for Labour and Social Security, after hearing the opinion of ENEA. The conditions for granting a licence, the information which the applicant must provide and the procedure for delivering the licence are specified in a Ministerial Decree of 1st March 1974. The licence is delivered by the Minister of Industry, Commerce and Crafts in agreement with the Ministers responsible for Agriculture and Forests, National Education, and Health, respectively, depending on whether the radioisotopes are intended for use in agriculture, education or diagnosis and therapy.

A Ministerial licence is required when the total activity level of the radioisotopes exceeds the values laid down for each group of radionuclides listed in the Annex to the Decree of 19th July 1967 amending the Decree of 27th July 1966 (Section 13 of the 1860 Act as amended by Decree No. 1704 of 30th December 1965). A licence to use sealed and unsealed sources is required when the radioactivity of the materials in question exceeds the levels laid down by this same Decree.

An approval certificate relating to health protection is required from the Prefect, on the recommendation of the Provincial Public Health Officer, the Regional Labour Inspectorate and, where appropriate, the Provincial Agricultural Inspectorate, Provincial Veterinary Service or the port authorities for institutes, laboratories, establishments or clinics in which industrial or scientific research activities are carried out, including activities for medical purposes, involving the use of natural or artificial radioactive substances, apparatus containing such substances, or producing ionizing radiation (Section 102 of DPR No. 185).

2. Trade

The basic principle is that trade in radioactive materials requires the *prior authorisation* of the Minister of Industry, Commerce and Crafts (Section 4 of Act No. 1860). The rules for exemption from the licensing procedure laid down in Act No. 1008 of 31st December 1969 apply also to radioactive materials (see the Ministerial Decree of 15th December 1970, amended on 7th March 1973).

The *import* and *export* of such materials also require a licence issued by the Minister for Foreign Trade with the approval of the Minister of Industry, Commerce and Crafts (Section 4).

The provisions of DPR No. 185 dividing trading activities involving radioactive materials into two categories — A and B — are the same as those, described above, applicable to ores and source materials. The procedure for obtaining the clearance certificate (*nulla osta*) is laid down in the above-mentioned Ministerial Decree of 26th October 1966.

3. Exemptions, Prohibitions and Sanctions

Section 1 of DPR No. 185 specified that its technical scope was to be defined in a Decree of the President of the Republic, adopted after consultation with the various competent Ministries, ENEA and the Interministerial Council for Consultation and Co-ordination; this was done by DPR No. 1303 of 5th December 1969 which specifies, for each group of radionuclides, the total radioactivity level above which the radionuclides fall within the scope of DPR No. 185.

DPR No. 1303 provides, on the other hand, that activities involving the use of certain radionuclides such as neodimium 144, samarium 147, rubidium 87, indium 115, renium 187 and natural potassium and its compounds are excluded from the scope of DPR No. 185 (Section 6).

A Decree of the Minister of Health, adopted on 14th July 1970 pursuant to Section 110 (exemptions) of DPR No. 185, provides for exemptions from the declaration obligations — or from the prohibitions — laid down by this Decree.

University institutes and other scientific institutes governed by public law which use radioisotopes exclusively for purposes of scientific research are exempt from the licence required for the use of radioisotopes (Act No. 1860, Section 13).

The production, import, sale, use or possession in whatever form, of products intended for health or cosmetic purposes, luminous signs, watch faces, paint or other luminous objects, or toys, which emit ionizing radiation are prohibited. It is also prohibited to use radioactive substances in the manufacture of such products and articles. Exceptions to this prohibition must be authorised by the Minister of Health (Section 91 of DPR No. 185), without prejudice to the exemptions laid down in Section 110 of DPR No. 185.

It is prohibited to subject persons to fluoroscopic observation or X-ray examination except for medical or scientific purposes. It is also prohibited to manufacture, import, distribute, lend or use television equipment or cathode-ray tubes which emit ionizing radiation in excess of the authorised limits (Sections 91 and 110 of DPR No. 185).

Both Act No. 1860 (Section 29, as amended by DPR No. 1704 of 30th December 1965) and DPR No. 185 (Chapter XI) provide for sanctions to punish persons engaging in trade in radioactive materials without a licence[9].

IV. GENERAL REGIME FOR THE IMPORT AND EXPORT OF NUCLEAR MATERIAL AND EQUIPMENT

This section deals with the provisions of the general law on international trade, insofar as they apply to the import and export of nuclear material and equipment.

In addition to the provisions of Act No. 1860 governing the import and export of ores, source materials and radioactive materials, the Minister for Foreign Trade has, together with the Minister of Finance, published various regulations dealing with the *export* of goods.

These measures were taken in pursuance of the Royal Decree of 16th January 1946, which gives the Minister for Foreign Trade certain powers with regard to the control and co-ordination of imports and exports, in liaison with the other ministerial departments concerned.

The basic text in this field is a Decree of 10th January 1975 grouping together the provisions applicable to goods the export of which is subject to a special licensing regime. The list of goods in question is reviewed periodically. An important review was effected by the Ministerial Decree of 27th May 1983 (Supplement to the Official Journal of 1st July 1983), followed by partial amendments (Decree of 22nd June 1984, corrected on 15th November 1984, Decree of 15th August 1985, Decree of 12th February 1986 and Decree of 24th December 1987). Extracts from the sections dealing with nuclear material and equipment are reproduced in *Annex III* to this chapter.

Appendix 1 to the Decree of 27th May 1983 contains a list of those goods (not marked with an asterisk) for which an export licence is left to the discretion of the competent Minister (the Minister for Foreign Affairs), and those (marked with one or several asterisks) for which a licence is either granted automatically or left to the discretion of the competent Minister depending on the country of destination (Common Market countries, for example).

Attention should also be drawn to the Decree on the procedure for importing goods into Italy of the Minister for Foreign Trade, adopted jointly with the Minister of Finance on 6th May 1976 (Supplement to the Official Journal of 16th June 1976) and amended on several occasions since. This Decree, which is of general scope, provides that the import of goods is unrestricted with the exception of those listed in Annex I thereof. The import of the different items listed in Annex I (and marked with the letter A) requires a special licence from the Minister for Foreign Trade, issued according to the country of origin (Appendix 1 to the Decree). It should be noted that these restrictions and imports are dictated by purely economic considerations.

As regards nuclear items, Annex I of the Decree of 6th May 1976 concerns, in particular, chemical and isotopic fissile elements; other radioactive chemical elements; their inorganic or organic compounds with a defined or undefined chemical composition; alloys or cermets containing those elements or isotopes or their inorganic or organic compounds: under customs tariff number 28.50: restrictions on importation from area B (socialist countries). Motor vehicles especially constructed for the transport of highly radioactive products are also included (customs tariff number 87.02).

Further, in compliance with the provisions of the EURATOM Treaty, a *declaration* with regard to the *import* of certain radioactive ores, radioactive chemical elements, radioisotopes, etc. must be made to the Minister of Industry, Commerce and Crafts (Finance Ministry Circular of 11th January 1960).

Moreover, import duty has been suspended on nuclear reactors, materials (especially nuclear fuels, moderators and coolants), apparatus, equipment and items designed for the construction and operation of nuclear reactors, which cannot be supplied by domestic firms and which are necessary for research and experimentation purposes or for the production of energy and fissile materials (Decree of the Minister of Finance of 13th December 1957).

V. TRANSPORT[10]

The general principle laid down by Act No. 1860 (Section 5 amended by Section 2 of DPR No. 1704 of 30th December 1965) is that the transport of special fissile materials or radioactive materials, when these latter exceed the limits laid down by the relevant regulations, is subject to prior authorisation and may be carried out only by transport firms duly authorised by Decree of the Minister of Industry, Commerce and Crafts, adopted in agreement with the Ministers responsible for Transport, Civil Aviation and the Merchant Navy.

Also in accordance with the above-mentioned Section 5 as amended, special transport operations of fissile materials exceeding the levels of radioactivity fixed by Decree No. 15 of 15th December 1970 or radioactive materials exceeding the levels of radioactivity laid down in the Decree of 27th July 1966[11] (amended on 19th July 1967), must be carried out by land, sea or air transport firms, licensed by Decree of the Minister of Industry, Commerce and Crafts, in agreement with the Minister concerned. Transport operations involving materials whose radioactivity is below the levels referred to above may be exempt from the licensing obligation; special notification must, however, be sent in advance by the carrier to the Prefect and the competent medical authorities in the regions of origin and destination respectively (see Section 5 of Act No. 1860).

Pending the planned adoption of safety and radiation protection regulations for nuclear transports — as provided by Section 5 as amended of the 1962 Act — such transports must be carried out in compliance with the relevant standards of DPR No. 185 of 1964.

Various Ministerial circulars determine standards of protection which must be complied with, conditions for approving containers and other technical specifications.

VI. PHYSICAL PROTECTION AND SAFEGUARDS

In order to implement the International Atomic Energy Agency recommendations on the physical protection of nuclear material (INFCIRC 225/Rev. 1), the Minister of Industry, Commerce and Crafts issued, on 19th April 1979, a Decree setting up within the Ministry an Interministerial Advisory Committee for the physical protection of nuclear material and installations. This body is responsible for establishing the criteria necessary for the adoption of physical protection measures, for examining the protection measures taken for the installations concerned and for determining and adopting the corresponding requirements. At present, Italy has no regulations dealing specifically with the physical protection of nuclear material; the appropriate instructions are given directly to the operator by the Minister of Industry, Commerce and Crafts, independently of the operating licence.

It may, however, be noted that ENEA is responsible for supervising the application of passive physical protection measures with respect to installations and nuclear material (Section 2 of the 1971 Act, as amended).

From the safeguards' viewpoint, ENEA has the task of checking inventories of fissile materials, source materials and ores. More generally, it ensures compliance with the international safeguards agreements signed by Italy and applying to such materials.

ENEA inspectors enjoy wide powers of verification for this purpose (DPR No. 185, Section 13).

VII. INTELLECTUAL PROPERTY IN THE NUCLEAR FIELD

Without prejudice to the application of the Community rules on the dissemination of information, the general rules on patents for invention and industrial designs in Italy are contained in a Decree of 29th June 1939 and in the provisions of the international Conventions on the protection of industrial property rights, incorporated into domestic legislation.

The Central Patents Office of the Ministry of Industry, Commerce and Crafts is responsible for carrying out the formalities provided for under Article 16 of the EURATOM Treaty (routine notification). To determine whether a patent application relates to a specifically nuclear object or is directly linked to the development of nuclear energy, the Central Patents Office may call upon experts from ENEA, a list of whom is drawn up by ENEA and approved by the Minister of Industry, Commerce and Crafts (Act No. 1860, Section 15).

The Central Patents Office must forward to ENEA all applications for patents for inventions or industrial designs acknowledged to be of a specifically nuclear nature or directly related and essential to the development of nuclear energy (Section 26).

The Minister of Industry, Commerce and Crafts may, if it is in the public interest, issue non-exclusive licences to ENEA for the use of patents for invention or usable designs (*modelli di utilità*). Non-exclusive licences may also be issued by the Minister, after consultation with ENEA, to a user of nuclear installations when they are essential to the development of nuclear energy in Italy. Any indemnity owing to the owner of the patent must then be determined by decree, account, however, being taken of any public funding of the research which led to the invention patented. In the event of a dispute relating to this indemnity, the person concerned may refer the matter to the courts (Section 27).

So far, Section 27 has not given rise to any concrete implementing measures, and the powers given under this Section to the Minister of Industry, Commerce and Crafts have not been used.

VIII. AGREEMENTS

1. Multilateral Agreements

As regards non-proliferation, Italy which, as stated above, is bound by the EURATOM Treaty obligations relating to safeguards, ratified the Treaty on the Non-Proliferation of Nuclear Weapons on 2nd May 1975[12].

Italy is also a Party to the Agreement of 5th April 1973 between EURATOM, IAEA and the Community Member States Party to the Treaty on the Non-Proliferation of Nuclear Weapons (so-called Verification Agreement).

As concerns physical protection, Italy has signed (as a Member State of EURATOM) but not yet ratified the Convention on the Physical Protection of Nuclear Material; an Act of 7th August 1982 has nevertheless been published, approving this ratification.

2. Bilateral Agreements

Italy has concluded a large number of bilateral agreements which cover, in broad terms, scientific, technical and economic co-operation in the nuclear field. Furthermore, industrial and scientific relations have been forged with many countries with a view to concluding contracts for the supply of installations and services in the nuclear field.

This section includes only those agreements which, directly or indirectly, generally or specifically, deal with nuclear trade.

a) Framework agreements for nuclear co-operation

Framework agreements for co-operation are concluded either by the Italian Government with the other government concerned, or by ENEA with the corresponding foreign body. The Ministry for Foreign Affairs is responsible for these agreements which are submitted to Parliament for ratification if they have financial implications. Administration of the agreements is entrusted to ENEA. Most such agreements are of unlimited duration or are renewed automatically.

- Agreement concluded with ***Brazil*** on 6th September 1958 (peaceful uses of nuclear energy).
- Agreement concluded between ENEA and the Atomic Commission of ***Argentina***, 1985 (peaceful uses of nuclear energy).
- Agreement concluded between CNEN (ENEA) and the ***Yugoslav*** Atomic Energy Commission, on 7th November 1960 — amended and extended on 9th May 1962 and 13th November 1965 (studies on nuclear material and the production of nuclear energy).

— Agreeement concluded between CNEN (ENEA) and the ***Greek*** Atomic Energy Commission, on 21st September 1961 (studies on nuclear material and the production of nuclear energy).

— Agreement concluded between CNEN (ENEA) and the ***Spanish*** Junta de Energia Nuclear on 25th June 1965 (peaceful uses of nuclear energy).

— Agreement concluded between CNEN (ENEA) and the ***USSR*** State Committee for the Use of Atomic Energy, on 22nd October 1965 (peaceful uses of nuclear energy).

— Agreement concluded between CNEN (ENEA) and the Atomic Energy Commission of ***Pakistan***, on 24th September 1966 (peaceful uses of nuclear energy).

— Agreement concluded between CNEN (ENEA) and the Atomic Commission of ***Iraq*** in 1976 (peaceful uses of nuclear energy).

— Agreement concluded with ***Indonesia*** on 17th March 1980 (framework agreement renewing a previous agreement of 1977).

— Co-operation agreements with ***Canada***, of 1965 (research and development) and 1977 (nuclear safety).

— Agreement concluded between ENEA and the ***Indian*** Atomic Commission in 1977 (peaceful uses of nuclear energy).

— Agreement concluded between ENEA and the Atomic Commission of the ***People's Republic of China*** in 1980 (peaceful uses of nuclear energy).

Furthermore, a series of agreements concerning more particularly nuclear safety have been concluded with the following countries: ***Poland*** (1963), ***USSR*** (1965), ***Israel*** (1972), ***United States*** (1975), ***Hungary*** (1976), ***France*** (1978), ***United Kingdom*** (1980), and ***Spain*** (1982).

Lastly, other co-operation agreements relating to the use of nuclear energy for peaceful purposes have been concluded with ***Bulgaria***, ***Columbia***, ***Egypt***, ***Romania*** and ***Zaire***, respectively.

As regards bilateral co-operation, several contracts dealing with the supply of equipment, installations and research laboratories have meant that Italy has had to conclude inter-governmental agreements in order to fulfil its non-proliferation commitments (Brazil, China, Indonesia, Iraq).

b) Industrial co-operation and supply agreements[13]

— Agreement concluded between CNEN (ENEA) and the ***Argentinian*** Atomic Energy Commission, on 11th February 1965 (supply of ores, radioisotopes and nuclear equipment).

— Memorandum of Understanding concluded on 10th January 1984 between the ***Federal Republic of Germany, Belgium, France, Italy*** and the ***United Kingdom*** relating to co-operation in the field of liquid metal fast breeder reactors.

NOTES AND REFERENCES

1. Act No. 1240 of 15th December 1971 amended by Act No. 84 of 5th March 1982, restructuring the National Committee for Nuclear Energy (CNEN), set up originally by Act No. 933 of 11th August 1960. (For further details, see *Regulatory and Institutional Framework for Nuclear Activities*, Vol. I, OECD/NEA, 1983.)
2. The licensing regime for nuclear installations falls outside the scope of this study and will not therefore be included. For further details, see *Licensing Systems and Inspection of Nuclear Installations*, OECD/NEA, 1986.
3. The definitions of these materials are as follows:
   - "Special fissile materials" means plutonium 239; uranium 233; uranium enriched in uranium 235 or uranium 233; and any substance containing one or more of the foregoing isotopes and such other fissile materials as may be specified by the Council, acting by a qualified majority on a proposal from the Commission; the expression "special fissile materials" does not, however, include source materials.
   - "Uranium enriched in uranium 235 or uranium 233" means uranium containing uranium 235 or uranium 233 or both in an amount such that the abundance ratio of the sum of these isotopes to isotope 238 is greater than the ratio of isotope 235 to isotope 238 occurring in nature.
   - "Source materials" means uranium containing the mixture of isotopes occurring in nature; uranium whose content in uranium 235 is less than the normal; thorium; any of the foregoing in the form of metal, alloy, chemical compound or concentrate; any other substance containing one or more of the foregoing in such a concentration as shall be specified by the Council, acting by a qualified majority on a proposal from the Commission.
   - "Ores" means any ore containing, in such average concentration as shall be specified by the Council acting by a qualified majority on a proposal from the Commission, substances from which the source materials defined above may be obtained by the appropriate chemical and physical processing.
4. It should also be noted that Act No. 1008 of 19th December 1969, amending Act No. 1860, specifies that the term "raw materials" means source materials and ores as defined in Article 197 of the EURATOM Treaty.
5. This Council was set up by DPR No. 185 within the Ministry of Industry, Commerce and Crafts. Composed of representatives from the different ministries concerned and from ENEA, it is competent with respect to all regulatory questions relating to nuclear safety and radiation protection.
6. *Single Section*: "By Decree of the Minister of Industry, Commerce and Crafts, in agreement with the Minister of Health, after consultation with the National Committee for Nuclear Energy (now ENEA), exemptions from declarations and authorisations prescribed by Act No. 1860 of 31st December 1962 may be allowed in respect of the possession of, trade in, and transport of small quantities of special fissile materials, raw materials and other radioactive materials, subject to precautions being taken for the protection of workers and the population at large against the dangers of ionizing radiation resulting from the peaceful uses of nuclear energy.
   Raw materials means source materials and ores as defined in Article 197 of the Treaty establishing the European Atomic Energy Community, approved by Act No. 1203 of 14th October 1957."
7. These provisions also cover trade in and the transport of such materials and of other radioactive materials.
8. A Ministerial Decree of 15th June 1966 lays down the levels of radioactivity for category A.
9. Section 29 of Act No. 1860 relating to penal provisions was declared unconstitutional by a judgment of the Constitutional Court dated 27th November 1974 (No. 665).
10. For further details, see *Regulations Governing the Transport of Radioactive Materials*, OECD/NEA, 1980.
11. Published on 14th October 1966 — not to be confused with the Ministerial Decree of the same date dealing with the possession of radioactive materials.
12. Italy has also adhered to the London Club Guidelines (INFCIRC/254, IAEA, 1978).
13. Italy is directly concerned by the agreements for peaceful co-operation and the supply of nuclear material concluded between EURATOM and the United States, Canada and Australia respectively; in particular, the agreements concluded with the United States on 28th July 1955 and 3rd July 1957 have been replaced by the EURATOM/ United States Agreements. The same is true for the Agreement of 28th December 1957 with the United Kingdom.

*
**

Il regime giuridico dell'impiego pacifico dell'energia nucleare, Vol. I, Normativa nazionale, ENEA, Rome, June 1986.

Annex I

EXEMPTIONS PROVIDED FOR BY THE MINISTERIAL DECREE OF 15TH DECEMBER 1970 (AMENDED BY DECREE OF 7TH MARCH 1973) FROM THE NOTIFICATION AND LICENSING OBLIGATIONS PRESCRIBED BY ACT No. 1860 OF 31ST DECEMBER 1962, IN IMPLEMENTATION OF ACT No. 1008 OF 19TH DECEMBER 1969*

Section 1

In accordance with Section 3(2) of Act No. 1860 of 31st December 1962, the following are exempted from notification:

1) Substances in the form of metals, alloys, chemical compounds, chemical mixtures, solutions, or gases, in which the content of natural or depleted uranium or thorium is below a total weight of 10 kg, or in which the content of natural or depleted uranium or thorium does not exceed a total of 0.05 per cent even if the 10 kg total limit in weight indicated above is exceeded.
2) Rare earths, their compounds, mixtures, or by-products which do not contain more than a total content of 0.25 per cent natural uranium or thorium.
3) Ores which do not contain a total of more than 10 kg natural uranium or thorium.
4) Thorium contained in the following equipment:
   a) incandescent gas-mantles;
   b) vacuum lamps;
   c) welding electrodes;
   d) electric light bulbs, providing that each single bulb does not contain more than 50 mg thorium; and
   e) germicide lamps, artificial sun-lamps, outdoor lamps or lamps for industrial lighting provided that each single lamp does not contain more than 2 g thorium.
5) Natural or depleted uranium or thorium contained in the following:
   a) any products made of vitrified ceramics, if the enamelling does not contain more than 20 per cent in weight uranium or thorium;
   b) any vitreous products, vitreous enamelling, vitreous or porous varnish which do not contain more than 10 per cent in weight uranium or thorium.
6) Any product or part thereof containing an alloy or dispersion of tungsten-thorium, or magnesium-thorium provided that the thorium contained does not exceed 4 per cent of the total weight.
7) Natural or depleted uranium contained in counter-weights in aircraft, whether already installed, stored, or being mounted or dismantled.
8) Thorium contained in already manufactured optical lenses provided that each lens does not contain more than 30 per cent thorium in the total weight and that they are not modified by any manufacturing, setting or polishing process.
9) Thorium contained in any accessories for aeroplane engines which are manufactured with a nickel-thorium alloy in the form of finely subdivided bioxide and that the thorium contained does not exceed 4 per cent of the weight.

The present provisions do not affect the obligation to comply with the provisions of Decree No. 185 of the President of the Republic in particular those laid down by Sections 30 and 31.

Section 2

The exemption provided by Section 1 of the present Decree does not apply to the facilities or storage buildings in a plant as determined by Section 8 of Decree No. 185 of the President of the Republic, of 13th February 1964.

* Unofficial translation.

ITALY

Section 3

Trade in raw materials or minerals, the total content of which does not exceed 3 kg of natural or depleted uranium or thorium is exempted from the licensing requirement laid down by Section 4 of Act No. 1860 of 31st December 1962. A licence is necessary, however, when the total quantity of uranium or thorium traded in the solar year exceeds 10 kg.

Trade in radioactive materials is also exempted from licensing provided that their activity for each particular bill of sale is equal to or less than the limits laid down by Sections 2(a), (b), (c), (d), 3 and 4 of the Ministerial Decree of 27th July 1966 (Official Journal No. 285, 4th November 1966), amended by the Ministerial Decree of 19th July 1967 (Official Journal No. 20, 11th August 1967). A licence is necessary, however, when more than 100 single transactions have been effected per solar year.

The present provisions do not affect the obligation to comply with the provisions of Decree No. 185 of the President of the Republic, of 13th February 1964, in particular those prescribed by Section 36.

Section 4

The carriage of special fissile materials whose total weight does not exceed the limits laid down by Section 1 of Decree No. 185 of the President of the Republic, of 13th February 1964, namely 15 grammes, is not subject to the authorisation prescribed by Section 5 of Act No. 1860 of 31st December 1962 amended by Section 2 of Decree No. 1704 of the President of the Republic, of 30th December 1965.

Annex II

MINISTERIAL DECREE OF 4TH NOVEMBER 1982

Conditions for notifying the possession, bringing up to date and accounting of special fissile materials and raw materials (source materials and ores)

Appendices

DENUNZIA DI DETENZIONE DI MATERIE FISSILI SPECIALI E MATERIE PRIME FONTI

(Art. 3 della legge n° 1860 del 31 dicembre 1962 e Artt. 30 e 31 del D.P.R. n° 185 del 13 Febbraio 1964)

ABM (1)

D W

Nome o Ragione sociale e indirizzo del Detentore

Luogo di Detenzione

ESTREMI DEL PROVVEDIMENTO AUTORIZZATIVO (2)

☐ AUTORIZZAZIONE ☐ NULLA OSTA ☐ LICENZA DI ESERCIZIO

AMMINISTRAZIONE, ESTREMI DEL PROVVEDIMENTO E DATA DEL RILASCIO

Data di scadenza del Provvedimento G M A

SCOPO DELLA DETENZIONE (2)

☐ SC immagazzinamento
☐ EC arricchimento
☐ RR reattore di ricerca
☐ RE reattore di potenza
☐ AT altro: ....

☐ DC trattamento combustibili irraggiati
☐ TC trasformazioni chimico-fisiche
☐ FC fabbricazione elementi di combustibile
☐ CH lavori di ricerca

RISERVATO

matricola fornitore

matricola vettore

Nome o Ragione sociale e indirizzo del Fornitore

Nome o Ragione sociale e indirizzo del Vettore

TIPO E QUANTITA' DELLE MATERIE

DESCRIZIONE:

	(3) PARTITA PO	CC	ID	(4) F	(5) NC	(6) ST	(7) EL	(9) PESO ELEMENTO	(11) UM	(8) IS	(10) PESO ISOTOPI FISSILI	(11) UM	DATA DI ENTRATA IN POSSESSO G	M	A
1															
2															
3															
4															
5															
6															
7															
8															

OSSERVAZIONI:

Nominativo del Detentore responsabile

Firma ....

NOTE PER LA COMPILAZIONE DELLA SCHEDA PER LA DENUNZIA DI DETENZIONE DI MATERIE FISSILI SPECIALI E MATERIE PRIME FONTI.

(1) Corrisponde alla sezione (2) dell'Allegato II del Regolamento EURATOM. Codice EURATOM dell'area di bilancio materie (ABM) che è entrata in possesso delle materie.

(2) Barrare la casella che interessa.

(3) Corrisponde alla sezione (8) o (19) dell'Allegato II del Regolamento EURATOM. Indicare nei primi tre caratteri (PO) il numero della partita omogenea mediante la quale saranno contabilizzate le materie ricevute; nei seguenti due (CC) la composizione chimica delle materie usando uno dei codici della tabella dei codici della composizione chimica; gli ultimi tre caratteri (ID) possono essere utilizzati secondo proprie esigenze di gestione.

Da (4) a (8) Per la codifica di: Forma (F), Natura Contenitori (NC), Stato (ST), Elemento (EL), Isotopo (IS), attenersi a quanto previsto per tali informazioni nelle note esplicative dell'Allegato II del Regolamento EURATOM.

(9) Corrisponde alla sezione (12) dell'Allegato II del Regolamento EURATOM. Indicare il peso in grammi per il plutonio e l'uranio arricchito; in chilogrammi per il torio, l'uranio naturale e l'uranio impoverito. Indicare le cifre decimali come risultano dalle registrazioni contabili.

(10) Corrisponde alla sezione (15) dell'Allegato II del Regolamento EURATOM. Va registrato soltanto per l'uranio arricchito. Usare la stessa unità di misura del corrispondente peso dell'elemento.

(11) Come Unità di Misura (UM) utilizzare «G» per i grammi e «K» per i chilogrammi.

DETENZIONE DI MATERIE FISSILI SPECIALI E MATERIE PRIME FONTI

(Art. 3 della legge 31-12-1962 n. 1860)

ALLEGATO II -
Pagina n°

	ABM (2)			
1	2	3	4	5
I				

Impianto dichiarante
(1) ....

RAPPORTO SULLE VARIAZIONI D'INVENTARIO

Periodo di dichiarazione
dal .... al ....

Impianto corrispondente
(1) ....

	Data G | M | A (3)	PCM (4)	Misura (5)	Tipo di var. d'inv. (6)	ABM corrispondente (7)	Designazione della partita (8)	Numero d'articoli (9)	Descriz. delle materie (10)	Elemento (11)	Peso dell'elemento (12)	Unità (13)	Isotopo (14)	Peso degli isotopi fissili (15)	Unità (16)	Impegno (17)	Uso (18)	Informazione corrispondente (19)	Scrittura (20)	Correzione (21)	Data originale G | M | A (22)	
	6 7 8 9 10 11	12	13	14 15	16 17 18 19	20 21 22 23 24 25 26 27	28 29 30 31	32 33 34 35	36	37 38 39 40 41 42 43 44 45	46	47	48 49 50 51 52 53 54 55 56	57	58	59 60	61 62 63 64 65 66 67 68	73	74	75 76 77 78 79 80	
1																					
2																					
3																					
4																					
5																					
6																					
7																					
8																					
9																					
10																					
11																					
12																					

Osservazioni (25)

Luogo e data d'invio del rapporto ....

Nome e qualifica del firmatario responsabile ....

Firma ....

ALLEGATO III -
Pagina n°

AGGIORNAMENTO ANNUALE DELLE MATERIE FISSILI SPECIALI E MATERIE PRIME FONTI
(Art. 3 della legge 31-12-1962 n. 1860)

RAPPORTO SUL BILANCIO MATERIE

	ABM (4)				Data G | M | A (5)					
1	2	3	4	5	6	7	8	9	10	11
M										

(1) Impianto: ....

(2) Inizio del periodo considerato: ....

(3) Categoria: ....

	Inform. d'invent. (6)		Elemento (7)	Peso dell'elemento (8)	Unità (9)	Isotopo (10)	Peso degli isotopi fissili (11)	Unità (12)	Correzione (13)	Osservazioni (14)
	14	15	36	37 38 39 40 41 42 43 44 45	46	47	48 49 50 51 52 53 54 55 56	57	74	
1										
2										
3										
4										
5										
6										
7										
8										
9										
10										
11										
12										
13										
14										
15										
16										
17										
18										
19										
20										

Luogo e data d'invio del rapporto ....

Nome e qualifica del firmatario responsabile ....

Firma ....

	ABM (2)	Data G | M | A (3)
1	2 | 3 | 4 | 5	6 | 7 | 8 | 9 | 10 | 11
P		

AGGIORNAMENTO ANNUALE DELLE MATERIE FISSILI SPECIALI E MATERIE PRIME FONTI

(Art. 3 della legge 31-12-1962 n. 1860)

SITUAZIONE DELL'INVENTARIO FISICO

ALLEGATO IV

Pagina n° ...

(1) Impianto ....

	PCM (4)	Misura (5)	Designazione della partita (6)	Numero d'articoli (7)	Descriz. delle materie (8)	Elemento (9)	Peso dell'elemento (10)	Unità (11)	Isotopo (12)	Peso degli isotopi fissili (13)	Unità (14)	Impegno (15)	Uso (16)	Correzione (17)	Osservazioni (18)
	12	13	20 | 21 | 22 | 23 | 24 | 25 | 26 | 27	28 | 29 | 30 | 31	32 | 33 | 34 | 35	36	37 | 38 | 39 | 40 | 41 | 42 | 43 | 44 | 45	46	47	48 | 49 | 50 | 51 | 52 | 53 | 54 | 55 | 56	57	58	59 | 60	74	
1															
2															
3															
4															
5															
6															
7															
8															
9															
10															
11															
12															

Luogo e data d'invio del rapporto ....

Nome e qualifica del firmatario responsabile .... **Firma** ....

ADDENDUM
PER LA COMPILAZIONE DELL'ALLEGATO II E PER LA DESIGNAZIONE DELLA PARTITA OMOGENEA.

a) Sezione (1): nella parte in alto a sinistra del formulario il detentore dovrà indicare il proprio nome o ragione sociale. Nella parte in alto a destra sarà indicato l'impianto o il fornitore delle materie nucleari; nel caso in cui il formulario contenga piú denuncie di detenzione di materie nucleari provenienti da diversi impianti o fornitori, questi ultimi saranno indicati nella sezione (25) — OSSERVAZIONI — facendo riferimento al numero del rigo del formulario.

b) Sezione (2): codice Euratom dell'area di bilancio materie che è entrata in possesso delle materie nucleari.

c) Sezione (3): giorno (colonne 6, 7); mese (colonne 8, 9); anno (colonne 10, 11) in cui il detentore è entrato in possesso delle materie nucleari.

d) Sezione (4): punto chiave di misura relativo alla ricezione delle materie nucleari, cosí come definito nelle Disposizioni particolari sul controllo Euratom.

e) Sezioni (5), (6), (7); sezioni da (9) a (18) e da (20) a (22): dovranno essere usati i codici descritti nelle note esplicative del Regolamento EURATOM n. 3227/76 del 19 ottobre 1976, pubblicato sulla Gazzetta Ufficiale delle Comunità europee del 31 dicembre 1976.

f) Sezione (8): nel caso di ricezione di materie nucleari da un impianto o fornitore situato in uno Stato terzo, cioé un qualunque Stato che non sia membro della Comunità Europea per l'Energia Atomica — codice RF della sezione (6) — il detentore compilerà la sezione (8) nella maniera seguente: nelle colonne 20. 21, 22 indicherà il numero della partita omogenea mediante laquale saranno contabilizzate le materie nucleari ricevute; nelle colonne 23, 24 indicherà la composizione chimica delle materie nucleari usando uno dei codici della tabella allegata. Le colonne 25, 26, 27 della sezione (8) saranno utilizzate dal detentore secondo proprie esigenze di gestione.

g) Sezione (19): nel caso di ricezione di materie nucleari da un impianto o fornitore situato in uno Stato membro della Comunità Europea per l'Energia Atomica — codice RD della sezione (6) — il detentore, dopo aver compilato la sezione (8), usando la designazione della partita scelta dal mittente, dovrà compilare la sezione (19) nella maniera seguente: nelle colonne 61, 62, 63 indicherà il numero della partita omogenea mediante la quale contabilizzerà le materie nucleari ricevute: nelle colonne 64, 65 indicherà la composizione chimica usando uno dei codici della tabella allegata. Le colonne 66, 67, 68 saranno utilizzate dal detentore secondo proprie esigenze di gestione.

N.B. Il detentore dovrà compilare le sezioni (8) e (19) secondo quanto stabilito dalle Note esplicative contenute nel Regolamento EURATOM, nei casi in cui è necessario registrare una «informazione corrispondente» e cioé: cambiamento di categoria (codice CC), cambiamento di impegno particolare (codice CR), cambiamento di uso (codice CU), modifica della partita (codice RB); in quest'ultimo caso il detentore dovrà compilare la sezione (8) secondo quanto descritto alla nota f) di cui sopra.

TABELLA DEI CODICI DELLA COMPOSIZIONE CHIMICA

Acetato di uranile	UH
Diuranato di ammonio	UW
Carbonati di uranio	UZ
Carburo di uranio	UR
Cloruri di uranio	UE
Esafluoruro di uranio	F6
Joduro di uranio	UJ
Lega uranio-alluminio	UA
Lega uranio-molibdeno	UK
Leghe varie di uranio	UL
Nitrato di uranile	UN
Nitruro di uranio	UI
Ossidi di uranio: UO_2	U2
Ossidi di uranio: U_3O_8	U8
Ossidi di uranio: UO_3	U3
Ossidi di uranio: Ossidi vari di U	UX
Ossidi misti uranio-gadolinio	UG
Solfato di uranio	US
Tetrafluoruro di uranio	F4
Uranio metallico	UM
Sali vari di uranio	UQ
Biossido di torio	T2
Carburo di torio	TR
Lega magnesio-torio	TV
Leghe varie di torio	TL
Nitrato di torio	TN
Ossalato di torio	TO
Ossidi vari di torio	TX
Sali vari di torio	TQ
Tetracloruro e cloruri vari di torio	TE
Tetrafluoruro di torio	T4
Torio metallico	TM
Biossido di plutonio	P2
Carburo di plutonio	PR
Lega plutonio-alluminio	PA
Lega plutonio-berillio	PB
Leghe varie di plutonio	PL
Nitrato di plutonio	PN
Nitruro di plutonio	PI
Solfati misti	SM
Plutonio metallico	PM
Solfato di plutonio	PS
Sali vari di plutonio	PQ
Carburi misti	RM
Cloruri misti	EM
Leghe miste	LM
Nitrati misti	NM
Nitruri misti	IM
Ossalati misti	OM
Ossidi misti	XM
Solfati misti	SM
Composizioni chimiche varie di uranio	VU
Composizioni chimiche varie di plutonio	VP
Composizioni chimiche varie di torio	VT
Composizioni chimiche varie	CV

(5496)

Annex III

MINISTRY FOR FOREIGN TRADE

Ministerial Decree of 27th May 1983*

Export List — Specific Provisions relating to Exportation of Goods**

The Minister for Foreign Trade
together with
The Minister of Finance

Considering Decree No. 12 of 16th January 1946 on delegation of authority relating to the tasks of the Ministry for Foreign Trade;

Considering Decree-Law No. 476 of 6th June 1956 converted with amendments into Act No. 786 of 25th July 1956, relating to new currency regulations and the establishment of a free market in foreign and national currencies;

Considering the Ministerial Decree of 10th January 1975 (published in the Ordinary Supplement of Official Journal, No. 31 of 1st February 1975) concerning the Export List and its subsequent modifications);

Considering the Ministerial Decree of 30th November 1982 (published in Official Journal, No. 352 of 23rd December 1982) concerning exportation of certain metallurgical products to the United States of America;

decree that

Single Section

Appendices 1 and 2 of the Ministerial Decree of 10th January 1975 are replaced by Appendices 1 and 2 of this Decree.

The Ministerial Decree of 30th November 1982 (concerning exportation of certain metallurgical products to the United States of America) constitutes Appendix No. 3 to the Ministerial Decree mentioned in the preceding paragraph.

This Decree will take effect on the fifteenth day following the date of its publication in the Official Journal of the Republic of Italy.

....

* Amended as at 12th February 1986. The Decree of 24th December 1987 (published in the Official Journal of 2nd April 1988) simply reclassifying items has not been taken into account in this list.

** Unofficial translation.

ITALY

EXTRACTS FROM THE EXPORT LIST

List of Goods whose Exportation is Subject
to Ministerial Licence

NOTES

1. For goods without an asterisk, a licence may be granted at the discretion of the appropriate Ministry.

2. For goods with one asterisk, a licence will be granted either automatically or at ministerial discretion, according to the country of destination, as follows:

* "automatic licence", for all destinations;

** "automatic licence", for Common Market countries a) and DOM b); discretionary licence for other countries;

**** "automatic licence", for other countries; by customs for Common Market countries a), and DOM b);

**** "discretionary licence", for other countries; by customs for Common Market countries a), and DOM b).

a) Common Market countries: Belgium, Denmark, France, Federal Republic of Germany, Greece, Great Britain and Northern Ireland (including the Channel Islands and the Isle of Man), Ireland, Luxembourg, the Netherlands.

b) DOM = Overseas French Departments: Guadaloupe, Guiana, Martinique, Reunion.

. . . .

3. For the exportation of materials destined for the armament and equipment of armed forces, the licence mentioned in Section 28, paragraph 2 of the Public Security Law (approved by Royal Decree No. 773 of 18th June 1931) is also necessary.

Customs tariff number	Description of goods

Section V

Mineral Products

Chapter 26

Metallurgical minerals, slags and ashes

ex 26.01	Source materials, in any form or present in any substance where the source material concentration exceeds 0.05 per cent by weight, excluding consignments of source materials in which the uranium content is: 1. up to 10 kg for any application, or 2. up to 100 kg for civil non-nuclear applications.
****26.03 ex C	Slags and ashes of copper, and its alloys.

. . . .

Chapter 27

Mineral fuels, mineral oils and products from their distillation bituminous substances, mineral waxes

. . . .

II) Biological, chemical and radioactive substances suitable for producing destructive effects on the population, livestock and crops, in the event of war.

Customs tariff number	Description of goods

Chapter 28

Inorganic chemical products; inorganic or organic compounds of precious metals, of radioactive elements, of rare earth metals, and of isotopes

(see also Ch.29 II)

I) Inorganic compounds of tantalum and niobium as follows:
1. compounds of tantalum and niobium of purity 98 per cent or more;
2. other compounds containing 20 per cent or more tantalum in which the ratio niobium/tantalum is less than 1:1000.

II) Inorganic compounds of hafnium (cf. ex 81.04 III), beryllium (cf. ex 77.04) and zirconium (cf. ex 81.04 VIII).

III) Inorganic compounds:
1. monocrystals of gallium excluding gallium phosphide, gallium arsenide, gallium phosphide-arsenide, and gallium nitride having all the following characteristics:
   a) wafers treated by diffusion;
   b) enriched with selenium, tellurium, silicon, sulfur, tin, and zinc;
   c) dislocation density EPD superior to 10 000 per cm^3;
   d) carrier concentration superior to $1x10^{16}$ per cm^3;
   e) carrier mobility less than 2000 cm^2 per Volt sec.
2. monocrystals of indium in any form;
3. hetero-epitaxials composed of an insulating monocrystalline substratum covered in an epitaxial way with silicon, gallium compounds, and indium compounds;
4. tellurium compounds with cadmium-mercury in any form.

IV) Borides with more than 98.5 per cent purity and with a fusion point 2000 ^{o}C or more and their compounds in raw or semi-worked forms.

(see also Sect. XV I)

V) Lithium as follows:
a) alloys containing 50 per cent or more of lithium, normal or depleted in Li 6 isotope or containing any quantity of lithium 6 enriched lithium;
b) any other material containing lithium 6 enriched lithium, including compounds, mixtures and concentrates, excluding:
   I) the following consignments on condition that none of these contains lithium 6 enriched lithium:
      1. 1 kg or less of metal contained or not contained in an alloy;
      2. 10 kg or less of hydrides;
      3. 50 grams or less of lithium deuteride.
   II) lithium 6 enriched lithium contained in thermoluminescent dosimeters.

28.01 A	Fluorine, excluding consignments of 25 kg or less.
28.04 C V b c (see also ex 38.19 IX)	Monocrystalline silicon with one of the following characteristics: 1. containing bismuth, indium, gallium, selenium or thallium with an average concentration of carriers superior to $10^{16}/cm^3$; 2. containing arsenic with an average concentration of carriers superior to $10^{16}/cm^3$ and less than $10^{13}/cm^3$; 3. with type P conductivity and 5 000 ohm-cm resistivity or more; 4. ingots with a resistivity of 50 ohm-cm or less for all types N and for the type P 1-1-1, or 100 ohm-cm or less for the type P 1-0-0.
28.04 C V d	Boron in any form.
28.05 A III	Lithium metal.
ex 28.09	Red smoking nitric acid containing nitrogen dioxide in solution.
28.13 ex D	Nitrogen tetroxide

Customs tariff number		Description of goods
28.14 ex B		Trifluoride of chlorine, excluding consignments of 5 kg or less.
28.8 ex A		Hydrazine with 70 per cent concentration or more, hydrazine nitrate, hydrazine perchlorate.
28.39 B ex VI		Thorium nitrate with a concentration of source materials superior to 0.05 per cent by weight, excluding consignments of 1000 kg or less if intended for the production of gas-burner sleeves.

. . . .

ex 28.50	I)	Fissile isotopes (U-233, U-235 and Pu-238, Pu-239, Pu-241) including any combination containing one or more of the above isotopes, excepting: 1. consignments of 1 effective gram or less by weight; 2. consignments of 3 effective grams or less by weight if contained in a sensing component of equipment; 3. quantities that are contained in cardiac pacemakers.
ex 28.50	II)	Tritium, compounds and mixtures containing tritium in which the ratio of tritium/hydrogen is over 1:1000, and products containing one or more of the aforesaid substances, excluding: 1. consignments of tritium, compounds, mixtures and separate products containing one or more of the aforesaid substances so long as they do not exceed 100 curies; 2. tritium contained in luminescent paint, luminescent products, gas and aerosol detectors, electronic tubes, lightning or static electricity devices, ion generating tubes, or cells for gas chromatography, and calibration devices; 3. tritium compounds and mixtures the components of which, when separated, cannot lead to the development of an isotopic hydrogen mixture where the ratio of tritium to hydrogen is higher than 1:1000 in atoms.
ex 28.51 A (see also 38.19 VI)		Deuterium and compounds, mixtures and solutions containing deuterium, including heavy water and heavy paraffins, in which the ratio of deuterium to hydrogen atoms is more than 1:5000 in numbers, excluding consignments of the aforesaid products with a deuterium content of 10 kg or less.
ex 28.56 B		Boron carbide, excluding powder with a boron content 70 per cent or more by weight, and its raw or semi-worked products.
28.57 ex A	I)	Hydride of boron (for example boranes) excluding sodium boro-hydride, potassium boro-hydride, monoborane, diborane and triborane;
	II)	Hydrides in which lithium, normal or lithium 6 enriched, is mixed with hydrogen or its isotopes.
28.57 ex C	I)	Boron azide with a compact hexagonal structure and white form, and its compounds in raw or semi-worked forms; other compounds of boron-nitrogen (for example borazon, borazine or boro-pyrozolidine).
	II)	Lead nitrides.

. . . .

Chapter 29

Organic chemical products

I) Organic boron compounds, including the boron organic metallic compounds that are not specifically mentioned in this list.

II) Tantalum and niobium organic compounds as follows:

1. tantalates and niobates of 98 per cent purity or more;
2. other compounds that contain 20 per cent or more of tantalum in which the ratio of niobium to tantalum is less than 1:1000.

Customs tariff number	Description of goods

III) Organic hafnium compounds (cf. 81.04 III), beryllium (cf. 77.04), and zirconium (cf. 81.04 VIII).

IV) Organic compounds:

1. monocrystals of gallium excluding gallium phosphide, gallium arsenide, gallium phosphide-arsenide, and gallium nitride having the following characteristics:
   a) treated plaquettes by diffusion;
   b) mixed with selenium, tellurium, silicon, sulfur, tin, and zinc;
   c) dislocation density EPD superior to 10 000 per cm^3;
   d) carrier concentration superior to $1x10^{14}$ per cm^3;
   e) carrier mobility less than 2000 cm^2 per Volt sec.
2. monocrystals of indium in any form;
3. hetero-epitaxials composed of an insulating monocrystalline substratum covered in an epitaxial way with silicon, gallium compounds or indium compounds;
4. tellurium compounds and cadmium-mercury in any form.

(see also Ch.28 I) — V) Lithium as follows:

a) alloys containing 50 per cent or more of lithium, normal or lithium 6 depleted or containing any quantity of lithium 6 enriched lithium;

b) any other material containing lithium 6 enriched lithium, including compounds, mixtures and concentrates, excluding:

I) the following consignments on condition that none of these contains lithium 6 enriched lithium:
1. 1 kg or less of metal contained or not contained in an alloy;
2. 10 kg or less of hydrides;
3. 50 grams or less of lithium deuteride;

II) lithium 6 enriched lithium contained in thermoluminescent dosimeters.

....

Chapter 37

Products for photography and cinematography

I) Plates, films (including cinematographic films) that are punched or non-punched, produced, undeveloped and developed, negative or positive, containing detailed technical information (technology) concerning plants for uranium enrichment, for irradiated fuel reprocessing, for heavy water production and their main critical components, which can be used for manufacturing nuclear weapons and other nuclear explosive devices.

....

Chapter 38

Various products of chemical industries

Customs tariff number	Description of goods
38.01 ex A (see also 69.03 ex A)	I) Nuclear-grade graphite, i.e. with a purity level less than 5ppm boron equivalent and density greater than 1.5 gr/cm^3, excluding separate consignments of 100 kg or less.
	II) Artificial graphite, with apparent density 1.90 or more compared to water at +15.5 ^oC.
ex 38.19	I) Chemical products and preparations containing 5 per cent or more of free or combined boron (excluding pharmaceutical specialities prepared for retail) specified in Chapter 28 IV and VV.DD.28.56 B, 28.57 ex A-I and 28.57 ex C-I.

....

Customs tariff number	Description of goods
	IV) Mixtures, compounds and concentrates that contain lithium 6 enriched lithium, excluding: *a)* the following consignments on condition that none of these contains lithium 6 enriched lithium: 1. 1 kg or less of metal contained or not contained in an alloy; 2. 10 kg or less of hydrides; 3. 50 grams or less of lithium deuteride; *b)* lithium 6 enriched lithium contained in thermoluminescent dosimeters.
	....
(see also ex 28.51 A)	VI) Deuterium and compounds, mixtures and solutions containing deuterium, including heavy water and heavy paraffins, in which the ratio of deuterium to hydrogen atoms is more than 1:5000 in numbers, excluding consigments of the aforesaid products with a deuterium content of 10 kg or less.
	....

Chapter 49

Printed matter and graphics

ex 49.01 B	Pamphlets and similar printed matter, even in single sheets, containing detailed technical information (technology) on plants for uranium enrichment, for irradiated fuel reprocessing, for heavy water production, and their main critical components that can be used for making nuclear weapons and other nuclear explosive devices, excluding published literature.
	....

Section XV

Base Metals and Their Products

(see also Ch.28 V)	I) Alloys containing 50 per cent or more of normal lithium, natural or lithium 6 depleted, or containing any quantity of lithium 6 enriched lithium. II) Alloys containing more than 60 per cent by weight of hafnium, excluding consignments of alloys with contained hafnium equal to 1 kg or less.
	....

Chapter 75

Nickel

	I) Nickel, porous metal with an average pore size of up to 25 micrometres and a nickel content of at least 99 per cent, excluding separate porous metal nickel plates of not more than 930 cm^2 to be used in batteries for civil applications.

Customs tariff number	Description of goods
	II) Nickel alloys containing a higher percentage of nickel by weight than any other element, as follows: 1. whose combined aluminium and titanium content is more than 11 per cent, or 2. reinforced by dispersion containing more than 1 per cent thorium, aluminium, yttrium, zirconium, cerium, or lanthanum oxydes, or 3. containing 0.05 per cent or more of scandium, yttrium, didymium, cerium, lanthanum, neodymium, or praseodymium.
****ex 75.01	Raw nickel (excluding the anodes mentioned in 75.05); wastes and nickel scraps.
ex 75.02	Nickel bars capable of producing energy: *a)* greater than $10x10^6$ gauss-oersteds, or; *b)* greater than $4.85x10^6$ gauss-oersteds or more and having a coercitive force equal to 1800 gauss-oersteds or more.
75.03 ex B	Nickel powder with a quantity of nickel equal to 99 per cent or more and a particle size less than 100 micrometres.

. . . .

Chapter 77

Magnesium, beryllium, (glucine)

Customs tariff number	Description of goods
ex 77.04 (see also Ch.28 II and 29 III)	Beryllium (glucine) as follows: metal, alloys containing more than 50 per cent of beryllium by weight, compounds containing beryllium and their products excluding: 1. metal windows for X-ray equipment; 2. finished or semi-worked devices of oxide that are built for parts of electronic components or as supports for electronic circuits; 3. shipped quantities of 500 grams or less of beryllium with purity equal to at least 99 per cent, or equal to at least 100 grams of beryllium with more than 99 per cent purity, on condition that the shipped quantities do not contain monocrystals; 4. shipped quantities of 5 kg or less of beryllium contained in compounds with less than 99 per cent purity.

. . . .

Chapter 81

Other base metals

Customs tariff number	Description of goods
ex 81.02	Molybdenum alloys containing 97.5 per cent or more of molybdenum, excluding wires.
ex 81.03	Tantalum and alloys of tantalum as follows: 1. tantalum powder containing less than 200 ppm of total metallic impurities and anodes made of this powder; 2. tantalum alloys containing 60 per cent or more tantalum and scraps of these alloys.
ex 81.04 C	I) Cobalt alloys (i.e. alloys containing a greater percentage of cobalt by weight than any other element), as follows: 1. containing 5 per cent or more tantalum, or 2. reinforced by dispersion containing more than 1 per cent thorium, aluminium, yttrium, zirconium or cerium oxydes; 3. containing 0.05 per cent or more of scandium, yttrium, didymium, cerium, lanthanum, neodymium or praseodymium.

Customs tariff number	Description of goods

II) Magnetic alloys of cobalt having one of the following characteristics:

1. initial permeability 120 000 gauss-oersteds (0.15 Henry/m) or more, and 0.0 or equivalent magnetic field;
2. 98.5 per cent of maximum remanence or more for materials with magnetic permeability;
3. capability of producing energy greater than 10×10^6 gauss-oersteds, or 4.85×10^6 gauss-oersteds or more and having coercitive force equal to 1800 oersteds (143 200 ampere/m) or more.

ex 81.04 F (see Ch.28 II, Ch.28 III)

III) Hafnium as follows: metal, alloys and compounds containing more than 60 per cent of hafnium by weight, and their products, excluding consignments of the aforesaid products not containing more than 1 kg of hafnium.

ex 81.04 H

IV) Niobium alloys containing 60 per cent or more niobium or niobium-tantalum; their scraps.

ex 81.04 K

V) Titanium alloys in raw, semi-worked form, and scraps having the following nominal compositions:

a) 6 per cent aluminium, 2 per cent tin, 4 per cent zirconium, 6 per cent molybdenum and the remainder titanium;
b) 12 per cent or more aluminium by weight.

ex 81.04 M

VI) Depleted uranium, excluding that especially made for the following civil applications:

1. safety shields;
2. packaging;
3. ballast;
4. counterweights.

ex 81.04 N

VII) Thorium alloys containing more than 5 per cent thorium by weight.

ex 81.04 O (see Ch.28 II, Ch.29 III)

VIII) Zirconium metal; alloys containing over 50 per cent zirconium by weight; compounds in which the ratio of hafnium/zirconium is less than 1:500 by weight, and products that are entirely made of these elements, excluding:

a) zirconium metal and alloys of zirconium in consignments of up to 5 kg;
b) sheets or plates of zirconium with a maximum thickness equal to 0.025 mm (0.00095 inch) for use in photographic flash bulbs and designated for such use in consignments of up to 200 kg.

....

Section XVI

Machinery and Equipment; Electrical Equipment

....

III) A) Complete systems, especially designed or prepared for the conversion of plutonium nitrate to plutonium oxide, adapted in particular so to avoid criticality and radiation effects and to minimise toxicity hazards, made up mainly of the following components:

a) storage and processing vessels;
b) calcination oven;
c) ventilation plant;
d) radioactive waste processing plant;
e) equipment for handling plutonium oxide powders (e.g. sifters, mixers etc.);
f) related control instrumentation.

B) Complete systems, especially designed or prepared for plutonium metal production, adapted in particular so to avoid criticality and radiation effects and to minimise toxicity hazards, made up mainly of the following components:

a) storage and processing vessels;
b) fluorination oven;
c) reactor for conversion/reduction of plutonium to metal;

Customs tariff number		Description of goods
		d) equipment for plutonium recovery from slags; *e)* ventilation plant; *f)* equipment for processing radioactive slags; *g)* equipment for handling the plutonium metal produced; *h)* related control instrumentation.
		The export of single components listed in A and B above is subject to ministerial authorisation only in cases where such components are part of the complete system.

Chapter 84

Boilers, machinery, mechanical equipment and devices

....

	VI)	Equipment especially designed for separating lithium isotopes.
(see also ex 85.22 VII)	VII)	Installations especially designed for producing uranium hexafluoride (UF_6)
(see also ex 85.22 VI)	VIII)	Equipment, made especially for military uses, for dissemination of biological, chemical and radioactive substances; and its main components.
	IX)	Installations and equipment especially designed for fabricating fuel elements for nuclear reactors.
	X)	Installations especially designed for fabricating tritium.

....

ex 84.17	II)	Equipment for the production of liquid hydrogen, excluding installations that produce less than 1.5 tons in 24 hours and not capable of producing of hydrogen solutions.
	III)	Equipment for the production of liquid fluorine.
	IV)	Heavy water, deuterium or deuterium compound production installations, and their especially designed or prepared equipment and components.
	V)	Equipment for continuous-type nitration especially designed for production of military explosives and solid propellants.
	VI)	Installations, machines and equipment especially designed for processing irradiated nuclear materials in order to isolate or recover fissile materials, such as machines for cutting nuclear reactor fuel elements, countercurrent solvent extractors, anticritical safety containers, and their parts and specific accessories.
	VII)	Heat exchangers that are used in: 1. laser equipment; 2. nuclear plants; consisting of aluminium, copper, nickel, or alloys containing more than 60 per cent nickel or any combination of these metals, in clad tubing designed to operate at a pressure below atmospheric pressure, with a leakage rate that is less than 10^{-4} atm per hour, with a pressure differential of 1 bar.
	VIII)	Jet nozzle separation units, capable of separating the isotopes from source materials, special fissile products, and other fissile products.
ex 84.18	I)	Centrifugal equipment, especially designed or prepared for use in plants for the reprocessing of irradiated fuel, resistant to the corrosive effects of nitric acid, in stainless steel, with a low carbon, titanium (and its alloys) and zirconium content.
	II)	Gas centrifuges or separation units using the vortex process capable of separating isotopes from source materials, from special fissile products and other fissile products, and their components as follows:

Customs tariff number	Description of goods
	1. Rotating components:
(see also ex 73.18 I, ex 76.06 I and Sect. XIII item III)	*a)* complete rotor assemblies made of thin-walled cylinders or a number of interconnected thin-walled cylinders with a thickness of 12 mm or less joined together by flexible bellows [see b)], a diameter of between 75 and 400 mm, manufactured from one or more of the following materials: — maraging steel capable of an ultimate tensile strength of 2.050×10^9 N/m^2 or more — aluminium alloys capable of an ultimate tensile strength of 0.460×10^9 N/m^2 or more
(see also Sect. VI item I and Sect. XIII item I)	— filamentary materials of an ultimate tensile strength equal to or greater than 0.3×10^6 N/m^2;
(see also ex 73.20, ex 76.07 and Sect. XIII item IV)	*b)* joined by bellows of wall thickness 3 mm or less, a diameter of between 75 and 400 mm, having a convolute and manufactured from materials listed in a) above (see also ex 82.05);
(see also ex 73.40 II, ex 76.16 I and Sect. XIII)	*c)* disc-shaped components of between 75 and 400 mm manufactured from materials listed in item V) a) above;
(see also ex 73.40 III, ex 76.16 II and Sect. XIII item VI)	*d)* top and bottom caps in the form of discs of a diameter between 75 and 400 mm shaped to contain the bearings referred to below (static components), manufactured from materials listed in a) above.
	2. Static components:
(see also ex 85.02)	*a)* magnetic suspension bearings consisting of ring-shaped magnets with a relation between outer and inner diameter smaller or equal to 1.6:1, in a form having an initial permeability of 0.15 Henry/m or more, or a remanence of 98.5 per cent or more or an energy product of greater than 80 000 joules/m^3 (10×10^6 gauss-oersteds);
(see also ex 73.40 IV)	*b)* dampers consisting of pivots of hardened steel shaped into a hemisphere at one end with a means of attachment to the bottom cap;
(see also ex 84.11 IV)	*c)* molecular pumps consisting of cylinders with 1 to 1 length to diameter ratio, with 75 to 400 mm internal diameter, 10 mm or more wall thickness, internal helical grooves, rectangular and 2 mm or more in depth and internal bores;
(see also ex 85.01 V)	*d)* ring-shaped motor stators consisting of multi-phase windings on a laminated low loss ion core comprised of thin layers 2 mm thick or less, especially designed for high speed multi-phase AC hysteresis (or reluctance) motors for synchronous operation within a vacuum in the frequency range of 600-2000 Hz and a power range of 50-1000 volts amps.
	Auxiliary systems:
(see also ex 73.24 II, ex 75.06 I, ex 76.11 II)	*a)* feed autoclaves capable of operating at up to 100 kN/m^2 pressure and at a rate of 1 kg/h or more, manufactured from one of the following materials resistant to uranium hexafluoride (UF_6): — stainless steel; — aluminium and its alloys; — nickel and its alloys containing more than 60 per cent nickel;
(see also ex 73.24 III, ex 75.06 II, 76.11 III)	*b)* Desublimers or cold traps capable of operating at up to 3 kN/m^2 pressure and at a temperature between -70 °C and +70 °C manufactured from the materials listed in a) above;
(see also ex 73.24 IV, ex 75.06 III, ex 76/11 IV)	*c)* stations for trapping UF_6 into containers manufactured from the materials listed in a) above;
(see also ex 73.18 ex 73.20, ex 75.04 I, ex 76.06, ex 76.07)	*d)* machine header piping systems with a piping network of varying forms (straight, curved, knee etc.), manufactured from the materials listed in a) above;
(see also ex 90.28 XIX)	*e)* UF_6 mass spectrometers: especially designed or prepared magnetic or quadrupole mass spectrometers capable of taking "on-line" samples from UF_6 gas streams and having all of the following characteristics: — unit resolution for mass greater than 320 — constructed of or lined with nichrome or monel or nickel plated — of the electron bombardment type — having a collector system suitable for isotopic analysis;

Customs tariff number	Description of goods
(see also ex 85.01 VI)	*f)* frequency changers (converters or inverters) especially designed or prepared to supply motor stators as defined in 2 d) above, or parts and components thereof having all of the following characteristics: — a multi-phase output of 600 to 2000 Hz — a frequency control better than 0.1 per cent — harmonic distortion less than 2 per cent; efficiency greater than 80 per cent;
(see also ex 73.18 II, ex 75.04 II, ex 76.06 II)	*g)* pipes with a 5 mm diameter for extracting UF_6, generally conforming to "Pitot pipes" and made of UF_6 resistant materials listed in a) above;
(see also ex 73.18 III, ex 75.04 III, ex 76.06 III)	*h)* housing in the form of cylinders with a wall thickness between 6 and 30 mm especially designed or prepared to house the rotors referred to in 1 a) above, manufactured from UF_6 resistant materials listed in a) above and shaped to mount the annular magnet and damper referred to in 2 a) and 2 b);
(see also ex 90.24)	*i)* pressure measurement instruments to measure the pressure of UF_6 gaseous streams manufactured from UF_6 resistant materials listed in a) above, capable of measuring pressures to 13 000 N/m^2 with better than 1 per cent accuracy.

. . . .

ex 84.59	VIII) Nuclear reactors, i.e. reactors capable of providing a self-sustaining controlled fission chain reaction; important component elements designed or prepared for use in a nuclear reactor, such as reactor pressure containment, reactor core support structures, coolant circulation pumps, fuel element handling apparatus, heat exchangers, control rods and related drive mechanisms, pressure tubes; apparatus for the production of energy and/or propulsion, not otherwise specified, especially designed for use with nuclear reactors.

. . . .

7. Machines with a horizontal axis, dual support and three cylinders, and a motor with a power equal to 45 kW or more to "spin form and flow form" the filamentary materials described in Sections VI-I and XIII-I of the Export List in force, as components for use in gas centrifuges for uranium enrichment.

XII) Solvent extractors (pecked or pulse, mixer-settlers columns) especially designed or prepared for use in irradiated fuel reprocessing plants, resistant to nitric acid corrosion effects, made of low carbon stainless steel, titanium (and its alloys) and zirconium content.

XIII) Holding or storage vessels especially designed or prepared for use in irradiated fuel reprocessing plants, resistant to nitric acid corrosive effects, made of low carbon stainless steel, titanium (and its alloys) and zirconium, equipped for operating and handling by remote control and having the following characteristics to avoid nuclear criticality:

a) for vessels of all forms, walls or internal structures, a boron equivalent of at least 2 per cent;
b) for cylindrical vessels, a maximum internal diameter of 7 inches (17.78 cm);
c) for paralelliped and annular vessels, a maximum width of 3 inches (7.62 cm).

. . . .

Customs tariff number		Description of goods

Chapter 85

Electrical machinery and equipment for electrotechnical uses

. . . .

IV) Electrochemical, semi conducting and radioactive devices for direct conversion of chemical, solar or nuclear energy as follows:

. . . .

3. Energy sources different from nuclear reactors and based on systems using radioactive materials, excluding:
   a) those having an output power less than 0.5 Watt and a total weight more than 90.7 kg;
   b) those designed and manufactured for medical uses within the human body.

. . . .

ex 85.22 (continued)	V)	Electrolitic cells for fluorine production, with a capacity of more than 250 g of fluorine per hour.
(see Ch.84 VII)	VI)	Apparatus especially designed for producing uranium hexfluoride (UF_6).
(see Ch.84 VI)	VII)	Apparatus especially designed for separating lithium isotopes.
	VIII)	Neutron generating systems, including tubes, constructed to function without external vacuum systems and with electrostatic acceleration for producing a tritium-deuterium nuclear reaction.

. . . .

Section XVIII

Optical Instruments and Equipment, Instruments for Photography and Cinematography, Measurement, Verification, Precision Instruments. Medical/Surgical Instruments and Equipment; Clocks, Musical Instruments; Sound Recorders, Videotape Recorders.

Chapter 90

Optical instruments and equipment, instruments for photography and cinematography, measurement, verification, precision instruments; medical/surgical equipment

ex 90.20

Flash impression X-ray systems including tubes having all of the following characteristics:
1. highest peak power 500 MW;
2. highest power output 500 kV;
3. pulse width less than 0.2 microsecond.

. . . .

Customs tariff number		Description of goods
ex. 90.28 (continued)	XVI)	Especially designed or prepared control instrumentation for reprocessing source materials, special fissile products and other spent fuels.
		....
(see also ex 84.18 IIIe)	XIX)	UF_6 magnetic or quadrupole mass spectrometers especially designed or prepared for on-line sampling of UF_6 gas streams, having all of the following characteristics: — unit resolution for mass greater than 320; — constructed or lined with nichrome or monel or nickel plated; — electron bombardment type; — having a collector system suitable for isotopic analysis.
		....

Chapter 92

Musical instruments or sound recorders, videotape recorders, and their components

ex 92.12	All types and forms of equipment for recording and reproducing, drums, records, cylinders, wax records, tapes, films, wires, matrices etc: 1. blank, excepting those manufactured for recording and reproducing voices and music; 2. recorded, containing detailed technical information (technological) on plants for uranium enrichment, for irradiated fuel reprocessing, for heavy water production and their main critical components, which can be used for the manufacture of nuclear weapons or other nuclear explosive devices.

JAPAN

TABLE OF CONTENTS

I. INTRODUCTION

Since the early fifties Japan has developed a vast nuclear programme based on the peaceful use of nuclear energy, ranging from nuclear power generation to radioisotope production. These nuclear activities have been supported from the start by a legal infrastructure ensuring that they are carried out in compliance with certain fundamental principles laid down in the 1955 *Atomic Energy Basic Law* (Basic Law)[1].

The overriding requirement is that nuclear energy be used exclusively for peaceful purposes in Japan, and the Basic Law specifies in Section 2 that 'the research, development and utilisation of atomic energy shall be limited to peaceful purposes ... the results therefrom shall be made public to contribute to international co-operation'. In addition, protection against radiation hazards must be ensured, nuclear activities controlled from the viewpoint of non-proliferation, and international co-operation furthered in all aspects of nuclear activities. These considerations are clearly reflected in the nuclear legislation.

A number of other laws were made under the Basic Law for the peaceful development of nuclear activities, in particular, the 1957 *Regulation Law*[2] which provides for control of nuclear material and equipment and the 1956 *Prevention Law*[3] whose purpose is to provide for radiation protection and secure public safety, *inter alia* by regulating the use, sale, disposal, etc. of radioactive materials and equipment.

These three laws constitute the basic framework for nuclear activities, including trade in materials and equipment, together with general import and export control legislation (which will be discussed below). In addition, at international level, non-proliferation commitments as well as export guidelines are complied with.

In describing how the regulation of nuclear trade is organised in Japan, this study will first discuss the Government's nuclear import and export policy and its responsibilities and will attempt to explain the different regulations and their interaction. It is important to note the different aspects of the legislation : that which governs trade in nuclear materials and equipment on the one hand and radiation protection on the other, and the regulations made under general trade law in respect of imports and exports.

II. NUCLEAR IMPORT/EXPORT POLICY

While Japan imports nuclear fuels, materials and technology, it also has a highly developed nuclear industry and the corresponding potential for supplying numerous nuclear and nuclear-related services and equipment, *inter alia*, engineering and technology know-how, nuclear steam supply systems and power plants ; it does in fact export equipment such as components for pressure vessels, tubes for fuel cladding, etc. (see under VIII below : Agreements).

Japan has a clearly defined nuclear export policy based on assurance of peaceful uses and non-proliferation, including compliance with the London Club Guidelines, elaborated by the Nuclear Suppliers Group (NSG)[4] of which Japan is a founder member.

Already in 1962, the Atomic Energy Commission issued a policy statement to the effect that nuclear materials, reactor cores and special nuclear materials reprocessing units exported from Japan be used solely for peaceful purposes, thus setting a basic principle for nuclear exports control, consistent with the principles of the Basic Law (Section 2). This statement is reproduced as *Annex I* to this chapter.

This statement was further supplemented by the establishment of more specific export criteria in conformity with the provisions of the Treaty on the Non-Proliferation of Nuclear Weapons and with the above-mentioned London Club Guidelines (see under Export regime below).

The "use" of nuclear fuel material and other internationally-controlled material[5] is subject to a licence granted by the *Prime Minister*, the Minister of International Trade and Industry (MITI) or the Minister of Transport (MOT) as the case may be (Regulation Law, Sections 52 and 61-3).

While the *Ministry of Foreign Affairs* (MOFA), is responsible for international co-operation in the field of the peaceful uses of nuclear energy, licences for nuclear imports and exports are issued by the *Minister of International Trade and Industry* (MITI). The *Science and Technology Agency* (STA), MITI and MOT formulate basic policies and promote measures to develop the peaceful uses of atomic energy and are responsible for nuclear safety regulations and for implementation of safety measures in this field[6].

In addition, the *Minister of State for Science and Technology* who heads the STA is competent for licensing the use, sale and disposal of radioisotopes (Prevention Law, Sections 3 and 4).

In short, control over nuclear imports and exports is implemented in two ways in Japan. Firstly, in accordance with the Regulation Law and the Prevention Law, no person other than the licence holder is allowed to use nuclear material, equipment and radioisotopes; further controls are imposed for specific procedures under these Laws.

Secondly, Government control is exercised through a general import and export scheme. Nuclear materials and equipment are classified as "exceptional items" subject to prior licensing requirements by the Government.

III. TRADE IN AND IMPORT/EXPORT OF NUCLEAR MATERIAL AND EQUIPMENT

As briefly mentioned, the sale, import and export of nuclear material is controlled on different levels by a licensing system instituted by nuclear law and by general law on trade. While permits for *dealings* in nuclear material are granted under nuclear legislation by the STA, MITI or MOT as the case may be, nuclear *import* and *export* licences proper are issued by the Minister of International Trade and Industry.

It should be noted that, in addition to the regulatory mechanism governing nuclear trade, various circular notices are issued by the different administrative departments; guidance (*gyohsei-Shidou*) is also provided by the authorities concerned. However, as these texts are not available, they have not been taken into account in the study.

The *Agency of Natural Resources and Energy* (ANRE), within the Ministry of International Trade and Industry (MITI), has general control over affairs concerning the research, development and utilisation of nuclear energy within the Ministry's jurisdiction. It is responsible for granting permission to receive import allotments (import quotas) of nuclear substances, radioactive isotopes and such substances.

Also, the *International Trade Administration Bureau* under MITI is in charge of affairs concerning the promotion, improvement and regulation of Japan's exports and imports. Its duties include inspection of the business procedures of trading firms to ensure compliance with the Foreign Exchange and Foreign Trade Control Law (Law No. 228 of 1949) and finally, it is responsible for overall control of approvals related to exports.

The following sections will discuss the licensing regimes under nuclear and general legislation.

1. Nuclear Licensing Regime

The Atomic Energy Basic Law lays down the principles for carrying out peaceful nuclear activities and provides for the enactment of laws specifically regulating their different aspects, which is the case of the Law for the Regulation of Nuclear Source Material, Nuclear Fuel Material and Reactors (Regulation Law). Thus, the Basic Law[7] and the Regulation Law as well as two Cabinet Orders made in their implementation lay down a detailed licensing system for nuclear activities in Japan. These are the Ordinance for the Definition of Nuclear Fuel Material, Nuclear Source Material, Reactors and Radiation (Cabinet Order No. 325 of 21st November 1957) and the Ordinance for the Enforcement of the Regulation Law (Cabinet Order No. 324 of 21st November 1957).

For purposes of efficiency, the system is standardised in the sense that the licensing procedure is the same for all nuclear materials with a number of additional requirements in respect of internationally-controlled material, as described below.

a) Licensing procedure

The Regulation Law provides that any person (i.e. nuclear operators) wishing to use, etc. nuclear fuel or internationally-controlled material must be granted a permit by the Prime Minister or the Minister of International Trade and Industry or the Minister of Transport in certain cases (Sections 52 and 61-3). Persons holding such a permit may transfer, import or export nuclear fuels (subject to the Import and Export Control Orders — see following section). Applications for a permit must contain the following particulars:

— name and address, and if it is a legal entity, the name of its representative;
— purpose and method of use;
— kind of nuclear fuel material/kind and quantity of internationally-controlled material;
— estimated period of use and location.

A permit is granted only after it is ascertained, *inter alia*, that the following requirements are met (Regulation Law, Section 53):

— the nuclear fuel material will not be used for non-peaceful purposes;
— the permit will not hinder planned research, development and use of atomic energy.

b) Further measures regarding internationally-controlled material

When internationally-controlled material is to be used for refining or fabrication purposes or for the establishment or operation of reactors, etc., *advance notification* of the kinds, quantity and period of use of such material must be made to the Prime Minister and in case of refining purposes, also to the Minister of International Trade and Industry (Regulation Law, Section 61-3).

Also, the Prime Minister may order the user of internationally-controlled material to return it or to transfer it when the international agreement in its respect has been superseded, has expired or has been terminated or if the supplier state exercises its option to recover the material in accordance with the terms of the agreement (Regulation Law, Section 61-9).

Finally, a limitation on the use or transfer of internationally-controlled material or any other conditions in implementation of the agreement in its respect may be attached to a permit (Section 62).

c) Safeguards measures

The Regulation Law lays down a series of provisions (Chapter VI) to ensure that careful accounts are kept of nuclear fuel material; in particular, users of such material must keep records of them, and in case of loss or theft, this must be reported immediately to the STA.

The *Safeguards Division* of the Nuclear Safety Bureau of the STA is in charge of safeguards and the STA inspectors may have access at all times to premises where nuclear fuel material is present for purposes of control. The Nuclear Safety Bureau's tasks include review of record-keeping, inspection planning and evaluation of results of inspections of nuclear fuel material. The Nuclear Materials Control Centre performs the technical work connected with these duties.

STA inspectors are authorised to inspect records, documents and any other articles necessary in the discharge of their verification work. They may also question the persons holding the nuclear fuel material concerned.

In addition, as regards *internationally-controlled material*, an official designated by the State having supplied such material may accompany an STA inspector and also inspect the relevant records and documents etc., in the same way as the inspector. This official is entitled to inspect the internationally-controlled material or collect samples thereof for testing purposes in accordance with the arrangements provided in this respect in the agreement concerning the material.

IAEA safeguards measures based on the Nuclear Non-Proliferation Treaty are applied to nuclear material and provision is made for further safeguards measures should the need arise.

d) Exemptions

Exemptions from permit requirements are also provided by the Regulation Law (Section 52) for certain specified quantities of nuclear fuel materials. A table of the materials exempted from licensing requirements is reproduced in *Annex II* to this chapter.

An exception is also made to the obligation to give advance notification to the Prime Minister for nuclear source material whose radioactivity or quantity of thorium or uranium does not exceed the limits fixed by Cabinet Order No. 324 of 21st November 1957 as amended (Regulation Law, Section 61-2)[8].

It should be noted, however, that where nuclear material is subject to international control, a permit is required from the Prime Minister for activities which are otherwise exempt from licensing requirements (Regulation Law, Section 61-3, Chapter VI-2, Ordinance No. 50 of 29th September 1961).

e) Sanctions

The Regulation Law, as amended by Law No. 73 of 27th May 1986, lays down a number of sanctions for violation of its provisions.

A prison term of not more than three years and/or a fine of not more than 1 000 000 yen is prescribed (Section 77) in respect of any person who has used nuclear fuel, without obtaining a permit or violates an order of suspension of its use.

A prison term of not more than one year and/or a fine of not more than 500 000 yen is imposed (Section 78) on any person who has violated restrictions on transfer or receipt of nuclear fuel or who has not complied with emergency measures to be taken where necessary, as provided by the Law.

A fine of not more than 300 000 yen is imposed on persons who have omitted to lay down safety regulations and to have them approved, as provided by the Law (Section 79).

Finally, a fine of not more than 200 000 yen is imposed on persons who have failed to maintain records of internationally-controlled material in their possession or who have not given advance notification of its particulars (Section 80).

2. General Licensing Regime

The import and export of nuclear materials and equipment are subject to the provisions of general trade law, namely, the *Foreign Exchange and Foreign Trade Control Law* (Law No. 228 of 1949) which is a framework act regulating foreign exchange and foreign trade in Japan. Two Cabinet Orders were made under that Law, for import and export respectively, to enforce its provisions and specify them further; these are the *Import Trade Control Order* (Cabinet Order No. 414 of 29th December 1949 as last amended by Cabinet Order No. 8 of 25th January 1985) and the *Export Trade Control Order* (Cabinet Order No. 378 of 1st December 1949 as last amended by Cabinet Order of 19th December 1986). The Import Trade Control Order is supplemented by the *Import Trade Control Regulations* (MITI Ordinance No. 77, December 1979 as last amended by MITI Ordinance No. 4 of 14th February 1986) while the Export Trade Control Order is for its part completed by the *Export Trade Control Regulations* (MITI Ordinance No. 64 of 1st December 1949 as last amended by MITI Ordinance No. 95 of 27th December 1986). These Ordinances detail the procedures for obtaining import and export licences and approvals.

The Foreign Exchange and Foreign Trade Control Law provides that trade is free in principle and any restrictions can be regarded as exceptional measures. Such restrictions may be imposed only where necessary for maintaining the balance of international payments, development of international trade or in the interests of the national economy. They take the form of export approvals by the Minister of International Trade and Industry (Section 47 and following).

As regards imports it is provided (Section 52) that in the interest of development of foreign trade and the national economy, persons importing goods may have to obtain prior approval therefor, as laid down by a Cabinet Order.

The following paragraphs briefly describe import and export procedures for nuclear materials and equipment.

a) Import regime

The *Import Trade Control Order* lays down the basic rules for import controls, while import procedures, as already mentioned, are provided for by the Import Trade Control Regulations (MITI Ordinance).

Persons wishing to import nuclear materials and equipment must obtain approval of such imports from the Minister of International Trade and Industry, in accordance with the procedure laid down in the MITI Ordinance.

The Import Trade Control Order (Section 3) provides in particular that the Minister shall designate the goods which are governed by an import quota system, the places of origin or shipment areas of goods for which import approval must be obtained etc. (see *Annex III* for list of nuclear or nuclear-related items)[9]. Persons intending to import goods covered by this quota system must obtain an allocation for such import from the Minister before applying for an import licence (Section 9). When approving an import or an import quota, the Minister may attach any conditions he considers necessary (Section 11).

Import licences are valid for six months unless otherwise decided by the Minister (Section 5). He may require the applicant to submit a report on the items concerned to check whether the import conforms to the laws and regulations in force (Sections 16 and 17).

Customs authorities must confirm to the Minister in accordance with his instructions that approval by licence has been duly obtained by the importer (Section 15).

Government agencies are not subject to the provisions of the Order when importing designated goods but have to consult with the Minister (Section 20).

The Import Trade Control Regulations (MITI Ordinance) lay down the following procedures for imports. Persons wishing to obtain an import approval must submit in duplicate to the Minister of International Trade and Industry, an application for import approval made out on the prescribed form (Section 2). Those wishing to obtain an import quota allocation must follow the same procedure as that for import approval also on the form prescribed for such allocations (Section 8).

Finally, persons intending to import or who have imported goods must submit to the Minister a report on the import on the prescribed form and through the bank dealing with the payment related to such import (Section 10).

b) Export regime

Any person who wishes to export items listed in Attachment I to the Export Trade Control Order must obtain approval from the Minister of International Trade and Industry (Section 1) in accordance with the procedure laid down by the Export Trade Control Regulations (MITI Ordinance).

Attachment I to the Export Trade Control Order contains a detailed and descriptive list of all products exported from Japan subject to licensing. An extract from the list representative of nuclear materials and nuclear-related equipment is reproduced as *Annex IV* to this chapter.

The Export Trade Control Order provides in particular that licences for the export of nuclear materials and equipment are valid for three months unless the Minister of International Trade and Industry decides otherwise (Section 8). He may require the applicant to submit a report on the items concerned to check whether their export conforms to the laws and regulations in force (Sections 7 and 10).

Customs authorities must confirm to the Minister of International Trade and Industry in accordance with his instructions, that the approval by licence has been duly obtained by the exporter (Section 5).

The provisions of the Order do not apply to items exported by the Minister of International Trade and Industry.

The Export Trade Control Regulations (MITI Ordinance) provide that applications for the export approval for nuclear materials or equipment must be made in triplicate to the Minister of International Trade and Industry (Section 1.1). The Minister may require the applicant to also attach in duplicate a list of the components to be exported, or as the case may be, an analysis table of the materials; both copies must be signed by the applicant (Section 1.2).

When the Minister approves an application, he returns one copy thereof to the applicant with an entry to this effect. This constitutes the *certificate of export approval* (Section 1.3).

Finally, persons intending to export goods must submit to Customs a report on the export in duplicate (export declaration and report), together with a copy of the invoice in the form stipulated by Ordinance No. 1 of 1967 of the Ministers of Finance and International Trade and Industry (Section 5). When the Customs authorities return a copy of the export report, this copy must be sent to the bank dealing with the export transaction (Section 6).

IV. TRADE IN AND IMPORT/EXPORT OF RADIOACTIVE MATERIALS

As already mentioned, the Law concerning Prevention from Radiation Hazards due to Radioisotopes, etc. (the Prevention Law) made under the Basic Law (Section 20), regulates for purposes of radiation protection the use, sale, etc. of radioisotopes.

The Prevention Law defines "radioisotopes" as isotopes that release radiation and their compounds, and matter containing them and "radiation-generating apparatus" as apparatus such as the cyclotron synchrotron, etc. which generates radiation by accelerating charged particles, as laid down by Cabinet Order (No. 259 of 30th September 1960).

Under the Prevention Law, persons engaging in the use or sale of radioisotopes and radiation-generating apparatus must obtain a licence from the Minister of State for Science and Technology (Sections 3 and 4). The application form must contain such particulars as the identity of the applicant, the kind of radioisotope, the location of the place of use or sale etc.

The licence is granted subject to the requirement that the site, etc. of the facility conform to the technical standards laid down by Order No. 56 of 30th September 1960 of the Prime Minister's Office. Other conditions may be imposed to prevent radiation hazards (Section 8).

The licence issued gives, *inter alia*, the name and address of the licensee, the kind and quantity of radioisotopes or the kind and characteristics of the radiation-generating apparatus and includes the conditions governing granting of the licence. Such licences are not transferable (Section 9).

Licences may be suspended or cancelled by the Minister of State for Science and Technology on the grounds of violation of the Prevention Law and Orders made in its implementation (Section 26).

a) Exemptions

The use, acquisition, transfer and export of sealed radioisotopes which do not exceed the quantities laid down by Cabinet Order No. 259 (less than 100 millicuries per establishment) require only advance reporting to the Minister of State for Science and Technology (Sections 3-2 and 29).

b) Sanctions

A prison term of not more than three years and/or a fine of not more than 500 000 yen is imposed on persons who have sold radioisotopes without a licence or who have disregarded an order to suspend such sale (Section 52).

A prison term of not more than one year and/or a fine of not more than 300 000 yen is imposed on persons who have transferred radioisotopes without authorisation or who have not reported any changes in their operations as compared with the conditions in their licence or have made such changes without obtaining an authorisation (Section 53).

A fine of not more than 200 000 yen is imposed on persons who have falsely reported the use of radioisotopes (Section 54).

A fine of not more than 100 000 yen is imposed on persons who have failed to submit a report on their activity to the Minister of Science and Technology if he requests such a report with a view to preventing radiation hazards or who have refused entry to their premises to an inspector designated for this purpose by the Minister (Section 55).

Finally, a fine of not more than 100 000 yen is imposed on persons engaged in selling radioisotopes who have not given their personnel the necessary instructions or training for radiation protection or who have not taken the measures required in respect of personnel who have been exposed to radiation (Section 55).

c) Medical uses of radioactive materials

It should be noted that the Prevention Law and Cabinet Order No. 259 of 30th September 1960 provide that radioisotopes and X-ray apparatus used for medical purposes fall into the category of medical supplies. The sale and import of radioactive medical supplies require a permit under the Medical Supplies Act (Act No. 145 of 10th August 1960). However, trade in X-ray medical apparatus is regulated by an Ordinance of the Ministry of Health and Welfare; it is specified that such trade requires reporting to the Governor of the Prefecture concerned. The Ministry of Health and Welfare is the authority responsible for granting permits for sale and import of radioactive medical supplies.

V. TRANSPORT

The legal framework for the transport by road and rail of radioactive materials in Japan is provided by the Basic Law, the Regulation Law and the Prevention Law. Sea transport of such materials is governed by the Ship Safety Law (Law No. 11 of 15th March 1933) while their transport by air is regulated by the Civil Aeronautics Law (Law No. 231 of 15th July 1952)[10].

The Basic Law (Section 12) provides that persons *transporting* nuclear fuel materials shall do so in accordance with regulations to be laid down by the Government.

Under the Regulation Law (Section 59-2) any person transporting nuclear fuel materials (unless by vessel or aircraft) must do so, as far as packaging requirements are concerned, in accordance with any relevant Order of the Prime Minister's Office and, with regard to the method of transport, in accordance with any relevant Order of the Minister of Transport.

The Prevention Law (Section 18-2) provides that persons transporting radioisotopes other than by vessel or aircraft shall do so in accordance with the technical standards laid down by Order of the Prime Minister's Office or, in the case of transport by rail or by automobile or light vehicle, by Order of the Minister of Transport.

The administrative requirements and safety standards applicable to all modes of transport of radioactive materials conform to the 1973 edition of the IAEA Regulations for the Safe Transport of Radioactive Materials.

VI. PHYSICAL PROTECTION

With regard to physical protection measures, a Special Committee of the Japanese Atomic Energy Commission has studied the situation, prepared a report and made a recommendation concerning the physical protection system to be implemented in Japan.

VII. INTELLECTUAL PROPERTY IN THE NUCLEAR FIELD

The Basic Law (Section 17) provides that if necessary in the public interest, the Government may take measures under the Patent Law (Law No. 121 of 13th April 1959) concerning patented inventions in the nuclear field.

JAPAN

Contracts under which patented techniques and inventions relating to atomic energy may be transferred abroad are subject to regulations laid down by the Government pursuant to the Patent Law (Section 18, Basic Law). The Government may grant awards, within budgetary limits, with respect to patented inventions or inventions for which an application for a patent has been filed (Section 19).

VIII. AGREEMENTS

In addition to multilateral agreements in the nuclear field, Japan has entered into a series of bilateral agreements on the peaceful uses of nuclear energy which can be divided into two types. The first type is an overall agreement generally covering the peaceful uses of nuclear energy ; and the second type of agreement covers specific areas in the nuclear field. Of the latter, only those which provide for the supply of information, nuclear material and equipment as well as technical/industrial co-operation are referred to below.

1. Multilateral Agreements

Japan ratified the Treaty on the Non-Proliferation of Nuclear Weapons (NPT) on 8th June 1976.

2. Bilateral Agreements

a) Exchange of notes on nuclear co-operation

Exchange of notes on the use of atomic energy for peaceful purposes between the Government of Japan and :

- the Government of the ***Federal Republic of Germany*** on 10th March 1959 ;
- the Government of ***France*** on 23rd July 1965 ;
- the Government of ***Sweden*** on 27th March 1973 ; and
- the Government of ***Italy*** on 26th October 1973.

b) Safeguards

- Agreement between the Government of Japan and the ***International Atomic Energy Agency*** on Safeguards under the NPT, signed on 4th March 1977 and entered into force on 2nd December 1977.

c) Agreements for nuclear co-operation

- Agreement between the Government of Japan and the Government of ***Canada*** on the use of atomic energy for peaceful purposes, signed on 2nd July 1959 and entered into force on 27th July 1960. A Protocol amending this Agreement was signed on 22nd August 1978, and entered into force on 2nd September 1980.

  The Agreement, which was automatically extended after its initial period of ten years, provides for the supply by Canada of natural uranium. It stipulates that use of the uranium is restricted to peaceful purposes, prohibits nuclear explosions and provides for full scope application of IAEA safeguards.

- Agreement between the Government of Japan and the Government of the ***United States*** on the use of atomic energy for peaceful purposes, signed on 26th February 1968 and entered into force on 10th July 1968. A Protocol amending this Agreement was signed on 28th March 1973 and entered into force on the same day.

  This Agreement, which was concluded for a period of 35 years, renewed and widened the 1958 Agreement. It provides for the supply by the United States of enriched uranium for the power reactors to be built in Japan. The Agreement covers, *inter alia*, exchange of information, transfer of material and facilities etc., and the application of IAEA safeguards.

- A new Agreement was concluded on 4th November 1987 between the Government of Japan and the Government of the ***United States*** concerning co-operation in the peaceful uses of nuclear energy. It stipulates that the above Agreement of 1968 will be terminated on entry into force of the present Agreement, whose provisions will apply to nuclear material and equipment subject to the former. The Agreement has an initial term of thirty years and expands the peaceful nuclear co-operation between the two countries.

  The Agreement provides for the transfer of material, nuclear material, equipment (including reactors) and components for nuclear research and nuclear power purposes. It is accompanied by an Implementing Agreement containing, *inter alia*, the prior consent of both Parties for reprocessing and storage in facilities within their territorial jurisdiction as listed in annex. Application of full-scope IAEA safeguards are required and implementation of both Parties' respective existing agreements with the IAEA will be considered as fulfilling this requirement.

— Agreement between the Government of Japan and the Government of the ***United Kingdom*** for the use of atomic energy for peaceful purposes, signed on 6th March 1968 and entered into force on 15th October 1968.

  This Agreement, which was concluded for a period of thirty years, renews and widens the Agreement signed in 1958. Under this further Agreement, the United Kingdom Atomic Energy Authority (UKAEA) is to carry out the chemical reprocessing of irradiated fuels from Japanese installations and supply other services in the fuel cycle. It stipulates conditions for co-operation similar to those in the Agreement with the United States.

— Agreement between the Government of Japan and the Government of ***Australia*** for the use of atomic energy for peaceful purposes, signed on 21st February 1972 and entered into force on 28th July 1972.

  A revision of this Agreement, which was concluded for a period of thirty years, was signed on 5th March 1982 and entered into force on 17th August 1982. The Agreement renews and widens the 1972 Agreement. The 1972 Agreement did not provide for reprocessing, but the revised agreement provides for 'generic consent' being given to reprocessing similar to that given to 'transfer' on condition that reprocessing is conducted under IAEA safeguards, and that the recovered plutonium be used within the scope of Japan's nuclear fuel cycle programme. Under the Agreement, Australia is to supply natural uranium.

— Agreement between the Government of Japan and the Government of ***France*** for the use of atomic energy for peaceful purposes, signed on 26th February 1972 and entered into force on 22nd September 1972.

  This Agreement, which was concluded for a period of ten years, covers exchange of information, transfer of material and facilities, supply of services and co-operation in mining and exploitation of natural uranium. Under this Agreement, France is to carry out the reprocessing of irradiated fuels from Japanese installations and supply natural uranium. It stipulates conditions for co-operation similar to those in the co-operation agreement with the United States. Following the initial ten-year period, it may be terminated by a six months advance notification.

— Agreement between the Government of Japan and the Government of the ***People's Republic of China*** for co-operation in the peaceful uses of nuclear energy, signed on 31st July 1985 and entered into force on 10th July 1986.

  The Agreement provides that co-operation between both countries shall be for peaceful utilisation of nuclear energy exclusively. The areas of co-operation include exchange of experts and information, as well as nuclear materials, equipment and facilities. IAEA safeguards and physical protection measures are to be applied and prior written consent is required for transfer of nuclear materials and equipment. This bilateral co-operation Agreement is the first concluded by Japan which considers its role as a supplier of nuclear materials and equipment. The Agreement will remain in force for fifteen years with automatic extension every five years thereafter.

d) Agreements for co-operation on research and development in the nuclear field

These agreements are of a technological nature and were not concluded at Government level but between both countries at ministerial level or by the national public or semi-public agencies competent in the area concerned.

Canada

— Agreement of 27th September 1971 on co-operation on heavy water reactor research concluded between the Japan Power Reactor and Nuclear Fuel Development Corporation and Atomic Energy of Canada Ltd (AECL).

France

— Arrangement of 15th March 1979 on co-operation in the field of light water reactor research concluded between the Atomic Energy Bureau of the Japan Science and Technology Agency (STA) and the French Atomic Energy Commission (CEA).

Federal Republic of Germany

— Arrangement of 3rd July 1976 on R and D in the field of light water reactor safety concluded between the Atomic Energy Bureau of the STA and Federal Ministry for Reseach and Technology (BMFT).

— Agreement of 16th January 1980 on the NSRR/PNS Project (Nuclear Safety Research Reactor/Projekt Nuklear Sicherheit) concluded between JAERI and the Karlsruhe Nuclear Research Centre (KfK). This Project covers exchange of information on fuel damage under conditions such as reactivity accidents, loss of coolant etc.

— Arrangement of 2nd February 1979 for co-operation concerning research and development in the field of high temperature gas-cooled reactors between the JAERI and the Jülich Nuclear Research Establishment (KFA).

United Kingdom

— Agreement of 15th June 1970 for co-operation on research and development in the field of fast-breeder reactors between the JAERI and the PNC and the United Kingdom Atomic Energy Authority (UKAEA).

United States

— Agreement of 1st January 1979 for co-operation in the field of research on fast breeder reactors between the PNC and the United States Department of Energy (DOE).

— Arrangement of 31st December 1985 for co-operation in the field of research on light water reactor safety, high-temperature gas reactor safety, fast breeder reactor safety, radioactive waste management and nuclear safety regulation between the Nuclear Safety Bureau of the STA, the Agency of Natural Resources and Energy of the MITI, and the United States Nuclear Regulatory Commission (NRC).

NOTES AND REFERENCES

1. Law No. 186 of 19th December 1955 as amended.
2. Law No. 166 of 10th June 1957 for the Regulation of Nuclear Source Material, Nuclear Fuel Material and Reactors, as amended, Section 1: "This Law ... is enacted for the purpose of providing the necessary regulations ... on the uses of internationally controlled material, to execute agreements or other international arrangements concerning the research, development and use of atomic energy [for peaceful uses]."
3. Law No. 167 of 10th June 1957 concerning Prevention from Radiation Hazards due to Radioisotopes, etc., as amended.
4. The NSG is a group of nuclear exporting countries having adopted a set of Guidelines (issued as IAEA document INFCIRC/254) which specify the guarantees required by an exporter country from an importer country in connection with the transfer of certain types of nuclear material, equipment and, technology to non-nuclear weapon States. For a detailed analysis of these questions see Volume I of this study dealing with international aspects of nuclear trade.
5. Section 2 of the Regulation Law specifies that internationally-controlled material means "nuclear source material, nuclear fuel material ... or other material or equipment to which safeguards are applied under agreements or other international arrangements".
6. For further details concerning these authorities see analytical study in the same series: *Regulatory and Institutional Framework for Nuclear Activities*, OECD/NEA, Vol. I, 1983.
7. Section 3 of the Basic Law gives the following definitions:

   "i) Atomic energy means all kinds of energy released from atomic nuclei in the process of nuclear transformation.

   ii) Nuclear fuel material means materials which release a large amount of energy in the process of nuclear fission such as uranium, thorium, etc.

   iii) Nuclear source material means materials which are raw materials for nuclear fuel materials, such as uranium ore, thorium ore, etc."

   It is interesting to note that the Regulation Law refers to the Basic Law for its definitions and adds a further definition — that of internationally-controlled material (Note 5).
8. These limits are:

   Nuclear source material which does not exceed limits specified by Cabinet Order (No. 324, Section 19) for the density of radioactivity or for the quantity of uranium or thorium it contains.For the concentration of radioactivity: 0.002 microcurie per gram (for solid nuclear source material: 0.01 microcurie per gram). For the quantity of uranium and that of thorium: 900 grams as may be determined by multiplying the quantity of uranium by three, in terms of thorium or by totalling all of these.
9. The nuclear and nuclear-related items covered by the import quota system are specified by MITI Notification No. 170 of 1966, as amended by MITI Notification No. 503 of 10th December 1985.
10. For further details, see analytical study in the same series: *Regulations Governing the Transport of Radioactive Materials*, OECD/NEA, 1980.

Annex I

POLICY STATEMENT ISSUED BY ATOMIC ENERGY COMMISSION IN 1962

Section 2 of The Atomic Energy Basic Law specifies that the research, development and utilisation of atomic energy in our country shall be limited to peaceful purposes. It is difficult to include "export" into "utilisation" here in this provision in terms of interpretation of the law.

It seems that, however, our country should observe the spirit of the Atomic Energy Basic Law even when our country involves the utilisation of atomic energy in foreign countries.

Therefore, it is necessary to ensure that nuclear source materials, nuclear fuel materials, reactor cores, and refining and reprocessing units of special nuclear material which our country supplies to foreign countries should be utilised only for peaceful purposes.

Annex II

SECTION 52(v) OF THE REGULATION LAW

Exemption of Nuclear Fuel Material used in the Kinds and Quantity as Provided by Cabinet Order No. 324 of 21st November 1957, Section 15*

Kind of Nuclear Fuel Material	Quantity
1. Uranium, of which the ratio of U-235 toU-238 is the same as the natural mixture rates, and its compounds	less than 300 grams of uranium
2. Uranium, of which the ratio of U-235 to U-238 is less than the natural mixture rate, and its compounds	less than 300 grams of uranium
3. Material which contains more than one of the above No. 2 materials and can be used as fuel in a reactor	less than 300 grams of uranium
4. Thorium and its compounds	less than 900 grams of thorium
5. Material which contains more than one of the above No. 4 materials and can be used as fuel in a reactor	less than 900 grams of thorium

* Unofficial translation by Japanese authorities.

Annex III

IMPORT NOTICE

(Ministry of International Trade and Industry Notification No. 170 of 1966 as Amended by Notification No. 503 of 10th December 1985)*

Excerpts

Customs tariff number	Description of goods
ex.26.01-8	Metal ores of radioactive elements
ex.28.50	Fissile chemical elements and isotopes; compounds, inorganic or organic, of such elements or isotopes, whether or not chemically defined; alloys, dispersions and cermets, containing any of these elements, isotopes, inorganic or organic compounds
28.52-1	Compounds, inorganic or organic, of thorium or of U-235-depleted uranium
81.04-1	U-235-depleted uranium and articles thereof
ex.81.04-2-(3)	Unwrought lumps, powders, flakes, waste and scraps of thorium
ex.81.04-3	Thorium and articles thereof; cermets containing thorium and articles thereof and tubes of zirconium
84.59-6	Nuclear reactors and parts thereof
ex.90.28-3	Instruments or apparatus for measuring or detecting alpha-, beta-, or gamma- or X-ray, cosmic or similar radiations
ex.90-29	Parts and accessories for instruments or apparatus for measuring or detecting alpha-, beta-, gamma- or X-ray, cosmic or similar radiations

* Unofficial translation by Japanese authorities.

Annex IV

EXPORT TRADE CONTROL ORDER

(Cabinet Order No. 378, 1st December 1949, as Amended on 26th January 1981)*

Excerpts from list of items in attachment I

....

4. Ground metals, half-finished products and primary products of nonferrous metal and their alloys and further, which fall under any one of those mentioned below.

   A. Ground metals, half-finished products or primary products of beryllium or beryllium alloy, which contain beryllium more than 50 per cent by total weight (hereinafter referred to as "ground metal, etc." in this paragraph).

   B. Ground metal, etc. of metal boron.

   C. Ground metal, etc. of titanium alloy and contents of aluminium, zirconium, molybdenum, zinc, and titanium are 6 per cent, 4 per cent, 6 per cent, 2 per cent and 82 per cent respectively by total weight or those of which the aluminium content is more than 12 per cent by total weight.

   D. Ground metal, etc. of cobalt alloy, of which the cobalt content is more than 50 per cent by total weight and, in addition, which fall under any one item mentioned below.

      1. Those, of which the tantalum content is more than 5 per cent.
      2. Those, which are types intensified by dispersion and whose contents of aluminium oxide, yttrium oxide, zirconium oxide, cerium oxide or thorium oxide is more than 1 per cent by total weight.
      3. Those, whose content of scandium, yttrium, lanthanum, cerium, praseodymium or neodymiam is more than 0.05 per cent by total weight.

   E. Ground metal, etc. of nickel alloys, whose nickel content is more than 50 per cent by total weight and, in addition, which fall under any one item mentioned below.

      1. Those, of whose content of aluminium and titanium is more than 11 per cent by total weight.
      2. Those, which are types intensified by dispersion and whose content of aluminium oxide, yttrium, zirconium oxide, lanthanum oxide, cerium oxide or thorium oxide is more than 1 per cent by total weight.
      3. Those, of whose content of scandium, yttrium, lanthanum, cerium, praseodymium or neodymium is more than 0.05 per cent by total weight.

   F. Ground metal, etc. of niobium alloy, whose content of niobium or total of contents of niobium and tantalum exceed 60 per cent by total weight.

   G. Ground metal, etc. of molybdenum alloy, whose content of molybdenum is more than 97.5 per cent by total weight (excluding wires).

   H. Ground metal, etc. of hafnium or hafnium alloy, whose hafnium content is more than 60 per cent by total weight.

   I. Ground metal, etc. of tantalum, whose purity is more than 99.98 per cent or tantalum alloy, whose tantalum content is more than 60 per cent by total weight.

5. Ground metal, half-finished products and primary products of lithium, zirconium and zirconium alloy and lithium alloy, which fall under any one of those mentioned below.

   A. Those, of which the ratio of lithium 6 to lithium 7 exceeds the natural ratio of mixture.

   B. Those, of which the lithium content exceeds 50 per cent by total weight.

....

* Unofficial translation by Japanese authorities.

18. Artificial graphite, the apparent specific gravity of which shows over 1.90 degrees at a temperature of 15.5 degrees (excluding those which are mentioned in item 19).

19. Synthetic graphite, whose boron content is less than 5 per 1 000 000 by total weight and, in addition, apparent (specific) gravity of which at a temperature of 15.5 °C is over 1°.50 (limited to those prepared for atomic reactors).

....

46. Boron, fluorine, hydrogen peroxide, ammonium perchlorate, nitrogen tetroxide, guanidine nitrate, guanidium perchlorate, hydrazine, hydrazine nitrate, hydrazine perchlorate, monomethylhydrazine, dimethylhydrazine, chlorine trifluoride, beryllium compounds, boron compounds, zirconium compounds (limited to those, whose content of hafnium is less than 1-500 of zirconium), niobium compounds, hafnium compounds, tantalum compounds, and boron mixtures.

47. Half-finished products and primary products of beryllium compounds, zirconium compounds mentioned in paragraph 46 and hafnium compounds (excluding half-finished products and primary products of beryllium oxide, which are to be used for parts of electronic machinery and tools).

48. Heavy hydrogen compounds, heavy hydrogen mixtures, tritium compounds, tritium mixtures, lithium compounds and lithium mixtures, which fall under any one of those mentioned hereunder and heavy hydrogen and tritium.

A. Heavy hydrogen compounds or heavy hydrogen mixtures, of which the ratio of number of atoms of heavy hydrogen to the number of atoms of hydrogen exceeds 1-5000.

B. Tritium compounds or tritium mixtures, of which the ratio of the number of atoms of tritium to the number of atoms of hydrogen exceeds 1-1000 (in the case of tritium mixtures and when tritium and hydrogen are separated, those, of which the ratio of the number of atoms of tritium to the number of atoms of hydrogen does not exceed 1-1000, are excluded).

C. Lithium compounds, which contain hydrogen, heavy hydrogen or tritium.

D. Lithium compounds or lithium mixtures and those, of which the ratio of lithium 6 to lithium 7 exceeds the natural ratio of mixtures.

....

51. Nuclear fuel materials and nuclear source materials.

....

62. Nuclear reactors, their parts and accessories, apparatus and apparatus for generation of electric power or propulsion, which are designed for nuclear reactors.

....

66. Apparatus for generating neutrons of accelerating static electricity type which is operated by nuclear reaction between tritium and heavy hydrogen and which is designed to be operated without using a vacuum pump.

....

66-2. Apparatus, its parts and control apparatus designed for separation or reprocessing of nuclear fuel material, nuclear source material or lithium, which were exposed to radiation.

....

JAPAN

76. Manufacturing equipment for heavy hydrogen or heavy hydrogen compounds (including concentrating equipment) and their parts and related equipment.

. . . .

80. Manufacturing equipment for uranium hexafluoride, equipment for separating isotopes of uranium and their related equipment and their parts.

81. Manufacturing equipment for uranium dioxide, separating equipment for lithium isotopes and equipment for manufacture and processing of nuclear fuel materials.

NETHERLANDS

TABLE OF CONTENTS

NETHERLANDS

I. INTRODUCTION

Although not direct exporters of nuclear reactors, the Netherlands are present in this market as suppliers of equipment, materials and services. In particular, they participate in the international uranium enrichment enterprise, URENCO.

International commitments undertaken by the Netherlands and concerning nuclear trade include their participation in the work of the Zangger Committee and of the Nuclear Suppliers' Group ("London Club"). The Netherlands is Party to the Treaty on the Non-proliferation of Nuclear Weapons.

As far as exports to non-nuclear-weapon States are concerned, the Netherlands have undertaken to act in compliance with the principles resulting from the work of the London Club (INFCIRC/254), laying down the guidelines applicable to the export of nuclear materials, equipment and technology. This undertaking is contained in two communications to the Parliament dated 30th March 1976 (Kamerstukken II, 1975/1976, 13865, No. 1), and 11th January 1978 (Kamerstukken II, 1977/1978, 13865, No. 2).

Netherlands legislation on nuclear trade is comprised partly of specifically nuclear texts, and partly of the general regulations concerning foreign trade. The basic provisions regulating nuclear activities are contained in the Nuclear Energy Act of 25th February 1963 (Stb.[1] 1963, No. 82) last amended in 1985 (Stb. 1985, No. 287). A whole series of decrees, implementing the Nuclear Energy Act, contain detailed regulations governing nuclear activities. In the interest of clarity, the titles of the most important of them are given below:

- Decree of 29th August 1969 on definitions (Stb. 1969, No. 358), amended by a Decree of 20th October 1986 (Stb. 1986, No. 533);
- Decree of 4th September 1969 on nuclear installations, fissile materials and ores (Stb. 1969, No. 403), last amended by a Decree of 19th September 1986 (Stb. 1986, No. 530);
- Decree of 4th September 1969 on the transport of fissile materials, ores and radioactive substances (Stb. 1969, No. 405), amended by a Decree of 4th June 1987 (Stb. 1987, No. 342); a Decree of 3rd September 1987 (Stb. 1987, No. 403) contains the full text of the Decree of 4th September 1969, as amended on 4th June 1987;
- Decree of 8th October 1969 on the registration of fissile materials and ores (Stb. 1969, No. 471);
- Decree of 16th October 1969 on the registration of radioactive materials and the costs of the Food and Drugs Inspectorate (Stb. 1969, No. 472);
- Decree of 20th October 1969 on national defence exemptions (Stb. 1969, No. 476), amended by a Decree of 5th November 1982 (Stb. 1982, No. 677), amended by a Decree of 16th December 1986 (Stb. 1986, No. 729);
- Decree of 22nd October 1969 on the duties of the Food and Drugs Inspectorate (Stb. 1969, No. 474);
- Decree of 12th November 1969 on the entry into force of the Nuclear Energy Act (Stb. 1969, No. 514);
- Decree of 17th June 1971 relating to nuclear secrecy (Stb. 1971, No. 420);
- Decree of 13th February 1976 on nuclear installations accidents (Stb. 1976, No. 138);
- Decree of 25th June 1981 on contributions (Stb. 1981, No. 455).
- Decree of 10th September 1986 on radiation protection (Stb. 1986, No. 465) (this text replaces the Decree of 10th September 1969 on radioactive materials — Stb. 1969, No. 404).

The Act regulating trade, exports and imports generally, is that of 5th July 1962 (Stb. 1962, No. 295), amended on several occasions.

Various regulatory and supervisory authorities are involved in applying this legislation (including, in particular, the Ministers for Economic Affairs; Housing, Regional Development and the Environment; Social Services and Employment; Welfare, Health and Cultural Affairs; Finance; Foreign Affairs; Transport; Construction[2], etc.), as are advisory bodies such as the Public Health Council.

The drafting of this study has essentially followed the distinction made within nuclear legislation as such between fissile materials, ores, equipment and radioactive materials, as well as the distinction between nuclear legislation and general legislation.

II. TRADE IN FISSILE MATERIALS, ORES, RADIOACTIVE MATERIALS AND APPARATUS EMITTING IONIZING RADIATION — NUCLEAR LEGISLATION

A. LICENSING REGIME

1. Fissile Materials[3], Ores and Equipment

The Nuclear Energy Act prohibits the possession or *transfer* of fissile materials or ores without joint authorisation from the Minister for Economic Affairs, the Minister for Social Services and Employment, the Minister of Welfare, Health and Cultural Affairs and the Minister for Housing, Regional Development and the Environment (Section 15 of the Nuclear Energy Act and Section 3 of the Decree of 4th September 1969 on nuclear installations, fissile materials and ores, Stb. 1969, No. 403). Similar authorisation is required to construct, bring on-line, operate or alter any establishment in which nuclear energy may be released or in which fissile materials may be manufactured or processed, or are stored.

The general procedure for applying for a licence is laid down in Section 3 of the Decree of September 1969 on nuclear installations, fissile materials and ores. Applications must be sent to the competent Ministers, and contain, *inter alia*, the following information :

— a detailed description of the uses to which the fissile materials, ores, installations or equipment will be put ;
— the name and address of the applicant ;
— an indication of the period for which the licence is requested ;
— the identification and description of the site on which the installation in question is to be located ;
— information relating to the particular establishment for which the licence is sought.

Specific provisions relating to information required for licence applications are contained in Sections 4, 5, 6, 7, 8, 9, 11, 12, 13 and 14 of the above-mentioned Decree. For example, applications for permission to possess fissile materials must contain information about the quantities, the chemical and physical state, and the form, content, degree of enrichment and activity of the materials in question.

Detailed conditions may be attached to the licence concerning, in particular, the protection of persons and property, national security, storage and surveillance of fissile materials and ores, and supplies (Section 19 of the Act of 21st February 1963, Stb. 1963, No. 82).

The Ministry for Economic Affairs keeps a general *register*, and any person transporting fissile materials or ores, or who has them in his possession or transfers them, must keep a *record* thereof and give notice for the purpose of their inclusion in the register (Sections 13 and 14 of the Act of 21st February 1963).

By way of exception, Sections 41 and 42 of the Decree of September 1969 on nuclear installations, fissile materials and ores, provide that no licence is required for having in an establishment non-irradiated fissile materials containing only natural or depleted uranium or thorium in quantities not exceeding 100 grammes of each of these elements, and no plutonium. No licence is required either for ores packed in water-tight metal containers or, if not packed, provided their specific activity does not exceed 0.37 kilobecquerels per gramme. The transfer of exempted materials does not require a licence either, nor does the transfer of fissile materials or ores to a person authorised to receive them (Section 43 of the September 1969 Decree on nuclear installations, fissile materials and ores).

2. Radioactive Materials and Radiation Emitting Apparatus[4]

The preparation, possession and use of radioactive materials are prohibited without a licence granted by the Minister for Social Services and Employment, the Minister of Welfare, Health and Cultural Affairs and the Minister for Housing, Regional Development and the Environment, in consultation with the other Ministers concerned (Decree implementing the Nuclear Energy Act relating to radiation protection, dated 10th September 1986, Stb. 1986, No. 465) ; examples of such Ministers include the Minister for Agriculture and Fisheries and the Minister of Transport.

Detailed provisions concerning the keeping of registers are laid down in a Decree implementing the Nuclear Energy Act and relating to the registration of radioactive materials and Food and Drugs Inspectorate costs, of 16th October 1969 (Stb. 1969 No. 472). This Decree also contains instructions for supplying information from the registers and for financing the costs incurred by the Inspectorate.

Any person who prepares, keeps, uses or transfers radioactive materials is required to keep a *record* thereof and to give notice for the purpose of registration in the above-mentioned registers (Section 28 of the Act of 21st February 1963). Sections 68-74 of the Radiation Protection Decree of 10th September 1986 (Stb. 1986, No. 465) govern the implementation of Section 28 of the 1963 Act.

Radiation-emitting equipment is also governed by the Radiation Protection Decree, which applies to X-ray apparatus, particle accelerators, etc. (Section 9). The use of heavy equipment of this type requires a licence from the Minister for Social Services and Employment, the Minister for Housing, Regional Development and the Environment, and the Minister of Welfare and Health and for Cultural Affairs (Sections 10-12). The application must include, in particular, a description of the equipment, its purpose and the protective measures which will be taken (Section 11).

The Decree on Radiation Protection of 10th September 1986 provides for exemptions from licensing and registration in exceptional cases, on condition that radiation protection measures are observed. A number of other detailed exemptions from the general licensing system are also listed in the Decree. These include radioluminous timepieces in compliance with the radiation protection norms adopted by the OECD Council (Section 54).

B. IMPORTS AND EXPORTS

1. Fissile Materials and Ores

Section 15(a) of the 1963 Nuclear Energy Act provides that it is prohibited to transport, possess, *import* or *export* into or out of the Netherlands, or cause to be so imported or exported, or dispose of fissile materials or ores without a licence. However, exemptions from this licence requirement are provided for by the Transport Decree of 4th September 1969 (Stb. 1969, No. 405), as amended by the Decree of 4th June 1987 (Stb. 1987, No. 342) on the transport of fissile materials, ores and radioactive substances.

Thus, the Decree provides that no licence is required under the Nuclear Energy Act to export or import into the Netherlands fissile materials or ores in the performance of a transport contract (Section 23 of the Transport Decree of 4th September 1969, as amended by the Decree of 4th June 1987). As a consequence of this general exemption the system applicable for the import and export of such materials is that laid down by the regulations on trade in strategic materials by virtue of the Act of 5th July 1962 (Stb. 1962, No. 295) on imports and exports in general (see the section on Trade in nuclear articles — general legislation).

Moreover, no licence under the Nuclear Energy Act is required to *import* or cause to be imported fissile materials or ores into the Netherlands other than in the performance of a transport contract, when the materials in question are :

— non-irradiated fissile materials, if they consist entirely of natural or depleted uranium or natural thorium and contain no plutonium, and if the quantity brought into the Netherlands on any particular occasion contains not more than 100 grammes of thorium or 100 grammes of uranium ;
— fissile materials that are held, or have been or may be imported, under a licence required by the national legislation of Belgium or Luxembourg, or in relation to which permission has been granted to transit those countries, provided the stipulations or conditions attached to this licence are observed (Section 23 of the Transport Decree of 4th September 1969, as amended by the Decree of 4th June 1987) ;
— special fissile materials not intended for Belgium or Luxembourg, which transit Netherlands territory, provided the materials are not unloaded on such territory from the means of transport used ;
— ores.

Applications for licences to import fissile materials or cause them to be imported into the Netherlands must be made in writing to the Minister for Economic Affairs, the Minister for Housing, Regional Development and the Environment, the Minister for Social Services and Employment, and the Minister of Welfare, Health and Cultural Affairs. In practice, applications are filed with the Minister for Housing, Regional Development and the Environment, with copies to the other Ministers concerned.

Licence applications must contain the following particulars :

— the name and address of the applicant ;
— whether the application covers importing or causing to be imported ;
— the name and address of the person to whom the fissile materials are consigned (ores being exempted from the licensing obligation by Section 23 of the Transport Decree of 4th September 1969 as amended by the Decree of 4th June 1987), and, if the said person is established in Belgium or Luxembourg, a statement signed by him certifying that he is authorised by the laws of his country to have the fissile materials concerned in his possession ;
— the quantity, chemical and physical state, form, content and degree of enrichment of the fissile materials ;
— the country of origin of the fissile materials ;
— the probable date on which the fissile materials will enter Netherlands territory or the period for which the licence is required ;
— the customs office through which the fissile materials will be brought into the Netherlands (Section 24 of the Transport Decree of 4th September 1969 as amended by the Decree of 4th June 1987).

Should one of the Ministers concerned consider that an application contains too few particulars for him to judge its merits, he may require any further information deemed necessary within a time limit to be set by him (Section 24).

The Transport Decree provides further that, with a view to the protection of persons, animals, plants and property, a licence to import fissile materials into Netherlands territory may only be granted subject to the following stipulations :

- fissile materials may be imported into Netherlands territory only if they are intended for a person who is authorised under Netherlands, Belgian or Luxembourg law to have these materials, or for a person in a country other than the Netherlands, Belgium or Luxembourg;
- fissile materials may only be imported into Netherlands territory across the frontier between the Netherlands and Belgium or through the designated customs office;
- the licence, or a certified copy thereof, must be submitted on request to the official responsible for inspection in this customs office.

Similar conditions may be attached to a licence to cause fissile materials to be imported into Netherlands territory (Section 25).

The Minister for Social Services and Employment, the Minister of Welfare, Health and Cultural Affairs and the Minister for Housing, Regional Development and the Environment may grant exemptions from the provisions of the Decree (Section 26). Such exemptions may be granted subject to certain restrictions or conditions.

2. Radioactive Substances

It is prohibited to *import* or *cause to be imported* radioactive substances into Netherlands territory without a licence (Section 29 of the Nuclear Energy Act).

However, the Transport Decree of September 1969 provides that this ban does not apply to the importation of radioactive substances in performance of a transport contract or to the importation:

- of radioactive substances which, in accordance with a licence required under Belgian or Luxembourg national legislation, are held, or have been or may be imported, or may transit one of these countries, provided the requirements and stipulations attached to the licence are observed;
- of radioactive substances not intended for Belgium or Luxembourg and which transit Netherlands territory, provided the materials are not unloaded in such territory from the vehicle used (Section 27).

When a licence is required, the application must be made in writing to the Minister for Housing, Regional Development and the Environment, the Minister for Social Services and Employment and the Minister of Welfare, Health and Cultural Affairs. Radioactive substances may only be *imported* or *caused to be imported* into Netherlands territory other than in performance of a transport contract if they are intended for a person who, under Netherlands, Belgian or Luxembourg law, is authorised to have these substances or for a person in a country other than the Netherlands, Belgium or Luxembourg (Section 31).

III. TRADE IN NUCLEAR ARTICLES — GENERAL LEGISLATION

In the Netherlands, nuclear trade with foreign countries is also regulated by the ordinary law in this field, in particular, the *Act of 5th July 1962 on Imports and Exports* (Stb. 295), most recently amended on 24th March 1976 (Stb. 215). A *Decree of 26th April 1963 on the Export of Industrial Products* (Stb. 128), adopted in pursuance of the Act, determines the materials, articles and equipment subject to licensing and inspection, and specifies that the competent authority in this respect is the *Minister for Economic Affairs*.

Section 2 of the 1962 Act provides for the adoption, in the interests of the national economy and national security and in implementation of the international agreements concluded by the Netherlands, of regulations governing the import and export of articles or materials to be specified in such regulations. The Act also provides for the adoption of regulations concerning the import and export of articles from or to certain countries.

Decrees relating to exports and imports, as well as any amendment or abrogation thereof, are promulgated by the Minister for Economic Affairs in consultation with the Ministers concerned (in particular, the Minister for Foreign Affairs), depending on the nature of the products in question. The Ministers consult, in their turn, the Economic and Social Council, the Commission set up by the Industrial Organisation Act (Stb. 1950, No. 22) or the body directly concerned by the Decree in question [Act of 1962, Section 2(3) and (4)].

This consultation procedure is not, however, required when an import or export Decree is drawn up for reasons of national security, or pursuant to an international Convention provided that, in the opinion of the Ministers concerned, such consultation would be against the public interest [Section 2(5)].

Decrees relating to imports and exports as well as any amendment or abrogation thereof are published in the Official Gazette (Section 8).

The implementing Decree of 26th April 1963 relating to exports of industrial products has been amended on numerous occasions due, in particular, to technological developments in the field of strategic materials.

It is prohibited to export articles or materials listed in *Appendix A* of the Decree without a licence from the Minister for Economic Affairs (Section 2).

Licences granted under Section 2 are subject to the following conditions (Section 7) :

— when materials or articles for which a licence has been given are being exported, the licence must be presented to the customs official responsible for collecting customs duty;
— if the licence is not kept by this official, it must immediately be returned to the Minister for Economic Affairs;
— the Minister must be kept informed of the use made of the licence during the period for which it was granted.

It is also prohibited to export materials or articles listed in *Appendix B* without presenting a form signed by or on behalf of the exporter concerned, established in compliance with the conditions laid down by the Minister, to the customs official responsible for collecting customs duty (Sections 3 and 6).

The Minister for Economic Affairs may grant exemptions in respect of the provisions of Sections 2 and 3.

A Decree of 7th October 1977 (Stb. 586) made the 1962 Act applicable to :

i) *articles entering* Netherlands territory (imports) other than those in direct transit or in course of carriage, destined for East European countries or socialist countries of South-East Asia[5]. Under a Decree of 9th March 1981 (Stcrt. 1981, No. 49)[6], consignments in transit for South Africa are subject to control;

ii) goods which enter, and remain in internal circulation temporarily before leaving Netherlands territory;

iii) goods which enter after having first been exported or taken out of Netherlands territory and which did not arrive at the destination specified in the licence.

Lastly, the Appendix to the *eighth Decree* amending the Decree of 1963 (*Decree of 12th June 1981 relating to the export of strategic materials* — Stb. 351) contains the Dutch version of the Trigger List of IAEA documents INFCIRC 209 and 254, completed by certain sections on ultracentrifugation technology. This list is revised regularly. The twelfth and most recent amendment was made in July 1987 and that list is reproduced in the *Annex* hereto. A Note is attached to the Decree, explaining the reasons for this amendment and also stipulating that it is prohibited to export the materials listed in the Appendix without permission from the Minister for Economic Affairs.

The Appendix draws a distinction between articles intended for military purposes, industrial articles and nuclear articles. It is specified that the "nuclear list" has been redrafted on the basis of the internationally approved terminology and in compliance with non-proliferation guidelines. Additional explanations are given for a number of items, especially those intended for nuclear applications; a number of articles which were previously subject to licence have, on the other hand, been exempted from this obligation provided that certain conditions for use are observed.

It should be noted that there is no special regime in this field for the *import* of nuclear material.

IV. TRANSPORT

A. GENERAL REGULATIONS

The provisions regulating the transport of radioactive and fissile materials in the Netherlands are contained in a Decree of 4th September 1969 (Stb. 1969, No. 405), as amended by a Decree of 4th June 1987 (Stb. 1987, No. 342), on the transport of fissile materials, ores and radioactive substances. Not only does this Decree deal with the carriage of radioactive materials by all modes of transport, it also regulates activities closely associated with such carriage such as the import and export of radioactive materials, and their storage during transport (see the previous section).

The Nuclear Energy Act of 1963 provides that it is prohibited to transfer (transport) fissile materials, ores or radioactive materials without a licence. Under the Transport Decree, a licence is required to transport or store during transport, certain high-activity substances unless they are packed in approved containers.

Given that in the Netherlands, the transport of radioactive materials implies the crossing of frontiers frequently, particular care has been taken to ensure that the national transport regulations are in harmony with the regulations governing international transport. In fact, for all modes of transport, the international regulations have been incorporated into the national ones.

Since the Nuclear Energy Act draws a distinction between fissile materials and ores on the one hand, and radioactive substances on the other, this distinction has been maintained in legislation based on the Act. For this reason, these two categories of radioactive materials will be dealt with separately in this section.

It should be noted that the Decree of 3rd September 1987 (Stb. 1987, No. 403) contains the full text of the basic 1969 Decree as amended on 4th June 1987.

1. Fissile Materials and Ores

The Nuclear Energy Act of 1963 provides that it is prohibited to transport, possess, import or export into or out of the Netherlands, or cause to be so imported or exported, or dispose of fissile materials or ores without a licence (see above).

As concerns the actual transport of such materials, the Transport Decree of 4th September 1969 as amended by the Decree of 4th June 1987, provides that fissile materials and ores are exempt from the licence requirement if no licence is required for their transport under the VSG, VLG or VBG Regulations[7] since, in that case, all that is necessary is that the general packing and approval procedures provided for under these Regulations be observed.

In those cases where a licence to transport fissile materials or to have them in storage during transport is required, the Transport Decree provides that application must be made in writing to the Minister for Economic Affairs and to the Minister of Social Services and Employment, the Minister of Welfare, Health and Cultural Affairs, and the Minister of Housing, Regional Development and the Environment although, in practice, it is submitted to this last-named Minister, with a copy to the other Ministers concerned.

Applications must include the name and address of the applicant, the name and address of the consignor, the name and address of the person to whom the fissile materials are consigned and, if this person is established in Belgium or Luxembourg, a statement signed by him to the effect that he is authorised by the laws of his country to have fissile materials in his possession; in addition, applications must indicate the route along which transport will take place, a description of the means of transport to be used, the probable date of transport or the period for which the licence is required, the quantity of fissile materials to be transported, certificates of approval or acceptance of the type of container to be used, the name and address of the person providing insurance cover or some other form of financial security, and lastly, if applicable, a detailed description of the place or places where the fissile materials concerned will be stored pending and during transport.

Should one of the above-mentioned Ministers consider that an application contains too few particulars for him to judge its merits, he may require any additional information deemed necessary to be furnished within a time-limit to be set by him (Section 3).

2. Radioactive Substances

In contrast to the system adopted for fissile materials and ores, the Nuclear Energy Act of 1963 does not contain any general ban on the transport of radioactive substances without a licence. However, under the Transport Decree of 4th September 1969, as amended by the Decree of 4th June 1987, a licence is required in order to transport or store during transport certain explosive radioactive substances, as well as certain substances of a high activity level unless these latter are packed in approved containers and their carriage has already been approved by the authorities of another country, provided that country is one which the Dutch authorities recognise as acting upon the relevant International Atomic Energy Agency recommendations (Section 5).

When a licence to transport radioactive substances or to have them in storage during transport is required, the application must be made in writing to the Minister for Housing, Regional Development and the Environment, the Minister for Social Services and Employment and the Minister of Welfare, Health and Cultural Affairs. A copy of the application must at the same time be sent to the Minister of Transport. The particulars to be included in the application are the same as those described above for fissile materials and ores, and again, any one of the Ministers concerned may require additional information if he considers it necessary in order to be able to judge the application (Section 6).

B. PARTICULAR MODES OF TRANSPORT

The Transport Decree of 4th September 1969, as amended by the Decree of 4th June 1987, contains detailed provisions according to the mode of transport: rail, road, inland waterway and sea, and air. Information relating to the competent authorities and an analysis of the national legislation have been published in the NEA Study of 1980 entitled "Regulations Governing the Transport of Radioactive Materials".

V. NUCLEAR SECURITY AND PHYSICAL PROTECTION

The provisions regulating national security questions in the Netherlands, and particularly those relating to the disclosure of information about nuclear activities, including trade, are contained in the Nuclear Energy Act. The Act provides for national control and security measures, in the interests of the State, for any activity requiring licensing of the use of fissile materials and ores (Section 19 of the Act of 21st February 1963). Section 19 specifies that conditions in this respect may be attached to licences with a view to ensuring State security or compliance with the international obligations undertaken by the Netherlands. However, the Decrees implementing the Act contain no such requirement relating to fissile materials and ores, nor any provisions about licences within the framework of Section 19.

Decrees issued pursuant to the Nuclear Energy Act may also require that information, equipment or materials used to produce nuclear energy or relating to the storage, manufacture or processing of fissile materials, be treated as an *official secret*, if such information, equipment or materials have been obtained subject to an obligation of secrecy either directly from the Government or with the approval of the competent authorities, or if the Ministers concerned should so decide (Section 68 of the Act of 21st February 1963). The Decree implementing Section 68 is the *Nuclear Secrecy Decree of 17th June 1971* (Stb. 420). The scope of application of the 1971 Decree, designed to protect industrial secrets and to prohibit the export of sensitive information, was broadened to include ultracentrifugation and reprocessing technologies, by a Directive of 24th September 1971 (Stcrt 1971, No. 107) promulgated jointly by the Minister for Foreign Affairs, the Minister of Social Services and Employment, the Minister of Welfare, Health and Cultural Affairs, the Minister for Housing, Regional Development and the Environment, and the Minister responsible for matters concerning science policy and university education.

Physical protection requirements are laid down during the licensing procedure regulated by the Nuclear Energy Act, and are based on the IAEA Recommendations (INFCIRC/225/Rev. 1).

VI. INTELLECTUAL PROPERTY IN THE NUCLEAR FIELD

There is no legislation in the Netherlands at present specifically governing patents in the nuclear field.

Annex I to the Almelo Treaty of 4th March 1970 between the Netherlands, the Federal Republic of Germany and the United Kingdom on co-operation in the field of uranium enrichment contains provisions concerning patents and other industrial property rights.

VII. AGREEMENTS

The Netherlands is Party to several multilateral and bilateral agreements covering scientific, economic and technical co-operation in the field of nuclear energy.

Only those agreements which, directly or indirectly, generally or specifically, deal with trade in nuclear materials, equipment and technology, are included in this chapter.

1. Multilateral Agreements

The following have been concluded by the Netherlands:

- 1968 Treaty on the Non-Proliferation of Nuclear Weapons (NPT), ratified by the Netherlands on 2nd May 1975;
- Agreement of 5th April 1973 between EURATOM, IAEA and the Member States Parties to the NPT (so-called Verification Agreement);
- Convention on the Physical Protection of Nuclear Material of 1980, signed but not yet ratified by the Netherlands;
- Agreement between the Netherlands, the Federal Republic of Germany and the United Kingdom on collaboration in the development and exploitation of the gas centrifuge process for producing enriched uranium (Almelo Treaty — 4th March 1970).

2. Bilateral Agreements

The collaboration, started in 1951, between the Foundation for fundamental material research (FOM) and ***Norway*** has, since 1955, continued between the RCN[8] and the Norwegian Institutt for Atomenergi (IFA). It covers scientific and technical research in the nuclear field, the development of reactors and exchanges of personnel and information. A further Agreement, dated 27th January 1959, was designed to promote and co-ordinate nuclear research in the two bodies : harmonisation of research programmes, exchange of scientific and technical information, creation of mixed research groups in each country working on joint projects in the nuclear centres of Petten (Netherlands) and Kjeller (Norway).

A Co-operation Agreement between the RCN, the ***Belgian*** Atomic Energy Commission and the ***USRR State Commissariat*** for the use of atomic energy was concluded in Moscow on 8th March 1965 ; it provides for the exchange of experts and information.

A Memorandum of Understanding between the Government of the Netherlands and the Government of the ***Federal Republic of Germany*** has, since 1967, regulated collaboration between the two countries in the field of the development and marketing of fast breeder reactors. (Belgium and Luxembourg have signed similar agreements with the Federal Republic of Germany).

On the basis of an exchange of letters, the ***United Kingdom Atomic Energy Authority*** (UKAEA) and the RCN concluded, on 22nd April 1968, an Agreement on collaboration in the peaceful uses of atomic energy. The Agreement provides for the exchange of scientific and technical information in the field of nuclear energy and the exchange of scientific personnel. It follows a previous Agreement (dated 14th March 1956) between the UKAEA and the RCN on collaboration on the construction and development of reactors. Other organisations in the Netherlands, listed in an Annex to the Agreement, are empowered to participate in the above-mentioned exchanges.

NOTES AND REFERENCES

1. Stb.: Staatsblad = Bulletin of Acts, Regulations and Decrees.
2. The current names and spheres of competence of these Ministries are used in this study.
3. Section 1 of the Nuclear Energy Act of 21st February 1963 (Staatsblad 1963, No. 82) and Section 1 of the Definitions Decree of 29th August 1969 (Staatsblad 1969, No. 358) define fissile materials as materials, except ores, containing by weight 0.1 per cent plutonium, 3 per cent thorium or 0.1 per cent uranium. Ores are defined in these same texts as ores, except monazite, containing by weight at least 0.1 per cent uranium or 10 per cent thorium.
4. Radioactive materials are defined in Section 1 of the 1963 Act as any matter which emits ionizing radiation as well as materials and objects containing such matter, except for fissile materials and ores. Apparatus is defined in Section 1 of the Decree of 10th September 1987 issued pursuant to the Nuclear Energy Act and relating to radioactive materials (Stb. 1987, No. 465), as any apparatus capable of emitting radiation with the exception of the spontaneous mutation of radioactive and fissile materials, and nuclear fission.
5. Albania, Bulgaria, the German Democratic Republic, Hungary, Cambodia, North Korea, Laos, Mongolia, Poland, Romania, Czechoslovakia, the USSR, Vietnam, the People's Republic of China.
6. Stcrt.: Staatscourant (second official publication of regulations in the Netherlands).
7. — Reglement voor het vervoer over de spoorweg van gevaarlijke goederen (VSG) (Rail transport) (Stcrt. 1982, 19)
   — Reglement voor het vervoer over land van gevaarlijke goederen (VLG) (Road transport) (Stcrt. 1979, 189)
   — Reglement voor het vervoer over binnenwateren van gevaarlijke goederen (VBG) (Inland waterway transport) (Stcrt. 1968, No. 207).
8. In 1976, the Reactor Centrum Nederland (RCN) became the Netherlands Energy Research Foundation (Energieonderzoek Centrum Nederland - ECN).

NETHERLANDS

Annex

APPENDIX TO THE DECREE OF 12TH JUNE 1981 ON THE EXPORT OF STRATEGIC MATERIALS (Stb. 351) — TWELFTH AMENDMENT DATED JULY 1987*

NUCLEAR GOODS

A. NUCLEAR MATERIALS

0151 Special and other fissile materials, excepting:

1. consignments of one effective gramme or less;
2. consignments of three effective grammes or less when contained in a sensing component in instruments.

Technical notes:

1. "Special fissile materials" is understood to mean: plutonium 239, uranium 233, uranium enriched in the isotopes 235 or 233, and any material containing these isotopes.

2. "Uranium enriched in the isotopes 235 or 233" is considered to be: uranium which contains the isotope 235, 233 or both in an amount such that the abundance ratio of the sum of these isotopes to the isotope 238 is greater than the ratio of the isotope 235 to the isotope 238 occurring in nature.

3. "Other fissile materials" is considered to be: isotopes of plutonium other than plutonium 239 and any material containing these isotopes.

4. "Effective gramme of special or fissile materials" is understood to be:
   a) for uranium 233 or plutonium: the weight of the element in grammes;
   b) for uranium enriched to 1 per cent or more in the isotope U-235: the element weight in grammes multiplied by the square of its enrichment, expressed as a decimal weight fraction;
   c) for uranium enriched to less than 1 per cent in the isotope U-235: the element weight in grammes multiplied by 0.0001;
   d) for americium 242m, curium 245 and 247 and californium 249 and 251: the element weight in grammes multiplied by 10.

5. For this item the term "obtained through reprocessing" is defined as any process intended to increase the concentration of the controlled isotope.

0152 Source materials in any form or present in any substance in which the concentration of the source material is greater than 0.05 per cent by weight, excepting consignments of:

1. *a)* source materials containing 10 kg uranium or less, regardless of the application;
   b) source materials containing 100 kg uranium or less, if intended for civilian, non-nuclear applications.
2. 50 kg thorium.
3. thorium alloys containing less than 5 per cent thorium by weight.
4. depleted uranium especially prepared for the following civilian applications:
   a) safety shields;
   b) packaging;
   c) ballast; or
   d) counterweights.

Technical note: "Source material" is understood to be: uranium which contains a mixture of isotopes such as occurring in nature; uranium depleted in the isotope 235; thorium; in any of the mentioned materials in the form of metal, alloy, chemical compound, or concentrates.

* Unofficial translation.

0153 Deuterium and deuterium compounds, mixtures and solutions which contain deuterium, including heavy water and heavy paraffins, in which the ratio of deuterium to hydrogen atoms is greater than 1: 5000, except consignments of the above-mentioned substances containing 10 kg deuterium or less.

0154 Zirconium (metal), alloys containing more than 50 per cent zirconium by weight, compounds, in which the hafnium/zirconium ratio is less than 1: 5000 by weight and products which are entirely manufactured thereof, except:

1. consignments of zirconium metal and alloy 5 kg or less;
2. consignments of zirconium 200 kg or less in the form of foil, or strip with a thickness not greater than 0.025 mm and specially prepared and intended for use in photo flash bulbs.

0155 Nickel powder and porous nickel metal:

A. powder with a nickel content of 99 per cent or more and a particle size less than 100 microns;

B. porous metal with an average pore diameter of 25 microns or less and a content of pure nickel of 99 per cent or more, excepting single plates of porous nickel, with a surface not less than 930 cm^2, intended for use in batteries for civilian applications.

Technical note: Subheading B of this entry refers to porous nickel metal which is manufactured of nickel power, as described in A, to form a metal material with fine pores interlinked throughout the overall structure.

N.B.: See item 1661.

Note 1: A short administrative export licence procedure may be allowed for shipments of nickel powder in uncompacted powder form in quantities of 4 000 kg or less for non-nuclear civilian applications.

Note 2: A short administrative export licence procedure may be allowed for shipments of nickel powder obtained by the carbonyl process to the People's Republic of China for non-nuclear civilian applications.

0156 Graphite suited for application in nuclear reactor, i.e. graphite with a purity level of more than 1 ppm boron equivalent and with a density greater than 1.5 g/cm^3, except individual consignments of 100 kg or less (see also item 1673).

0157 Lithium, as follows:

A. metal, hydrides or alloys containing lithium enriched in the 6 isotope to a concentration greater than that occurring in nature (7.5 per cent on an atom percentage basis);

B. any other materials containing lithium enriched in the 6 isotope (including compounds, mixtures and concentrates) except lithium enriched in the 6 isotope contained in thermoluminescent dosimeters.
(For natural lithium deuteride or lithium enriched in the 7 isotope, see item 0153.)

0158 Hafnium metal, alloys and compounds containing more than 60 per cent hafnium by weight, and manufactures thereof, excepting consignments of the above having a hafnium content of 1 kg or less.

0159 Beryllium metal, alloys containing more than 50 per cent beryllium by weight and compounds containing beryllium and manufactures thereof, excepting:

1. beryllium metal windows for X-ray equipment;
2. beryllium oxide shapes in fabricated or semi-fabricated forms, specially designed for electronic assemblies or as substrates for electronic circuits;
3. consignments of 500 g or less of beryllium with a purity of 99 per cent or less, or 100 g or less of beryllium with a purity of 99 per cent or greater, provided these consignments do not contain monocrystals;
4. consignments of 5 kg or less of beryllium, in compounds with a purity less than 99 per cent.

0162 Tritium, tritium compounds and mixtures containing tritium, in which the ratio of tritium to hydrogen by atoms is greater than 1: 10^3, as well as products which contain one or more of the foregoing, excepting:

1. consignments of tritium, tritium compounds, and mixtures as well as individual products which contain one or more of the foregoing, with a radioactivity of 3 700 giga becquerel (100 curie) or less;
2. tritium in luminescent paint, self-luminescent products, gas and aerosol detectors, electron tubes, lightning and static elimination devices, detector cells for gas chromatography, and calibration devices;
3. tritium and tritium compounds where the separation of the tritium from its compounds cannot result in the evolution of an isotopic mixture of hydrogen in which the ratio of tritium to hydrogen by atoms is greater than 1:1000.

0163 Materials for nuclear heat sources, as follows:

A. plutonium in any form with a plutonium isotopic assay of plutonium 238 of more than 50 per cent, except:
   1. consignments with a plutonium content of one gramme or less;
   2. consignments of three effective grammes or less when contained in a sensing component in instruments;
   3. plutonium 238 contained in cardiac pacemakers.

B. “previously separated” neptunium 237 in any form, except consignments with a neptunium 237 content of one gramme or less.

Technical note: For the purpose of this item, “previously separated” is defined as the application of any process intended to increase the concentration of the controlled isotope.

0164 Specially designed or prepared materials for the separation of isotopes of natural uranium and depleted uranium, and special and other fissile materials.

N.B.: See item 0170 for isotopic separation plants.

B. NUCLEAR INSTALLATIONS

0170 A. Installations for the separation of isotopes, source materials, special and other fissile materials, such as:

1. gas centrifuge assemblies;
2. jet nozzle separation units;
3. vortex separation units;
4. laser isotopic separation units;
5. chemical exchange separation units;
6. electromagnetic separation units;
7. plasma separation units;
8. gaseous diffusion separation units.

B. Components specially designed for the above, including:

1. valves with a diameter of 0.5 cm or greater and with bellow seals, which are made of or lined with aluminium, nickel, or an alloy containing more than 60 per cent nickel;
2. blowers and compressors (turbo, centrifuge, and axial types) completely made of or lined with aluminium, nickel or an alloy containing 60 per cent or more nickel, with a capacity of 1.7 m^3 per minute or greater, including compressor seals (blowers, compressors, and compressor seals with different specifications are not included under this entry);
3. heat exchangers made of aluminium, copper, nickel or alloys containing more than 60 per cent nickel or combinations of these metals in the form of clad tubes, designed for use at pressures of less than 1 atm with a leakage rate of less than 10 Pa (0.1 millibar) per hour at a pressure differential of 1 bar (heat exchangers with different specifications are not included in this item);
4. gaseous diffusion barriers;
5. gaseous diffuser housings.

C. Components as described here below, specially designed for use in gas centrifuges:

1. Rotating components:

a) complete rotors, that is thin-walled cylinders or a number of interconnected thin-walled cylinders, made of “material” with a high strength to density ratio;
Note: this includes subassemblies;

b) rotor tubes, specially designed thin-walled cylinders with a wall thickness of 12 mm or less, a diameter between 75-400 mm and fabricated in material with a high strength to density ratio;

c) rings or bellows specially designed, either for strengthening a rotor tube at certain places or for joining a number of rotor tubes and made of a material with a high strength to density ratio;

d) disc-shaped components with diameter between 75-400 mm, specially designed to be mounted inside the centrifuge rotor tube and made of a material with a high strength to density ratio;

e) bottom and top caps in the form of disc-shaped components with a diameter of 75-400 mm specially designed to fit to the ends of a rotor tube and made of a material with a high strength to density ratio

Technical note 1: The materials used for centrifuge rotating components are:

a) maraging steel capable of an ultimate tensile strength of 2.050 x 10^9 N/m^2 or more,

b) aluminium alloys capable of an ultimate tensile strength of 0.460 x 10^9 N/m^2 or more,

c) filamentary elements, for use in composite structures as meant in item 1763A.

Technical note 2: The bellows is a short cylinder of wall thickness of 3 mm or less, a diameter of between 75-400 mm and with a convolute.

2. Static components:

a) specially designed bearing assemblies, consisting of an annular magnet suspended in a housing containing a damping medium, where the housing is made of a UF_6 resistant material;

b) specially designed bearings comprising a pivot/cup assembly mounted on a damper;

c) molecular pumps in specially designed or prepared cylinders with extruded helical grooves and internally machined bores.

Technical note: Typical dimensions are as follows:

1. 75-400 mm internal diameter;
2. wall thickness of 10 mm or more;
3. ratio length/diameter of 1:1;
4. the grooves are typically rectangular in cross-section and 2 mm or more in depth.

d) specially designed ring-shaped stators for high speed multiface AC hysteresis motors (or reluctance) for synchronous operation in vacuum with the following characteristics:

1. a frequency range of 600-2000 Hz;
2. a power range of 50-1000 Va; and
3. consisting of multi-face windings surrounding a thin layer core with:
   i) a thickness of 2 mm or less,
   ii) low magnetic losses.

D. Specially developed accessories, apparatus or components for ultra-centrifuge enrichment plants, as described hereunder, and constructed entirely of and coated with UF_6 resistant materials:

1. specially developed feed-systems and systems for withdrawing enriched or depleted gas streams including:

   a) feed autoclaves or stations used for passing UF_6 to the centrifuge cascades with a maximum pressure of 100 KN/m^2 and at a rate of 1 kg/h or more;

   b) desublimers (or cold traps) used to remove UF_6 from the cascades at a pressure up to 3 KN/m^2 and which can be chilled to 203 K (-70 °C) or heated up to 343 K (70 °C);

   c) stations for enriched or depleted gas streams, used to trap UF_6 in containers;

2. specially developed piping systems or headers for handling UF_6 in the cascades;

3. specially developed mass spectrometers capable of taking on line samples of UF_6 feed streams, of depleted and enriched UF_6 gas streams with all the following characteristics:

   a) unit resolution for mass greater than 320;
   b) ion sources made of or lined with nicrome or monel or nickel plated;
   c) electron bombardment ionization sources;
   d) having a collector system suitable for isotopic analysis.

4. frequency changers (also known as convertors or invectors) specially designed to supply motor stators for ultracentrifuge enrichment with all the following characteristics, and specially designed components therefor:

   a) a multiface output of 600 Hz to 2 kHz;
   b) frequency control better than 0.1 per cent;
   c) harmonic distortion of less than 2 per cent; and
   d) an efficiency greater than 80 per cent.

E. Other components for ultra centrifuge enrichment plants:

1. components specially designed for housing the complete rotor of an ultracentrifuge as referred to in C.1.a including upper and bottom bearings and motor stator;

2. UF_6 pressure measurement devices or apparatus specially designed for measuring pressures up to 13 KN/m^2 with an accuracy better than ± 1 per cent and with pressure sensors made of UF_6 resistant materials;

3. specially designed scoops of maximum 5 mm diameter for extraction of UF_6 gas from a rotor tube by means of the pitot-tube principle, suitable for connection with the central gas extraction system and made of UF_6 resistant materials.

F. Equipment specially developed for the construction of rotor components of gas centrifuges:

1. equipment specially designed for making up rotor tube components, discs and caps as referred to in C.1.b and e;

....

3. equipment specially designed to balance rotors in three or more planes using vacuum test chambers and suitable for very precise handling of gas centrifuge rotors at velocities of more than 300 m/sec., as referred to in C.1.a;

4. equipment specially designed for the fabrication of rings or bellows as referred to in C.1.c.

Technical note: "UF_6 resistant materials" are for example stainless steel, aluminium alloys, nickel or alloys of more than 60 per cent.

Note 1: See item 0151 for the definition of "special fissile materials" and "other fissile materials".

Note 2: See item 0164 for specially designed or prepared materials for the separation of isotopes.

0171 Plants for the reprocessing of irradiated nuclear reactor fuel elements and specially designed or prepared equipment and components thereof, including:

A. fuel element chopping machines, i.e. remote control equipment for the cutting or chopping of irradiated nuclear reactor fuel assemblies, bundles or rods;

B. 1. critically safe tanks (for example annular or slab tanks with a small diameter), specially designed or prepared for the dissolution of irradiated nuclear reactor fuel, which can withstand hot, highly corrosive fluids, and which can be remotely loaded and maintained;

....

C. countercurrent solvent extractors, specially designed or prepared for use in an installation for the reprocessing of irradiated natural or depleted uranium and irradiated special and other fissile materials ...;

D. instruments for the control of processes, specially designed or prepared for the monitoring or control of the reprocessing of irradiated natural or depleted uranium and irradiated special and other fissile materials;

E. systems specially designed for the conversion of plutonium nitrate into plutonium oxide;

F. systems specially designed for the production of plutonium metal.

Technical note: A "plant for the reprocessing of irradiated nuclear reactor fuel elements" contains equipment and components which as a rule are in direct contact with and directly control the irradiated fuel and the major nuclear material and fission product processing streams.

Note 1: See item 0151 defining "special" and "other" fissile materials.

Note 2: See item 0181 for counterflow liquid extraction equipment specially designed for use with nuclear propulsion equipment. See item 0170 B for other counterflow liquid extraction equipment.

0172 Nuclear reactors, i.e. reactors which can maintain a controlled, self-sustained fission chain reaction, and equipment and components, specially designed or prepared for use with a nuclear reactor including:

A. pressure vessels, i.e. metal vessels either as complete units or as the principal prefabricated components thereof, which are specially designed or prepared to contain the core of a nuclear reactor and which are capable of withstanding the operating pressure of the primary coolant, including the top plate of the reactor pressure vessel;

B. equipment for fuel element handling, including charging and discharging equipment for reactor fuel;

C. control rods, i.e. rods specially designed or prepared to control the reaction rate in a nuclear reactor, including the neutron absorption part and the support or suspension structures therefor and control rod guide tubes;

D. electronic controls to control the power levels in nuclear reactors, including control rod drive mechanisms and instruments for the detection and measurement of radiation for the determination of the neutron flux levels;

E. pressure tubes, i.e. tubes specially designed or prepared to contain fuel elements and the primary coolant in a nuclear reactor at an operating pressure of more than 50 bar;

F. coolant pumps, i.e. pumps specially designed or prepared for circulating the primary coolant of nuclear reactors;

G. internal parts specially designed or prepared for the operation of nuclear reactors, including but not limited to the reactor core support structures, thermal shields, baffles, core grid plates and diffuser plates;

H. heat exchangers.

Technical note: A "nuclear "reactor" contains the parts in or directly affixed to the reactor vessel, the equipment which controls the power level in the reactor core, as well as components which usually contain the primary coolant of the reactor core, are in direct contact with or control the primary coolant.

0173 Plants and specially designed equipment for the fabrication of nuclear reactor fuel elements.

Technical note: A "plant for the preparation of nuclear reactor fuel elements" contains equipment which:

a) as a rule is in direct contact with or directly processes or controls the production flow of nuclear material;
b) seals the nuclear material within the cladding;
c) checks the integrity of the cladding or the seal;
d) checks the final treatment of the solid fuel.

0174 Plants for the production of heavy water, deuterium and deuterium compounds and specially designed or prepared equipment and components therefor.

0175 Plants for the preparation of uranium hexafluoride (UF_6) as well as specially designed or prepared equipment (including equipment for the purification of UF_6) as well as specially designed or prepared components therefor.

C. NUCLEAR-RELATED EQUIPMENT

0180 Neutron generator systems, including neutron generator tubes, designed to operate without an external vacuum system and use electrostatic acceleration to induce a tritium-deuterium nuclear reaction.

Note: A short administrative export licence procedure may be allowed for shipment of tubes and systems covered by this item provided that they are for civilian use.

0181 Power generating or propulsion equipment specially designed for use with military, space, marine or mobile nuclear reactors.

Technical note: This item does not apply to conventional power generating equipment which, although designed for use in a particular nuclear plant, could in principle be used in conjunction with conventional systems.

0182 Electrolytic cells with a production of fluorine greater than 250 g per hour.

0183 Equipment for the separation of lithium isotopes.

0184 Equipment specially designed for the production or recovery of tritium.

GOODS IN WHICH TECHNOLOGY IS SPECIFIED

2000 Printed matter and other written material, and other goods intended or suited for the transfer of knowledge, insofar as they contain technology pertaining to the design, preparation or use of the goods as specified in this Appendix, unless this has been made known in generally accessible publications known to us.

NORWAY

TABLE OF CONTENTS

NORWAY

I. INTRODUCTION

In Norway, trade in nuclear and radioactive materials and equipment is governed by several considerations, in particular, the non-proliferation of nuclear weapons (safeguards), nuclear safety and physical protection on the one hand and on the other, protection against radiation hazards. These various considerations are reflected in the legislation in force.

Such trade is subject to a system of permits laid down by Act No. 28 of 12th May 1972 on Nuclear Activities. In addition, the Decree of 2nd May 1984, made in implementation of that Act (Section 6) lays down regulations for the physical protection of nuclear materials and therefore has a bearing on their commerce.

Nuclear trade is also governed by ordinary trade law and the Act of 13th December 1946 relating to exports is generally applicable, as it covers all exports from Norway. In particular, the Ministry of Trade issued Regulations on 1st November 1983 concerning implementation of regulatory measures regarding imports and exports; the Regulations provide (Section 1) that the Ministry shall prepare lists of those materials that are subject to licensing. These lists which are updated at regular intervals are contained in reports published by the Ministry and include nuclear items.

Trade in radioactive materials, namely radioisotopes, is dealt with by the Regulations of 1st March 1983 on production, imports and sales of radioisotopes. It should be noted that these Regulations, made in pursuance of the Act of 18th June 1938 concerning the Use of X-rays and Radium etc. (Sections 1 and 5), govern such trade for purposes of radiation protection.

The above legislation provides the regulatory framework for nuclear trade in Norway, while the authorities responsible for granting the licences and permits required are the *Ministry of Petroleum and Energy* under the 1972 Act on Nuclear Activities, the *Ministry of Trade* under the 1946 Act on Exports and finally, the *National Institute of Radiation Hygiene* (*Statens Institutt for Stralehygiene — SIS*)[1] under the 1983 Regulations on production, imports and sales of radioisotopes.

In the description of the regulation of nuclear trade in Norway, the Government's policy on nuclear exports and imports will first be discussed and then followed by an analysis of the pertinent nuclear and general regulations in the field. As already mentioned, the regulations governing trade in radioactive materials do so from the radiation protection viewpoint and will therefore be analysed separately to distinguish between the different objectives underlying adoption of the legislation concerned. The transport of radioactive materials and their physical protection as well as industrial property in the nuclear context will also be discussed. Finally, reference will be made to agreements of relevance to nuclear trade.

II. NUCLEAR EXPORT AND IMPORT POLICY AND PROCEDURES

Three concerns are at the root of Norway's export and import policy and may be summarised as follows: nuclear material and equipment should not be diverted to non-peaceful purposes, nuclear activities are to be conducted in a safe manner and finally, national obligations under international treaties must be complied with.

It should be noted here that the Institute for Energy Technology (*Institutt for Energiteknikk — IFE*)[2], by an agreement of 16th December 1970 with the Government, acts as the national safeguards body. IFE is responsible for implementing international safeguards in Norway under a Royal Decree of 6th November 1969. It has a licence to possess and operate nuclear installations which includes a standing permit to possess nuclear material. One of the conditions for granting of this licence is that IFE make provision for implementing international safeguards in accordance with the obligations set out in agreements concluded by Norway with other States or with international organisations. The Nuclear Energy Safety Authority (*Statens Atomtilsyn — SAT*)[3] supervises that this condition is complied with.

1. Export Regime

As a matter of principle, Norway has since 1980 restricted its exports of nuclear material and equipment to countries where all nuclear activities are under the International Atomic Energy Agency's Safeguards System.

In addition, Norway as a member of the Nuclear Exporters Committee (so-called Zangger Committee)[4] complies with the trigger list for exports of nuclear materials and equipment adopted by that Committee. The Ministry of Foreign Affairs drew up procedures for implementing the Zangger Committee requirements on 4th December 1975.

Furthermore, in accordance with COCOM[5] requirements, applications for export licences (sent to the Ministry of Trade) must be accompanied by an import certificate issued by the trade authorities in the receiving country. It should be noted that COCOM's "Atomic Energy List" originally formed the basis of the Ministry of Trade's regulation of nuclear exports. Since the Zangger Committee's list was made applicable, additional materials have been made subject to export licensing requirements (see section III.2 below).

Regarding the particular case of heavy water of which Norway is a producer, if the exported quantity of heavy water exceeds 50 kg, an end use statement, issued by the importer must be attached to the export licence application. In any event, all applications for the export of heavy water are submitted to the IFE before a licence is granted.

In the context of its standing permit to possess nuclear material, IFE has been granted the right to export such material. In effect, IFE is practically the sole possessor of nuclear material in Norway.

If nuclear material of United States origin is to be exported, approval by the United States Department of Energy (US DOE) must be given in advance. IFE, acting on behalf of the Government of Norway, obtains this approval via the Norwegian embassy in Washington. After a shipment has taken place, IFE makes a report on the shipment to the IAEA (and to US DOE in the case of nuclear material of United States origin).

If the amount of exported nuclear material exceeds one effective kilogram of plutonium and uranium, IFE must notify the International Atomic Energy Agency (IAEA) at least two weeks before the nuclear material is prepared for shipping.

An owner of nuclear material (apart from IFE) may not send the material out of the country until such a transfer has been approved by SAT and IFE. If US DOE approval is required, IFE must be informed at least five months before the planned transfer. The owner shall upon shipment immediately notify IFE in writing of the date of shipment and the exact weight of the materials shipped.

In Norway, international movements of nuclear material have until now essentially involved despatch from IFE of irradiated fuel for reprocessing and storage, and of fresh fuel for regeneration and return. The remaining nuclear exports have involved heavy water and zirconium tubes; however, the production of zirconium tubes has now been stopped.

Finally, the Customs Tariff refers by letter code to obligatory licences required under the 1946 Act on Exports, giving information to the Customs authorities requiring them to determine that the necessary export licence has been obtained. Nuclear or nuclear-related items are referred to under letter code E and require export licences.

2. Import Regime

Norwegian import of nuclear material essentially involves imports by IFE of reactor fuel materials, including test fuels for the Halden Reactor Project[6]. Remaining nuclear imports mainly concern zirconium tubes.

Before an import takes place, IFE provides the exporting country with an Import Certificate issued by the Ministry of Trade and Shipping in accordance with COCOM requirements.

IFE must report to IAEA all receipts of nuclear material in Norway. If the amount of expected transfer of nuclear material to Norway exceeds one effective kilogram, IFE must notify IAEA of the transfer as far in advance as possible, and in any case no later than the date of arrival.

An importer of nuclear material (apart from IFE) must, upon receipt of the material, immediately notify IFE in writing of the date of arrival and the exact weight of the material received. He may not transfer the material to other persons in Norway without SAT and IFE approval of the transfer.

The granting of a permit by the Ministry of Petroleum and Energy to import nuclear material is subject to the condition that the importer accepts certain obligations concerning the accounting and reporting of such material to ensure that it is placed under satisfactory safeguards.

III. TRADE IN NUCLEAR MATERIAL AND EQUIPMENT

The regulatory aspects of nuclear trade can be considered from two angles : the purely nuclear regulations, namely the 1972 Act on Nuclear Activities and, in the context of general trade law, the Act of 13th December 1946 relating to exports together with the 1983 Regulations made in its implementation and more recently, an Act relating to the control of strategic goods, services and technology (1987).

NORWAY

1. Nuclear Regulations

The *Act of 1972 on Nuclear Activities* gives the following definitions of nuclear and radioactive substances [Section 1(a), (b) and (c)] :

"*(a)* Nuclear fuel means :
fissionable material in the form of uranium or plutonium metal, alloy or chemical compound, and such other fissionable material as the Ministry [of Petroleum and Energy] may determine ;

(b) radioactive products means :
other radioactive material (including wastes) which is made, or has become radioactive by radiation incidental to the production or utilization of nuclear fuel ;

(c) nuclear substance means :
nuclear fuel, other than natural uranium and depleted uranium, as well as radioactive products, except radioisotopes used for industrial, commercial, agricultural, medical or scientific purposes or which are intended for, and are directly usable for such a purpose".

The Act provides (Section 5) that it is unlawful to possess plutonium and enriched uranium without a permit from the Ministry of Petroleum and Energy. A permit to possess such materials does not include the right to export them, unless this is specially indicated.

A permit may include the right to own, store, handle, transport, sell or otherwise possess plutonium and enriched uranium. The permit may be granted generally for a definite or indefinite period, or on an individual basis, and it may be restricted to cover a special authorisation for one of the activities mentioned above (Section 5).

In the context of administrative provisions, the Act stipulates (Section 6) that the King may make rules regarding the ownership, sale, etc. of nuclear substances or other types of nuclear fuel or radioactive products.

The granting of a permit for owning, handling, selling etc. nuclear substances is subject to such conditions as are considered necessary from the viewpoint of safety (Section 8). The Nuclear Energy Safety Authority (SAT) is the authority responsible for supervising that such conditions are complied with where necessary, by means of inspections, and that nuclear activities are conducted on a sound basis (Sections 13 and 14).

A permit is not required from the Ministry of Petroleum and Energy for the possession of natural uranium, depleted uranium or thorium (Section 2).

Finally, the Act provides (Section 55) that violation of its provisions may be sanctioned by a fine or imprisonment for one year or by both.

2. General Trade Regulations

The *Act of 13th December 1946 on Exports* controls the exports of nuclear materials and equipment. The Act is general in character and bans exports of foods or articles from Norway without a licence or exemption therefrom by the King (Section 1). It specifies that statements of exports and other relevant documents must be submitted to the competent Ministry (Section 3) and provides that the King may make more detailed regulations in implementation of the Act (Section 4).

By Royal Decree of 12th December 1947, the Ministry of Trade was given power to exercise such authority under the Act, and introduced compulsory licences for the export of a number of materials, including nuclear material.

The Ministry's *Regulations of 1st November 1983* made under the 1946 Act lay down provisions with regard to export licences and the conditions to be complied with by applicants. As already mentioned, the Regulations (Section 1) provide that the Ministry shall draw up lists of items requiring an export licence which will be regularly updated and published in reports.

The Atomic Energy List established by the Ministry of Trade includes the nuclear and nuclear-related items subject to an export licence. This List, which is reproduced in *Annex I*, contains items from both the Zangger Trigger List and the COCOM Atomic Energy List.

An Act relating to the control of strategic goods, services and technology entered into force on 18th December 1987. It complements the above Act of 1946 and is relevant, *inter alia*, to the export of nuclear material, equipment, sensitive nuclear technology and services. In effect, it provides for strict controls and verification of certain exports.

There are no specific regulations regarding import licences for nuclear items apart from the requirements contained in the Regulations of 1st March 1986 relating to import and sales of radioisotopes analysed below.

IV. TRADE IN RADIOACTIVE MATERIALS

The *Regulations of 1st March 1983 relating to Production, Import and Sales of Radioisotopes* issued by the Ministry of Social Affairs apply to radioisotopes used for industrial, commercial agricultural, medical or scientific purposes and regulate such uses with a view to radiation protection.

Under the Regulations (Sections 3 and 4), imports and sales of radioisotopes require a permit from the National Institute of Radiation Hygiene (SIS).

The Institute may issue detailed rules concerning registration and reporting of imports and may stipulate conditions governing the granting of permits in connection with imports by individual companies for their own use and for trading purposes (Section 3).

Applications for a permit to import and trade in radioisotopes must be filed with SIS. As a rule such applicants are dealers, but end-users may also apply. Permits are issued on a case-by-case basis and may also be delivered as a general permit covering several years. The main criteria for obtaining a general permit are demonstration of the need therefor and observance of the relevant radiation protection regulations. It should be noted that the Institute for Energy Technology (IFE) has a general permit for the import and sale of all types of radioisotopes. (A model of the general permit is contained in *Annex II* to this chapter.)As mentioned above, SIS is empowered to issue specific conditions governing imports and sales of radioisotopes and they are set out in a document of 20th June 1984 entitled "Conditions for production, import and sale of radioactive material in Norway". These conditions are general and concern, *inter alia*, internal safety procedures, quality control and a reporting system to SIS.

Such conditions must in principle be complied with by licensees. In addition, licensees may only sell radioisotopes to users approved by SIS.

However, given the wide variety of radioactive materials from the viewpoint of both activity and hazard, SIS considered that it was not possible to establish conditions applicable indiscriminately to all cases. Accordingly, to assist licensees, SIS has prepared comments on the conditions to facilitate their interpretation, e.g. "Further interpretation of conditions for the import and sale of smoke detectors".

Finally, if conditions stipulated by the Ministry of Health and Social Affairs or SIS are not complied with, the latter may withdraw the permit concerned.

V. ORES

The General Concessions Act (No. 16) of 14th December 1917 on the acquisition of waterfalls, mines and other immovable property provides (Chapter II) that prospecting activities may be undertaken by the State, local authorities and Norwegian nationals and companies. Such activities require a permit from the Ministry of Trade but the State and local authorities are exempted from this requirement. In addition, uranium and thorium ores are subject to export licences being granted by the Ministry.

At present, uranium prospecting is almost entirely carried out by the State.

VI. TRANSPORT[7]

The Act of 12th May 1972 on Nuclear Activities provides the basic framework for regulating the transport of nuclear materials in Norway ; the *Act of 18th June 1983 concerning the Use of X-rays and Radium* governs the transport of radioactive and nuclear materials from the radiation protection viewpoint. In addition, the Physical Protection Regulations of 1984, described under the following heading, must be complied with during transport operations.

The National Institute of Radiation Hygiene (SIS) is competent for delivering the permits and certificates required in accordance with the IAEA Regulations for the Safe Transport of Radioactive Materials; both packaging (transport containers) and the transport itself must be approved by SIS with respect to radiation protection criteria.

The Nuclear Energy Safety Authority (SAT), which is responsible for the physical protection aspects of transport operations (see below), issues permits for the transport of nuclear material (1972 Act, Section 5).

It should be noted that, before any export takes place, a financial security certificate and approval by the competent national bodies are required for the safe transport of radioactive materials in transit and to recipient countries. The IFE applies for such documents.

VII. PHYSICAL PROTECTION

A *Royal Decree of 2nd May 1984*, made in pursuance of the 1972 Act on Nuclear Activities (Section 6) lays down *Regulations for the Physical Protection of Nuclear Material*. Their purpose is to establish conditions which will minimise the possibilities of theft of nuclear material and sabotage of nuclear plants, as well as facilitate recovery of stolen materials.

As already mentioned, the Nuclear Energy Safety Authority (SAT) is competent for the physical protection of nuclear material, while the National Institute of Radiation Hygiene (SIS) is responsible for radiation protection aspects.

In addition, if theft or sabotage are reported, the Ministry of Petroleum and Energy acts as the co-ordinating body for the steps to be taken by the Ministry of Justice and Police and the Ministry of Foreign Affairs. The Ministry of Justice and Police is for its part responsible for initiating the operations to counteract such theft or sabotage, and the Ministry of Foreign Affairs is charged with providing information on the subject to other countries in accordance with Norway's obligations under the 1980 Convention on the Physical Protection of Nuclear Material (Section 13).

Persons responsible for nuclear material are required to establish and maintain a system for physical protection of such material during storage, processing and transport. They must also prepare a safety report on physical protection for the approval of the Ministry of Petroleum and Energy, on the basis of a recommendation by SAT (Section 12).

They must in addition appoint one or more persons to be responsible for the physical protection aspects of stored materials, as well as equipment and material being processed or shipped (Section 12). In particular, for each individual shipment, they must appoint a transport co-ordinator responsible for preparing the shipment involved [Section 17(b)].

The Regulations lay down specific requirements for protecting nuclear material in storage and divide the material into three categories (I, II, and III) according to their radioactivity and weight (Appendix 1).

The Regulations also detail fundamental rules for physical protection of nuclear material during transport by road and as appropriate, by other means of transport (Section 17).

The physical protection of all shipments must be approved by SAT which must authorise them in advance. Such authorisation contains the conditions and requirements applying to each particular shipment. However, SAT may give a general permit only for shipment of categories II and III materials, in which case no further notification is required for individual shipments [Section 17(c)].

An External Transport Control, established by the sender of the materials, maintains telephone/radio contact with the transport vehicle or the escorting vehicle and with the recipient of the materials and will give instructions to the transport personnel, the police or the highway authorities if any irregularities occur during the transport operation [Section 17(e)].

The Regulations specifically provide that, to reduce any risks in connection with transport of nuclear material, it must be ensured that shipments remain as short a time as possible in transit, that few reloadings and temporary storages occur on the way and that shipments do not take place at regular, known times. Only authorised persons may proceed with shipments and the person responsible (the "operator" under the 1972 Act), together with the authorities concerned must be cautious in dealing with information which could jeopardise physical protection. Shipments of category I materials must be treated as confidential in accordance with security instructions issued by Royal Decree of 17th March 1972 [Section 17(a)].

Shipments of nuclear material are subject to agreements being concluded prior to the shipment between the sender and the recipient on the one hand, and the sender and the transport firm on the other; also at least

24 hours' notice of the transport operation must be given to the recipient and the sender must keep the recipient informed of the estimated time of arrival. In case the shipment does not arrive at that time, the recipient must inform the External Transport Control accordingly. The transport route must be decided in advance, and an alternative route planned [Section 17(f) and (i)].

SAT, in co-operation with the Institute for Energy Technology (IFE) and the sender (for exports) or the recipient (for imports) must ensure that the nuclear material during shipment in the exporting country or shipment to the importing country and in countries of transit will as a minimum be subject to a level of physical protection as set out in Appendix 3 to the Regulations[8]. Also, SAT, in co-operation with IFE, must reach agreement with the exporting or importing country and with the countries of transit regarding the point of transfer of responsibility for physical protection from the authorities of one country to those of the other [Section 17(k)].

IFE, which has knowledge of the transport operation, initiates SAT's contact with foreign authorities. SAT contacts the Ministry of Foreign Affairs in order to obtain statements in connection with transit through countries which have not signed the Convention on the Physical Protection of Nuclear Material.

Special, more stringent, rules apply to the transport of category I materials as regards transport by road, rail, sea and air, e.g., road transport equipment must be designed and built to resist attack, the position of the vehicle on the road must be reported to the External Transport Control several times an hour, and shipments by rail must be placed in a goods train or a separate waggon in a passenger train and must have a police escort (Section 18).

It should be noted that international shipments of nuclear material must be carried out on the basis of the IAEA Regulations on the Safe Transport of Radioactive Materials (Section 18).

It is specified that the Regulations on the Physical Protection of Nuclear Material are additional to those already applying to the storage and transport of radioactive substances or dangerous goods (Section 18).

VIII. INTELLECTUAL PROPERTY IN THE NUCLEAR FIELD

Although the Act of 15th December 1967 on Patents contains no special provisions concerning the nuclear field, it is provided that the Government may order, when in the public interest, that the right to a particular invention be surrendered to the State.

Also, the 1972 Act on Nuclear Activities (Section 53) provides that persons who have had knowledge of technical or business secrets during the course of their activities must preserve such secrets and, in particular, may not use this information for commercial purposes.

IX. AGREEMENTS

In addition to the international Conventions to which it is a Party, Norway has concluded a number of agreements in the nuclear field. Only those agreements which have a bearing on nuclear trade are mentioned below. However, no reference is made to international agreements concerning general trade or transport.

1. Multilateral Agreements

The following Conventions providing for international control measures which affect nuclear trade have been ratified by Norway:

— Treaty of 1st July 1968 on the Non-Proliferation of Nuclear Weapons (NPT), ratified by Norway on 5th February 1969;

— Convention of 3rd March 1980 on the Physical Protection of Nuclear Material, ratified by Norway on 15th August 1985.

2. Bilateral Agreements

The following agreements refer to general nuclear co-operation or to co-operation in a specific area:

a) Framework agreements

— Agreement between Norway and the ***United States*** for Co-operation in the Peaceful Uses of Nuclear Energy, signed on 12th January 1982 and entered into force on 2nd July 1984 for thirty years.

This Agreement covers, *inter alia*, transfer of information, material (source material, special nuclear material and by-product material), components and equipment for reactors and other nuclear installations as well as moderator material.

It is specified that none of the items transferred under the Agreement shall be used for military or explosive purposes. Furthermore, any reprocessing or enrichment of transferred material is subject to agreement by the other Party and prior consent by the other Party is required concerning any transfers whatsoever to third parties.

With regard to activities under the Agreement, both Parties undertake to apply IAEA safeguards under the Non-Proliferation Treaty as well as physical protection measures in accordance with IAEA document INFCIRC/225/Rev.1.

b) Supply agreements

— Agreements between Norway, the ***United States*** and the ***International Atomic Energy Agency (IAEA)*** for supply of nuclear material or equipment; the first of this series of agreements was concluded on 1st April 1961 and the latest on 10th April 1967.

c) Safeguards agreements

— Agreement between Norway and the ***IAEA*** for Application of Safeguards in connection with the NPT, signed on 1st March 1972.

NOTES AND REFERENCES

1. SIS, whose supervisory authority is the Ministry of Health and Social Affairs, is the body competent for radiation protection in Norway. It is empowered to licence all facilities and devices emitting ionizing radiation with regard to radiation protection and may issue the necessary regulations for this purpose.
2. IFE is an independent foundation under the Ministry of Petroleum and Energy. It is the national centre for nuclear research and development and produces and distributes radioisotopes. For further details on SIS and IFE, see *Regulatory and Institutional Framework for Nuclear Activities*, Volume II, OECD/NEA, 1984.
3. SAT (Statens Atomtilsyn) was set up by the 1972 Act on Nuclear Activities and is placed under the Ministry of Petroleum and Energy for administrative purposes. It is the highest specialised agency on nuclear safety questions and is the supervisory authority in that field. See publication quoted in Note 2 for further details.
4. The Zangger Committee was set up in 1970, following the entry into force of the Treaty on the Non-Proliferation of Nuclear Weapons, under the auspices of the IAEA, to interpret the safeguards clause (Article III) of the Treaty. The Committee's agreement on the definition of those items whose export "triggers" application of IAEA safeguards is known as the Trigger List. For further details see Volume I of this study on international regulation of nuclear trade.
5. COCOM (Co-ordinating Committee for Multilateral Export Controls) co-ordinates export controls for NATO countries (except Iceland) plus Japan. COCOM maintains three lists of products and technologies whose export to the USSR and other Communist countries is embargoed or controlled through export licensing, one of which being the Atomic Energy List. See Volume I of this study for further details.
6. The Halden Boiling Water Reactor is an international project set up under the auspices of the OECD Nuclear Energy Agency and is operated under the direction of IFE.
7. For further details see *Regulations Governing the Transport of Radioactive Materials*, OECD/NEA, 1980.
8. Appendix 3 to the Regulations is based on Appendix I to the Convention on the Physical Protection of Nuclear Material.

Annex I

ATOMIC ENERGY LIST
ESTABLISHED BY THE MINISTRY OF TRADE (1987)*

A. NUCLEAR MATERIAL

A1 Special and other fissionable materials:

a. Plutonium all isotopes, alloys, compounds, and any material containing the foregoing;

b. Uranium 233, uranium enriched in the isotopes 235 or 233, alloys, compounds and any material containing the foregoing;

Note: "Uranium enriched in the isotopes 235 or 233" is defined as uranium containing the isotopes 235 or 233, or both, in an amount such that the abundance ratio of the sum of these isotopes to the isotope 238 is greater than the ratio of the isotope 235 to the isotope 238 occurring in nature.

A2 Source materials:

Any of the following source materials in any form or incorporated in any substance in which the concentration of source material by weight exceeds 0.05 per cent

a. Uranium containing the mixture of isotopes occurring in nature;

b. Uranium depleted in the isotope 235;

c. Thorium;

d. Any of the foregoing in the form of metal, alloy, chemical compound or concentrate.

Exceptions:

i) Source materials having an uranium content of:
  1. 10 kg or less for any application; or
  2. 100 kg or less for civil, non-nuclear applications;

ii) 1 000 kg or less of thorium nitrate (mantle grade) for use in the production of thoriated gas mantles;

iii) Thorium alloys containing less than 5 per cent thorium by weight;

iv) Depleted uranium specially fabricated for the following civil applications:
  1. Shielding;
  2. Packaging;
  3. Ballasts;
  4. Counter-weights.

A3 Deuterium, and compounds, mixtures and solutions containing deuterium, including heavy water and heavy paraffins, in which the ratio of deuterium atoms to hydrogen atoms exceeds 1:5000 by number.

Exception:

Shipments of the above having a deuterium content of 10 kg or less.

A4 Zirconium metal, alloys containing more than 50 per cent zirconium by weight, compounds, in which the ratio of hafnium to zirconium is less than 1:500 parts by weight, and manufactures wholly thereof.

Exceptions:

i) Zirconium metal and alloy in shipments of 5 kg or less;

ii) Zirconium in the form of foil or strip having a thickness not exceeding 0.025 mm (0.00095 in.) and specially fabricated and intended for use in photo flash bulbs, in shipments of 200 kg or less.

* Unofficial translation by Norwegian authorities.

NORWAY

A5 Nickel powder and porous nickel metal, as follows:

a. Powder with a nickel purity content of 99 per cent or more and a particle size of less than 100 micrometres;

b. Porous metal material with a mean pore size of 25 micrometres or less, and a nickel purity content of 99 per cent or more.

Exception:

Single porous nickel metal sheets not exceeding 930 cm^2 in size, intended for use in batteries for civil applications.

Note: Sub-item b above refers to porous nickel metal manufactured from nickel powder defined in sub-item a above which has been compacted and sintered to form a metal material with fine pores interconnected throughout the structure.

A6 Nuclear-grade graphite, i.e. graphite having a purity level better than five parts per million boron equivalent and with a density greater than 1.5 g/cm^3.

Exception:

Individual shipments of 100 kg or less.

A7 Lithium, as follows:

a. Metal, hydrides or alloys containing lithium enriched in the 6 isotope to a concentration higher than the one existing in nature (7.5 per cent on an atom percentage basis);

b. Any other materials containing lithium enriched in the 6 isotope (including compounds, mixtures and concentrates), *except* lithium enriched in the 6 isotope incorporated in thermoluminescent dosimeters.

A8 Hafnium, as follows: metals, alloys and compounds of hafnium containing more than 60 per cent hafnium by weight, and manufactures thereof.

Exception:

Shipments of the above having a hafnium content of 1 kg or less.

A9 Beryllium, as follows: metal, alloys containing more than 50 per cent beryllium by weight, compounds containing beryllium and manufactures thereof.

Exceptions:

i) Metal windows for X-ray machines;

ii) Oxide shapes in fabricated or semi-fabricated forms specially designed for electronic component parts or as substrates for electronic circuits;

iii) Shipments of 500 g or less of beryllium having a purity of 99 per cent or less, or 100 g or less of beryllium having a purity greater than 99 per cent, provided shipments exclude single crystals;

iv) Shipments of 5 kg or less of beryllium contained in compounds with a purity of less than 99 per cent.

A12 Tritium, compounds and mixtures containing tritium in which the ratio of tritium to hydrogen by atoms exceeds 1 part in 1 000, and products containing one or more of the foregoing.

Exceptions:

i) Shipments of tritium, compounds, mixtures and individual products containing one or more of the foregoing substances not exceeding 100 curies;

ii) Tritium contained in luminous paint, self-luminous products, gas and aerosol detectors, electron tubes, lightning or static elimination devices, ion generating tubes, detector cells of gas chromatography devices, and calibration standards;

iii) Compounds and mixtures of tritium, where the separation of the constituents cannot result in the evolution of an isotopic mixture of hydrogen in which the ratio of tritium to hydrogen by atoms exceeds 1 part in 1 000.

B. NUCLEAR FACILITIES

B1 Plants for the separation of isotopes of source material, special and other fissionable materials, and specially-designed or prepared equipment and components therefor, including:

a. Units specially designed for separating isotopes of source material, special and other fissionable materials, such as:

1. Gas centrifuges;
2. Jet nozzle separation units;
3. Vortex separation units;
4. Laser isotopic separation units;
5. Chemical exchange separation units;
6. Electromagnetic separation units;
7. Plasma separation units;
8. Gaseous diffusion separation units;

b. Specially designed components for the above, including:

1. Valves wholly made of or lined with aluminium, aluminium alloys, nickel or alloy containing 60 per cent or more nickel, 0.5 cm or greater in diameter, with bellows seals:

Exception: Valves not so defined.

2. Blowers and compressors (turbo, centrifugal and axial flow types) wholly made of or lined with aluminium, aluminium alloys, nickel or alloy containing 60 per cent or more nickel and having a capacity of 1 700 litres (1.7 m^3) per minute or greater, including compressor seals :

Exception: Blowers and compressors not so defined.

3. Gaseous diffusion barriers;
4. Gaseous diffusion housings;
5. Heat exchangers made of aluminium, copper, nickel or alloys containing more than 60 per cent nickel, or combinations of these metals at sub-atmospheric pressure with a leak rate of less than 10 pascal (0.1 millibar) per hour under a pressure differential of 10^5 pascal (1 bar):

Exception: Heat exchangers not so defined.

B2 Plants for the reprocessing of irradiated nuclear reactor fuel elements, and specially designed or prepared equipment and components therefor, including:

a. Fuel element chopping machines;

b. Critically safe tanks (e.g. small diameter, annular or slab tanks);

c. Process control instrumentation specially designed or prepared for monitoring or controlling the reprocessing of irradiated source and special and other fissionable materials.

Note: A plant for the reprocessing of irradiated nuclear reactor fuel elements includes equipment and components which normally come into direct contact with and directly control the irradiated fuel and the major nuclear material and fission product processing streams.

B. Nuclear reactors, i.e. reactors capable of operation so as to maintain a controlled, self-sustaining fission chain reaction, and equipment and components specially designed or prepared for use in connection with a nuclear reactor, including:

a. Pressure vessels, i.e. metal vessels as complete units or as major shop-fabricated parts therefor;

b. Fuel element handling equipment, including reactor fuel charging and discharging machines;

c. Control rods, including the neutron absorbing part and the support or suspension structures therefor, and control rod guide tubes;

d. Electronic controls for controlling the power levels in nuclear reactors, including reactor control rod drive mechanisms and radiation detection and measuring instruments to determine neutron flux levels;

e. Pressure tubes;

f. Coolant pumps;

g. Internals specially designed or prepared for the operation of a nuclear reactor, including but not limited to core support structures, thermal shields, baffles, core grid plates and diffuser plates;

h. Heat exchangers.

Note : A "nuclear reactor" includes the items within or attached directly to the reactor vessel, the equipment which controls the level of power in the core, and the components which normally contain or come into direct contact with or control the primary coolant of the reactor core.

B4 Plants for the production of heavy water, deuterium, or deuterium compounds, and specially designed or prepared equipment and components therefor.

B6 Plants for the production of uranium hexafluoride (UF_6) and specially designed or prepared equipment (including UF_6 purification equipment) and components therefor.

NORWAY

C. NUCLEAR-RELATED EQUIPMENT

C1 **Neutron generator systems, including tubes, designed for operation without an external vaccum system and utilizing electrostatic acceleration to induce a tritium-deuterium nuclear reaction.**

C2 **Power generation or propulsion equipment specially designed for use with military nuclear reactors.**

C3 **Electrolytic cells for the production of fluorine with a production capacity greater than 250 g of fluorine per hour.**

C4 **Equipment specially designed for the separation of isotopes of lithium.**

C5 **Equipment specially designed for the production of tritium.**

C6 **Frequency changers (converters or inverters) specially designed or prepared to supply motor stators for gas centrifuge enrichment, having all of the following characteristics, and specially designed components therefor:**

a. A multiphase output of 600 Hz to 2 kHz;

b. Frequency control better than 0.1 per cent;

c. Harmonic distortion of less than 2 per cent; and

d. An efficiency greater than 80 per cent.
(See also item B1 on this List.)

Annex II

PERMIT TO IMPORT AND SELL RADIOISOTOPES

Pursuant to the Regulations of 1st March 1983 relating to production, imports and sales of radioisotopes

[Name and address of firm]

is given permission to import and sell radioisotopes.

The permit includes:

[Description of nuclide, activity, etc.]

The general provisions for the permit are given in "Conditions for Production, Imports and Sales of Radioactive Materials in Norway" issued by the National Institute of Radiation Hygiene on 20th June 1983. Interpretation of the conditions for your use of radioisotopes is provided in the enclosed: "Further Interpretation of Conditions for Imports and Sales of ... [type or radioactive source or product, e.g. Smoke detectors]".

The permit is conditional on ...

The permit is valid until ......

SPAIN

TABLE OF CONTENTS

SPAIN

I. INTRODUCTION

In the 1950s and 1960s, Spain set up institutions and introduced legislation designed to promote the peaceful uses of nuclear energy.

The creation of the *Junta de Energia Nuclear* (JEN)[1] (Nuclear Energy Commission) in 1951, a body placed under the authority of the Ministry of Industry and Energy, together with Act No. 25 of 29th April 1964 on nuclear energy (1964 Act), constituted the basis for the development of nuclear activities in Spain.

The Junta de Energia Nuclear had powers in respect of all the activities connected with the nuclear fuel cycle ranging from the stage of prospecting for and mining radioactive ores to the management of waste. This body was also entrusted with nuclear research and given powers in the field of nuclear safety and radiation protection.

When it was restructured, a whole range of enterprises and bodies were created, and these now constitute the public sector of the nuclear energy industry in Spain.

Thus, in 1980, responsibility for all the activities of the fuel cycle, except final disposal of radioactive waste, was transferred to the National Uranium Enterprise (*Empresa Nacional del Uranio S.A. — ENUSA*)[2].

Also in 1980, the *Nuclear Safety Council* (*Consejo de Securidad Nuclear*) was created[3]. This body is directly answerable to Parliament and is the competent authority in the field of nuclear safety and radiation protection.

Lastly, in 1984, the National Radioactive Waste Enterprise (*Empresa Nacional de Residuos Radioactivos, S.A. — ENRESA*)[4] was set up in order to administer radioactive waste management in Spain.

In order to ensure supplies to Spain's nuclear reactors, ENUSA is responsible for acquiring enough uranium concentrates and enrichment services to meet domestic demand for a minimum period of ten years[5]. It must also establish reserve stocks of an amount and on conditions determined by the Ministry of Industry and Energy.

The electricity companies operating nuclear power plants are, for their part, obliged to keep a reserve stock of fuel elements in compliance with the conditions laid down in Royal Decree No. 1611 of 17th July 1985.

From the administrative viewpoint, the authority in charge of energy policy and responsible for drafting the corresponding regulations is the *Ministry of Industry and Energy* (MIE). Nuclear foreign trade policy is normally determined within "Delegate Commissions" in which the various Ministries concerned are represented and which are placed under the authority of the Prime Minister[6].

As regards non-proliferation, Spain ratified the Treaty on the Non-Proliferation of Nuclear Weapons on 5th November 1987. On that date, the so-called 1973 Verification Agreement (Tripartite) between IAEA, EURATOM and Community Member States also became applicable[7]. In any event, all nuclear installations in Spain were already subject to the IAEA safeguards.

As yet, Spain has not ahered to the Nuclear Suppliers Group Guidelines (so-called London Club), although this option is at present being considered.

From the nuclear trade viewpoint, Spain takes an active part in trade in this field, principally as an importer of nuclear material and services relating to the front end of the fuel cycle.

Restrictions on the export of nuclear material and equipment which are sensitive from the nuclear non-proliferation viewpoint do not feature in Spanish nuclear legislation, properly so-called. On the other hand, after Spain recently became a member of the European Communities, the regulations on foreign trade were amended. The provisions concerning trade in nuclear items contained in nuclear legislation proper, and those in the general law will be dealt with separately.

This study will also include a brief mention of the regulations on transport and intellectual property as well as on agreements relating to nuclear trade.

II. TRADE IN, AND IMPORT AND EXPORT OF NUCLEAR MATERIAL AND EQUIPMENT

1. Nuclear Legislation

a) Mining

Two systems have been applied successively in this field. The first (Order of 4th October 1945) was characterised by a monopoly situation in which the State retained, temporarily, the exclusive right to mine the uranium deposits in fourteen Spanish Provinces in which such deposits were known to exist. In 1948, these exclusive rights were extended (Decree of 23rd December 1948, Section 2) to all of metropolitan Spain and were conferred, in 1951, on the Junta de Energia Nuclear upon its creation (Constitutive Decree of

22nd October 1951). Prospecting was encouraged and could legally be undertaken by private individuals who had, however, to report any deposits to JEN and who were paid compensation for their find.

This system was abolished in 1958 by the Freedom of Mining Act (Act of 17th July 1958 amending the Decree of 22nd October 1951). Private firms were allowed to mine deposits outside the areas reserved to JEN. They had first, however, to obtain the necessary authorisations and concessions from the Ministry responsible for Industry. The General Directorate of Mines informed the General Directorate for Energy of any prospecting licences issued. This latter Directorate, in turn informed JEN.

Under the current law, the Ministry of Industry and Energy is responsible for supervising these activities. This Ministry keeps a record of the quantities of radioactive ores mined[8].

ENUSA takes part in prospecting activities as a member of uranium prospecting groups set up in Spain by private enterprises. The contracts concluded for this purpose specify the conditions on which ENUSA may acquire the ores should the work of prospecting prove fruitful.

b) Trade in ores and concentrates

Under the Nuclear Energy Act of 1964, the Junta de Energia Nuclear enjoyed wide prerogatives in this field which have lapsed since the creation of ENUSA and the reorganisation of the nuclear fuel cycle (see also the Order of the Minister of Industry and Energy of 12th May 1983).

As is the case for mining and manufacturing activities, the Ministry of Industry and Energy keeps a record of sales of concentrates[9] (Nuclear Energy Act of 1964, Section 23).

Spanish purchasers and sellers are authorised to trade freely in radioactive ores and concentrates of domestic origin as long as the ores do not leave the country. Such persons must, however, notify the Ministry of Industry and Energy of their commercial transactions (1964 Act, Sections 22 and 23).

The import and export of radioactive ores, on the other hand, as well as commercial transactions carried out with foreigners require a licence from of the Ministry of Industry and Energy (Section 22).

c) Licensing and control of radioactive materials and nuclear fuel

Possession and use

The basic provisions governing the safe use of radioactive materials and nuclear fuel are contained in the 1964 Nuclear Energy Act, the Regulations on nuclear and radioactive installations of 21st July 1972 and the Act of 22nd April 1980 setting up the Nuclear Safety Council[10].

Radioactive materials and nuclear fuel may be stored and used in Spain only by persons or firms expressly licensed to do so by the Ministry of Industry and Energy (Section 31 of the 1964 Act).

Licences are automatically rescinded in the event of non-compliance with the prescribed conditions and timetable, in the same way as licences relating to nuclear and radioactive installations. These licences may also be rendered null and void by decision of the Council of Ministers, on the proposal of the Ministry of Industry and Energy, for exceptional reasons of national interest. In such an event, the operator is compensated in accordance with the provisions of the law on compulsory purchase (Section 32 of the 1964 Act).

Radioactive materials and nuclear fuels used or possessed by persons or firms without a licence may be seized, without prejudice to any other penalty (Section 43 of the 1964 Act). The opening of an inquiry into breaches of the foregoing provisions may, with the prior agreement of the Ministry of Industry and Energy, lead to the immediate seizure of the materials and fuel and a ban on acquiring further fuel or materials for as long as the reasons for the seizure continue to exist.

Manufacture

Persons may also undertake the manufacture of radioactive materials if they have obtained a licence from the Minister of Industry and Energy (Sections 28 and 31 of the 1964 Act).

Licences for the manufacture in Spain of apparatus and equipment intended for specifically nuclear or radioactive purposes, are granted by the Minister of Industry and Energy (Section 34 of the 1964 Act).

d) Trade in radioactive materials and nuclear fuel

Role of ENUSA

As pointed out in the Introduction, the powers of the National Uranium Enterprise extend to all the commercial and industrial activities of the front end of the nuclear fuel cycle.

While ENUSA is responsible for ensuring the supply of Spanish nuclear reactors for the ten years to come, the Ministry of Industry and Energy, for its part, approves contracts dealing with the supply of uranium concentrates and of conversion and enrichment services.

The licence for each import or export of nuclear material pursuant to the contracts submitted for the approval of the Ministry of Industry and Energy, is issued by the Ministry responsible for Economy, Finance and Trade.

Trade in radioactive materials, nuclear fuel and equipment

Radioactive materials and nuclear fuel may only be stored or used, within Spain, by persons in possession of a licence from the Ministry of Industry and Energy. This provision applies also to the transfer or sale of such materials or fuel (Section 31 of the 1964 Act).

Any such licence may lapse in the event of non-compliance with the prescribed time-table or conditions. Moreover, it may be revoked by the Council of Ministers for reasons of national interest, on payment of compensation in compliance with the law on compulsory purchase (Section 32 of the 1964 Act).

Commercial companies must report all sales of apparatus or equipment capable of emitting ionizing radiation to the Ministry of Industry and Energy so as to allow the competent departments of the Ministry to verify the conditions of their installation and the competence of the persons who are to work with the apparatus or equipment (Section 33 of the 1964 Act).

Possession and use of materials and equipment for medical purposes

The use and acquisition of radioisotopes and radioactive sources for medical purposes, including radiotherapy, are subject to a licence granted by the Ministry of Industry and Energy after first hearing the opinion of the Nuclear Safety Council.

X-ray apparatus used for medical purposes is subject to licensing and supervision on conditions to be determined by the Ministry of Industry and Energy and the Nuclear Safety Council respectively.

2. General Legislation on Foreign Trade

Pursuant to becoming a member of the European Communities at the beginning of 1986, Spain is proceeding with the adaptation of its trade legislation, especially with regard to tariffs, to bring it into line with Community regulations. At present, foreign trade is regulated by a Ministerial Order of 21st February 1986 which entered into force on 1st March of the same year.

a) Imports

The new requirements laid down by the Government in this field are contained in the *Order of 21st February 1986* of the Minister of Trade and Finance regulating the procedure relating to, and performance of import operations (amended by an Order dated 23rd April 1986). This text was amended more recently by an Order by the Director-General for Foreign Trade dated *16th March 1987* (which entered into force the day following its publication in the Official Journal, namely on 22nd April 1987). The main purpose of this Order is to combine in a single Annex, Annexes II and IV of the Order of 21st February 1986.

In accordance with Community practice, the Order classifies countries from which goods originate in four geographical zones : (Annex I of the Order) : zone A (European Community countries) ; zone B (European Free Trade Association countries and A.C.P. States) ; zone C (countries belonging to GATT) ; and zone D (Socialist countries).

The Order of 21st February 1986 also makes a distinction between import operations which may be undertaken freely (which is the rule), and those subject to a system of administrative licence (which is the exception).

Some goods which are allowed to be imported freely may, however, be made subject to a prior statistical control. This involves an obligation to send to the General Directorate for Foreign Trade a document entitled "*prior import notification*" (reproduced in Annex III to the Order). The notification is lodged with the General Register of the Secretary of State for Trade or with those of the territorial or provincial Departments of the economy and trade. Compliance with this formality is enforced by the Director-General for Foreign Trade. Notifications must be amended in the event of a change in the import operation in question (Sections 3 and 4 of the Order of 21st February 1986).

The General Directorate for Foreign Trade is also competent to issue import certificates when such a document is required for certain types of import (Section 5 of the Order of 21st February 1986).

Items whose importation requires an *administrative licence* (the relevant form is reproduced in Annex V to the Order) vary in line with the classification by territorial zone, and are listed in Annex IV to the Order of 21st February 1986. These licences are issued by the Director-General for Foreign Trade ; formalities are entered in the General Register of the Secretary for State for Trade (Section 6 of the 1986 Order).

The documents proving that prior import notification has been made and the administrative licence received are stamped by the customs offices concerned (Section 17 of the 1986 Order).

The goods subject to the prior notification or administrative licence procedure are designated in Annexes II and IV to the Order of 21st February 1986 by means of reference figures. The nuclear items on this list are numbered as follows : 28.50, 28.51 and 28.52. As mentioned above, Annexes II and IV were combined by the Order of 16th March 1987, under which the above-mentioned items are all subject to the administrative import licence procedure. The *Royal Decree of 19th December 1986* (Official Journal, supplement to No. 307 of 24th December 1986), the purpose of which was to modify the customs tariffs for the year 1987, gives a list of these numbered references (see the *Annex* to this Chapter).

b) Importation of dual-purpose technology

The regulations on this point, contained in an *Order of 5th June 1985*, concern certain items of strategic importance which may not be re-exported without the prior authorisation of the supplier countries concerned.

In such cases, the importation and, where appropriate, re-exportation of these items must, under the Order, be preceded by the issuing of an *international import certificate* (the relevant form is reproduced in Annex I to the Order). This certificate is issued at the request of the importer by the Ministry of the Economy and Finance (General Directorate for Tariff Policy and Imports). The goods involved may not be re-exported without the agreement of the Ministry (Annex III to the Order).

It is also provided that the customs authorities should, upon importation and at the request of the country of origin of the goods or of the importer, issue an *entry certificate* (Annex II to the Order).

c) Exports

The relevant legislation here is *Royal Decree No. 2701 of 27th December 1985* regulating the export trade and an *Order, also dated 21st February 1986*, which governs the procedure relating to, and performance of export operations.

The basic principle laid down in Decree No. 2701 is that trade should be free although the Minister of the Economy and Finance is empowered to make exceptions to this rule for certain types of product which are then made subject to the system of administrative licence.

Reference is also made in the Decree to the application of regulations relating, in particular, to the re-exportation of dual-purpose technology.

The procedure laid down in the Order of 21st February 1986 relating to exports is, on the whole, analogous to that contained in the Order of the same date regulating imports. In particular, it is once again the General Directorate for Foreign Trade which is the competent authority with regard to the administrative formalities relating to prior notice of export and to the administrative licence.

The nuclear items for which prior notice of export is required are the same as those mentioned above with regard to import operations and bearing the references 28.50 and 28.51 for zones A-1 and A-2.

With regard to the administrative export licence, the items concerned are those listed under the reference numbers 28.50 and 28.51 as well as 26.01 : nuclear source materials in whatever form or constituting part of any substance of which the nuclear source material content exceeds 0.05 kg in weight, except for consignments of nuclear source materials in which the uranium content is 10 kg or less, for whatever type of application; 100 kg or less, for non-nuclear non-military applications.

d) New Regulations on import, export and re-export of dual-purpose products and technology

These Regulations, recently adopted to implement the relevant COCOM recommendations (see Volume I of this study) are contained in *Royal Decree No. 480 of 25th March 1988* (Official Journal of 21st May 1988).

The primary object of this Decree is to set up an *Interministerial Regulatory Commission for Foreign Trade in Defence Materials and Dual-Purpose Products and Technology (Junta Interministerial Reguladora del Commercio Exterior de Material de Defensa y Productos y Technologias de Doble Uso)*, called the Junta here below. This body is responsible for controlling all imports and exports of such materials and technology and recommends the appropriate measures in this field. In parallel, a Sub-Directorate for Control of Foreign Trade was also set up in the Foreign Trade General Directorate of the Ministry of the Economy and Finance (Royal Decree No. 485 of 6th May 1988).

Setting aside materials for national defence purposes, nuclear equipment and technology in the dual-purpose category (military and civil) are subject to Junta control as well as to the procedures prescribed by the Royal Decree of 25th March 1988 (Section 1).

That Decree lays down the condition that, prior to export operations, the names of persons involved must be entered in a special *register* for exports of defence materials and dual-purpose products and technology; this register is kept by the Foreign Trade General Directorate (Section 6).

As regards rules for *imports* (Section 9), the entry into Spanish territory of dual-purpose products and technology from countries requiring final destination control, is subject to delivery by the Foreign Trade General Directorate of an international import certificate (a model of which is reproduced in Annex II of the Decree) and, where necessary, of an entry control certificate (Annex III of the Decree).

As for rules for *exports* and re-exports (Sections 11 to 14), the corresponding operations require an administrative export licence in accordance with the Order of 21st February 1986 (mentioned under c) above). According to the circumstances and the country of destination, delivery of the licence may be subject to the exporter supplying an international import certificate for the dual-purpose products and technology concerned, as well as a final destination certificate from the importing country. In certain cases, an entry control certificate (from the country of destination) may also be required by the Junta.

The Foreign Trade General Directorate notifies the persons concerned, the police authorities *(Guardia Civil)*, the Ministry of Defence and the Customs Offices of its approval of the import or export licences.

The Royal Decree of 25th March 1988 supplements, without affecting its application, the above-mentioned Order of 5th June 1985 regulating the import of dual-purpose technology (see under b) above).

III. TRANSPORT

Provisions dealing specifically with the transport of radioactive materials are to be found in the outline Nuclear Energy Act of 1964, and several different regulations complete these provisions with regard to the various modes of transport (Decrees Nos. 1999 of 1979, 881 of 1982 and 1749 of 1984, regulating the transport of goods by road, rail and air, respectively).

While the Ministry of Transport and Communications has general competence in the field of transport, it is the Ministry of Industry and Energy which is responsible for issuing approval certificates and licences for consignments of radioactive materials. The Nuclear Safety Council, for its part, enforces compliance with the technical safety requirements and acts as an advisory body to the Ministry[11].

IV. NATIONAL SECURITY AND PHYSICAL PROTECTION MEASURES

1. National Security and Non-Proliferation

The provisions regulating national security in the nuclear field are contained in the 1964 Act and a Decree of 21st July 1972; they do not, however, enter into great detail. The Ministry of Industry and Energy is kept informed of operations involving nuclear material, and keeps a register in which to record the movements of such materials.

Any loss, abandonment or theft of radioactive substances must be notified to the competent authorities as soon as possible, and offences are punishable by criminal or administrative penalties.

The 1964 Act provides that prison sentences may be passed on persons who, without the required licence, supply, receive, possess or trade in nuclear material (Section 86).

Criminal penalties are also applied to persons who disclose without authorisation, violate, steal or use without permission any secret information relating to nuclear energy (Section 87).

The Centre for Research on Energy, the Environment and Technology — CIEMAT (formerly the Junta de Energia Nuclear), a body answerable to the Ministry of Industry and Energy, is responsible for maintaining the foreign relations necessary for the application of safeguards (within the meaning of the IAEA Statute) in Spain.

CIEMAT has the task of supervising all movements of nuclear material within Spain.

2. Physical Protection

There is, at present, no special legislation in Spain on the physical protection of nuclear installations and of nuclear material during transport.

Plans for the physical protection of nuclear installations are submitted for approval to the Ministry of Industry and Energy.

The Nuclear Safety Council assists in drawing up the criteria which must be met by plans for the physical protection of nuclear and radioactive installations, and participates also in the approval procedure for such plans (Act of 22nd April 1980).

V. INTELLECTUAL PROPERTY IN THE NUCLEAR FIELD

Provisions relating to patents, trademarks and inventions in the nuclear energy field, have been included in the outline Nuclear Energy Act of 1964.

Patent applications are filed in accordance with the normal procedure laid down by Spanish legislation on industrial property (Section 81).

Patents are issued by the Industrial Property Registration Office, after it has examined a report by the CIEMAT (Section 82).

On the basis of a report by the CIEMAT, the Ministry of Industry and Energy may grant exemption from the need to provide evidence of implementation and operation, as required by the law on industrial property, to any patent owner who has submitted a request to this effect to the Industrial Property Registration Office (Section 83).

VI. AGREEMENTS

1. Multilateral Agreements

As already mentioned, Spain became a Party to the Treaty on the Non-Proliferation of Nuclear Weapons on 5th November 1987.

The Convention on the Physical Protection of Nuclear Material has been approved by Parliament and the Spanish Government is preparing to ratify it.

2. Bilateral Agreements

Spain is party to numerous bilateral agreements covering, as broadly defined, scientific, technical and economic co-operation in the field of nuclear energy.

Only those agreements which, directly or indirectly, generally or specifically, deal with trade in nuclear material, equipment and technology have been included in this section.

a) Framework agreements for nuclear co-operation

As a consequence of Spain's joining the European Atomic Energy Community, a whole series of bilateral agreements will have to be revised.

The various co-operation agreements currently in force and relating to the peaceful use of nuclear energy were concluded with the following countries: ***Chile*** (1972), ***Portugal*** (1973), ***United States*** (1974), ***Peru*** (1976), ***Ecuador*** (1978), ***Argentina*** (1979), ***Federal Republic of Germany*** (1979), ***Uruguay*** (1979), ***Colombia*** (1980, subject to ratification), ***Brazil*** (1983, subject to ratification), ***Venezuela*** (1984) and ***People's Republic of China*** (1985).

b) Industrial co-operation agreements

In 1966, Spain concluded with ***France*** an Agreement on the construction in Catalonia of a natural uranium reactor (Vandellos power plant).

c) Safeguards agreements

A safeguards transfer Agreement had been concluded between the ***International Atomic Energy Agency***, Spain and the ***United States*** on 9th December 1966 entering into force on the same day. This Agreement transferred to the IAEA responsibility for administering the safeguards provided for in the successive co-operation agreements concluded between Spain and the United States, to promote and develop the use of atomic energy for peaceful purposes.

It is recalled that when Spain ratified the Non-Proliferation Treaty, the provisions of the Tripartite Agreement of 1973 between IAEA, EURATOM and the non-nuclear weapon Member States of the Community which are party to the Non-Proliferation Treaty became applicable to it.

NOTES AND REFERENCES

1. The Junta has recently been reorganised and renamed (Act No. 13 of 14th April 1986) "Centro de Investigaciones Energeticas Medioambientales y Tecnologicas" (CIEMAT).
2. Set up by Royal Decree No. 2967 of 7th December 1975.
3. Act No. 15 of 22nd April 1980.
4. Royal Decrees No. 1522 of 4th July 1984 and No. 1899 of 1st August 1984. For further details see *Regulatory and Institutional Framework for Nuclear Activities*, Volume II, OECD/NEA, 1984.
5. Royal Decree No. 2967 of 7th December 1979, as amended by Royal Decree No. 1611 of 17th July 1985.
6. Delegate Commissions in the field of international trade include the Government Delegate Commission for Foreign Policy *(Comision Delegada del Gobierno para la Politica Exterior)* and the Delegate Commission for Economic Questions *(Comision Delegada del Gobierno para los Asuntos Economicos)*.

   Questions relating to national security fall within the jurisdiction of the Government Delegate Commission for State Security *(Comision Delegada del Gobierno para la Seguridad del Estado)*. This Commission, chaired by the Prime Minister, is composed of the Ministers of Foreign Affairs, of Justice, of Defence, of the Interior, as well as the Prime Minister's Deputy and the Director-General for State Security. However, given that nuclear energy in Spain is used exclusively for peaceful purposes, this Commission does not normally intervene in questions of nuclear trade.
7. On signing the accession Treaty to the European Communities, Spain had made the following Declaration:

   "The Kingdom of Spain, not having acceded to the Treaty on the Non-Proliferation of Nuclear Weapons, undertakes to seek actively and as rapidly as possible in close co-operation with the Commission and the Council, the most appropriate solution calculated, whilst taking into account the Community's international commitments, to observe fully the obligations flowing from the Treaty establishing the European Atomic Energy Community, in particular with respect to nuclear supplies and to the movement of nuclear material within the Community." (Published in the Spanish Official Journal on 1st January 1986).
8. "Radioactive ore" means any ore containing uranium or thorium (Section 2 of the 1964 Act).

   Henceforth, radioactive ores are considered to be the same as other ores and are subject to the general mining legislation, which includes:
   - Mining Act No. 22 of 21st July 1973 (Offical Journal No. 176 of 24th July 1973);
   - General Mining Regulations (Royal Decree No. 2857 of 25th August 1978, Official Journal Nos. 295 and 296 of 11th and 12th December 1978);
   - Act No. 54 of 5th November 1980, amending the 1973 Mining Act (deals in particular with energy resources);
   - Royal Legislative Decree No. 1303 of 28th June 1986 relating to the adaptation of the said Act of 1973 to the European Economic Community legislation (Chapter VII).
9. "Concentrate" means any product resulting from the treatment of radioactive ores which has a uranium or thorium content exceeding that of the materials in their natural state (Section 1 of the 1964 Act).
10. "Radioactive material" means any material containing substances which emit ionizing radiation.

    "Nuclear fuel" means any material which can be used to produce energy by a nuclear fusion chain reaction (1964 Act).
11. For further details, see *Regulations Governing the Transport of Radioactive Materials*, OECD/NEA, 1980.

Annex

ROYAL DECREE OF 19th DECEMBER 1986 AMENDING THE CUSTOMS TARIFF FOR THE YEAR 1987*

(Extracts)

Chapter 28

INORGANIC CHEMICALS; INORGANIC AND ORGANIC COMPOUNDS OF PRECIOUS METALS, RADIOACTIVE ELEMENTS, OF RARE EARTH METALS AND ISOTOPES

. . . .

Notes:

. . . .

6. Only the following products should not be considered as falling within Item 28.50:

a) the following fissile chemical elements and isotopes: natural uranium and its isotopes U-233 and U-235, plutonium and its isotopes;

b) the following radioactive chemical elements: technecium, prometheum, polonium, astatine, radon, francium, actinium, protactinium, neptunium, americium, and other elements with higher atomic numbers;

c) all other natural and artificial radioactive isotopes (including those of precious or base metals in Sections XIV or XV);

d) organic and inorganic compounds of these elements and isotopes, whether or not of a defined chemical composition, including mixtures thereof;

e) alloys (other than ferro-uranium), dispersions and cermets containing these isotopes or their organic or inorganic compounds;

f) spent (irradiated) fuel rods from nuclear reactors.

The term "isotopes", mentioned above and in the text of Items 28.50 and 28.51 includes enriched isotopes except, however, chemical elements existing in nature in the form of pure isotopes as well as U-235-depleted uranium.

. . . .

DESCRIPTION OF ITEMS

28.50 CHEMICAL ELEMENTS AND FISSILE ISOTOPES; OTHER CHEMICAL ELEMENTS AND RADIOACTIVE ISOTOPES: THEIR INORGANIC OR ORGANIC COMPOUNDS WHETHER OR NOT OF A DEFINED CHEMICAL COMPOSITION; ALLOYS; DISPERSIONS AND CERMETS CONTAINING THESE ELEMENTS OR ISOTOPES OR THEIR INORGANIC OR ORGANIC COMPOUNDS:

A. Chemical elements and fissile isotopes; their compounds, alloys, dispersions and cermets, including spent (irradiated) fuel rods from nuclear reactors (EURATOM).

B. The other elements.

* Unofficial translation.

28.51 ISOTOPES OF CHEMICAL ELEMENTS APART FROM THOSE REFERRED TO UNDER 28.50; THEIR INORGANIC OR ORGANIC COMPOUNDS WHETHER OR NOT OF A DEFINED COMPOSITION:

A. Deuterium; deuterium oxide (heavy water) and other deuterium compounds; hydrogen and its compounds, enriched in deuterium; mixtures and solutions containing those products (EURATOM).

B. The other elements.

28.52 INORGANIC OR ORGANIC COMPOUNDS OF THORIUM, U-235-DEPLETED URANIUM AND RARE EARTH METALS OF YTTRIUM AND SCANDIUM, INCLUDING MIXTURES OF THOSE SUBSTANCES:

A. Thorium, U-235-depleted uranium, including mixtures of those substances.

B. The other elements.

Chapter 84

BOILERS, MACHINERY, MECHANICAL APPARATUS AND EQUIPMENT

....

Notes:

....

4. (EURATOM)

The term "nuclear reactor" (in Part 84.59.B) means all the apparatus and devices contained within a biological shield, which includes, in this case, the shield itself as well as the devices relating to the articles located within the actual containment (essentially the control rods and the control and command equipment inasmuch as it is connected with the rods and/or other equipment located within the containment).

LIST OF ITEMS

84.14 INDUSTRIAL FURNACES AND LABORATORY OVENS, EXCLUDING ELECTRIC FURNACES REFERRED TO UNDER 85.11:

A. Specially designed for the separation of spent (irradiated) nuclear fuel, for radioactive waste treatment or for recycling spent (irradiated) fuel (EURATOM).

....

84.17 APPARATUS AND EQUIPMENT, EVEN ELECTRICALLY HEATED, FOR TREATMENT OF MATERIALS IMPLYING TEMPERATURE CHANGES SUCH AS: PREHEATING, COCTION, TORREFACTION, DISTILLATION, RECTIFICATION, PASTEURIZATION, DRYING, EVAPORATION, VAPORIZATION, CONDENSATION, COOLING, ETC...

....

C. Heat exchangers.

....

II. Others:

a) specially designed for nuclear power plants ...
b) metal plates for heat exchangers.

....

84.18 CENTRIFUGES AND CENTRIFUGE DRYERS: APPARATUS FOR FILTRATION OR LIQUID PURIFICATION AND GAS SCRUBBING:

A. For separating uranium isotopes (EURATOM).

B. Specially designed for separating spent (irradiated) nuclear fuel, radioactive waste treatment or spent (irradiated) nuclear fuel reprocessing (EURATOM).

....

aa) To obtain products referred to in 28.51.A (deuterium and its compounds).

b) Apparatus (not centrifuges) for filtration or purification of liquids or gas scrubbing:

1. Apparatus for obtaining products referred to in 28.51.A (deuterium and its compounds).

....

84.59 MACHINERY, MECHANICAL APPARATUS AND EQUIPMENT, NOT EXPRESSLY REFERRED TO OR INCLUDED IN THE OTHER SECTIONS OF THIS CHAPTER:

A. To obtain products referred to in 28.51.A (EURATOM).

B. Nuclear reactors (EURATOM).

C. Specially designed for spent (irradiated) nuclear fuel recycling (mixed radioactive metal oxides, shielding, etc.) (EURATOM).

SWEDEN

TABLE OF CONTENTS

I. INTRODUCTION

In the context of nuclear trade, Sweden may be considered as a supplier of services and equipment and as an importer of nuclear material. Nuclear activities, including trade in nuclear equipment and material, are governed by the Act of 12th January 1984 on Nuclear Activities (SFS[1] 1984 :3) which came into force on 1st February 1984, replacing the Atomic Energy Act of 1956. In addition, the Ordinance on Nuclear Activities (SFS 1984 :14), which also came into force on the same date, details the procedures for trade in such equipment and material. Trade in nuclear and radioactive materials from the viewpoint of protection against radiation hazards is regulated by radiation protection legislation.

It is a fundamental principle contained in the 1984 Act (Section 3) that nuclear activities must be conducted in such a way as to ensure that safety and radiation protection requirements are met and that Sweden's obligations stemming from agreements preventing the proliferation of nuclear weapons are fulfilled. It should be noted that this Act, which is particularly aimed at providing for safety in connection with nuclear activities also provides for their close supervision — all such activities are regulated by provisions governing permits, licences and conditions.

Different regulations have a bearing on nuclear trade, in particular, those on ores, transport, safeguards and physical protection. They will be described in this chapter, in addition to the national policy on such trade and to import and export provisions. The agreements concluded by Sweden in the nuclear field will also be mentioned.

II. NUCLEAR EXPORT POLICY AND GOVERNMENT CONTROL

Sweden is a Party to the Treaty on the Non-Proliferation of Nuclear Weapons (NPT) and has undertaken, in accordance with the Treaty, neither to develop nuclear weapons or nuclear devices nor to contribute to other countries' development of them by its exports. Sweden is also a member of a group of nuclear supplier countries which have agreed to follow Guidelines for the export of nuclear material, equipment and technology transfers (so-called London Club). (These international control systems are described in detail in Volume I of this study.) Accordingly, the export of nuclear material and equipment from Sweden is carried out in compliance with a list regarding the export of sensitive nuclear material and certain categories of equipment in accordance with the NPT and the London Guidelines trigger list[2]. In fact, the Government has chosen to apply even stricter requirements than those laid down in the Guidelines.

In addition to the material and equipment referred to in the 1984 Act on Nuclear Activities as requiring a licence (Section 1), the list in the Annex to the 1984 Ordinance concerning exports includes technology transfers and certain dual-use nuclear-related products (equipment not initially designed or prepared for use in the nuclear field but which can be used for the manufacture of nuclear devices). The equipment and materials in the list are items which cannot be exported from Sweden without Government permission.

It is a feature of Government in Sweden that decision-making is a collective procedure involving all the Cabinet and not simply the Minister who is competent in the area concerned. The Minister makes proposals regarding matters for which his Ministry is responsible and advises the Government on decisions to be taken.

The *Ministry of Energy and the Environment* is generally responsible for the use of nuclear energy in Sweden and in this connection it oversees the licensing procedure for nuclear activities, including nuclear trade.

The supervisory authority is the *Swedish Nuclear Power Inspectorate* — SKI (*statens kärnkraftinspektion*), the national body responsible for administering the licensing procedure under the 1984 Act on Nuclear Activities (Section 16) ; it also supervises compliance with the Act and any directives or conditions issued thereunder. Under the 1984 Ordinance on Nuclear Activities, applications for licences to acquire, possess, transfer or otherwise have dealings with nuclear material and equipment must be filed with SKI.

III. TRADE IN NUCLEAR MATERIAL AND EQUIPMENT

As already mentioned, Sweden has established a system of licensing, permits and notifications concerning all dealings with nuclear material and equipment, both at national and international levels. The principles of the system are contained in the 1984 Act on Nuclear Activities which provides that a licence under the Act is required for such activities; the different procedures are laid down in the 1984 Ordinance. In addition, reference is made, where appropriate, to the provisions of the 1958 Radiation Protection Act regarding measures to be taken for protection against radiation.

The 1984 Act on Nuclear Activities (Section 1) includes the following in its definition of nuclear activities:

- the acquisition, possession, transfer, handling, processing, transport of or other dealings with nuclear material or nuclear waste;
- import of nuclear material;
- export of nuclear material or minerals containing such materials, products made from nuclear material or goods containing such material, equipment or materials that have been specially designed or prepared for the processing, use or production of nuclear material or which are otherwise of essential importance to the production of nuclear devices, to the extent prescribed by the Government; and
- the granting or transfer of a right to manufacture outside Sweden such equipment or materials as referred to above and is manufactured within Sweden, to the extent prescribed by the Government.

The Act [Section 2(2)] goes on to define nuclear material as:

- uranium, plutonium or any other material or substance that is or can be used for the generation of nuclear energy, (nuclear fuel) or any compound containing such material[3];
- thorium or any other substance that is suitable for conversion to nuclear fuel or any compound containing such material; and
- spent nuclear fuel that has not been placed in a final repository.

As mentioned above, the 1984 Ordinance on Nuclear Activities provides for a system of notification and licensing, according to the activity/category of nuclear material and equipment to be imported and exported. Such material and equipment are listed in the Ordinance and its Annex (see *Annex I* hereto) which specifies as follows the type of procedure to be complied with in each case:

Government permission for the export of materials and equipment described in the Annex to the Ordinance, (Section 2).

Applications for export licences must be submitted to the SKI which obtains the necessary information from companies, authorities etc. and, where appropriate, consults the Swedish Defence Research Institute. SKI then submits the documents in the case, together with its own recommendation to the Ministry of Energy and the Environment for consideration — in consultation with the Ministry for Foreign Affairs — and final decision by the Government. The Government's decision is made public.

Although each application for an export licence is considered on a case-by-case basis, it is the Governments' policy to grant licences for nuclear products and materials only for non-nuclear weapon States which have ratified the Treaty on the Non-Proliferation of Nuclear Weapons or have accepted equally comprehensive IAEA Safeguards for all their nuclear activities.

Actual supervision that no transfer of commodities subject to export control takes place without a licence is carried out by the Customs Offices.

Licence to be obtained from the *Swedish Nuclear Power Inspectorate* (SKI) for the acquisition, possession or transfer or conveyance into Sweden of defined quantities of uranium, plutonium and thorium (Section 16). In addition, a licence is also required for the export of smaller quantities of materials also as defined in the Ordinance (Section 17). Further details concerning those requirements are to be found in *Annexes II and III* to this chapter.

Advance notification to the SKI of the acquisition, possession, transport, import, etc. of certain given quantities of e.g. enriched uranium (no more than 15 grams) or natural or depleted uranium (no more than 5 kilograms) (Section 4).

Such dealings with natural or depleted uranium or compounds containing them for use as counterweights in aircraft or for producing radiation shielding devices as well as alloys intended for use other than nuclear fuel (when the uranium content does not exceed one per cent by weight) also require advance notification (Section 8).

Finally, thorium (or compounds containing thorium) for producing activation compounds for electrodes, incandescent mantles, lenses of filters and alloys in which the thorium content does not exceed five per cent by weight may be acquired, transported, imported etc. after notifying the SKI (Section 9).

Also, universities and scientific and technological institutes may, for scientific use and after notifying the SKI, acquire, possess, import, etc. or otherwise have dealings with natural or depleted uranium or compounds containing them as well as thorium or other substances intended to be converted to nuclear fuel (Section 5). Uranium, plutonium or other substances used as nuclear fuel may be conveyed into Sweden, after notifying the SKI, by a person licensed under the 1984 Act to acquire, possess, transfer or otherwise have dealings with such a substance (Section 14).

In addition, uranium, plutonium or thorium or compounds containing them may, after the SKI has been notified, be transferred to a person who may, under the 1984 Act or Ordinance, acquire or possess such substances in the quantities entailed by such transfer (Section 10).

*
**

The 1984 Ordinance also specifies that no special licence or notification under the nuclear legislation is required for possession, transfer or other dealings with or import of deuterium, tritium and lithium to use the substances for purposes other than to bring about self-sustaining nuclear reactions. It should be noted that while no special application for a licence is required, there is an obligation to obtain a "general licence". Dealings with instruments or medical preparations containing these substances are also permitted. In addition, any person may process, and have dealings with substances whose content of natural or depleted uranium or thorium does not exceed 200 grams per ton (Sections 6 and 11).

The 1984 Act on Nuclear Activities lays down a series of sanctions for violation of its provisions, and in particular for conducting a nuclear activity without a licence, namely fines or imprisonment for a maximum of two years (Section 25).

As regards the illicit import or export of nuclear substances, material or equipment the 1984 Act (Section 25) provides that such transgressions are governed by the Act on penalties for the smuggling of goods (1960 :418).

*
**

The import of radioactive materials is controlled by customs officials under Ordinance 1958 No. 652 made by the general Customs Administration in agreement with the National Institute of Radiation Protection.

IV. TRADE IN RADIOACTIVE MATERIALS

For purposes of clarity, a distinction is made between trade in nuclear material and that in radioactive materials, the first being governed by security and control considerations while the second is governed primarily by radiation protection considerations. It should be noted nevertheless that radiation protection aspects are also taken into account in the legislation concerning nuclear trade, as described below.

Radiation protection legislation was until recently embodied in the Radiation Protection Act No. 110 of 14th March 1958 as amended[4]. The Act (Section 2) provides that trade in radioactive materials (including imports) may not be carried out without a licence issued by the competent authority. The 1984 Ordinance on Nuclear Activities (Section 3) provides furthermore that a licence under the Radiation Protection Act is required for the acquisition and possession or other dealings with materials subject to advance notification to the Swedish Nuclear Power Inspectorate.

In addition, the Ordinance (Section 7) prescribes that nuclear waste, as defined by the 1984 Act on Nuclear Activities, in the small quantities or with the low contents of radioactivity referred to in the Act may be acquired, possessed, imported etc. to be used for instruction, research or for medical, agricultural, industrial or commercial purposes, subject to a licence being granted under the 1958 Radiation Protection Act.

It should be noted that (unless otherwise specified) a licence under the Radiation Protection Act is not normally required for an activity licensed under the 1984 Act on Nuclear Activities. However, when such licence is granted, the radiation protection authority (see below) prescribes the conditions necessary for radiation protection.

The *National Institute of Radiation Protection — SSI* (statens stralskyddsinstitut), under the Ministry of Energy and the Environment, is the body responsible for all aspects of radiation protection and enjoys wide powers under the 1958 Radiation Protection Act. It attaches such conditions as are necessary from the radiation protection viewpoint to licences issued under the 1984 Act on Nuclear Activities, as provided by the 1958 Act.

Control of the import of radioactive materials is the responsibility of customs officials, acting in accordance with regulations made by the General Customs Administration in Agreement with the SSI (Ordinance 1958 No. 652).

V. ORES

Under the Act (No. 890) of 13th December 1974 (Section 1) concerning Certain Mineral Deposits, a special licence (concession) is required for the exploration for or exploitation of deposits of minerals containing uranium or thorium.

Applications for concessions are submitted to the National Industrial Board and considered by the Government or authority appointed by the Government (Section 2).

A concession may be granted only to someone who is considered suitable from the standpoint of the public interest to carry on the exploration or exploitation to which the concession refers (Section 6).

A concession may be combined with stipulations necessary for protecting public interests or individual rights or which are otherwise required in order to promote prospecting for and the preservation of natural resources in a manner serving the interests of the public (Section 10). It may be stipulated in the concession that the State shall be entitled to participate in the undertaking.

The Inspectors of Mining exercise supervision over compliance with the provisions in, or made by virtue of, the Act relating to exploration and exploitation. Concession-holders or others carrying on activities under the Act shall on demand furnish the Inspectors of Mining with such information and documents as are needed for supervision (Section 40).

It is expected that new legislation on these subjects will be adopted by Parliament in the near future.

VI. TRANSPORT[5]

The transport of nuclear material and equipment is governed by the 1984 Act and Ordinance on Nuclear Activities in connection with licensing and notification requirements. In addition, provisions concerning transport are laid down in the 1982 Act on the Transport of Dangerous Goods (SFS 1982 :84). Uranium, plutonium, thorium or compounds containing them may transit through Sweden if the necessary transport permits have been granted.

The 1958 Act on Radiation Protection provides that the National Institute of Radiation Protection (SSI) shall lay down regulations concerning transport, customs control and transit of such material and equipment.

VII. SAFEGUARDS AND PHYSICAL PROTECTION

There are no specific regulations in Sweden concerning safeguards or the physical protection of nuclear material, but the 1984 Act on Nuclear Activities stipulates [Section 4(2)] that safety measures are to be maintained by taking the necessary measures to prevent illicit dealings with nuclear material or waste. The Swedish Nuclear Power Inspectorate organises the safeguards and the physical protection of such material and equipment.

In addition, the 1984 Ordinance (Section 21) provides that the Inspectorate may issue directives on inspection of nuclear facilities and devices for the possession, handling, etc. of nuclear substances. These directives are issued on a case-by-case basis and cover accounting of nuclear material from the viewpoint of non-proliferation and safeguards.

VIII. INTELLECTUAL PROPERTY IN THE NUCLEAR FIELD

Co-ordinated Acts on Patents have been in force since 1st January 1968 in Sweden, Denmark, Finland and Norway. The Swedish Act (No. 837 of 1st December 1967) contains no special provisions as regards patents in the nuclear field.

IX. AGREEMENTS

1. Multilateral Agreements

Sweden ratified the 1968 Treaty on the Proliferation of Nuclear Weapons on 9th January 1970 and also ratified the 1980 Convention on the Physical Protection of Nuclear Material on 1st August 1980.

2. Bilateral Agreements

Sweden has entered into a number of bilateral agreements in the nuclear field and has pledged to its most important suppliers that it shall obtain prior approval before re-exporting material or equipment included in the agreement concerned. These framework agreements for nuclear co-operation are listed below.

— Agreement between the Government of Sweden and the Government of ***Austria***, signed on 25th August 1970 and entered into force immediately for an indefinite duration. The Agreement covers exchange of information, delivery of equipment and nuclear fuel, etc.

— Agreement between the Government of Sweden and the Government of ***Australia***, signed on 18th March 1981 and entered into force on 22nd May 1981 for a period of thirty years which is extended if not denounced. The Agreement covers delivery of nuclear material and equipment, etc.

— Agreement between the Government of Sweden and the Government of ***Canada***, signed on 17th November 1978 and entered into force on 27th September 1981 for a period of twenty years. The Agreement covers exchange of information, delivery of nuclear material and equipment, etc.

— Agreement between the Government of Sweden and the Government of ***Finland***, signed on 5th October 1968, supplemented by an Exchange of Notes of 4th March 1983, and entered into force immediately for an indefinite duration. The Agreement covers exchange of information, delivery of nuclear material and equipment, etc. For further details see the section on agreements in the chapter on Finland in this Volume.

— Agreement between the Government of Sweden and the Government of the ***Soviet Union***, signed on 12th January 1970 and entered into force on 12th November 1970 for a period of thirty years. The Agreement covers exchange of information, delivery of nuclear material and equipment, etc.

— Agreement between the Government of Sweden and the Government of the ***Swiss Confederation***, signed on 14th February 1968 and entered into force on 16th January 1969 for a period of ten years, renewed if not denounced.

— Agreement between the Government of Sweden and the Government of the ***United Kingdom***, signed on 16th May 1984 and entered into force immediately for an indefinite period. This Agreement supplements an original Agreement for co-operation signed in 1957, covering exchange of information, delivery of nuclear material and equipment; it concerns implementation of the Guidelines set out in IAEA document INFCIRC/254 for the export of nuclear material, equipment and technology (London Club Guidelines).

— Agreement between the Government of Sweden and the Government of the ***United States of America***, signed on 19th December 1983 and entered into force for a period of thirty years which is renewable. The Agreement covers exchange of information, delivery of nuclear material and equipment.

— The Government of Sweden concluded a framework Agreement with the Government of the ***People's Republic of China*** covering industrial and scientific co-operation, also in the nuclear field. This Agreement entered into force on the date of its signature, 5th December 1978, for a period of ten years which is renewable every five years thereafter.

NOTES AND REFERENCES

1. SFS: Svensk Författningssamling: Swedish Code of Statutes.
2. A list of items whose export "triggers" application of IAEA Safeguards.
3. It should be noted that the Swedish "kärnämne" (nuclear material) also includes deuterium, lithium, tritium etc. and compounds including such substances which might in future be used for fusion energy.
4. A new Radiation Protection Act and Radiation Protection Ordinance are scheduled to enter into force on 1st July 1988, replacing the previous texts on the subject. At present no further details on the new Act and Ordinance are available but the radiation protection principles remaining unchanged the 1958 Act is therefore mentioned in this study.

   The new legislation will be described in the OECD/NEA Nuclear Law Bulletin in due course.
5. For further details see *Regulations Governing the Transport of Radioactive Materials*, OECD/NEA, 1980.

***

New Swedish Nuclear Legislation, Ministry of Industry, Stockholm, 1984.

Annex I

ANNEX OF ORDINANCE ON NUCLEAR ACTIVITIES (SFS 1984:14)

List of equipment or material etc. that may not be conveyed out of Sweden without the permission of the Government

I. Equipment or material that has been specially designed or prepared for the processing, use or production of nuclear substances etc.

1. Nuclear reactors.
2. Equipment for nuclear reactors:
   a) reactor pressure vessels, assembled or in the form of prefabricated parts,
   b) machines for the loading or replacement of fuel in reactors,
   c) reactor control rods,
   d) pressure tubes intended for the containment of fuel elements and coolant at a pressure exceeding 5 000 kilopascals,
   e) tubes for fuel elements of zirconium or zirconium alloy in which the content of hafnium is less than five hundredths of the constitutent quantity of zirconium, insofar as the weight of the tubes conveyed out of Sweden exceeds 500 kilograms per year,
   f) main coolant pumps for the recirculation of coolant in the form of liquid metal.
3. Gaseous hydrogen containing heavy hydrogen (deuterium), if the weight ratio between deuterium and light hydrogen (protium) exceeds 1: 2500 and the weight of deuterium in the gas exceeds 2 kilograms on each export occasion.
4. Water containing heavy water (deuterium oxide) if the weight ratio between deuterium and light hydrogen (protium) exceeds 1: 2500 and the weight of deuterium oxide in the water exceeds 10 kilograms on each export occasion.
5. Graphite for reactor purposes whose impurity content amounts to no more than five millionths boron, counted as neutron poison, and whose density exceeds 1 500 kg/m^3, insofar as its weight exceeds 5 000 kilograms on each export occasion.
6. Plants for the reprocessing of irradiated fuel elements.
7. Equipment for plants for the reprocessing of irradiated fuel elements:
   a) machines for cutting up of fuel elements,
   b) tanks for dissolution of irradiated reactor fuel.
8. Plants for the fabrication of fuel elements.
9. Plants for the enrichment of uranium.
10. Equipment designed for the enrichment of uranium.
11. Plants for the production of heavy water.
12. Equipment designed for the production of heavy water.

II. Equipment or material for which the right to manufacture may not be assigned or transferred.

Such equipment and such material as is stipulated under I, points 1, 2 and 6-12.

Annex II

SUBSTANCES FOR WHICH A LICENCE IS REQUIRED UNDER THE 1984 ORDINANCE ON NUCLEAR ACTIVITIES

The type and quantities of the substances used as nuclear fuel for which the Swedish Nuclear Power Inspectorate can consider licence applications to acquire, possess, transfer, handle, process or otherwise have dealings with or convey into Sweden, are defined as follows (Section 16):

1) enriched uranium or compounds containing such uranium, if the content of the isotope uranium 235 amounts to no more than 5 kilograms;
2) no more than 5 kilograms of the isotope uranium 233 in pure or compound form;
3) no more than 5 kilograms of plutonium in pure or compound form;
4) natural or depleted uranium or compounds containing natural or depleted uranium; or
5) thorium or compounds containing thorium.

The Ordinance (Section 1) defines as natural uranium that which contains the mixture of isotopes occurring in nature; enriched uranium as that in which the content of the isotope uranium 235 is higher than in natural uranium and depleted uranium as that in which the content of uranium 235 is lower than in natural uranium.

Annex III

SMALL QUANTITIES OF SUBSTANCES FOR WHICH AN EXPORT LICENCE IS REQUIRED UNDER THE 1984 ORDINANCE

The SKI considers applications for licences to export from Sweden the smaller quantities of uranium, plutonium, thorium or tritium in pure form or in the form of an alloy, compound or mixture on each occasion of such an export:

1) no more than 10 kilograms of enriched uranium containing no more than 5 per cent of the isotope uranium 235;
2) no more than 100 grams of enriched uranium containing more than 5 per cent of the isotope uranium 235;
3) no more than 10 grams of the isotope uranium 233;
4) no more than 10 grams of plutonium;
5) no more than 50 kilograms of natural uranium or uranium depleted of the isotope uranium 235;
6) no more than 50 kilograms of thorium; or
7) no more than 1 gram of tritium.

SWITZERLAND

TABLE OF CONTENTS

SWITZERLAND

I. INTRODUCTION

As regards nuclear trade, Switzerland occupies a middle position as compared to the biggest European supplier countries (such as France and the Federal Republic of Germany). It has, for the size of the country, a relatively large nuclear power programme. Although Switzerland has long been a manufacturer of conventional electrical apparatus, it has not developed capacity with regard to the complete nuclear fuel cycle, its activities in this sphere being essentially confined to the manufacture of heavy equipment, the production of heavy water and the supply of services.

Before considering the regulation of nuclear trade, some general remarks are necessary. Nuclear legislation in Switzerland is based on the *Act of 23rd December 1959 on the peaceful use of atomic energy and protection against radiation*, the partial revision of which in 1987 is important from the trade viewpoint[1]. This revision introduces, in particular, an express reference to non-proliferation among the licensing criteria for the import and export of nuclear material and equipment. The provisions of this basic Act are essentially supplemented by two Ordinances regulating in a distinct manner two aspects of nuclear trade : the non-proliferation of nuclear weapons, and protection against radiation. The first aspect concerns trade in source materials and large nuclear equipment and is covered by the *Ordinance of 18th January 1984 on definitions and licences in the atomic energy field*, twice amended in 1987 to take account of amendments to the Atomic Energy Act[2]. The second aspect, relating to radioactive materials, is dealt with by the Radiation Protection Ordinance of 30th June 1976, as amended by the Ordinance of 28th November 1983.

Different regulations apply to each of these aspects of nuclear trade since it is a question, in the first case, of items which are sensitive from the viewpoint of national security or of Switzerland's international commitments, whereas trade in radioactive materials is regulated for radiation protection purposes.

If this study is to be complete, account must also be taken of regulations which are not specifically nuclear, insofar as they affect nuclear trade. This applies essentially to the *Federal Act of 25th June 1982 on external economic measures*, to the *Ordinance of 16th December 1985 on the export and transit of goods*[3] (adopted in implementation of that Act) and to the regulatory requirements concerning the transport of dangerous goods.

II. TRADE IN NUCLEAR MATERIAL AND EQUIPMENT

1. Import and Export Policy and Competent Authorities

Switzerland imports all the nuclear material required for its reactors. Its active co-operation with foreign countries extends also to reprocessing. Furthermore, there are several enterprises in the country which produce and export nuclear equipment ; Switzerland must therefore comply scrupulously with the international aspects of radiation protection and the non-proliferation of nuclear weapons.

In this connection, Switzerland has signed and ratified the 1968 Treaty on the Non-proliferation of Nuclear Weapons and is a member of the Group of Nuclear Supplier Countries (so-called London Club). The Swiss Government intends to take the measures promoting non-proliferation corresponding to its international commitments. In addition, Switzerland has ratified the 1980 International Convention on the Physical Protection of Nuclear Material.

The Federal Council, which already plays an important role in the organisation and conduct of nuclear activities in general, is expressly authorised under the Atomic Energy Act as amended to conclude bilateral agreements concerning the import and export of nuclear articles and technology. In addition, the Federal Council is now empowered to decide on general regulations in this field without requiring the approval of Parliament.

The competent authorities with regard to trade in nuclear material and equipment are as follows :

— the Federal Energy Office for the granting of licences to import and export nuclear articles ;
— the Principal Nuclear Safety Division with regard to the granting of certificates for the transport of nuclear material ;
— the Import and Export Division of the Federal Office of External Economic Affairs for the control of exports of strategic materials and equipment ;
— the Federal Department of Foreign Affairs as regards obtaining the confirmations required from the countries of destination in the case of export.

2. Nuclear Regulations

The Atomic Energy Act contains general provisions on the licensing procedure with regard to trade in nuclear materials and equipment, provisions that are supplemented by those of the Ordinance of 18th January 1984 on definitions and licences in the atomic energy field as amended. This legislation must be read together with relevant regulations that are not specifically nuclear.

Moreover, and in addition to the licensing procedure for import, export and transit, the 1984 Ordinance as amended requires that the export of certain sensitive categories of materials be notified.

a) Scope of licensing regime and criteria for granting licences

i) Nuclear fuel and wastes

Under Section 4 paragraph 1(c) of the Atomic Energy Act, a licence must be obtained from the Confederation for the import, transit and export of nuclear fuel and radioactive waste. Under this provision, the Ordinance of 18th January 1984 as amended (Section 11) set up a licensing system for trade in nuclear fuel and radioactive waste (Annex 1 of the Ordinance). These terms are defined in Sections 1 and 2, respectively, of the Ordinance[4]. It specifies that both placing goods in a customs depot and withdrawing them are treated as equivalent to transit operations.

Applications for licences for such operations are assessed with regard to several criteria. In the first place, the application must take into account the requirements laid down by Section 5 of the Atomic Energy Act, namely:

- Switzerland's external security and its international commitments essentially for non-proliferation purposes;
- physical protection;
- non-proliferation of nuclear weapons;
- compliance with the insurance provisions of the Act of 18th March 1983 on Nuclear Third Party Liability. The transport of nuclear fuel and radioactive products and waste must be covered by the third party liability insurance policy of the Swiss nuclear installation sending or receiving such fuel, products or waste. As regards transit, a third party liability insurance cover of at least SF 50 million is required, to which is added insurance by the Confederation for risks not covered by the private company;
- permission to export may be refused on grounds of national interest. In practice, no refusal has ever been made on this ground.

Secondly, in addition to the requirements laid down by the Atomic Energy Act, the Ordinance provides that the following must also be taken into account:

- radiation protection conditions;
- international conventions on co-operation in the peaceful uses of nuclear energy ratified by Switzerland;
- international conventions on the transport of dangerous goods to which Switzerland is a Party.

Finally, when nuclear fuel is exported or when plutonium and uranium enriched to more than 20 per cent are in transit and new technical measures regarding transport are applied on Swiss territory, the competent authority shall ensure that the licence applications conform to the London Club Guidelines[5].

These Guidelines on transfers of nuclear items provide for restrictions in trade based on physical protection and non-proliferation (safeguards) considerations. They are reproduced in Annex 3 to the 1984 Ordinance.

This licensing regime also makes it possible to effect the national control of materials which Switzerland undertook to carry out pursuant to Article III.1 of the Non-Proliferation Treaty; control procedures are dealt with in an Agreement with the IAEA, concluded on 6th September 1978 in compliance with INFCIRC/153 of the IAEA.

*
**

Furthermore, under the second paragraph of Section 4 of the Atomic Energy Act as amended, the Federal Council may decree that a licence is required to import, carry in transit and export equipment, products, apparatus and materials needed for nuclear technology as well as source materials to be used in producing nuclear fuel, and to export technology[6]. In accordance with this provision, Sections 12, 13 and 14 of the 1984 Ordinance as amended lay down a licensing regime for the following:

- reactors and related equipment, installations and equipment for fuel element fabrication (Section 12);
- other installations, equipment and material (Section 13);
- technology (Section 14).

ii) Nuclear reactors, related equipment and installations and equipment for fuel element fabrication

As mentioned above, under Section 12 of the 1984 Ordinance as amended, a licence is required for the export of nuclear reactors and equipment specially designed or prepared in their connection; a licence is also needed for installations for fuel element fabrication and equipment specially designed or prepared therefor.

The authority responsible for issuing the licence takes into account three criteria already mentioned with regard to nuclear fuel and waste, namely the requirements under Section 5 of the Atomic Energy Act, the international conventions on peaceful nuclear co-operation and the London Club Guidelines.

iii) Other installations, equipment and material

In accordance with Section 13 of the 1984 Ordinance as amended, a licence is required for the export — and when new technical measures regarding transport are applied on Swiss territory — for the transit of :

— installations and equipment specially designed or prepared for enrichment or reprocessing of nuclear fuel or production of heavy water, deuterium or deuterium compounds (Annex 2.III and IV of the Ordinance) ;
— heavy water, deuterium and nuclear graphite (Annex 2.I of the Ordinance).

The licence will again be granted on the basis of the criteria laid down by Section 5 of the Atomic Energy Act, the international conventions on peaceful nuclear co-operation and the London Club Guidelines.

iv) Technology

The export of nuclear technology is also subject to licensing (Ordinance, Section 14). Applications for a licence are also assessed according to the requirements of Section 5 of the Atomic Energy Act and Switzerland's international commitments as already mentioned.

The list of materials and equipment referred to in Sections 11, 12, 13 and 14 of the 1984 Ordinance as amended is reproduced in *Annex I* to this chapter.

Section 15 of the 1984 Ordinance as amended provides that the competent authority for granting licences is the *Federal Energy Office*. Decisions concerning export licence applications of particular political or economic importance are taken jointly by the Office, the *Federal Department of Foreign Affairs* and the *Federal Office of External Economic Affairs*.

At the border, the nuclear material and equipment subject to licensing must be inspected by the main Customs offices (Section 17, paragraph 2 of the 1984 Ordinance as amended).

A fee of between SF 200 and 2 000 is payable for licences (Sections 13 and 14 of the Ordinance of 30th September 1985 on fees in the nuclear energy field).

b) Information which licence applications must contain

Under Section 16 of the Ordinance of 18th January 1984 as amended, applications must contain information concerning :

— the composition and properties of the materials ;
— technical details about the equipment ;
— the type of technology and its scope according to the Trigger List of the London Club Guidelines ;
— the place of manufacture ;
— the place of destination and the recipient ;
— the anticipated use ;
— the purchase or sale conditions ;
— transport.

The Federal Energy Office may also require the applicant to provide additional information and request the necessary certificates from the authorities in the country of destination. The Federal Department of Foreign Affairs is responsible for obtaining certificates from abroad.

c) Obligation to notify the export of certain categories of sensitive goods

Under Section 18(1) of the Ordinance of 18th January 1984 as amended, certain sensitive goods intended for use in installations for enriching or reprocessing nuclear fuel or for the production of heavy water, deuterium or compounds of deuterium may be exported without a licence but must be notified to the Federal Energy Office at least twenty days before being despatched. These goods belong to the following categories :

— components whose foreseeable use will bring them into direct contact with nuclear fuel ;
— components that are essential, for radiation protection purposes, for the working of the process in question ;
— components needed to record and control material flowrates, inasmuch as they are specially designed or prepared for the process in question ;
— goods listed in Annex 2.III (see *Annex I* hereto) as being subject to mandatory notification which are likely to be used in installations not under the control of the International Atomic Energy Agency (IAEA).

When notification is made less than twenty days before despatch, the export operation may take place only with the agreement of the Federal Energy Office.

If the export of goods subject to mandatory notification also requires a licence under the Ordinance of 16th December 1985 on the export and transit of goods (see 3, below : Regulations concerning foreign trade), the lodging of a licence application with the Import and Export Division is treated as equivalent to notification, provided that the exporter specifies in his application that the goods in question require to be notified.

Under Section 18(5) of the 1984 Ordinance as amended, the Federal Council may, on the proposal of the Federal Department of Transport, Communications and Energy (after consultation with the Federal Department of Foreign Affairs and the Federal Department of the Economy), prohibit such exports or impose special conditions on them if the country of destination does not appear sufficiently determined to prevent proliferation. Should there be reason to suppose that these provisions might apply, the Federal Office informs the interested parties of this fact.

d) Offences

Breaches of the licencing procedure and the obligation to notify certain exports are regulated by Section 35 of the Atomic Energy Act. Under this Section, breaches of these provisions are punishable by a maximum fine of SF 20 000 unless the facts of the case amount to a more serious offence. Attempted offences and aiding and abetting are also punishable.

3. Regulations Concerning Foreign Trade

In addition to the licensing regime introduced by the Atomic Energy Act and the Ordinance of 1984 as amended, the Ordinance of 16th December 1985 on the export and transit of goods (nuclear and non-nuclear) — adopted in pursuance of the Act of 25th June 1982 on External Economic Measures — provides that the export and transit of certain articles which are technologically important for the Swiss economy require a licence. The list of such articles in the Annex to the 1985 Ordinance is much wider than that of the 1984 Ordinance as amended since it includes goods other than strategically important nuclear items[7] (extracts from this list concerning nuclear items are given in *Annex II* to this chapter). On the other hand, certain articles are covered by the 1984 Ordinance but not by that on the export and transit of goods. A licence may therefore be required in respect of a given item either under one only of these two texts, or under both at the same time. In this latter event, the two licences are in principle granted independently of each other and the economic operator must be in possession of both of them if the export or transit operation is to take place.

The competent authority for granting the licence required under the Export and Transit of Goods Ordinance is the Import and Export Division of the Federal Office of External Economic Affairs.

The relevant criteria for the granting of a licence under the Ordinance on the export and transit of goods are different from those applied in respect of the 1984 Ordinance as amended. The latter's criteria result from Switzerland's international commitments, especially with regard to the non-proliferation of nuclear weapons, whereas the objective of the Ordinance on the export and transit of goods is to control the export or transit of goods from countries having agreements with Switzerland and which only allow such goods to be exported or transited to Switzerland on condition that the latter guarantees not to re-export them without the consent of the countries in question.

Breaches of the Ordinance of 16th December 1985, whether committed intentionally or by negligence, are punishable by a maximum fine of SF 100 000. In cases of intentional breach, the judge may, in the most serious cases, also impose a prison sentence of up to one year. Attempted offences and aiding and abetting are also punishable (Section 7 of the Act of 25th June 1982).

III. TRADE IN RADIOACTIVE MATERIALS

The Radiation Protection Ordinance of 30th June 1976, as amended by the Ordinance of 28th November 1983, lays down technical radiation protection provisions covering all radioactive substances[8] as well as apparatus and articles containing such substances but does not regulate the control procedures applicable to radioactive waste and nuclear fuels, these being subject to the licensing regime provided for in the Ordinance of 18th January 1984 on definitions and licences in the atomic energy field as amended (see section II of this chapter). The Radiation Protection Ordinance of 30th June 1976 as amended introduces two distinct control procedures depending on the potential contamination risks linked to the various applications of the radioactive substances covered : a licensing procedure and a mandatory declaration procedure. The Ordinance also provides that a register must be kept and reports made.

The 1976 Ordinance as amended does not apply to transport operations. These are governed by regulations applying specifically to each mode of transport (cf. section V of this chapter).

Special provisions concerning foodstuffs are contained in the Ordinance on foodstuffs and everyday articles of 26th May 1936 (as modified on 12th May 1986), adopted in pursuance of the Federal Act of 8th December 1905 on trade in foodstuffs and various everyday articles.

1. Licensing Regime

Under Section 3 of the Ordinance of 30th June 1976 as amended, a licence is required to receive, deliver, export or import radioactive substances or apparatus and objects containing such substances (other than radioactive waste and nuclear fuels) whose absolute activity is more than 100 times the exemption limit specified in Appendix 4, column 2 of the Ordinance (see *Annex III* to this chapter) and whose specific activity as regards solid radioactive substances exceeds :

— 20 picocuries per gramme for alpha emitters, or
— 20 nanocuries per gramme for beta emitters.

This licencing regime also applies to radioisotopes intended for medical uses. However, users and acquirers of such substances normally have a general licence to use radioactive materials, and a special licence is not therefore necessary in every case. Licences are granted by the *Federal Office of Public Health.*

Further, under Section 17(2) of the 1976 Ordinance as amended, a licence is required to assemble, operate or use substances, apparatus or articles approved for restricted use by the Federal Office of Public Health. The Office may, however waive the need for such a licence and, if applicable, the mandatory declaration.

Approval of apparatus and articles for *restricted use* is the alternative category to approval for *general use* which applies to apparatus and articles containing radioactive substances with which, in normal conditions of use, it is impossible to enter into contact and which are constructed in such a way as to ensure that no person is exposed to radiation or inadmissible contamination (Section 16 of the 1976 Ordinance as amended).

Equipment emitting ionizing radiation may be approved for restricted use when the environmental dose rate produced exceeds 0.5 millirem per hour at a distance of 5 centimetres from the surface, on condition that no person is exposed to any radiation or inadmissible contamination when the substances, apparatus and articles are used for the purposes for which they were intended (Section 16).

Under Section 18(2), substances, apparatus and articles approved for restricted use by the Federal Office of Public Health must be marked with a distinctive sign determined by the Office and may not be delivered to the purchaser unless accompanied by a copy of the licence, which must be kept for inspection by the supervisory authorities.

The Ordinance lays down the details of the licensing procedure and the conditions to which licences are made subject.

Under Section 10, licence applications must be submitted in duplicate to the Federal Office of Public Health, accompanied by certificates and information concerning :

— the identity of the applicant and, where appropriate, the expert responsible for radiation protection ;
— a description of the substances, objects, equipment and apparatus involved, the premises in which they are kept and the nature of the activity envisaged ;
— the radiation protection measures envisaged and, in particular, relevant internal instructions and the proposed method of disposing of the radioactive waste.

The conditions for granting licences are specified in Section 5. Thus, a licence, subject when necessary to conditions and duties, is granted when :

— the applicant or the expert he has appointed to ensure radiation protection provides proof that he has the technical qualifications required by Sections 6 to 9[9] ;
— the enterprise has at its disposal the required number of experts ;
— such persons inspire complete confidence ;
— all aspects of radiation protection are guaranteed in compliance with this Ordinance.

If radiation protection cannot be sufficiently guaranteed, even by imposing special conditions and obligations, the licence is refused.

Licences may not be transferred and may be revoked by the issuing body if they were obtained on the basis of inaccurate or incomplete information or if the conditions to which they were made subject are not, or are no longer being observed (Section 13).

Furthermore, the import and export of radioactive substances and apparatus containing such substances are subject to control at the frontier by the Federal Office of Public Health. The General Customs Directorate designates the Customs Offices which are to process such imports and exports (Section 22).

2. Mandatory Declaration Procedure

The procedure for mandatory declaration to the Federal Office of Public Health, laid down in Section 14 of the 1976 Ordinance as amended, applies to the possession of radioactive materials and apparatus exempted from the licensing procedure, and to radioactive substances and apparatus approved for general use — defined above — but not exempted from the declaration requirements.

Like apparatus and articles for restricted use, those approved for general use should in principle be marked with a distinctive sign determined by the Federal Office of Public Health. The Federal Department of the Interior may, however, exempt certain categories of apparatus and articles from this obligation. Any change in the circumstances on which the licence application was based must also be notified to the Federal Office of Public Health.

Section 17(3) specifies that any change made to the substances, apparatus and articles approved for general or restricted use must be notified without delay if it results in an increased risk of irradiation or a basic change in the type of construction approved.

3. Obligation to Register Radioactive Materials

Section 15 of the Ordinance of 30th June 1976 as amended specifies that persons trading in radioactive substances or articles containing such substances (except for radioactive waste and nuclear fuels) — trading is defined as supplying and acquiring — must make appropriate entries in a register and submit an annual report to the Federal Office of Public Health containing the following information :

- a description of the radionuclides and, where appropriate, their chemical composition ;
- a description of the apparatus and articles containing such substances ;
- the addresses of the suppliers in Switzerland and abroad together with the activity level of each radionuclide received ;
- the addresses of the recipients in Switzerland and abroad together with the activity level of each radionuclide delivered.

Section 35 of the Atomic Energy Act applies to *breaches* of the provisions of the 1976 Ordinance as amended. Section 35 provides, in particular, that any person who, without being licenced, carries out actions for which a licence is necessary, or who does not comply with the conditions and duties imposed on the granting of a licence is punishable by a maximum fine of SF 20 000 unless the facts of the case amount to a more serious offence. Attempted offences and aiding and abetting are also punishable.

4. Special Licensing Regime for Foodstuffs

Trading in irradiated foodstuffs is regulated by the Foodstuffs Ordinance of 26th May 1936 (as amended on 12th May 1986), adopted in implementation of the Federal Act of 8th December 1905 on trade in foodstuffs and various everyday articles.

Under Section 11b of the Ordinance of 26th May 1936 as amended, foodstuffs treated by means of ionizing radiation may not be marketed unless such treatment has been authorised by the Federal Office of Public Health, something which, for the moment, is not envisaged. This provision also applies to imported foodstuffs even though it is more difficult to exercise control in such cases.

Breaches of this provision are punishable by a term of imprisonment not exceeding three months or a maximum fine of SF 1 000 (Section 41 of the Federal Act of 8th December 1905 on trade in foodstuffs and various everyday articles).

IV. NATIONAL SECURITY AND PHYSICAL PROTECTION

With regard to national security, Switzerland, as already mentioned, ratified on 9th March 1977 the Treaty on the Non-Proliferation of Nuclear Weapons (NPT) and undertook to apply in their entirety the Guidelines of the Group of Nuclear Supplier Countries (the London Club) on nuclear transfers, including, since the 1987 revision of the Atomic Energy Act, the provisions on the transfer of nuclear technology.

There is no legislation dealing specifically with national security but special provisions are contained in the Atomic Energy Act and in the 1984 Ordinance on definitions and licences in the atomic energy field as amended, as was indicated in section II on trade in nuclear material and equipment. Decisions on the granting of licences are made on the basis of non-proliferation considerations and the London Club Guidelines.

In addition, and within the context of penal sanctions which, generally speaking, are applicable to persons who intentionally transgress the atomic energy provisions of the Atomic Energy Act, Section 34 provides that the betrayal of secrets concerning the peaceful use of atomic energy is an offence which is judged more or less severely depending on whether or not the secrets were passed on to a foreign agency or enterprise. In serious cases, particularly when the offender acted on behalf of an official or private foreign agency or a private foreign enterprise, or of their agents, the judge may pronounce a sentence of long-term imprisonment (*réclusion*). Offences committed through negligence are punishable by a prison sentence of up to one year or a fine.

There is no Swiss legislation dealing specifically with physical protection considerations, i.e. measures to prevent the unlawful acquisition and use of nuclear material. However, as seen in section II, the Ordinance of 18th January 1984 on definitions and licences in the atomic energy field, as amended, contains a reference to the London Club Guidelines on nuclear transfers which include special physical protection provisions. In addition, on 9th January 1987, the Swiss Government ratified the International Convention on the Physical Protection of Nuclear Material.

V. TRANSPORT

Under the Atomic Energy Act (Section 4 b) and the 1984 Ordinance on definitions and licences in the atomic field as amended (Section 9), a licence is required for the transport, delivery, acceptance or any other form of possession of radioactive residues or nuclear fuels. This prior authorisation is granted by the Federal Energy Office in accordance with the criteria laid down in Section 5 of the Atomic Energy Act, including, in particular, the need for insurance cover, and guarantees with respect to physical protection and Switzerland's external security and international non-proliferation commitments. There are, in addition, regulations governing each specific mode of transport which adopt, more or less without amendment, the contents of the international Conventions on the transport of dangerous goods[10].

There is no special licensing regime for radioactive materials, and their transport is governed solely by the above-mentioned regulations on the transport of dangerous goods.

The Principal Nuclear Safety Division of the Federal Energy Office is empowered to issue transport certificates for all nuclear materials in compliance with the transport of dangerous goods regulations.

VI. INTELLECTUAL PROPERTY IN THE NUCLEAR FIELD

Apart from a transitional provision in the legislation on patents and a few reservations in international agreements, Switzerland has not drafted any special regulations dealing with nuclear industrial property rights. Consequently, the ordinary law on patents for inventions applies in the nuclear field.

It is true that Section 34 of the Atomic Energy Act amounts to a specific penal provision applicable to the betrayal of secrets relating to nuclear energy, but this Section is of very limited application compared to the penalties applying under the ordinary law on professional secrecy and State secrets (Article 273 of the Penal Code), the betrayal of manufacturing or trade secrets (Article 162) and treason (Article 267). To date, Section 34 of the Atomic Energy Act has never been applied.

VII. AGREEMENTS

1. Multilateral Agreements

On 9th March 1977, Switzerland ratified the Treaty on the Non-Proliferation of Nuclear Weapons and informed the IAEA that it undertook to apply the Guidelines of the Nuclear Suppliers Group (London Club). On 6th September 1978, Switzerland concluded a safeguards agreement with the IAEA in implementation of the Non-Proliferation Treaty.

On 9th January 1987, Switzerland ratified the Convention on the Physical Protection of Nuclear Material.

2. Bilateral Agreements

- Agreement concluded with the Government of the ***United States of America*** on 21st June 1956 and renewed on 30th December 1965, on the exchange of information, the transfer of apparatus and equipment and the transfer of fissile materials for research purposes.
- Co-operation Agreement with ***Canada*** on the peaceful uses of atomic energy, dated 6th March 1958 and renewed in 1964, 1969 and 1971. A provision has now been included that the Agreement will be automatically renewed every year, unless one of the Parties indicates otherwise at least six months before termination on the 31st July of the year in question. The Agreement deals with the supply of nuclear fuels, the exchange of information and the supply of equipment. A new Agreement on co-operation in the peaceful uses of nuclear energy was concluded with Canada on 22nd December 1987 (not yet in force).
- Co-operation Agreement of 11th August 1964 with the Government of the ***United Kingdom*** for the

peaceful uses of atomic energy dealing with the supply of nuclear fuels, the exchange of information and the transfer of materials and equipment.

— Co-operation Agreement of 26th May 1965 with ***Brazil*** for the peaceful uses of atomic energy dealing with the exchange of information and staff and the reciprocal supply of materials and equipment.

— Co-operation Agreement with ***Sweden*** of 16th February 1968 for the use of atomic energy for peaceful purposes. This Agreement provides for the exchange of information and services, and the supply of equipment, installations, nuclear source materials, special nuclear materials and fuel.

— Co-operation Agreement with ***France*** for the peaceful uses of atomic energy, signed on 14th May 1970. Under this Agreement, Switzerland and France undertake to co-operate in the field of the processing of spent fuel, and the reciprocal supply and import of nuclear materials and equipment. It also promotes the development of co-operation between the nuclear industries of the two countries.

— Agreement with ***Egypt*** on co-operation in the peaceful uses of nuclear energy, signed on 13th November 1984. The Parties express the desire to widen co-operation in the nuclear field between the public and private organisations of the two States. This collaboration is placed in the context of the rules on non-proliferation. The conditions for co-operation were negotiated within the framework of the Non-proliferation Treaty and the London Club (Guidelines on nuclear transfers). They include the undertaking by each Party not to use the nuclear articles exchanged except for exclusively peaceful purposes, to submit them to IAEA control, not to re-export them to a third country except on the same conditions and finally, to guarantee the physical protection of these items.

— Co-operation Agreement with ***Australia*** signed on 28th January 1986. This Agreement regulates the non-proliferation safeguards required for establishing peaceful nuclear co-operation between the two countries regarding the exchange of nuclear materials, equipment and technology. The safeguards include, in particular, the undertaking by each Party to use the goods exchanged exclusively for peaceful and non-explosive purposes, to allow verification of this use by the IAEA, not to re-export these items to a third country unless precise conditions are met, and to ensure their safety.

— Co-operation Agreement with the ***People's Republic of China***, signed on 12th November 1986. This Agreement regulates the non-proliferation safeguards required for developing co-operation between both countries for the exchange of nuclear materials, equipment and technology. Such safeguards include in particular the commitment of the two Parties to use the items exchanged exclusively for peaceful, non-explosive, purposes, to re-export such items to a third country only subject to specific conditions, including their safety. Both Parties have also undertaken to submit items considered sensitive to IAEA control.

SWITZERLAND

NOTES AND REFERENCES

1. Act of 9th October 1986 amending the Federal Act of 23rd December 1959 on the peaceful use of atomic energy and protection against radiation. This amendment entered into force on 1st April 1987. Given that the revision officially adopts the shortened title of the "Atomic Energy Act", this shortened title will, for convenience, be used in the rest of this chapter.
2. The first amendment of 2nd March 1987 (RO 1987-547) entered into force on 1st April 1987 and the second, dated 28th October 1987 (RO 1987-838), entered into force on 1st January 1988.
3. This Ordinance amends the Ordinance of 7th March 1983 on the export of goods.
4. Nuclear fuel is defined as:

   a. The following source materials:
   1. natural uranium, i.e. uranium with the mixture of isotopes found in nature;
   2. depleted uranium, i.e. uranium with an uranium 235 content lower than natural uranium;
   3. thorium;
   4. substances containing the above-mentioned materials in whatever form.

   b. The following special fissile materials:
   1. plutonium 239;
   2. plutonium 241;
   3. uranium 233;
   4. enriched uranium, i.e. uranium in which the uranium 233 or uranium 235 content, or that of these two isotopes combined is higher than the uranium 235 content in natural uranium;

   a. 5. substances containing the above-mentioned materials in whatever form.

   The following are not considered as nuclear fuels:

   a. uranium and thorium ores;
   b. source materials that are not used for energy production, namely those used for analyses, shields or for the manufacture of industrial products and such products;
   c. special fissile materials whose activity does not exceed 100 kilobecquerels.

   Residues are defined as radioactive materials (including activation products) whose activity does not exceed 100 gigabecquerels and which are produced in the nuclear transmutation processes occurring within nuclear fuels.
5. See Volume I of the study on international regulations in which the Guidelines are analysed in detail.
6. The Act defines technology as technical data in a physical form to which the public has no access and which are important with regard to the design, construction, operation or maintenance either of the actual installations for enriching or reprocessing nuclear materials or for heavy water production, or of the main and vital component parts of such installations.
7. Goods indicated by the figure 1) may be exported without a licence when the amount in question does not exceed SF 2 000. Exceptions are regulated by the Federal Department of the Economy. The Federal Department of the Economy may limit the export of certain goods in order to ensure domestic supply. Should important interests be at stake, export may be authorised.

   Under Section 3 of the 1985 Ordinance, when exporting goods which, while coming under one of the tariff numbers in the Annex are not mentioned expressly, the exporter is required to indicate in the export declaration that such goods are not subject to the licensing regime.
8. In its Appendix I, this Ordinance defines radioactive substances as substances or mixtures of whatever chemical composition and physical state containing radionuclides whose activity level exceeds the thresholds permitted under the Ordinance.
9. Sections 6 to 9 cover medical and chiropractic uses, uses by dental practitioners and dental surgeons trained abroad to a level not equivalent to the Federal Dental Surgeon diploma but authorised to practice by the Cantons, and other applications.
10. For further details, see the Analytical Study *Regulations Governing the Transport of Radioactive Materials*, OECD/NEA, 1980.

Annex I

ORDINANCE OF 18TH JANUARY 1984 ON DEFINITIONS AND LICENCES IN THE ATOMIC ENERGY FIELD AS AMENDED*

(Amendement of 28th October 1987)

The List of Nuclear Material and Equipment Requiring a Licence or Notification

Annex 1
(Section 11)

Customs Tariff Number	Description of goods
	Nuclear fuel
ex. 2844.1000/5000	— Uranium (natural, enriched or depleted uranium) and uranium isotopes — Thorium — Plutonium and plutonium isotopes
	Substances containing the above in any form
	Spent fuel elements (irradiated)
ex. 8401.3000	Unirradiated fuel elements

Prior remarks on Annexes 1 and 2

When goods are exported under a customs tariff number mentioned in Annexes 1 and 2 but are not listed therein, the notification of export should specify that the goods concerned are not subject to an export licence.

* Unofficial translation.

Annexe 2 *
(art. 12 à 14, 18)

Numéro du tarif[1]	Désignation de la marchandise
	I. Matériaux pour usage nucléaire
2845.1000	Eau lourde (oxyde de deutérium)
ex 2845.9000	Deutérium (hydrogène lourd) et ses composés
ex 3801.1000	Graphite nucléaire
	II. Réacteurs nucléaires et leurs équipements
ex 7304.4111/9020[2] ex 7305.3110/9020[2] ex 7306.4011/9020[2]	Tubes de force en acier allié destinés à contenir en même temps le combustible et le fluide caloporteur dans un réacteur nucléaire
ex 8109.9000[2]	Tubes de force en alliage de zirconium destinés à contenir en même temps le combustible et le fluide caloporteur dans un réacteur nucléaire
ex 8401.1000[2]	Réacteurs nucléaires, à l'exception des réacteurs de puissance nulle, c'est-à-dire dont la capacité de production de plutonium ne dépasse pas 100 g par année
ex 8401.3000[2]	Gainages en zirconium dans lesquels le rapport pondéral hafnium/zirconium est inférieur à 1/500, en envois dépassant 500 kg brut
ex 8401.4000[2]	Composants de réacteurs nucléaires: – cuves de pression complètes ou leurs parties importantes préfabriquées (d'un poids unitaire de plus de 1000 kg) – barres de réglage (barres d'arrêt et de commande) – tubes de force destinés à contenir en même temps le combustible nucléaire et le fluide caloporteur
ex 8413.1900[2] 8110/8130[2]	Pompes de circulation pour métaux liquides utilisés comme caloporteurs dans certains réacteurs nucléaires
ex 8426.1110/1920[2] ex 8428.9010/9020[2]	Dispositifs servant à charger ou à décharger le combustible d'un réacteur

[1] RS **632.10** annexe

[2] Les marchandises énumérées à ce numéro peuvent être exportées sans autorisation si le poids brut de l'envoi ne dépasse pas 20 kg.

* Note by the Secretariat: List available in French only.

Numéro du tarif	Désignation de la marchandise	Autorisation obligatoire selon art. 13	Notification obligatoire selon art. 18
	III. Equipements servant à l'enrichissement de l'uranium		
ex 6806.9000 ex 6903.1000/ 9000	Fibres utilisées dans des matériaux composites servant à la fabrication de cylindres rotatifs (bols) pour centrifugeuses et ayant un module d'élasticité rapporté à la masse spécifique de 12.3×10^6 m^2/s^2 ou plus		×
ex 6815.1000	Fibres de carbone ou de graphite utilisées dans des matériaux composites servant à la fabrication de cylindres rotatifs pour centrifugeuses et ayant un module d'élasticité rapporté à la masse spécifique de 12.3×10^6 m^2s^2 ou plus et une charge limite de rupture rapportée à la masse spécifique de 0.3×10^6 m^2/s^2 ou plus		×
ex 7207/7212 ex 7218/7220 ex 7224/7226	Produits en acier martensitique («maraging steel») laminés en plat et ayant une charge limite de rupture de 2.050×10^9 N/m^2 ou plus		×
ex 7304/7306	Tubes en acier martensitique («maraging steel») et ayant une charge limite de rupture de 2.050×10^9 N/m^2 ou plus		×
ex 7304.4111/4922 9010/9020 ex 7305.3110/9020 ex 7306.4011/4022 6010/9020 ex 7307.1910/2920 ex 7507.1100/2000 ex 7608.1000/2000 ex 7609.0000	Tubes et leurs accessoires, pour des systèmes servant à conduire et à distribuer l'hexafluorure d'uranium à l'intérieur de cascades de centrifugeuses, en acier inoxydable, en nickel ou en alliages contenant au moins 60 pour cent en poids de nickel ou en aluminium ou ses alliages; tubes de prélèvement servant à extraire l'hexafluorure d'uranium de l'intérieur de cylindres rotatifs ou de chambres, en acier inoxydable, en nickel ou en alliages contenant au moins 60 pour cent en poids de nickel ou en aluminium ou ses alliages	×	×
ex 7326.1910/1920 9021/9034	Pièces forgées en acier martensitique («maraging steel») et ayant une charge limite de rupture de 2.050×10^9 N/m^2 ou plus		×
ex 7608.2000	Tubes en alliages d'aluminium ayant une charge, limite de rupture de 0.460×10^9 N/m^2 ou plus		×
ex 7616.9010 ex 7616.9090	Pièces forgées en alliages d'aluminium ayant une charge limite de rupture de 0.460×10^9 N/m^2 ou plus		×

Numéro du tarif	Désignation de la marchandise	Autorisation obligatoire selon art. 13	Notification obligatoire selon art. 18
ex 8102.9300 ex 8102.9900	Fibres de molybdène utilisées dans des matériaux composites servant à la fabrication de cylindres rotatifs de centrifugeuses et ayant un module d'élasticité rapporté à la masse spécifique de 12.3 × 10^6 m^2/s^2 ou plus et une charge limite de rupture rapportée à la masse spécifique de 0.3 × 10^6 m^2/s^2 ou plus		×
ex 8108.9000	Fibres de titane utilisées dans des matériaux composites servant à la fabrication de cylindres rotatifs de centrifugeuses et ayant un module d'élasticité rapporté à la masse spécifique de 12.3 × 10^6 m^2/s^2 ou plus et une charge limite de rupture rapportée à la masse spécifique de 0.3 × 10^6 m^2/s^2 ou plus		×
ex 8401.2000[1]	Compresseurs et leurs composants, utilisés pour la séparation des isotopes d'uranium	×	
ex 8401.2000	Centrifugeuses à gaz utilisées pour la séparation des isotopes d'uranium	×	
	Composants et pièces détachées de centrifugeuses à gaz utilisés pour la séparation des isotopes d'uranium:	×	
	1. Les pièces suivantes, en acier martensitique («maraging steel») ayant une charge limite de rupture de 2.050 × 10^9 N/m^2 ou plus, en alliages d'aluminium ayant une charge limite de rupture de 0.460 × 10^9 N/m^2 ou plus ou en matériaux fibreux des numéros ex 6806.9000, ex 6903.1000/9000, ex 6815.1000, ex 8102.9300, ex 8102.9900 et ex 8108.9000 du tarif douanier, utilisés dans des matériaux composites: – assemblages rotors complets – cylindres rotatifs, ayant une paroi de 12 mm ou moins d'épaisseur et un diamètre compris entre 75 et 400 mm – anneaux et soufflets servant à renforcer ou à relier les cylindres rotatifs – chicanes à monter dans les cylindres rotatifs – bouchons d'extrémité supérieurs et inférieurs pour les cylindres rotatifs		

[1] Les marchandises énumérées à ce numéro peuvent être exportées sans autorisation si le poids brut de l'envoi ne dépasse pas 20 kg.

Numéro du tarif	Désignation de la marchandise	Autorisation obligatoire selon art. 13	Notification obligatoire selon art. 18
	2. Supports de suspension magnétique pour rotors, en acier inoxydable, en aluminium ou ses alliages, en nickel ou en alliages contenant 60 pour cent en poids de nickel ou plus		
	3. Dispositifs pour paliers et amortisseurs de rotors		
	4. Cylindres dont la paroi interne présente des rainures hélicoïdales usinées et des orifices (pompes moléculaires)		
	Bâtis pour centrifugeuses à gaz servant à la séparation des isotopes d'uranium, pour montage d'assemblages rotors avec les supports et paliers correspondants et le stator du moteur		×
	Unités de séparation à tuyère (ou buses), unités de séparation à vortex, barrière de diffusion des gaz (membranes) et leurs bâtis, utilisés pour la séparation des isotopes d'uranium	×	
ex 8419.5010/5092 8910/8992	Autoclaves d'alimentation servant à introduire l'hexafluorure d'uranium dans les cascades de centrifugeuses; appareils de condensation ou pièges à froid servant à prélever l'hexafluorure d'uranium des cascades centrifugeuses. Stations servant à transférer l'hexafluorure d'uranium dans des conteneurs	×	
ex 8454.3000 ex 8456.1010/9093 ex 8457.1010/3030 ex 8458.1110/9930 ex 8459.1010/6930 ex 8460.1110/2930 4010/9030 ex 8461.1010/3030 5010/9030 ex 8462.1010/9930 ex 8463.9010/9030 ex 8465.1010/9530 9910/9930 ex 8477.1010/1020 4010/4020 5910/8020	Machines et appareils servant à fabriquer les anneaux et soufflets destinés à soutenir ou à relier les cylindres rotatifs des centrifugeuses à gaz		×
ex 8462.2110/2930	Machines à dresser servant à aligner sur un même axe les composants des assemblages rotors des centrifugeuses à gaz		×

Numéro du tarif	Désignation de la marchandise	Autorisation obligatoire selon art. 13	Notification obligatoire selon art. 18
ex 8463.9010/9030	Presses à emboutir et laminoirs à extrusion, modèles à support double ou à triples galets, à broche horizontale, construites pour un moteur d'entraînement de 45 kW ou plus ou équipées d'un tel moteur, et servant à la fabrication de cylindres rotatifs pour les centrifugeuses à gaz		×
ex 8477.5910/5920	Bobineuses pour fibres et filament, coordonnées et programmées sur trois axes ou plus, pour la fabrication, à partir de matériaux composites, de cylindres rotatifs pour les centrifugeuses à gaz		×
ex 8479.8910/8920	Machines et appareils servant au montage des cylindres rotatifs de centrifugeuses à gaz (assemblage de composants de rotors, chicanes, bouchons d'extrémité supérieurs et inférieurs), y compris mandrins et pinces de serrage de précision et dispositifs de frettage		×
ex 8481.1090 3090 4090 8090	Soupapes revêtues ou entièrement faites d'aluminium, de nickel ou d'alliages contenant au moins 60 pour cent en poids de nickel, avec joint à soufflet, et d'un diamètre nominal de 5 mm ou plus		×
ex 8503.0091/0093	Stators pour moteurs à haute vitesse (à hystérésis ou à réluctance) alimentés en courant polyphasé, pour un fonctionnement synchrone sous vide dans une gamme de fréquence de 600 à 2000 Hz et dans une gamme de puissance de 50 à 1000 VA, pour les centrifugeuses à gaz servant à la séparation des isotopes d'uranium	×	
ex 8504.4010/4030 9010/9030	Convertisseurs de fréquence, et leurs composants, pour moteurs à haute vitesse (à hystérésis ou à réluctance) alimentés en courant polyphasé et ayant une sortie polyphasée de 600 à 2000 Hz, une stabilité élevée (écarts de fréquence inférieurs à 0,1%), une faible distorsion harmonique (inférieure à 2%) et un rendement supérieur à 80 pour cent, pour les centrifugeuses à gaz servant à la séparation des isotopes d'uranium	×	
ex 9026.2000 9000	Instruments et appareillages, y compris les capteurs de pression appropriés, servant à mesurer ou contrôler la pression de l'hexafluorure d'uranium jusqu'à une valeur de		×

Numéro du tarif	Désignation de la marchandise	Autorisation obligatoire selon art. 13	Notification obligatoire selon art. 18
	13 000 N/m^2 avec une précision supérieure à 1 pour cent, au moyen de capteurs de pression en acier inoxydable, en bronze au phosphore, en aluminium ou ses alliages, en nickel ou en alliages contenant 60 pour cent en poids de nickel ou plus		
ex 9027.3000	Spectromètres de masse pour l'hexafluorure d'uranium, présentant une résolution unitaire pour des masses supérieures à 320, sources d'ions, constituées ou recouvertes de nichrome, monel ou nickel, source à bombardement électronique et système collecteur adapté à l'analyse isotopique	×	
ex 9031.1000	Equilibreuses pour rotors de centrifugeuses à gaz à trois étapes ou plus, avec chambres de contrôle sous vide, pour l'équilibrage de précision de rotors dont la vitesse périphérique est supérieure à 300 m/s.		×

Numéro du tarif	Désignation de la marchandise
	IV. Equipements pour la fabrication d'éléments combustibles
Chapitre 84/85, 90	Installations et équipements pour la fabrication d'éléments combustibles
	V. Equipements servant au retraitement d'éléments combustibles usés (irradiés)
ex 7310.1000[1)] ex 7310.2900[1)] ex 8108.9000[1)] ex 8109.9000[1)] ex 8419.5021/5092[1)] 8921/8992[1)] ex 8479.8110/8920[1)]	Récipients spéciaux, à géométrie anti-criticité pour la dissolution de combustible irradié ou pour le stockage des substances dissoutes, en acier inoxydable, titane, zirconium et autres matériaux de haute qualité, résistant à la corrosion par l'acide nitrique et dont les parois ou les structures internes contiennent au moins 2% de bore ou ont un diamètre de 17,78 cm (7 pouces) au plus pour les récipients cylindriques ou une largeur maximale de 7,62 cm (3 pouces) pour les récipients annulaires ou en forme de disque
ex 8419.4021/4092 8921/8992 ex 8421.1910/1920 2910/2930 ex 8479.8110/8920	Appareils et dispositifs d'extraction des dissolvants (colonnes avec garnissage, colonnes pulsées, décanteurs centrifuges, mélangeurs-décanteurs), en acier inoxydable, titane, zirconium et autres matériaux de haute qualité

1) Les marchandises énumérées à ce numéro peuvent être exportées sans autorisation si le poids brut de l'envoi ne dépasse pas 20 kg.

Numéro du tarif	Désignation de la marchandise
ex 8456.1010/1030[1] ex 8461.5010/5030[1] ex 8462.3110/3930[1] ex 8479.8110/8120[1]	Machines à débiter les éléments de combustible usés (irradiés)
Chapitre 84/85	Systèmes de conversion complets pour la transformation de nitrate de plutonium en oxyde de plutonium, construits spécialement pour éviter les accidents de criticité et réduire les risques liés aux radiations et à la toxicité; Systèmes complets de production de plutonium métallique, construits spécialement pour éviter les accidents de criticité et réduire les risques liés aux radiations et à la toxicité
	VI. Equipements pour la production d'eau lourde
ex 8401.2000[1]	Appareillage et dispositifs servant à produire de l'eau lourde (oxyde de deutérium), du deutérium (hydrogène lourd) et des composés de deutérium.

[1] Les marchandises énumérées à ce numéro peuvent être exportées sans autorisation si le poids brut de l'envoi ne dépasse pas 20 kg.

Annex II

ORDINANCE OF 16TH DECEMBER 1985 ON THE EXPORT AND TRANSIT OF GOODS*

Extracts from the List of Goods the Export and Transit of which Require a Licence

Customs Tariff Number	Description of goods
ex.2532.30	Lithium ores
ex.2601.80	Uranium-bearing ores (including uraninite and pitchblend), thorium ores (monazite, uranothorianite, thorite, autunite (calco-uranite), brannerite, carnotite, davidite, parsonite, tobernite (cupro-uranite, chalcolite), tuyamunite, beryllium ores, niobium ores (columbium), tantalum ores
....	....
ex.2603.01	Ash and residue containing uranium, thorium, zirconium, lithium, hafnium (celtium), beryllium, niobium (columbium), tantalum, titanium or compounds of these metals
....	....
ex.2804.32	Boron, tellurium of 99.9 per cent or higher purity
ex.2805.10	Lithium
....	....
ex.2812.01	Boron oxide of 99.9 per cent or higher purity
ex.2813.30	Nitrogen peroxide, oxygenated fluorine compounds
ex.2814.01	Bromium fluoride, iodium fluoride, trifluorides of chlorine, phosphorous and nitrogen, chlorine pentafluoride, nitryl perchlorate, boron trifluoride
....	....
ex.2829.10	Beryllium fluoride
ex.2830.80	Lithium chloride
ex.2839.80	Beryllium nitrate
ex.2842.60	Beryllium and lithium carbonates
....	....
ex.2850.01	Fissionable chemical elements: natural uranium, plutonium; fissionable isotopes: uranium 235, uranium 233, U-235 and U-233 enriched uranium, plutonium 239, 241; inorganic or organic compounds, of defined chemical composition or not, of mechanical elements and fissionable isotopes; alloys, dispersions and cermets containing these elements or their compounds; spent (irradiated) fuel elements; alloys of uranium and plutonium; tritium
ex.2851.01	Deuterium (heavy hydrogen) and deuterium compounds; lithium isotopes and their compounds
ex.2852.01	Inorganic and organic compounds of thorium and U-235-depleted uranium
....	....
ex.2856.30	Aluminium carbide, beryllium carbide, boron carbide, tantalum carbide, zirconium carbide of 99.5 per cent or higher purity

* Unofficial translation.

Customs Tariff Number	Description of goods
ex.2857.01	Boron and lithium hydrides; borides, aluminium nitride, boron nitride; silicon nitride, tantalum nitride, zirconium nitrate of 99.5 per cent or higher purity
....	....
ex.3801.01	Nuclear graphite
....	....
ex.7302.30	Ferro-uranium
....	....
ex.7324.10/20	Multiple-partition iron or steel vessels for the transporting or storing of liquid fluorine[1]
ex.7501.10	Crude nickel of 99 per cent or higher purity, nickel alloys whose combined aluminium and titanium content is more than 11 per cent by weight; intermetal nickel-aluminium compounds whose aluminium content is 10 per cent or more by weight[1]
....	....
ex.7502.10/ 7503.40	Bars, sections, wire, sheets, plates, foil, strips, powders and chaffs: — in pure nickel of 99 per cent or higher purity or — in nickel alloys whose combined aluminium and titanium content is more than 11 per cent by weight or — in nickel alloys whose aluminium content is more than 10 per cent by weight or — in intermetal nickel-aluminium compounds whose aluminium content is 10 per cent or more by weight[1]
ex.7504.01	*a.* Tubes, pipes, hollow rods and piping accessories: — in pure nickel of 99 per cent or higher purity or — in nickel alloys whose combined aluminium and titanium content is more than 11 per cent by weight or — in nickel alloys whose aluminium content is 10 per cent or more by weight or — in intermetal nickel-aluminium compounds whose aluminium content is more than 10 per cent by weight[1] *b.* Seamless tubes, pipes and hollow rods having an outside diameter greater than 60 mm, in nickel alloys with a chromium content 19 per cent or more by weight, a molybdenum content of 7.4 per cent or more by weight, containing at most 6 per cent iron by weight and 3 per cent or more niobium by weight (columbium) or combined niobium-tantalum[1]
ex.7506.12	Multiple-wall nickel vessels for transporting or storing liquid fluorine[1]
....	....
ex.7611.01	Multiple-wall aluminium vessels for transporting or storing liquid fluorine
....	....
ex.7704.01	Beryllium (glucinium) crude or worked
....	....
ex.8104.12/22	Thorium U-235 depleted uranium Cadmium Gallium Germanium Indium Cobalt Niobium (columbium) Titanium Hafnium (celtium) Zirconium Vanadium — crude or in bars, wire, filaments foil, sheet, tubes

Customs Tariff Number	Description of goods
ex.8104.12/40	Hafnium (celtium), zirconium: their products[1]
....	....
ex.8410.60/84	Pumps to circulate liquid metal used to cool nuclear reactors[1]
ex.8411.10/84	*a.* Compressors for the separation of uranium isotopes;
	b. Blowers and compressors (turbo-compressors, centrifugal or axial-type) made entirely of aluminium, nickel or alloys containing 60 per cent or more nickel or coated with these substances, with a suction volume of 1.7 m^3 or more per minute; vacuum pumps at less than 10^{-6} Pascal; cryogenic pumps
	c. Parts and spare parts of items listed under letter a above[1]
....	....
ex.8417.10/14	*a.* Equipment and devices for the production of heavy water (deuterium oxide), deuterium (heavy hydrogen), deuterium and tritium compounds; heat exchangers of aluminium, copper, nickel or alloys containing more than 60 per cent nickel, designed to operate at a pressure below atmospheric pressure, with a leakage rate of 0.1 mbar per hour, with a pressure difference of 1 bar; equipment and devices for the production of uranium hexafluoride (UF_6); equipment for the production of liquid fluorine; nitration equipment[1]
	b. Equipment for the production of masks or for the production or processing of semi-conductor elements (wafers) or microcircuits[1]
	c. Equipment for separating isotopes
	d. Special vessels for reprocessing irradiated (spent) fuel elements[1]
	e. Parts and spare parts for items listed under letters a and c[1]
ex.8418.30/84	*a.* Gas diffusion barriers (membranes) and their frames, for the separation of isotopes
	b. Other equipment for the separation of isotopes, extractors of liquid used in an installation for reprocessing irradiated or fissile material
	c. Centrifugal equipment for tests with a useful load of more than 100 kg
	d. Parts and spare parts of items listed under letter b
ex.8422.60/84	Reactor fuel element handling equipment, including loading and unloading devices; machines and equipment (robots) for handling and/or positioning of materials, parts etc. except for: — those whose movement is controlled purely mechanically, or — simply positioned, or — whose return signal is based exclusively on the values of current, voltage, length or pressure[1]
....	....
ex.8445.10/30	....
	b. Cutters for irradiated (spent) fuel element reprocessing; isostatic presses (hydrostatic) whose pressure chamber inner diameter is 127 mm or more[1]
....	....
ex.8459.60/84	*a.* Non-irradiated fuel elements; special vessels for the reprocessing of irradiated (spent) fuel elements; nuclear reactors and their parts and spares such as pressure vessels, regulating rods (control and monitoring rods) and force tubes designed or prepared to contain fuel elements and the heat-carrying fluid simultaneously; dehydrating presses, extruding presses, cutting machines and mixers for the production of military explosives or solid fuels
....	....
ex.8503.12	Electrochemical fuel batteries (cells) operating at temperatures of 250°C or under; primary elements and batteries with a switch-on device and a life of three years or more; molten salt electrolyte-type elements and batteries; elements and batteries utilising a lithium anode dissolved in an electrolyte (non-aqueous) with an energy density of more than 220 Wh/kg; electrical energy sources based on radioactive material systems except those used for medical purposes inside the human body[1]

Customs Tariff Number	Description of goods
ex.8511.10/16	*a.* Industrial furnaces for fuel element production
ex.8519.10/18	*a.* Control instrumentation designed to monitor or control the reprocessing of irradiated (spent) fuel or fissile material
ex.8522.10/18	*a.* Equipment and apparatus for the production of heavy water (deuterium protoxide), deuterium (heavy hydrogen) and compounds of deuterium and tritium
ex.8702.20/24,28	Motor vehicles with multiple-wall vessels for transporting liquid fluorine[1]
ex.9020.10/30	*a.* Quick discharge X-ray systems, including tubes, with a peak power of 500 MW, with an output voltage in excess of 500 kV and with a pulse width of less than 0.2 microsecond; X-ray spectrometers[1] *b.* Equipment and apparatus to rectify quartz crystals using X-rays[1]
ex.9028.30/40	*a.* Electronic controls for regulation and control of power levels of nuclear reactors; automatic regulators and control devices for items covered under numbers 8411.10/84, 8444.01, 8445.10.30 letter b, 8459.60/84 letter d, 8511.10/16 letter c, 8511.20/24 letter d[1] *b.* Synchros and resolvers;[1]

1. The items under these numbers may be exported without a licence when the amount does not exceed SF 2 000. The Federal Office of Public Health rules on exceptions.

Annex III

ORDINANCE OF 30th JUNE 1976 ON PROTECTION AGAINST RADIATION AS AMENDED*

Activity limits
(Sections 3, 73, 111)

Toxicity class	Exemption limit Absolute activity[1]	Maximum activities permitted in laboratories of type		
		C	B	A
(1)	(2)	(3)	(4)	(5)
1	1 pCi	10 nCi	1 μCi	[2]
2	10 pCi	100 nCi	10 μCi	[2]
3	100 pCi	1 μCi	100 μCi	[2]
4	1 nCi	10 μCi	1 mCi	[2]
5	10 nCi	100 μCi	10 mCi	no limit
6	100 nCi	1 mCi	100 mCi	no limit
7	1 μCi	10 mCi	1 Ci	no limit
8	10 μCi	100 mCi	10 Ci	no limit
9	100 μCi	1 Ci	100 Ci	no limit
	Specific activity[1]			
α emitters	20 pCi/g			
β emitters	20 nCi/g			

1. Absolute activity limits may be exceeded if the specific values are not reached.
2. An activity limit for fissile nuclides may be deduced from their criticality.

*Unofficial translation.

UNITED KINGDOM

TABLE OF CONTENTS

UNITED KINGDOM

I. INTRODUCTION

Although the United Kingdom has not in recent years been a major participant in the nuclear reactor market, its role in nuclear world trade is significant as an exporter of nuclear fuels, in the provision of nuclear fuel cycle services particularly enrichment and reprocessing and as an exporter of radioisotopes (for medical and industrial use).

The United Kingdom commitment to non-proliferation is evidenced by its adherence to the 1968 Treaty on the Non-Proliferation of Nuclear Weapons (NPT) and to the EURATOM Treaty, by participation in the Zangger Committee and the Nuclear Suppliers Group (the London Club) and its use of the COCOM Atomic Energy List. All nuclear exports are undertaken within the framework of the NPT and London Club Guidelines.

This study will look at the regulation of nuclear trade in the United Kingdom in the context of policy statements defining the national approach to import and export of nuclear material and technology. It will give a description of the competent national regulatory and administrative authorities whose decisions and policies affect import and export and the commercial and other civil use of nuclear material and technology within the United Kingdom. The principal legislative provisions which provide the legal framework within which the nuclear industry functions will be briefly examined with particular reference to import and export and to the use within the United Kingdom of nuclear material and radioactive substances and equipment. Procurement, transport, safeguards, physical protection and industrial property and other provisions including multilateral and bilateral international agreements will also be discussed in relation to their impact on trade in nuclear material, radioactive substances and equipment.

II. THE UNITED KINGDOM NUCLEAR INDUSTRY

The United Kingdom's present absence from the export market for nuclear reactors has not diminished its importance as a key actor in other aspects of international nuclear business, especially in the areas of fuel and radioisotope supply. Moreover the United Kingdom nuclear industry has worldwide industrial intellectual property rights by no means confined to the technology relating to the first generation Magnox reactors. The United Kingdom mines and mills uranium through its conglomerate Rio Tinto Zinc. British Nuclear Fuels plc[1] is involved in fuel fabrication and in the back-end of the nuclear fuel cycle by providing reprocessing services not only in relation to the arisings of the United Kingdom industry but also for foreign customers. It is also involved in uranium enrichment services including activities carried on by way of participation in an international undertaking, URENCO[2]. CENTEC Centrifuge Techniques Limited (CENTEC), another company formed to implement the Almelo Treaty, is also engaged in the exploitation of the centrifuge process for uranium enrichment[3]. Amersham International plc[4] is a world leader in the field of medical and industrial radioisotope production.

III. GOVERNMENT POLICY

Government policy has always supported the objectives of non-proliferation. The central theme is to develop and protect the essentials of the United Kingdom nuclear programme and to share the benefit of its technological achievements whilst obviating the risks of weapons proliferation ("... to enable all countries to share in the benefits of nuclear science through trade in equipment and technology, wherever this can be done in conformity within the NPT without giving rise to the danger of proliferation of nuclear explosive technology")[5].

In August 1980, on the occasion of the second review conference of the NPT, the then Minister of State for Foreign and Commonwealth Affairs remarked "... the Treaty has created an international climate hostile to proliferation ...". Similarly, in August 1985 on the occasion of the third NPT review conference, the then Minister of State for Foreign and Commonwealth Affairs emphasised the United Kingdom's commitment to nuclear disarmament under NPT Article VI consistently with intention to retain nuclear defence capability as vital to national security. He went on to say that nuclear disarmament, multilateral or otherwise must await an appropriate moment and that the United Kingdom is opposed to the acquisition of nuclear weapons by any additional states.

As will be seen in more detail below the relevant United Kingdom legislation is exceedingly fractionated. No single Minister or government department has undivided overall responsibility for nuclear energy and radioactive substances. The Secretaries of State for Energy and for the Environment are respectively concerned with the general development and the intrinsic safety aspects on the one hand and with the protection of the environment on the other. But those two Secretaries of State[6] share some of their powers and responsibilities with other Ministers when nuclear energy matters overlap into areas covered by those other Ministers' portfolios. The Secretary of State for Foreign Affairs has general responsibility for international relationships including the essentially important fields of NPT and the 1980 Convention on the Physical Protection of Nuclear Material. Although the Secretary of State for Trade and Industry is responsible for the granting of import and export licences under general legislation, statutory instruments and administrative powers and for generally supporting United Kingdom industry including its overseas endeavours, his decisions are, where appropriate, taken in consultation with other Ministers and departments. The position may be broadly summarised as follows :

— *Secretary of State for Energy and Department of Energy* — overall supervision of United Kingdom nuclear policy; general control over the United Kingdom Atomic Energy Authority (UKAEA). The Secretary of State for Energy owns the shares in BNFL although the 1971 Act contains provision enabling a minority shareholding to be transferred to the private sector;

— the *Secretary of State for Foreign Affairs/the Foreign and Commonwealth Office (FC)*. Concerned primarily with arms control and non-proliferation aspects of nuclear export policy. Co-ordinates United Kingdom participation in international energy policy. Shares interest in safeguards with the Department of Energy although the latter takes the detailed lead as regards implementation of safeguards in the United Kingdom;

— the *Secretary of State for the Environment/Department of the Environment*. Concerned with control of pollution. Primary regulatory authority as respects environmental discharge but shares responsibility with the Department of Agriculture, Fisheries and Food which has an interest in the marine environment. Scottish and Welsh and Northern Irish Secretaries of State and their departments also share these responsibilities and interests;

— the *Secretary of State for Defence/Ministry of Defence* — concerned with defence policy, interested in export questions only insofar as the possibility of unlawful proliferation or diversion might be a factor in the decision making process;

— the *Secretary of State for Health and Social Security* has responsibility for the National Health Service and for the conduct of the medical and auxiliary professions. Administers the Medicines Act 1968. References to the "Health Ministers" are to a collective term used to include also Scottish and Welsh departmental responsibilities.

The Secretary of State for Energy may, with the consent of the Treasury, render certain financial assistance to BNFL under the Nuclear Industry (Finance) Act 1977. General financial assistance for undertakings which engage in the export of goods of any sort may be made available through the Export Credits Guarantee Department, an executive agency responsible to the Secretary of State for Trade and Industry. Assistance is granted on a case-by-case basis.

IV. THE LEGISLATIVE BACKGROUND AND HISTORICAL PERSPECTIVE

The *Atomic Energy Act 1946* was passed by the United Kingdom Parliament on 6th November 1946, little more than a year after the ending of World War II. At that time, the distinction between the development of nuclear technology and the production and use of atomic energy and radioactive substances for defence purposes on the one hand and for peaceful purposes on the other was very much less clear cut that it has subsequently become. The Act has to be read in that context and is mentioned here as the first of a series of Acts of Parliament which came to be read and cited together as "the Atomic Energy and Radioactive Substances Acts 1946 to 1954".

The 1946 Act represented the first peacetime legislation dealing with the emergent nuclear industry. It concentrated control in the hands of the Minister of Supply and in particular contained provision for the control of export or import. In fact the export/import control powers in that Act, although they still remain on the Statute Book, have not been utilised. Instead of using the specific powers under the 1946 Act control of the export and import of nuclear material, technology and equipment was *and still is* exercised under general legislation which had its origin in World War II controls. So it is that the Import, Export and Customs Powers (Defence) Act 1939 is the legislative base whereby the Government in the person of the Secretary of State for Trade and Industry exercises control over the whole field of import and export. It is significant that the Radioactive Substances Act 1948 contains alternative machinery for the imposition of import/export controls but expressly provides that such machinery shall not become capable of activation until the expiry of the 1939 Act[7]. The 1948 Act also contains power to regulate the safe disposal of radioactive waste products and the transport of radioactive substances.

Other Statutes which affect or have affected the structure and/or functioning of the United Kingdom nuclear industry include the following:

- the *Atomic Energy Authority Act 1954*: set up the United Kingdom Atomic Energy Authority to take over the activities of the Minister of Supply and conferred the specific functions of developing and carrying out research into, and producing, atomic energy and radioactive substances;
- the *Radioactive Substances Act 1960*: regulates the keeping and use of radioactive material and apparatus and the disposal and accumulation of radioactive waste;
- the *Nuclear Installations Act 1965 as amended*: provides for the licensing of nuclear sites and imposes duties on licensees and provides legal remedies for the breach of those duties and gives effect to the Paris Convention and Brussels Supplementary Convention on third party liability in the nuclear field;
- the *Radiological Protection Act 1970*: establishes the National Radiological Protection Board as the governmental body to undertake research and provide advice and services in connection with radiation hazards;
- the *Health and Safety at Work etc. Act 1974*: contains exceedingly wide powers over the whole field of industrial etc. safety and includes power to modify and/or make regulations as respects nuclear safety;
- the *Control of Pollution Act 1974*: includes power to regulate discharges of radioactive waste;
- the *Food and Environmental Protection Act 1985*: includes powers to regulate discharges into the environment, including the territorial and high seas which incidentally control/restrict United Kingdom operators of radioactive discharges and/or the dumping of radioactive wastes.

V. TRADE IN NUCLEAR MATERIAL, TECHNOLOGY AND EQUIPMENT

1. Import Controls

Section 1 of the Import, Export and Customs Powers (Defence) Act 1939 (as modified by the Secretary of State for Trade and Industry Order 1970)[8] empowers the Secretary of State by Order to make such provisions as he may think expedient for prohibiting or regulating in all cases or in specified classes of cases, and subject to such exceptions, if any, as may be made *by or under the Order*, "the importation ... to the United Kingdom ... of all goods or goods of any specified description". The sanctions applicable under the Act for contravention are forfeiture of goods and a customs penalty. Officers of the Customs and Excise service are empowered to require any persons possessing or having control of goods to furnish proof that their importation is not unlawful.

The Import of Goods (Control) Order 1954 made under the 1939 Act prohibits all goods (other than those proved to have been consigned from the Channel Islands) from being imported into the United Kingdom except under the authority of a licence granted by the Secretary of State for Trade and Industry. Licences so granted may be particular (i.e. enabling a specified importer or class of importers to import specified goods) or general (i.e. enabling an individual or persons generally to import certain goods from certain countries without the need to apply for a particular licence). Import licensing procedure is by way of application to the Import Licensing Branch of the Department of Trade as provided for in Article 2 of the 1954 Order. The making of false statements or the furnishing of false documents or information is a criminal offence and any licence granted or obtained as a result is null and void *ab initio*.

2. Export Controls

Although theoretically other powers exist (see above) United Kingdom export control is exercised by means of Orders made under the Import, Export and Customs Powers (Defence) Act 1939. The Order making power as respects exports is in identical terms (*mutatis mutandis*) as the power in respect of imports. However, for obvious reasons, the way in which the power has been exercised and the administrative criteria applied are more complex, particularly as a result of international obligations not only of NPT and EURATOM but also of supply agreements imposing restrictions on end use and/or re-exportation. Amendments made from time to time in the Orders reflect advances in relevant technology and in international obligations relating thereto. For example the Export of Goods (Control) Order 1978 was amended by the Export of Goods (Control) (Amendment No. 3) Order 1979 and the Export of Goods (Control) (Amendment No. 4) Order 1979 to include centrifuge equipment and UF_6 plant among the categories of goods specified in the Schedule to the Order as requiring an export licence.

The current Order is the Export of Goods (Control) Order 1987 (SI 1987 No. 2070). The effect of the Order is to make the exportation of "scheduled" goods without a licence subject to restrictions of varying degrees of severity ranging from total prohibition to any destination to prohibition as respects specified destinations and/or prohibitions designed to give effect to re-exportation embargoes imposed in connection with the importation of the goods into the United Kingdom. The Order is general in character and its application is in no way confined to nuclear goods and technology. An extract from the Schedule to the Order giving the text of Groups 2 A and B of Part II (Atomic Energy Minerals and Materials and Nuclear Facilities Equipment and Appliances respectively) is reproduced in *Annex I* hereto. The restrictions applying to Groups 2 A and B apply to related technological documents as respects their exportation to "Communist Bloc" countries and to the People's Republic of China. The specifications in Groups 2 A and B were last reproduced and published as administrative guidance in British Business Supplement dated December 1987, issued under the auspices of the Department of Trade and Industry (DTI). In that guidance the specifications are referred to as the "Atomic Energy List". Export applications in respect of the Atomic Energy List are dealt with by an Export Licensing Branch. Criteria adopted in granting or withholding licences are governed *inter alia* by the United Kingdom's adherence to NPT and EURATOM and to any restrictions imposed by the originating exporter.

As regards criteria generally the situation is principally influenced by the "Guidelines for Nuclear Transfers" which is the appendix to IAEA INFCIRC/254 of February 1978. Special mention should be made of United States re-export controls: prospective United Kingdom exporters are reminded in the DTI guidance of United States assertion of control as respects re-exports from other countries of exports of United States origin or exports including components of United States origin and exporters are advised where appropriate to seek guidance from the Commercial Section of the United States Embassy in London.

VI. TRADE IN RADIOACTIVE SUBSTANCES AND APPARATUS

The possession of and trade in radioactive substances is governed by the Radioactive Substances Act 1948, the Medicines Act 1968 and the Radioactive Substances Act 1960. Certain provisions of these Acts, however, do not apply to nuclear installations licensed under Nuclear Installations Act 1965 e.g. reactors, fuel fabrication and reprocessing plants and fuel enrichment plants including those which hold plutonium extraction permits under Section 2 of the 1965 Act and accordingly are "specified bodies corporate" within the meaning of Schedule 1 to the 1965 Act (as inserted by the Schedule to the Atomic Energy Authority Act 1971) and those which are designated companies under Section 19 of the 1971 Act (companies established in connection with agreement on gas centrifuge process) to which stringent security provisions apply (see section II above). This avoids unnecessary duplication between the provisions of the licensing etc. regime and those applying in the ordinary way to premises not so subject. It is, however, the case that the Ionising Radiations Regulations 1985 (SI 1985 No. 1333), which lay down the rules relating to the supervision and conduct of health physics and other precautions in relation to persons who are in contact with radiation are of general application.

The Acts of 1948 and 1968 are mainly the concern of the Secretary of State for Health and Social Security and deal with the keeping and use of radioactive apparatus and substances for medicinal and therapeutic purposes. The Radioactive Substances Act 1960, on the other hand, is mainly the concern of the Secretary of State for the Environment and deals with the use and keeping of such substances from the point of view of environmental protection. The definition of "radioactive substance" is common to each of three Acts, *viz* "... any substance which contains any radioactive chemical element whether natural or artificial".

As noted in section IV above, the 1948 Act contains an additional alternative power to control the importation and exportation of radioactive substances but this is subject to provision that the power cannot be exercised until such time as the Import, Export and Customs Powers (Defence) Act 1939 expires.

Other provisions of the 1948 Act have been superseded by the Medicines Act 1968 which introduces a comprehensive system of control relating to medicinal products etc. by licensing and certification. The system includes three subordinate instruments which relate to trade in and use of radioactive substances intended for medicinal and/or therapeutic purposes.

The first of these is the Medicines (Radioactive Substances) (Order) 1978 (SI 1978 No. 1004) which extends the application of the Medicines Act to articles and substances that are, contain or generate radioactive substances and that are designed to be inserted into the human body or body cavities or to be brought into contact with the human body or are for administration to human beings for the purposes of diagnosis, research or tests[9]. The second is the Medicines (Committee on Radioactive Products) Order 1978 (SI 1978 No. 1005); this Order establishes the Committee on Radiation from Radioactive Medicinal Products for the purpose of giving advice to the Government with respect to the safety, quality and efficiency in relation to radiation of any relevant radioactive substance. The third is the Medicines (Administration of Radioactive Substances) Regulations 1978 (SI 1978 No. 1006); these Regulation were made under the Medicines Act 1968 and also under the European Communities Act 1972[10] and came into force partly on 1st January 1979 and partly on 1st July 1980. The Regulations prohibit the administration of radioactive medicinal products except by doctors or dentists holding a certificate issued by the "Health Ministers"[11] in respect of such products or by persons acting under the direction of such a doctor or dentist and except in accordance with descriptions or classes of products which may be administered and as to purposes for which they may be administered.

The Radioactive Substances Act 1960 regulates the keeping and use of radioactive material and mobile radioactive apparatus and makes provision as to the disposal and accumulation of radioactive wastes and as to liquid and gaseous discharges into the environment. In general, users of radioactive material are required to be registered but the UKAEA and holders of nuclear site licences are exempt from registration. The responsible Minister may also grant further exemptions (a list of the exemptions currently granted is given in *Annex II* hereto). The provisions of the 1960 Act do not in general bind the Crown but hospitals and other institutions within the National Health Service (ordinarily regarded as a Crown Service) are expressly bound.

Mobile radioactive apparatus may only be kept, used, lent or let out on hire by a person who has been granted registration by the responsible Minister. The UKAEA is exempt from the requirements of registration and the responsible Minister may grant exemption to classes of persons and/or in respect of descriptions of apparatus.

The 1960 Act prohibits the disposal of radioactive waste except in accordance with a Ministerial Authorisation. Only radioactive waste arising from luminised clocks or watches is expressly exempted from this requirement but the responsible Minister may grant exemption as respects particular descriptions of waste. The Act also prohibits the accumulation of radioactive waste except in accordance with an authorisation granted by the responsible Minister. The UKAEA and Nuclear Site Licensees are expressly exempt.

The Act also makes provision enabling the Minister to arrange for the provision of facilities for the disposal of radioactive waste. However current government policy has endorsed the "polluter pays" principle and the government has endorsed[12] the establishment by the nuclear industry of United Kingdom Nuclear Industry Radioactive Waste Executive Limited (NIREX)[13] to establish sites and facilities for radioactive waste disposal. It is envisaged that such facilities will be brought within the licensing regime of the 1965 Act.

The 1960 Act further provides for the appointment of inspectors to ensure that its provisions are observed. Such inspectors have special rights of entry as respects relevant premises. Breaches of any of the requirements of the 1960 Act are criminal offences punishable by a fine and/or imprisonment.

VII. CONTROLS FOR THE PROTECTION OF WORKERS AND OTHERS

The Safety and Health at Work etc. Act 1974 established a comprehensive and integrated system of control as respects all aspects of work activities, provided for comprehensive regulations and codes of practice as respects all industrial undertakings (including Nuclear Installations) and created a general body the Health and Safety Commission (HSC) served by an executive the Health and Safety Executive (HSE) which became responsible *inter alia* for formulating regulations to be made by the Secretary of State and for codes of practice and for the control and supervision of various industrial inspectorates including the Nuclear Installations Inspectorate (NII). Inspectorates having dealings with the United Kingdom nuclear industry, which do not now function under the 1974 Act are the inspectorates (separate for England and Wales and for Scotland) which supervise the observance of the requirements of the Radioactive Substances Act 1960 (in England and Wales the "Radio-Chemical Inspectorate" and in Scotland the "Anti-Pollution Inspectorate").

VIII. TRANSPORT[14]

The transport of radioactive materials is governed by different regulations, depending on the mode of transport used. Essentially, however, all the Regulations reflect the IAEA Regulations for the Safe Transport of Radioactive Materials, 1973 Edition (as amended in 1979). The Regulations also provide the various categories of certificates of approval required in the United Kingdom for the domestic transport of radioactive materials.

In the case of international transport of radioactive materials the provisions of RID[15] and ADR[16] with respect to certificates of approval are applied for rail and road transport respectively. For air transport, the Civil Aviation Authority's authorisation is required for any air operator to carry any radioactive materials on board an aircraft into, out of, or within the United Kingdom. This authorisation is required over and above any certificates issued in accordance with IATA regulations. A further mechanism of *de facto* control exists by virtue of the practice of insurers to insist on compliance with international standards, for example IAEA's Safety Series No. 6, parts of which are, where appropriate, effectively incorporated as conditions of insurance policies.

IX. SAFEGUARDS AND PHYSICAL PROTECTION

The Atomic Energy Act 1946, the Atomic Energy Authority Act 1954 and the Nuclear Installations Act 1965 (as amended by the Atomic Energy Act 1971) enable the Government authorities to exercise wide powers to prevent any improper use of special nuclear material[17].

Moreover by virtue of the United Kingdom's adherence to NPT and EURATOM and its participation in international supply agreements the United Kingdom nuclear industry is subject to stringent regimes of inspection and accounting particularly those imposed by or under the EURATOM Treaty.

The United Kingdom is a signatory (with EURATOM and the other Member States of EURATOM) of the 1980 Convention on the Physical Protection of Nuclear Material. The Nuclear Materials (Offences) Act 1983 was passed to enable the United Kingdom to ratify the Convention. It extends territorial jurisdiction exercisable in respect of certain offences of a serious nature involving nuclear material so as to cover acts done outside as well as inside the territorial limits of the United Kingdom.

X. INTELLECTUAL PROPERTY IN THE NUCLEAR FIELD

The Patents Act of 1977, which repealed Section 12 of the Atomic Energy Act conferring rights on the Secretary of State for Energy in relation to atomic energy patents, now contains provisions relating to the Secretary of State's rights in relation to patents generally (Sections 55 to 59).

XI. AGREEMENTS

1. Multilateral Agreements

The United Kingdom is a Party to the 1968 Treaty on the Non-Proliferation of Nuclear Weapons, having ratified the Treaty on 27th November 1968.

It has also signed the 1980 Convention on the Physical Protection of Nuclear Material as a Member State of EURATOM.

It is a party to the Co-operation Agreement with the ***Federal Republic of Germany*** and the ***Netherlands*** on collaboration in the development and exploitation of the gas centrifuge process for producing enriched uranium (the Almelo Treaty), signed on 4th March 1970.

It is also a party to the Memorandum of Understanding for Co-operation in the Field of Liquid Metal Fast Reactors with ***Belgium***, ***France,*** the ***Federal Republic of Germany***, and ***Italy***, signed on 10th January 1984.

2. Bilateral Agreements

— Agreement of 19th January 1961 with ***Spain*** for Co-operation in the Peaceful Uses of Atomic Energy, Cmnd.[18] 1427.

— Agreement of 11th August 1964 with the Government of the Confederation of ***Switzerland*** for Co-operation in the Peaceful Uses of Atomic Energy.

— Agreement of June 1968 with ***Finland*** for Co-operation in the Peaceful Uses of Atomic Energy, Cmnd. 3972.

— Agreement of 15th October 1968 with ***Japan*** for Co-operation in the Peaceful Uses of Atomic Energy, Cmnd. 3935.

— Agreement of 18th November 1968 with ***Chile*** for Co-operation in the Peaceful Uses of Atomic Energy, Cmnd. 4239.

— Agreement of 18th September 1975 with ***Romania*** for Co-operation in the Peaceful Uses of Atomic Energy, Cmnd. 6462.

— Agreement of 20th September 1977 with ***Sweden*** for Co-operation in the Peaceful uses of Atomic Energy, Cmnd. 290.

— Agreement of 14th March 1979/4th April 1979 with the ***Federal Republic of Germany*** on the Exchange of Information on Measures for the Safety of Nuclear Installations.

— Agreement of 24th July 1979 with ***Australia*** for Co-operation in the Peaceful Uses of Atomic Energy, Cmnd. 7768.

— Memorandum of Understanding signed on 2nd December 1981 with the Government of ***Brazil*** on the Development of Peaceful Uses of Nuclear Energy.

— Agreement of 3rd June 1985 with the Government of the ***People's Republic of China*** for Co-operation in the Peaceful Uses of Nuclear Energy, Cmnd. 9664.

3. Safeguards Agreements

— Agreement of 6th September 1976 between the United Kingdom, ***EURATOM*** and the ***IAEA*** for the Application of Safeguards in the United Kingdom in Connection with the Treaty on the Non-Proliferation of Nuclear Weapons.

NOTES AND REFERENCES

1. British Nuclear Fuels, plc incorporated under English Law, originally as a private limited company (Ltd.) and subsequently transformed into a public limited company (plc). This company pursuant to the Atomic Energy Authority Act 1971 became the transferee of a substantial part of the United Kingdom Atomic Energy Authority's (UKAEA's) undertaking consisting of the part of the production group concerned with fuel fabrication and reprocessing. The shares in the company were originally vested in the UKAEA but were transferred to the Secretary of State by the British Nuclear Fuels Limited (Transfer of Shares) Order 1981 (SI 1981 No. 868) made under Section 11 of the 1971 Act. That Act as amended by the Nuclear Industry (Finance Act) 1977 makes special provision for loans to the company by the Government. BNFL is a specified body corporate for the purposes of the Schedule to the Nuclear Installations Act 1965 (as inserted by Schedule 1 to the 1971 Act) by virtue of the Nuclear Installations (Application of Security Provisions) Order 1971 (SI 1971 No. 569) made under Section 2(IB) of the 1965 Act as inserted by Section 17 of the 1971 Act.
2. URENCO Ltd. is subject to security provisions by virtue of the URENCO Limited (Registration) Order 1971 (SI 1971 No. 1434) made under Section 19 of the Atomic Energy Authority Act 1971.
3. CENTEC — this company is similarly subject to security provisions by virtue of the CENTEC Centrifuge Techniques (Designation) Order 1973 (SI 1973 No. 17) made under Section 19 of the Atomic Energy Authority Act 1971.
4. Originally called the Radiochemical Company Ltd., incorporated under English Law as a private limited company subsequently transformed into a public limited company and now wholly owned by private sector shareholders. The company was transferee of a substantial part of the UKAEA's undertaking consisting of the part of the production group concerned with the production of radioisotopes. The "paving" legislation for the privatisation was the Atomic Energy (Miscellaneous Provisions) Act 1981 and the Amersham International Limited (Transfer of Shares) Order 1981 (SI 1981 No. 850).
5. Statement by the Secretary of State for Social Services, House of Commons Debate 895 (16th July 1978).
6. As a matter of United Kingdom constitutional theory the office of the Secretary of State is not generally divisible. The expression "... Secretary of State ..."in an Act of Parliament or Statutory Instrument means "... one of Her Majesty's Principal Secretaries of State" (Interpretation Act 1978, Schedule 1).
7. Section 9(3) of the 1939 Act contains a provision that the Act "... shall continue in force until such date as [His] Majesty may by Order in Counsel provide".
8. SI 1970 No. 1537— The Board of Trade i.e. the successor to the Commissioner of Trade and Plantations (Civil List and Secret Service Money Act 1782) was a Committee of the Privy Council constituted by an Order in Council dated 23rd August 1786 (see Hansard House of Commons 24th April 1923). Historically this committee had oversight of all United Kingdom trade both internal and external. Gradually its functions became for practical purposes exercisable by a Government Minister — the President of the Board of Trade and the 1970 Order devolved all that Minister's functions to the Secretary of State.
9. This wide definition covers both the use of radioactive sources externally and such techniques as implantation.
10. Thus the Regulations were designed to serve not only national purposes but also to conform to EEC requirements — see Directive 87/22/EEC.
11. The Secretary of State for Health and Social Security and the Secretary of State for Scotland in his capacity as Head of the Scottish Home and Health Department.
12. The policy underlying this initiative is set out in the White Paper "Radioactive Waste Management" Command paper (Cmnd) 8607.
13. United Kingdom Nuclear Industry Radioactive Waste Executive Limited: established under English Law as a private limited company with the Central Electricity Generating Board (CEGB); BNFL; the South of Scotland Electricity Board (SSEB); and UKAEA as members together with the Government who hold a special "golden"class share which gives them ultimate control over the land on which waste disposal facilities are sited if need be in perpetuity.
14. For further details see analytical study in the same series: *Regulations Governing the Transport of Radioactive Materials*, OECD/NEA, 1980.
15. International Regulations concerning the Carriage of Dangerous Goods by Rail.
16. European Agreement concerning the International Carriage of Dangerous Goods by Road.
17. The UKAEA is effectively controlled by the 1954 Act and the Schedule to the 1965 Act applies similar security controls to reprocessing activities.
18. Cmnd. =Command paper.

Annex I

EXPORT OF GOODS (CONTROL) ORDER 1987 (SI 1987 No. 2070) (Extracts)

Group 2

Atomic Energy Minerals and Materials, and Nuclear Facilities, Equipment and Appliances

Note 1: Goods specified in the heads of this Group may also be specified in Group 3 of this Part of this Schedule.

Note 2: The definitions applying to crude or semi-fabricated forms are those given under Group 3H.

GROUP 2A

Atomic Energy Minerals and Materials

A1 A13 Nuclear materials, the following:

(1) Special and other fissile materials, the following:

(a) plutonium, all isotopes, alloys, compounds and any material containing any of the foregoing .... A

(b) uranium 233, uranium enriched in the isotopes 235 or 233, alloys, compounds and any material containing any of the foregoing .... A

(c) americium 242m, curium 245 and 247, and californium 249 and 251, and any material containing the foregoing .... A

In this entry "Uranium enriched in the isotopes 235 or 233" is defined as uranium containing the isotopes 235 or 233, or both, in an amount such that the abundance ratio of the sum of these isotopes to the isotope 238 is more than the ratio of the isotope 235 to the isotope 238 occurring in nature.

A2 Source material, the following:

Natural and depleted uranium, in any form, or incorporated in any substance in which the concentration of uranium exceeds 0.05% .... A

Note: "Natural uranium is defined as uranium containing the mixture of isotopes occurring in nature; "Depleted uranium" is defined as uranium depleted in the isotope 235 below that occurring in nature.

— Source material, the following:

Thorium, in any form, or incorporated in any substance in which the concentration of thorium exceeds 0.05% .. A

A3 Deuterium, heavy water, deuterated paraffins and other organic and inorganic compounds, mixtures and solutions containing deuterium, in which the isotopic ratio of deuterium to hydrogen exceeds 1:5000 .... A

A4 Zirconium in which the ratio of hafnium content to zirconium content is less than one part to five hundred parts by weight, the following:

(1) Zirconium and alloys containing more than 50% zirconium, in crude or semi-fabricated forms .... A

(2) Zirconium compounds, except zirconium oxide thermally stabilised with calcium oxide or magnesium oxide or both .... A

(3) Manufactures wholly of any of the foregoing .... A

A5 Nickel powder having a nickel content of 99% or more and a mean particle size of less than 100 micrometers, whether compacted or not .... A

A6 Graphite, nuclear grade, having a purity level less than 5 parts per million boron equivalent and with a density greater than 1.5g/cm^3 .... A

A7 Lithium, the following:

(1) Lithium and alloys containing 50% or more of lithium, in crude or semi-fabricated forms .... A

(2) Lithium and alloys, mixtures, concentrates and compounds, containing lithium enriched in the lithium 6 isotope .... A

(3) Hydrides in which lithium, whether normal, depleted or enriched in the lithium 6 isotope, is compounded with hydrogen or its isotopes or complexed with other metals or aluminium hydride .... A

(4) Substances not specified above containing lithium enriched in the lithium 6 isotope .... A

A8 Hafnium, the following:

(1) Hafnium and alloys containing more than 60% of hafnium, in crude or semi-fabricated forms .... A

(2) Hafnium compounds containing more than 60% of hafnium .... A

(3) Manufactures of any of the foregoing .... A

A9 Beryllium, the following:

(1) Beryllium and alloys containing more than 50% of beryllium, in crude or semi-fabricated forms .... A

(2) Beryllium compounds .... A

(3) Manufactures of any of the foregoing except metal windows for medical X-ray machines .... A

— Fluorine .... A

— Chlorine trifluoride .... A

A12 Tritium, compounds and mixtures containing tritium, in which the ratio of tritium to hydrogen by atoms exceeds 1 part in 1 000, and products containing one or more of the foregoing .... A

except

(1) labelled compounds not exceeding 100 curies per shipment (in this entry "labelled compounds" means compounds in which one of the atoms is a different isotope from that found normally);

(2) luminous paint, self luminous products, gas and aerosol detectors, electron tubes, lightning or static electricity gradient meters, devices designed for the ionisation of air including static elimination devices, ion generating tubes, detector cells of gas chromatography devices, calibration standards, or apparatus and instruments not elsewhere specified in this Schedule incorporating such products or devices, provided that each product or device contains not more than 40 curies of tritium in any chemical or physical form; and

(3) compounds and mixtures of tritium, where the separation of the constituents cannot result in the evolution of an isotopic mixture of hydrogen in which the ratio of tritium to hydrogen by atoms exceeds 1 part in 1 000.

A13 Neptunium 237 in any form for nuclear heat sources .... A

A14 Specially designed or prepared materials for the separation of isotopes of natural uranium, and depleted uranium, and special and other fissile materials referred to in heads A1, A2 and A3 of this Group including specially designed chemical exchange resins .... A

— Specially designed or prepared materials for the separation of isotopes of thorium, including specially designed chemical exchange resins .... A

(For isotopic separation plants, see the entry in Group 2B relating thereto.)

— Calcium containing both less than 100 parts per million by weight of impurities other than magnesium and less than10 parts per million by weight of boron .... A

— Alloys containing a higher percentage of magnesium than of any other element and 10% or more of lithium .... A

GROUP 2B

Nuclear Facilities, Equipment and Appliances

B1 Plants for the separation of source material and special and other fissile materials, and specially designed orprepared equipment and components therefor, including:

(1) Valves wholly made of or lined with nickel, nickel alloy, phosphor bronze, stainless steel, aluminium or aluminium alloy, corrosion resistant to uranium hexafluoride (UF_6) or hydrogen fluoride (HF), 0.5 cm or greater in diameter with bellows seal .... A

(2) Units capable of separating isotopes of natural uranium, depleted uranium and special or other fissile materials, such as:

(a) Gas centrifuges .... A
(b) Jet nozzle separation units .... A
(c) Vortex separation units .... A
(d) Laser isotopic separation units .... A
(e) Chemical exchange separation units .... A
(f) Electromagnetic separation units .... A
(g) Plasma separation units .... A
(h) Gaseous diffusion separation units .... A

(3) Blowers and compressors (turbo, centrifugal and axial flow types) wholly made of or lined with nickel, nickel alloy, phosphor bronze, stainless steel, aluminium or aluminium alloy, corrosion resistant to uranium hexafluoride (UF_6) or hydrogen fluoride (HF) and having a capacity of 1 700 litres (1.7 m^3) per minute or greater, including compressor seals, except blowers and compressors not so defined .... A

(4) Heat exchangers made of aluminium, copper, nickel or nickel alloys, separately or together, and heat exchangers incorporating tubing clad with aluminium, copper, nickel or nickel alloys, separately or together, and in which the other parts are made wholly of the foregoing materials, separately or together, designed to operate at sub-atmospheric pressure with a leak rate of less than 10 pascal (0.1 millibar) per hour under a pressure differential of 10^5 pascal (1 bar) except heat exchangers not so defined .... A

(5) Gaseous diffusion barriers .... A

(6) Gaseous differ housings .... A

For specially designed or prepared materials for the separation of isotopes, see the entry in Group 2A relating thereto.

B2 Plants for the reprocessing of irradiated nuclear fuel and equipment and components specially designed or prepared therefor, or capable of being adapted for use therein, including:

(1) Fuel element chopping or shredding machines .... A

(2) Critically safe tanks (e.g. small diameter, annular or slab tanks) .... A

(3) Countercurrent solvent extractors and ion exchange processing equipment .... A

(4) Process control equipment or instrumentation specially designed or prepared for monitoring or controlling the reprocessing of irradiated source and special and other fissile materials .... A

(For process control equipment for lithium, see the entry in this Group relating thereto.)

B3 Nuclear reactors, i.e. reactors capable of operation so as to maintain a controlled, self-sustaining fission chain reaction, and equipment and components specially designed or prepared for use in connection with a nuclear reactor, including:

(1) Pressure vessels, i.e. metal or other vessels as complete units or as major shop-fabricated parts therefor ... A

(2) Fuel element handling equipment, including reactor fuel charging and discharging equipment .... A

(3) Control rods, including the neutron absorbing part and the support or suspension structures therefor, and control rod guide tubes .... A

(4) Electronic controls for controlling the power levels in nuclear reactors, including reactor control rod drive mechanisms and radiation detection and measuring instruments to determine neutron flux levels .... A

(5) Pressure tubes .... A

(6) Coolant pumps .... A

(7) Internals specially designed or prepared for the operation of a nuclear reactor, including core support structures, thermal shields, baffles, core gridplates, diffuser plates .... A

(8) Heat exchangers .... A

B4 Plants specially designed for the fabrication of nuclear reactor fuel elements and specially designed equipment therefor .... A

B5 Plants for the production or concentration of heavy water, deuterium, or deuterium compounds, and specially designed or prepared equipment and components therefor .... A

B6 Plants for the production of uranium hexafluoride (UF_6) and specially designed or prepared equipment (including UF_6 purification equipment) and components therefor .... A

C1 Neutron generator systems, including tubes, designed for operation without an external vacuum system and utilising electrostatic acceleration to induce a tritium-deuterium nuclear reaction .... A

C2 Power generating or propulsion equipment specially designed or adapted for use with military, space, marine or mobile nuclear reactors .... A

C3 Electrolytic cells for the production of fluorine, with a production capacity greater than 250 g of fluorine per hour .... A

C4 Equipment specially designed for the separation of isotopes of lithium .... A

(For plants for the separation of isotopes other than lithium, see the entry for such plants in this Group.)

C5 Equipment specially designed for the production or recovery of tritium .... A

C6 Frequency changers (converters or inverters) capable of a multi-phase electrical output of between 600-2 000 Hz and specially designed components therefor for use in gas centrifuge plants .... A

— Equipment specially designed for the manufacture or assembly of gas centrifuges capable of the enrichment or separation of isotopes and specially designed parts, components and equipment therefor .... A

(For gas centrifuge plants, see the entry for plants for separation of isotopes in this Group.)

— Mass spectrometers and mass spectrometer sources designed for measuring the isotopic composition of uranium hexafluoride (UF_6) gas, uranium and uranyl compounds .... A

— Pressure gauges capable of measuring pressures to 100 Torr (13332.2 newtons per square metre) or less having sensing elements of nickel, nickel alloy, phosphor bronze, stainless steel, aluminium or aluminium alloy, corrosion resistant to uranium hexafluoride (UF_6) or hydrogen fluoride (HF); and such sensing elements .... A

— Process control equipment or instrumentation specially designed or prepared for monitoring or controlling the reprocessing of irradiated lithium .... A

Annex II

LIST OF EXEMPTION ORDERS UNDER THE RADIOACTIVE SUBSTANCES ACT 1960

ENGLAND AND WALES

1. **The Radioactive Substances (Exhibitions) Exemption Order 1962 (SI 1962 No. 2645)**

   This Order gives conditional exemption from registration under Section 1 of the 1960 Act in respect of the keeping and use for demonstration purposes at an exhibition of radioactive material of limited radioactivity.

2. **The Radioactive Substances (Storage in Transit) Exemption Order 1962 (SI 1962 No. 2646)**

   This Order gives exemption (in some cases conditionally) from registration under Section 1 of the 1960 Act in respect of radioactive material securely packaged. It also gives exemption (in some cases conditionally) from the provision of Section 7 (prohibition of accumulation of radioactive waste without authorisation) in respect of securely packaged radioactive waste which is stored during transit. In certain cases there are limits on the number of packages and the period during which they may be stored or accumulated.

3. **The Radioactive Substances (Phosphatic Substances, Rare Earths Etc.) Exemption Order 1962 (SI 1962 No. 2648)**

   This Order gives exemption unconditionally from registration under Section 1 of the 1960 Act in respect of the keeping and use of radioactive substances consisting of substances (including phosphatic substances and rare earths) containing limited amounts of radioactive elements and articles made from such substances. It also gives unconditional exemption as regards disposal and accumulation of certain descriptions of radioactive waste arisings.

4. **The Radioactive Substances (Lead) Exemption Order 1962 (SI 1962 No. 2649)**

   This Order gives exemption unconditionally from registration under Section 1 of the 1960 Act in respect of the keeping and use of radioactive material consisting of or containing lead of the kind in common use. It also gives unconditional exemptions as respects disposal and accumulation of certain descriptions of radioactive waste arisings.

5. **The Radioactive Substances (Uranium and Thorium) Exemption Order 1962 (SI 1962 No. 2710)**

   This Order gives exemption (in some cases conditionally) from registration under Section 1 of the 1960 Act in respect of the keeping and use of radioactive material consisting of substances containing natural uranium and/or natural thorium and of articles made from such substances. It also gives exemption (in some cases conditionally) as respects disposal and accumulation of radioactive waste arisings.

6. **The Radioactive Substances (Prepared Uranium and Thorium Compounds) Exemption Order 1962 (SI 1962 No. 2711)**

   This Order gives exemption conditionally from registration under Section 1 of the 1960 Act in respect of the keeping and use for specified purposes and in amounts appropriate to laboratory work of radioactive material consisting of compounds of prepared thorium and prepared thorium and other related substances. It also gives exemption (in some cases conditionally) as respects disposal and accumulation of radioactive waste arisings.

7. **The Radioactive Substances (Geological Specimens) Exemption Order 1962 (SI 1962 No. 2712)**

   This Order gives exemption from registration under Section 1 of the 1960 Act in respect of the keeping and use for specified purposes of radioactive material consisting of specimens of natural rocks or natural materials containing uranium and/or thorium. It also gives exemption (in some cases conditionally) as respects disposal and accumulation of radioactive waste arisings.

8. **The Radioactive Substances (Waste Closed Sources) Exemption Order 1963 (SI 1963 No. 1831)**

   This Order gives exemption (conditionally and subject to exceptions) as respects disposal and accumulation of radioactive waste consisting of closed sources.

9. **The Radioactive Substances (Schools, Etc.) Exemption Order 1963 (SI 1963 No. 1832)**

   This Order gives exemption from registration under Section 1 of the 1960 Act in respect of the keeping and use at educational establishments of radioactive material consisting of or containing certain closed sources, open sources (containing no strontium 90 or alpha emitters). It also gives exemption (in most cases conditionally) as respects disposal and accumulation of radioactive waste arisings.

10. **The Radioactive Substances (Hospitals' Waste) Exemption Order 1963 (SI 1963 No. 1833) as amended by the Radioactive Substances (Hospitals' Waste) Exemption (Amendment) Order 1974 (SI 1974 No. 501)**

This Order (as amended) gives exemption as respects the disposal and accumulation of solid and liquid radioactive wastes (except those containing strontium 90 or alpha emitters) arising from relevant activities at hospitals and other medical establishments.

11. **The Radioactive Substances (Precipitated Phosphate) Exemption Order 1963 (SI 1963 No. 1836)**

This Order gives exemption from registration under Section 1 of the 1960 Act in respect of the keeping and use for specified purposes of radioactive material of limited radioactivity consisting of or containing precipitated phosphate.

12. **The Radioactive Substances (Electronic Valves) Exemption Order 1967 (SI 1967 No. 1797)**

13. **The Radioactive Substances (Smoke Detectors) Exemption Order 1980 (SI 1980 No. 953)**

This Order gives conditional exemption from registration under Section 1 of the 1960 Act in respect of the keeping and use of radioactive material consisting of smoke detectors incorporating sources of limited radioactivity. It also gives conditional exemption as respects disposal and accumulation of radioactive waste arisings.

14. **The Radioactive Substances (Gaseous Tritium Light Devices) Exemption Order 1985 (SI 1985 No. 1047)**

This Order deals with exemptions and exclusions under the Radioactive Substances Act 1960 in respect of certain articles containing tritium gas.

15. **The Radioactive Substances (Luminous Articles) Exemption Order 1985 (SI 1985 No. 1048)**

This Order (which revokes and replaces an earlier Order) deals with exemptions and exclusions under the Radioactive Substances Act 1960 in respect of radioactive luminous instruments and indicators.

16. **The Radioactive Substances (Testing Instruments) Exemption Order 1985 (SI 1985 No. 1049)**

This Order (which revokes and replaces an earlier one) deals with exemptions and exclusions under the Radioactive Substances Act 1960 in respect of testing instruments and radioactive sources used in conjunction therewith.

17. **The Radioactive Substances (Substances of Low Activity) Exemption Order 1986 (SI 1986 No. 1002)**

This Order (which revokes and replaces a number of previous Orders) deals with exemptions and exclusions under the Radioactive Substances Act 1960 in respect of certain substances of low radioactivity so as to give unconditional exemption from registration under Section 1 and excludes from disposal restrictions certain solid, liquid or gaseous materials below specified levels of radioactivity.

SCOTLAND

1. **The Radioactive Substances (Lead) Exemption Order 1962 (SI 1962 No. 2762)**
2. **The Radioactive Substances (Storage in Transit) Exemption Order 1962 (SI 1962 No. 2765)**
3. **The Radioactive Substances (Uranium and Thorium) Exemption Order 1962 (SI 1962 No. 2766)**
4. **The Radioactive Substances (Exhibitions) Exemption Order 1962 (SI 1962 No. 2768)**
5. **The Radioactive Substances (Phosphatic Substances, Rare Earths Etc.) Exemption Order 1962 (SI 1962 No. 2769)**
6. **The Radioactive Substances (Geological Specimens) Exemption Order 1962 (SI 1962 No. 2771)**
7. **The Radioactive Substances (Prepared Uranium and Thorium Compounds) Exemption Order 1962 (SI 1962 No. 2772)**
8. **The Radioactive Substances (Waste Closed Sources) Exemption Order 1963 (SI 1963 No. 1877)**
9. **The Radioactive Substances (Schools, Etc.) Exemption Order 1963 (SI 1963 No. 1878)**
10. **The Radioactive Substances (Hospitals' Waste) Exemption Order 1963 (SI 1963 No. 1869) as amended by the Radioactive Substances (Hospitals' Waste) Exemption (Amendment) Order 1974 (SI 1974 No. 487)**
11. **The Radioactive Substances (Precipitated Phosphate) Exemption Order 1963 (SI 1963 No. 1882)**
12. **The Radioactive Substances (Electronic Valves) Exemption Order 1967 (SI 1967 No. 1803)**
13. **The Radioactive Substances (Smoke Detectors) Exemption Order 1980 (SI 1980 No. 1599)**
14. **The Radioactive Substances (Gaseous Tritium Light Devices) Exemption Order 1985 (SI 1985 No. 1047)**
15. **The Radioactive Substances (Luminous Articles) Exemption Order 1985 (SI 1985 No. 1048)**
16. **The Radioactive Substances (Testing Instruments) Exemption Order 1985 (SI 1985 No. 1049)**
17. **The Radioactive Substances (Substances of Low Activity) Exemption Order 1986 (SI 1986 No. 1002)**

UNITED KINGDOM

NORTHERN IRELAND

1. **The Radioactive Substances (Lead) Exemption Order 1962 (SI 1962 No. 240)**
2. **The Radioactive Substances (Prepared Uranium and Thorium Compounds) Exemption Order 1962 (SI 1962 No. 242)**
3. **The Radioactive Substances (Uranium and Thorium) Exemption Order 1962 (SI 1962 No. 244)**
4. **The Radioactive Substances (Storage in Transit) Exemption Order 1962 (SI 1962 No. 246)**
5. **The Radioactive Substances (Geological Specimens) Exemption Order 1962 (SI 1962 No. 248)**
6. **The Radioactive Substances (Phosphatic Substances, Rare Earths Etc.) Exemption Order 1962 (SI 1962 No. 249)**
7. **The Radioactive Substances (Exhibitions) Exemption Order 1962 (SI 1962 No. 250)**
8. **The Radioactive Substances (Attachments to Lightning Conductors) Exemption Order 1963 (SI 1963 No. 216)**
9. **The Radioactive Substances (Hospitals' Waste) Exemption Order 1963 (SI 1963 No. 217)**
10. **The Radioactive Substances (Precipitated Phosphate) Exemption Order 1963 (SI 1963 No. 218)**
11. **The Radioactive Substances (Schools, Etc.) Exemption Order 1963 (SI 1963 No. 219)**
12. **The Radioactive Substances (Thorium X) Exemption Order 1963 (SI 1963 No. 221)**
13. **The Radioactive Substances (Waste Closed Sources) Exemption Order 1963 (SI 1963 No. 222)**
14. **The Radioactive Substances (Electronic Valves) Exemption Order 1967 (SI 1967 No. 313)**
15. **The Radioactive Substances (Tokens for Vending Machines) Exemption Order 1968 (SI 1968 No. 139)**
16. **The Radioactive Substances (Vouchers for Encashment Machines) Exemption Order 1968 (SI 1968 No. 140)**
17. **The Radioactive Substances (Smoke Detectors) Exemption Order 1980 (SI 1980 No. 304)**
18. **The Radioactive Substances (Gaseous Tritium Light Devices) Exemption Order 1986 (SI 1986 No. 10)**
19. **The Radioactive Substances (Luminous Articles) Exemption Order 1986 (SI 1986 No. 11)**
20. **The Radioactive Substances (Testing Instruments) Exemption Order 1986 (SI 1986 No. 12)**

UNITED STATES

TABLE OF CONTENTS

UNITED STATES

I. INTRODUCTION

Since the inauguration of President Eisenhower's "Atoms for Peace" programme in 1953 and the passage of the Atomic Energy Act of 1954, the United States has engaged in peaceful nuclear co-operation with other nations to share the benefits of civilian nuclear energy. Such co-operation has been intended to prevent and take into account the risks of proliferation — the spread of nuclear explosives. The nuclear export control regime plays a major role in minimising this risk. In the United States this regime calls for United States controls continuing after export, recipient assurances that exports intended for peaceful uses will not be diverted to an explosives programme, the maintenance of international safeguards and United States prior consent rights over subsequent use of the exported facilities or materials. It also restricts the export of weapons-useable material, sensitive facilities, and classified and sensitive nuclear technology.

The licensing and regulation of nuclear materials and equipment is governed by the Atomic Energy Act of 1954, as amended. That statute, enacted by the United States Congress in 1954 and amended on numerous occasions, replaced the Atomic Energy Act of 1946, a statute enacted after the close of World War II, during which the United States military had developed and utilised atomic weapons.

The 1946 Act had established the Atomic Energy Commission, a body of five members, to be appointed by the President. The function of the Atomic Energy Commission under the 1946 Act was focused on research and development and governmental control of production, ownership and use of fissionable materials to assure the common defence and security. The Federal Government owned atomic energy facilities and materials. The Atomic Energy Act of 1954[1] permitted private participation in the development of uses of atomic facilities and materials and set up a framework for co-operation with other nations in peaceful uses of the atom. That Act permitted private persons to build and operate production and utilisation facilities[2] subject to licensing and regulation by the Atomic Energy Commission.

The Atomic Energy Commission was abolished by the Energy Reorganization Act of 1974 and its licensing and related regulatory functions were transferred to the newly created Nuclear Regulatory Commission (NRC)[3]. All other functions of the Atomic Energy Commission were transferred to the Energy Research and Development Administration, whose functions were subsequently transferred to the Department of Energy[4].

The purpose of this study is to describe the regulation of trade in nuclear materials and facilities and other nuclear or nuclear-related equipment in the United States, at both national and international levels[5]. Particular emphasis will be placed on exports and their controls and, in addition to the licensing of transfers, other pertinent provisions of the legislation and regulations in force will also be analysed, namely those governing physical protection, transport and radiation protection. In addition, criteria for co-operation agreements will be discussed and the agreements on the peaceful uses of nuclear energy concluded by the United States are listed in *Annex III*.

II. NUCLEAR EXPORT AND IMPORT : LICENSING AND REGULATION

Prior to enactment of the Nuclear Non-Proliferation Act on 10th March 1978, the United States legal framework for exports of nuclear facilities, material and technology was relatively simple. Under the 1954 Atomic Energy Act, exports of production and utilisation facilities and special nuclear material were permitted under an agreement for co-operation provided for in Section 123 of that Act. Issuance of export licences and negotiation of agreements for co-operation were assigned to the Atomic Energy Commission.

1. Atomic Energy Act

The NRC had been given the function of export licensing of facilities, special nuclear material, source material and by-product material under the Energy Reorganization Act, as mentioned above. In addition to the requirement that export of facilities and special nuclear material be made under an agreement for co-operation, exports (or "distribution" by ERDA, later the Department of Energy) could be made upon a finding that the export would not be inimical to the common defence and security[6].

The *Nuclear Non-Proliferation Act* of 1978 (NNPA)[7] made significant changes in statutory licensing requirements for exports of nuclear commodities. It amended the Atomic Energy Act to add requirements for an NRC licence for the export of component parts of facilities and other items or substances especially relevant from the standpoint of export control because of their significance for nuclear explosive purposes as determined by the NRC. The NNPA also made significant changes in United States nuclear export criteria and procedures[8].

New export licensing procedures were incorporated in Section 126 of the Nuclear Non-Proliferation Act, in Commission regulations in 10 CFR Part 110, and in procedures published by Executive Branch agencies in the Federal Register pursuant to Section 126.

The procedural requirements for issuance of licences are : NRC transmittal of the licence application to the *Departments of State, Energy, Defence, Commerce*, and the *Arms Control and Disarmament Agency*. Within fifteen days, each agency must advise the State Department as to whether its preliminary view favours issuance, as well as what additional steps need be taken. Within fifteen days from that date, the State Department circulates a proposed Executive Branch judgment. A response by each agency is required within ten days from receipt of the proposed judgment. Unless the Secretary of State authorises additional time in the national interest and so informs the Congress, an Executive Branch judgment must be transmitted to the NRC within sixty days from receipt of the application. The judgment must specifically address the extent to which the export criteria in the NNPA are met and the extent to which the recipient country has adhered to its agreement for co-operation. Meanwhile, the Commission considers the licence application concurrently with Executive Branch consideration. The Commission must act on the application within sixty days after receipt of the Executive Branch judgment.

As required by the NNPA, Executive Branch procedures for the preparation of the Executive Branch judgment on licence applications have been published in the Federal Register. Those procedures establish certain categories of exports for which no findings or co-ordination are required because they lack significance for nuclear explosive purposes and thus are not inimical to the common defence and security. Those procedures also established an "*Interagency Sub-group on Nuclear Export Co-ordination*" (SNEC) to monitor and facilitate interagency processing of review of licence applications, among other things.

An Executive Branch judgment that the export would be inimical to the common defence and security *requires* NRC denial of the licence application. The Commission *must* issue the licence if it finds either that the statutory criteria and other requirements are met or finds that there is no material changed circumstance associated with a new application from those existing at the time of the last application for export to the same country if that application was approved under the Nuclear Non-Proliferation Act (NNPA).

If the NRC fails to act within the prescribed sixty day period, the applicant must be informed of the reason for the delay. If the NRC has not acted on an application within an additional sixty days, the President may authorise the export upon finding that further delay would be excessive and that withholding the export would be seriously prejudicial to United States non-proliferation objectives or would otherwise jeopardise the common defence and security (unless procedures for public participation have been commenced or further information has been requested of the Executive Branch). The Presidential authorisation is subject to Congressional review.

If the NRC cannot, based upon a reasonable evaluation of the assurances provided and other information available to the United States government, make the finding that the statutory criteria or their equivalent are met, the Commission must issue its decision to that effect and submit the licence application to the President. The President may authorise the export by Executive Order if he finds that denial would be seriously prejudicial to achievement of United States non-proliferation objectives or would otherwise jeopardise the common defence and security. The Executive Order may be overriden by a joint resolution of both houses of Congress within sixty days of continous session of Congress.

Pursuant to the direction in Section 304(b) of the Nuclear Non-Proliferation Act, the Commission has established procedures for public participation in export licensing. Those procedures are set out in Subparts H, I and J of Part 110. The procedures give the Commission discretion to hold a hearing or otherwise permit public participation if it finds that such a hearing or participation would be in the public interest and would assist the Commission in making the required statutory determinations. Part 110 provides that hearings may be oral or consist of written submissions. As authorised by Section 304(c) of the NNPA, the procedures for public participation do *not* include on-the-record, trial type provisions such as cross-examination and discovery and the Commission's decision is not required to be made on the basis of the hearing record.

In addition to the foregoing procedures, the Omnibus Diplomatic Security and Antiterrorism Act of 1986 (Public Law 99-399), 27th August 1986, added a new Section 133 to the Atomic Energy Act. That Section provides that, in addition to other applicable requirements, a licence may be issued by the NRC for the export of more than 2 kilograms of plutonium or more than 20 kilograms of uranium enriched to more than 20 per cent; and approval may be granted by the Secretary of Energy under Section 131 of the Act (discussed *infra*) for the transfer of such material only after the Secretary of Defence has been consulted on whether the physical protection of that material during the export or transfer will be adequate to deter theft, sabotage, and other acts of international terrorism which would result in the diversion of that material. If, in the view of the Secretary of Defence based on all available intelligence information, the export or transfer might be subject to a genuine terrorist threat, the Secretary must provide to the Commission or the Secretary of Energy, as appropriate, his written assessment of the risk and a description of the actions the Secretary of Defence considers necessary to upgrade physical protection measures.

a) Criteria for issuance of licences to export facilities, special nuclear material and source material

The applicable criteria for export of facilities, special nuclear material and source material are found in Sections 127 and 128 of the Atomic Energy Act, added by the NNPA, and other sections of the Atomic Energy Act relating to licensing of facilities and materials (Sections 103a and d and 104a and d for facilities, Sections 53a, 54c and 57c(2) and d for special nuclear material and Section 64 for source material). The criteria in the NNPA prescribe specific requirements which must be met. The Act does not define the factors that enter into the other general criterion of "not inimical to the common defence and security". However, experience in applying this criterion indicates to some extent the factors that may be considered.

Section 127 criteria

The criteria set out in Section 127 of the Atomic Energy Act were drafted so as largely to be satisfied under the basic requirements in the then current agreements for co-operation. The language of the Senate Report on the NNPA Bill (S.897) and the language of Section 126a(2), which requires that the criteria *or their equivalent* be determined to be met, makes this clear. The criteria need not be satisfied only by provisions in United States agreements for co-operation, but may be satisfied by other means, such as adherence to the Treaty on the Non-Proliferation of Nuclear Weapons (NPT) or the provision of supplementary assurances. The criteria in this Section (and Section 128) do not apply to licences for non-nuclear end uses, as noted above.

Criterion 1 calls for IAEA safeguards, as required by Article III.2 of the NPT, to be applied with respect to source material, special nuclear material and production or utilisation facilities, proposed to be exported, previously exported under the applicable agreement for co-operation, and to special nuclear material used in or produced through the use of such facilities or material.

Criterion 1 does not apply to exports to nuclear-weapon States, because Article III.2 of the NPT requires that provision of source or special fissionable material and equipment or material especially designed and prepared for processing, use, or production of special fissionable material by any party to the Treaty to *any non-nuclear weapon State* for peaceful purposes be subject to IAEA safeguards.

Criterion 1 is, of course, satisfied by the importing country having an NPT-type safeguards agreement with the IAEA (an INFCIRC/153-type agreement), but it does not preclude exports to countries having only INFCIRC/66 Rev.2-type safeguards agreements with the IAEA and the United States. This is consistent with the interpretation of Article III.2 of the NPT.

Criterion 2 requires that no exported materials and facilities proposed to be or previously exported under the applicable agreement for co-operation and no special nuclear material produced through their use, be used for any nuclear explosive device or for research on or development of any nuclear explosive device. Criterion 2 applies to *all* States, not only non-nuclear weapon States. Non-nuclear weapon States party to the NPT satisfy this criterion by reason of their ratification of that Treaty. Nuclear-weapon States party to the NPT are committed to not assisting other countries to acquire a nuclear explosive device.

Non-NPT countries and nuclear-weapon States may provide assurances of no nuclear explosive uses through ad hoc assurances or some other mechanism such as voluntary offers to apply IAEA safeguards to their peaceful nuclear activities, or application of EURATOM safeguards in the case of nuclear-weapon States (the United Kingdom and France). Agreements for co-operation uniformly preclude use of United States origin exported or produced materials for atomic weapons or for any other "military purpose". The United States position has been that this provision precludes use of United States exports for any so-called "peaceful" nuclear explosive device, since the technology of such devices is not distinguishable from that of weapons. Agreement with this position by States not party to the NPT having agreements for co-operation with the United States has been considered equivalent to meeting the stated criterion.

Criterion 3 requires that adequate physical security measures must be maintained with respect to exported or produced materials and to exported facilities.

It also provides that following the effective date of regulations promulgated by the NRC, as required by Section 304(d) of the Nuclear Non-Proliferation Act, physical security measures shall be deemed adequate if they provide a level of protection equivalent to that required by NRC regulations.

The Commission has promulgated regulations which prescribe physical security measures deemed adequate to satisfy this criterion. Consistent with Congressional direction in Section 304(d) of the NNPA, that the NRC promulgate regulations establishing levels of physical security which are not less strict than those established by any international guidelines to which the United States subscribes and which, in its judgment, provide adequate protection to nuclear facilities and source and special nuclear material, the Commission's regulations (10 CFR Section 110.43) require that as a minimum, physical security measures in a recipient country provide protection comparable to that in IAEA publication INFCIRC/225, Rev. 1.

None of the United States agreements for co-operation in effect when the NNPA came into force had provisions pertaining to physical security. Determinations that criterion 3 is met have been made by consideration of available information, including country visits and by written assurances that the required physical protection will be maintained. Assurances that levels specified in the Nuclear Suppliers' Group (so-called London Club)[9] physical security guidelines are being met have been accepted by the Commission as equivalent to the criterion specified in Part 110.

Criterion 4 requires that no exported material, facilities, sensitive nuclear technology, or special nuclear material produced through the use of exported material, will be retransferred to another nation or group of nations except with the prior approval of the United States. It does not require a United States veto right over retransfer of special nuclear material produced through use of non-United States origin material in United States supplied reactors.

All agreements for co-operation now contain a United States veto right over retransfer of United States supplied material. With respect to retransfer of produced special nuclear material, United States agreements for co-operation also presently provide rights of approval for the United States in some form. [Some agreements provide that United States-origin produced special nuclear material may be retransferred: 1) to a recipient having an appropriate agreement for co-operation with the United States, or 2) under safeguards acceptable to the United States. The criterion has been considered to be satisfied in such cases by virtue of the fact that the United States must agree that the agreement for co-operation is "appropriate" or that the safeguards in the recipient nation are "acceptable".]

Criterion 5 requires that the United States have prior approval rights over the reprocessing of United States supplied material or special nuclear material produced from such material, and on the alteration in form or content of irradiated fuel elements containing United States-supplied fuel removed from a reactor. Like criterion 4, criterion 5 does not require United States consent to reprocessing of non-United States origin fuel irradiated in United States-supplied reactors.

The bilateral co-operation agreement with the IAEA did not give the United States prior approval rights over either retransfers or reprocessing and the agreement with EURATOM did not give the United States prior approval rights over reprocessing. However, Section 126 of the Atomic Energy Act gives the President authority to exempt these groups of nations from criteria 4 and 5 upon a determination that failure to continue co-operation would be seriously prejudicial to the achievement of United States non-proliferation objectives or would otherwise jeopardise the common defence and security. The agreement with the IAEA has been amended to provide for United States approval rights. The Commission of the European Communities and the United States are presently engaged in discussions concerning their agreement for co-operation. The exemption of EURATOM from application of the reprocessing approval criterion during these discussions provided by Section 126a(2) of the Atomic Energy Act has been extended by the President yearly until 10th March 1988. Further annual extensions are permitted by the Act upon making the requisite findings. Some agreements provide that reprocessing may be performed upon a joint determination of the parties that safeguards may be effectively applied in a reprocessing facility in the recipient country. Since under this type of provision, the United States can withold consent by declining to make a "joint" determination, the criterion has been deemed satisfied.

Criterion 6. For export of sensitive nuclear technology, the foregoing conditions are applicable to any nuclear material or equipment produced or constructed under the jurisdiction of any recipient nation or group of nations by or through the use of any such exported sensitive nuclear technology.

Section 128 criterion

Section 128 of the Atomic Energy Act provides that licence applications for export to a non-nuclear-weapon State filed after 10th September 1979 or any such application under which the first export would occur after 10th March 1980, meet the criterion of "full-scope safeguards" — this is, that IAEA safeguards be maintained on all peaceful nuclear activities in the State at the time of the export. All NPT parties which have entered into safeguards agreements with IAEA satisfy this criterion. The criterion in Section 128 does *not* require recipients to be parties to NPT, or to have NPT safeguards agreements (INFCIRC/153-type agreements), but requires that, as a *factual* matter, a non-nuclear-weapon State recipient have all its peaceful nuclear activities under IAEA safeguards, thus permitting continued exports to non-NPT countries with no unsafeguarded facilities.

b) Non-inimicality to the common defence and security

The Nuclear Non-Proliferation Act (NNPA), while mandating additional criteria for issuance of export licences, retained the Atomic Energy Act criterion that exports not be inimical to the common defence and security. However, the report on the NNPA (before enactment), S 897, stated that in the absence of unusual circumstances, it was believed that any proposed export meeting the criteria set forth in Sections 127 and 128 would also satisfy the non-inimicality standard.

The "non-inimical" criterion has been used to consider policies which are consistent with (but not mandated by) the NNPA, such as reduction of the amount of highly enriched uranium exported. Decisions on exports of sensitive material — even though meeting the specific criteria in Sections 127 and 128 — are reviewed for their overall impact on the common defence and security. Thus, this criterion is used as a mechanism for ensuring that nuclear export decisions are consistent with and supportive of United States national security interests.

c) Criteria for issuance of licences to export components or items or substances especially relevant from the standpoint of export control because of their significance for nuclear explosive purposes (Section 109 of the Atomic Energy Act)

Exports of reactor components *not* classified as a production or utilisation facility (defined in 10 CFR 110.2), but specially designed or prepared for use in such a facility, or other substances or items especially relevant from the standpoint of export control because of their significance for nuclear explosive purposes are now subject to NRC licensing. Prior to enactment of the NNPA, such items were subject to licensing by the Department of Commerce. The statutory licensing criteria for export of items are four of those discussed above : *a)* application of IAEA safeguards as required by Article III.2 of the NPT ; *b)* no use in or for research and development of a nuclear explosive device ; *c)* no retransfer without United States prior consent and *d)* non-inimicality to the common defence and security.

The Commission has specified components, items and substances subject to the Section 109 licensing criteria in 10 CFR Part 110, Section 110.8. The components, items and substances include, among other things : *a)* heavy water production plants, nuclear reactor fuel fabrication plants and specially designed or prepared equipment, parts or components for such plants and for production or utilisation facilities ; *b)* heavy water (deuterium) ; and *c)* nuclear grade graphite.

All of the items subject to NRC licensing under Section 109 and 10 CFR Part 110 are not, *per se*, necessarily the subject of an IAEA safeguards agreement. Such items are determined to meet the first criterion by reference to application of IAEA safeguards to the facility in which they are used, or to the material in conjunction with which they are used. United States controls over retransfers are established by inclusion in an agreement for co-operation or by separate assurances.

The procedures for obtaining an export licence for components and other Section 109 items are the same as those described above for facilities, special nuclear and source material.

Termination of exports : Section 129 of the Atomic Energy Act sets out conditions under which export of source or special nuclear material, nuclear facilities or items subject to Section 109 shall be terminated. Although the provisions of Section 129 of the Act do not constitute specific criteria for issuance of export licences by the NRC, that Section does, as a practical matter, impose criteria that require termination, by the President, of licences to export nuclear materials and equipment still in the United States. These "criteria" are included in Section 110.45 of NRC regulations.

The conditions for termination of licences in Section 129 are : for non-nuclear weapon States, detonation of a nuclear explosive device ; termination or abrogation of IAEA safeguards ; material violation of an IAEA safeguards agreement ; activities involving source or special nuclear material and having direct significance for manufacture or acquisition of nuclear explosive devices ; and failure to take steps to terminate such activities. For all countries, the circumstances under which exports will be terminated are : 1) material violation of an agreement for co-operation with the United States or an agreement under which United States equipment or material has been exported ; 2) assistance to a non-nuclear weapon State to engage in activities involving source or special nuclear material having direct significance for manufacture or acquisition of a nuclear explosive device and failure to take steps toward terminating such assistance ; 3) conclusion of an agreement for transfer of reprocessing equipment, materials or technology to the sovereign control of a non-nuclear weapon State, except in connection with an international fuel cycle evaluation in which the United States is a participant or pursuant to a subsequent international agreement or understanding to which the United States subscribes.

The President must make a determination that the above described actions have occurred after 10th March 1978. The President may "waive" cessation of exports, subject to Congressional review, if he determines that cessation would be seriously prejudicial to the achievement of United States non-proliferation objectives or would otherwise jeopardise the common defence and security.

The Omnibus Diplomatic Security and Antiterrorism Act of 1986, *supra*, added a new Section 132 to the Atomic Energy Act authorising the President to suspend nuclear co-operation with any nation or group of nations which has not ratified the Convention on the Physical Protection of Nuclear Material.

d) Exports of by-product material

Exports of by-product material are not subject to the Nuclear Non-Proliferation Act (NNPA). Therefore, as a matter of law, no Executive Branch review is required. However, NRC regulations in Section 110.41 of 10 CFR Part 110 provide for Executive Branch review of exports of more than 100 curies of tritium, the initial export of nuclear material or equipment to a foreign reactor, and an export to a restricted or embargoed destination. A general licence is provided in 10 CFR Section 110.23 for export of certain kinds and quantities of by-product material. The criterion for issuance of export licences for by-product material is that the export not be inimical to the common defence and security.

e) Limitation on export of source or special nuclear material for enrichment or components of enrichment, fuel reprocessing or heavy water production facilities

Section 402(a) of the NNPA imposes special additional requirements on enrichment of exported material. That Section prohibits subsequent enrichment of United States origin special nuclear material or source material except with the prior approval of the United States and prohibits export for enrichment or reactor fuelling to any nation or group of nations which has, after 10th March 1978, entered into a new or amended agreement for co-operation with the United States except pursuant to this agreement[10].

Under Section 402(b) of the NNPA, major critical components of an enrichment, reprocessing or heavy water production facility cannot be exported under any agreement for co-operation unless the agreement specifically designates such components as items to be exported pursuant to the agreement.

f) Effects of exports on the public health, safety and environment

Statutory criteria for exports of facilities and materials in the Atomic Energy Act include the criterion that the export will not be inimical, or present a hazard, to the health and safety of the public[11]. However, the NRC has interpreted this criterion to apply only to the health and safety of the United States public. Similarly, it has interpreted the National Environmental Policy Act to require consideration only of environmental effects in the United States and on the "global commons" — high seas and Antarctica, [3 NRC 563 (1976), 5 NRC 1332 (1977)][12].

g) Assistance to foreign atomic energy activities

Section 57b of the Atomic Energy Act provides that :

"It shall be unlawful for any person to directly or indirectly engage in the production of any special nuclear material outside of the United States except : 1) as specifically authorised under an agreement for co-operation made pursuant to Section 123, including a specific authorisation in a subsequent arrangement under Section 131 of this Act, or 2) upon authorisation by the Secretary of Energy after a determination that such activity will not be inimical to the interest of the United States : *Provided*, that any such determination by the Secretary of Energy shall be made only with the concurrence of the Department of State and after consultation with the Arms Control and Disarmament Agency, the Nuclear Regulatory Commission, the Department of Commerce, and the Department of Defence."

Section 57b is implemented by the Department of Energy in its regulation 10 CFR Part 810. That regulation indicates what activities have been generally authorised by the Secretary, which activities require a specific authorisation by the Secretary, and how to request such authorisation.

Technology relating to reprocessing, enrichment, heavy water production or plutonium fuel fabrication requires a specific authorisation. However, furnishing information or assistance to prevent or correct a current or imminent radiological emergency posing a significant danger to public health and safety, is generally authorised, provided the Department of Energy is notified in advance.

When a specific authorisation by the Secretary of Energy is sought, he must determine that the activity for which the export will be utilised "will not be inimical to the interest of the United States". When a request for such an authorisation is received, it is distributed by the Department of Energy to the Arms Control and Disarmament Agency (ACDA), the Departments of State, Commerce, and Defence, and the NRC to review in accordance with substantially the same procedures used for consideration of NRC licences. If unanimous concurrence is not obtained, dispute resolution procedures through the Interagency Sub-Group on Nuclear Export Co-ordination (SNEC) are available ; however, in the case of such authorisations, the Secretary of Energy by statute may act after consultation with the concerned agencies and with the concurrence of the State Department.

h) Subsequent arrangements

Subsequent arrangements are defined by Section 131 of the Atomic Energy Act as arrangements entered into by any agency or department of the United States Government with respect to co-operation with any nation or group of nations (but not purely private or domestic arrangements) involving nuclear supply contracts, approvals for retransfer under an agreement for co-operation, arrangements for physical security, safeguards, or the storage or disposition of irradiated fuel elements and any other arrangements which the President finds to be important from the standpoint of preventing proliferation.

It is through the subsequent arrangement process that the United States exercises its consent rights in agreements for co-operation over retransfer and reprocessing of nuclear material and equipment subject to such agreements, and enters into enrichment and other supply contracts and safeguards arrangements.

A request for a subsequent arrangement is filed with the Department of Energy or in certain cases initiated by the Department of Energy which transmits the request to ACDA, the Departments of State, Commerce, and

Defence, and the NRC. No later than fifteen days after receipt of each request the five agencies must review the request and provide the Department of Energy with preliminary views, including whether the request will involve more extensive consideration than normal or whether additional information is required.

Thereupon, within fifteen days the Department of Energy prepares and transmits to the other agencies its proposed subsequent arrangement or other course of action. Within twenty days of receipt of a subsequent arrangement proposed by the Department of Energy, all agencies must provide written views to the Office of Nuclear Affairs at the Department of Energy. The ACDA response must state whether it intends to prepare an unclassified Nuclear Proliferation Assessment Statement (NPAS), which in the case of a subsequent arrangement may be prepared if, in the Director's view, a proposed subsequent arrangement might significantly contribute to proliferation.

After receipt of all agency views and, if necessary, the NPAS, the Secretary of Energy with the concurrence of the Secretary of State, decides whether to enter into the proposed subsequent arrangement. This decision, along with the determination of the Secretary of Energy that the arrangement will not be inimical to the common defence and security, must be published in the Federal Register. Subsequent arrangements for approval of reprocessing or retransfer of produced plutonium in quantities greater than 500 grams to a non-nuclear weapon State require a further determination by the Secretary of Energy that such activities "will not result in a significant increase in the risk of proliferation"; and must be reported to the Congress and not take effect for a period thereafter of fifteen days of continuous session. Any subsequent arrangement involving the transfer of spent power reactor fuel to the United States for storage or disposition is subject to a special congressional review mechanism set forth in Section 131.

If any disagreements arise during the Executive Branch processing of a subsequent arrangement, they are settled using the same procedures as for NRC licences.

2. Export Administration Act

Under the Export Administration Act of 1979, the United States *Department of Commerce* regulates the export of dual-use, nuclear-related goods and technology. Section 309(c) of the Nuclear Non-Proliferation Act (NNPA) provides for the publication of procedures regarding the control by the Department over all export items, other than those licenced by the NRC which could be, if used for purposes other than those for which the export is intended, of significance for nuclear explosive purposes. The procedures must provide for prior consultation with the Departments of State, Energy and Defence, the ACDA, and NRC.

Dual-use items referred to in the NNPA are contained in the Nuclear Referral List that is included in the Commodity Control List in Commerce Department regulations. (Extracts from this list are reproduced in *Annex I*; *Annex II* gives the country groups listed for export control purposes.) The Nuclear Referral List includes commodities which could be of direct or indirect use in the production of special nuclear material, nuclear explosive development and testing, e.g., state-of-the-art computers, flash X-rays, lasers, or high-speed cameras. Exports of such items require a validated licence. To obtain an export licence, an application is filed with the Commerce Department. Any application for an item on the Nuclear Referral List is generally referred to the Department of Energy for technical review, and the Department of Energy will concur in the proposed export if no proliferation problem is present. In such cases the Commerce Department will issue the licence; however, applications which, in the view of the Department of Energy or the Commerce Department, raise policy considerations or other concerns are referred to the Interagency Sub-Group on Nuclear Export Co-ordination (SNEC) for review by the concerned Executive Branch agencies and the NRC. The SNEC provides the Department of Energy with guidance concerning the type of cases which should receive full review. Any disagreements with respect to approval of the application are settled using the same dispute settlement procedures as for consideration of NRC licences.

There are no express statutory criteria which need to be met in the licensing of dual-use items. When evaluating an export licence application for dual-use equipment, the Department of Commerce considers *a)* the stated end use; *b)* the sensitivity of the particular item and its availability elsewhere; *c)* the assurances given in the particular case; and *d)* the non-proliferation credentials of the importing country.

3. Arms Export Control Act

Section 38 of the Arms Export Control Act, 22 USC 2778, authorises the President to control the import and export of defence articles and defence services and to provide foreign policy guidance to persons in the United States involved in the export and import of such articles and services. The President is authorised to designate those items which shall be considered as defence articles and defence services and to promulgate regulations for the import and export of such articles and services. The items so designated shall constitute the United States *Munitions List*. The Arms Export Control Act was amended by Section 509 of the Omnibus Diplomatic Security and Antiterrorism Act of 1986, *supra*, to prohibit export of items on the Munitions List to any country which the Secretary of State has determined for purposes of Section 6(j)(1)(A) of the Export Administration Act of 1979, has repeatedly provided support for acts of international terrorism. The prohibition is subject to waiver by the President upon his determination that the export is important to the national interests of the United States. He must submit a report to Congress justifying his determination and describing the proposed export. Any waiver expires at the end of ninety days unless Congress enacts a law extending the waiver.

The Comprehensive Anti-Apartheid Act of 1986, 22 USC 5001 *et seq.*, provides in Section 317 that no item on the Munitions List subject to United States jurisdiction may be exported to South Africa, except an item not covered by United Nations Security Council Resolution 418 (imposing an international arms embargo on South Africa) and which the President determines, and certifies to the Congress, is exported solely for commercial purposes and not for the armed forces, police or other security forces of South Africa. If the Congress, within thirty days after the President so certifies, enacts a joint resolution disapproving such export, the item may not be exported.

Decisions on issuing export licences under Section 38 are made in co-ordination with the Director of the Arms Control and Disarmament Agency (ACDA), taking into account the Director's opinion as to whether the export of an article will contribute to an arms race, increase the possibility of outbreak or escalation of conflict, or prejudice the development of bilateral or multilateral arms control arrangements.

Subsection (b) requires every person (other than an officer or employee of the United States Government acting in an official capacity) who engages in the business of manufacturing, exporting, or importing any defence articles or defence services to register with the United States Government agency charged with the administration of Section 38 and pay a registration fee which shall be prescribed by regulations.

The functions of the President under this provision have been delegated to the Secretary of State, and are carried out by the *Office of Munitions Control* of the State Department.

The *International Traffic in Arms Regulations* (ITAR) which carry out the purposes of Section 38 are found in Title 22, Parts 120-130 of the Code of Federal Regulations (CFR). As to the relationship with Department of Commerce regulations under the Export Administration Act, Section 120.4 of 22 CFR Part 120 expressly provides that if an article or service is placed on the Munitions List, its export is regulated exclusively by the Department of State.

22 CFR Part 121 is the United States Munitions List. The four main categories of items included on the List relevant to nuclear purposes are as follows :

1) Category VI(e) of that part lists naval nuclear propulsion plants, their land prototypes and special facilities for their construction, support, and maintenance, including any machinery, device, component, or equipment specifically developed, designed or modified for use in such plants or facilities.

2) Category XVI lists :
   a) Any article, material, equipment or device which is specifically designed or modified for use in the design, development, or fabrication of nuclear weapons or nuclear explosive devices.
   b) Any article, material, equipment, or device which is specifically designed or modified for use in the devising, carrying out, or evaluating of nuclear weapons tests or any other nuclear explosions, except such items as are in normal commercial use for other purposes.

Under 22 CFR Part 123, titled "Licences for the Export of Defence Articles", the export of any article on the United States Munitions List requires a licence from the Office of Munitions Control prior to the export unless a specific regulatory exemption applies. Such an exemption for equipment in Category VI(e) and Category XVI is contained in 22 CFR Section 123.21, which excepts equipment in such categories to the extent that it is under the export control of the Department of Energy or the Nuclear Regulatory Commission pursuant to the Atomic Energy Act of 1954, as amended, and the Nuclear Non-Proliferation Act of 1978.

Further, 22 CFR Part 125, titled "Licences for the Export of Technical Data and Classified Defence Articles", also provides that the provisions of the ITAR do not apply to technical data related to articles in Category VI(e) and Category XVI, because controlled by the Department of Energy and the NRC under the Atomic Energy Act of 1954, as amended and the Nuclear Non-Proliferation Act of 1978.

3) Additionally Category XII(f) on the Munitions List includes energy conversion devices for producing electrical energy from nuclear, thermal, or solar energy, or from chemical reaction which are specifically designed or modified for military application.

4) Category XIV includes, in paragraphs d) and e) :
   d) Nuclear radiation detection and measuring devices, manufactured to military specification ; and
   e) Components, parts, accessories, attachments, and associated equipment specifically designed or modified for the articles in paragraph d) of this category.

The items in Categories XII and XIV are not eligible for exemption from the provisions of the ITAR as are the items in Categories VI(e) and XVI.

4. Comprehensive Anti-Apartheid Act of 1986

The Comprehensive Anti-Apartheid Act of 1986, 22 USC 5001 *et seq.*, prohibits, in Section 307,

- the issuance by NRC of any licence for the export to South Africa of production or utilisation facilities, any source or special nuclear material or sensitive nuclear technology, or any component parts, items, or substances which the Commission has determined, pursuant to Section 109b of the Atomic Energy Act, to be especially relevant from the standpoint of export control because of their significance for nuclear explosive purposes;
- the issuance of any licence for the export to South Africa of any goods or technology which have been determined, pursuant to Section 309(c) of the NNPA, to be of significance for nuclear explosive purposes for use in, or judged by the President to be likely to be diverted to, a South African production or utilisation facility;
- any authorisation by the Secretary of Energy under Section 57b(2) of the Atomic Energy Act for any person to engage, directly or indirectly, in the production of special nuclear material in South Africa; and
- approval of the retransfer to South Africa of any goods, technology, source or special nuclear material, facilities, components, items, or substances referred to above by the NRC.

These prohibitions will terminate if the Secretary of State determines and certifies to the Speaker of the House of Representatives and the chairman of the Committee on Foreign Relations of the Senate that the Government of South Africa is a party to the NPT, or otherwise maintains IAEA safeguards on all its peaceful nuclear activities, as defined in the NNPA. The Section does not preclude

- any export, retransfer, or activity generally licensed or generally authorised by the NRC or the Departments of Commerce or Energy; or
- assistance for the purpose of developing or applying IAEA or United States bilateral safeguards, for International Atomic Energy Agency programmes generally available to its Member states, for reducing the use of highly enriched uranium in research or test reactors, or for other technical programmes for the purpose of reducing proliferation risks, such as programmes to extend the life of reactor fuel and activities envisaged by Section 223 of the Nuclear Waste Policy Act of 1982, or which are necessary for humanitarian reasons to protect the public health and safety.

The above described prohibitions do not apply with respect to a particular export, retransfer, or activity, or a group of exports, retransfers, or activities, if the President determines that to apply the prohibitions would be seriously prejudicial to the achievement of United States non-proliferation objectives or would otherwise jeopardise the common defence and security of the United States and, if at least sixty days before the initial export, retransfer, or activity is carried out, he submits to the Speaker of the House of Representatives or the Chairman of the Committee on Foreign relations of the Senate a report setting forth that determination, together with his reactions therefor.

5. Omnibus Diplomatic Security and Antiterrorism Act (Antiterrorism Act)

The Antiterrorism Act, in addition to the provisions described *supra*, contains other provisions pertaining to nuclear exports. Section 601 directs the President to 1) seek universal adherence to the Convention on the Physical Protection of Nuclear Material; 2) conduct a review to determine whether the recommendations on Physical Protection of Nuclear Material published by the International Atomic Energy Agency (INFCIRC/225, Rev. 1) are adequate to deter theft, sabotage, and the use of nuclear facilities and materials in acts of international terrorism, and 3) transmit the results of this review to the Director General of the IAEA.

He is also directly to take, in concert with United States allies and other countries, such steps as may be necessary a) to keep to a minimum the amount of weapons-grade nuclear material in international transit, and b) to ensure that when any such material is transported internationally, it is under the most effective means for adequately protecting it from acts or attempted acts of sabotage or theft by terrorist groups or nations. Agreement must be sought in the United Nations Security Council to establish an effective regime of international sanctions against any nation or subnational group which conducts or sponsors acts of international nuclear terrorism, as well as measures for co-ordinating responses to all acts of international nuclear terrorism, including measures for the recovery of stolen nuclear material and the clean-up of nuclear releases.

Federal Government agencies are specifically assigned tasks by the Antiterrorism Act. Section 604 provides that the Secretaries of Energy, Defence, and State, and the Director of the Arms Control and Disarmament Agency, and the Nuclear Regulatory Commission shall each review the adequacy of the physical security standards currently applicable with respect to the shipment and storage (outside the United States) of plutonium and uranium enriched to more than 20 per cent in the isotope 233 or the isotope 235, which is subject to United States prior consent rights, with special attention to protection against risks of seizure or other terrorist acts. The agencies had to not later than six months after the date of enactment (27th February 1987), each submit a written report to the Committee on Foreign Affairs of the House of Representatives and the Committee on Foreign Relations of the Senate setting forth the results of the review conducted pursuant to this Section, together with appropriate recommendations.

6. Imports of Nuclear Facilities and Materials

The NRC has authority, under Sections 103 and 104 of the Atomic Energy Act, to issue licences for the import of utilisation or production facilities. The NRC is also authorised to issue licences for the import of special nuclear material, source material, and by-product material (Sections 53, 62, 81) Unlike the export of such items, the statutory criteria for import under 10 CFR Part 110 include "no unreasonable risk to the public health and safety" as well as "not inimical to the common defence and security".

The Nuclear Non-Proliferation Act does not apply to nuclear imports and no consultation with other agencies is required.

For nuclear material imports, NRC regulations 10 CFR Part 110 provide a general licence to any person to import by-product, source or special nuclear material, other than 100 kilograms or more of irradiated fuel, if the consignee is authorised to possess the material under a) a contract with the Department of Energy or b) an exemption from licensing requirements issued by the Commission or a general or specific licence issued by the Commission or an Agreement State (see note 15). Importers of special nuclear material under this general licence must provide advance notification of imports to the Commission as specified in Part 73, discussed *supra*.

An environmental impact statement is required for import of spent power reactor fuel [10 CFR Part 51, Section 51.22(c)(15)].

If a hearing is requested in an import licensing proceeding by a person whose interest may be affected, and the request is granted, the Commission will consider, as provided in 10 CFR Section 110.84(b), the nature of the alleged interest; how that interest will be affected by the proceeding; and the possible effect of any order on that interest, including whether the relief requested is within the Commission's authority, and if so, whether granting relief would redress the alleged injury. As in the case of export licensing proceedings, the licensing decision will be based on all relevant information, including information which might go beyond that in the hearing record.

The Comprehensive Anti-Apartheid Act of 1986, however, prohibits import into the United States of uranium or uranium oxide that is produced or manufactured in South Africa. The prohibition took effect on 1st January 1987. The NRC has carried out the direction of this statute by amendments to 10 CFR Part 110.

That statute also provides (Section 303) that no article which is grown, produced, manufactured by, marketed, or otherwise exported by a parastatal[13] organisation of South Africa may be imported into the United States, 1) except for agricultural products during the twelve-month period from the date of enactment; and 2) except for those strategic minerals for which the President has certified to the Congress that the quantities essential for the economy or defence of the United States are unavailable from reliable and secure suppliers and except for any article to be imported pursuant to a contract entered into before 15th August 1986 (however, no shipments may be received by a national of the United States under such contract after 1st April 1987).

III. LICENSING AND REGULATION OF TRANSFER OF NUCLEAR MATERIAL AND EQUIPMENT

As explained in the Introduction, the licensing of nuclear materials and equipment, whether for domestic or import and export purposes, is governed by the Atomic Energy Act of 1954, as amended. The Act confers licensing and regulatory functions on the Nuclear Regulatory Commission. The licensing provisions of the Act together with the relevant Commission regulations and functions are described below.

1. Transfers of Fissionable Material (Special Nuclear Material)

Sections 51, 53, and 57 of the Atomic Energy Act authorise the Nuclear Regulatory Commission (NRC or Commission) to license and regulate the domestic possession and use of special nuclear material — plutonium, uranium 233, uranium enriched in the isotope 235, any other material which the Commission determines to be special nuclear material pursuant to Section 51 and any material artificially enriched by any of the foregoing, excluding source material[14].

Section 53a authorises the NRC to issue licences to transfer or receive in interstate commerce, transfer, deliver, acquire, possess, own, receive possession of or title to, import or export under the terms of an agreement for co-operation arranged pursuant to Section 123, special nuclear material.

The Act provides that the Commission shall establish, by rule, minimum criteria for the issuance of specific or general licences for among other things, the transfer of special nuclear material depending upon the degree of importance to the common defence and security or to the health and safety of the public.

The Atomic Energy Act requires that each licence issued pursuant to Section 53 contain and be subject to such conditions as :

- no right to the special nuclear material shall be conferred by the licence except as defined by the licence ;
- neither the licence nor any right under the licence shall be assigned or otherwise transferred in violation of the provisions of the Act ; and
- special nuclear material shall be distributed only pursuant to such safety standards as may be established by rule of the Commission to protect health and to minimise danger to life or property.

Section 57a of the Act provides that unless authorised by a general or specific licence issued by the Commission, no person may transfer or receive in interstate commerce, transfer, deliver, acquire, own, possess, receive possession of or title to, or import into or export from the United States any special nuclear material. Subsection c of Section 57 prohibits the Commission from issuing a licence pursuant to Section 53 to any person within the United States if the Commission finds that the issuance of such licence would be inimical to the common defence and security or would constitute an unreasonable risk to the health and safety of the public.

Subsection d of Section 57 authorises the Commission to establish classes of special nuclear material and to exempt certain classes or quantities of special nuclear material or kinds of uses or users from the requirements for a licence set forth in Section 57 when it makes a finding that the exemption of such classes or quantities of special nuclear material or such kinds of uses or users would not be inimical to the common defence and security and would not constitute an unreasonable risk to the health and safety of the public. The Commission was given the authority in Subsection d to permit the exemption of such items as heart pacemakers powered with plutonium 238 and plutonium-powered batteries in space applications, marine instruments and remote location instrumentation.

Regulations promulgated pursuant to the above-described provisions of the Atomic Energy Act concerning special nuclear material are found in Title 10 of the Code of Federal Regulations, Parts 70-73.

2. Domestic Licensing of Special Nuclear Material

10 CFR Part 70 is a basic regulation which establishes procedures and criteria for the issuance of licences to possess, use and transfer special nuclear material, and establishes the terms and conditions upon which the NRC will issue such licences.

Certain persons are exempt from licensing requirements pursuant to Part 70. Section 70.11, with certain exceptions set out in the Energy Reorganization Act, exempts the Department of Energy or any prime contractor of the Department to the extent that such contractor, under his prime contract with the Department receives title to, owns, acquires, delivers, receives, possesses, uses or transfers special nuclear material for :

- the performance of work for the Department at a United States Government-owned or controlled site, including the transportation of special nuclear material to or from such site and the performance of contract services during temporary interruptions of such transportation ;
- research in, or development, manufacture, storage, testing or transportation of, atomic weapons or components thereof ; or
- the use or operation of nuclear devices in a United States Government-owned vehicle or vessel. In addition, any prime contractor or subcontractor of the Department (or the Commission) is exempt from the requirements for a licence when the Commission determines that the exemption of the prime contractor or subcontractor is authorised by law ; and that, under the terms of the contract or subcontract there is adequate assurance that the work thereunder can be accomplished without undue risk to the public health and safety.

Section 70.12 of 10 CFR Part 70 exempts from licensing requirements common and contract carriers, freight forwarders, warehousemen, and the United States Postal Service to the extent that they transport special nuclear material in the regular course of carriage for another or storage incident thereto. This exemption does not apply to the storage in transit or transport of material by persons covered by the general licence issued under Section 70.20a and Section 70.20b, discussed below.

Section 70.13a exempts from licensing requirements persons who carry special nuclear material (other than plutonium) in aircraft of the armed forces of foreign nations subject to 49 USC 1508(a).

Part 70 also deals with general licences for the possession or use of special nuclear material. A "general licence" is a licence, provided by regulation, and effective without the filing of an application with the Commission or the issuance of licensing documents to particular persons.

Section 70.19 provides a general licence to receive title to, own, acquire, deliver, receive, possess, use and transfer, plutonium in calibration or reference sources to *a)* any person in a non-agreement state[15], *b)* any Government agency, or *c)* any person in an Agreement State licensed by the Commission who holds a specific licence to receive, possess, use and transfer by-product, source, or special nuclear material.

The general licence applies only to calibration or reference sources which have been manufactured or initially transferred in accordance with the specifications contained in a specific licence issued by the Commission or by an Agreement State which authorises manufacture of the sources for distribution to persons generally licensed by the Agreement State.

Section 70.20 provides a general licence to receive title to and own special nuclear material. Persons generally licensed under this Section are not authorised to acquire, deliver, receive, possess, use, transfer, import or export special nuclear material, except as authorised in a specific licence.

Section 70.20a issues a general licence to common or contract carriers, or warehousemen, to possess formula quantities[16] of strategic special nuclear material[17] and irradiated reactor fuel subject to certain Sections of the NRC's Regulation on physical protection of plants and materials. Carriers generally licensed under Section 70.20b are exempt from this Section, as are carriers of irradiated fuel for the Department of Energy. The general licence is subject to specified Sections of Part 70; however, it is not subject to certain other parts of NRC regulations except as specified.

Persons generally licensed under Section 70.20a must have submitted and received approval of a transportation security plan; this includes a plan for the selection, qualification, and training of armed escorts, or the specification and design of a specially designed truck or trailer as appropriate. The licensee must assure that the transportation is in accordance with the applicable physical protection requirements of 10 CFR Part 73 (see under Physical Protection below). Applicants for a licence to possess, use, transport or deliver to a carrier for transport formula quantities of strategic special nuclear material, who prepare a physical security, safeguards (in the sense of physical protection) contingency, or guard qualification training plan must protect these plans and related information from unauthorised disclosure.

The Commission will issue a licence to possess, receive, use, and transfer special nuclear material to an applicant if it determines that the application meets the requirements of the Atomic Energy Act and of the Commission's regulations[18].

Each licence issued under 10 CFR Part 70 is subject to the following pertinent conditions:

- no right to the special nuclear material shall be conferred by the licence except as defined by the licence;
- neither the licence nor any right under the licence shall be assigned or otherwise transferred in violation of the Atomic Energy Act;
- the licence shall be subject to, and the licensee shall observe, all applicable rules, regulations and orders of the Commission.

The Commission may incorporate in any licence such additional conditions and requirements with respect to the licensee's ownership, receipt, possession, use, and transfer of special nuclear material as it deems appropriate or necessary in order to:

- promote the common defence and security;
- protect health or to minimise danger to life or property;
- protect Restricted Data;
- guard against the loss or diversion of special nuclear material;
- require such reports and the keeping of such records, and to provide for such inspections of activities under the licence as may be necessary or appropriate to effectuate the purposes of the Atomic Energy Act and regulations thereunder.

The licensee must maintain records of changes to its material control and accounting programme made without prior Commission approval and furnish to the NRC a report containing a description of each change within specified periods.

The licensee can make no change which would decrease the effectiveness of its plan for physical protection of specified special nuclear material in transit, except that licensee may make changes to the plan for physical protection of special nuclear material without prior Commission approval if these changes do not decrease the effectiveness of the plan. A description of each change must be reported to the NRC.

Each licensee who possesses a formula quantity of strategic special nuclear material, or who transports, or delivers to a carrier for transport, a formula quantity of strategic special nuclear material or more than 100 grams of irradiated reactor fuel shall ensure that physical security, safeguards[19] contingency, and guard qualification and training plans and other related safeguards (i.e., physical security) information are protected against unauthorised disclosure.

UNITED STATES

Under 10 CFR Section 70.36, no licence granted under Part 70 and no right to possess or utilise special nuclear material granted by any such licence may be transferred, assigned or in any manner disposed of, either voluntarily or involuntarily, directly or indirectly, through transfer of control of any licence to any person unless the Commission shall, after securing full information, find that the transfer is in accordance with the provisions of the Atomic Energy Act, and give its consent in writing.

Section 70.42 of Part 70 contains provisions respecting transfer of special nuclear material. That Section provides that, except as otherwise provided in the licence and subject to the Section, a licensee may transfer special nuclear material :

- to the Department of Energy ;
- to the agency in any Agreement State which regulates radioactive materials, pursuant to an agreement with the Commission under Section 274 of the Act, if the quantity transferred is not sufficient to form a critical mass ;
- to any person exempt from the licensing requirements of the Act and regulations in Part 70 to the extent permitted under such exemption ;
- to any person in an Agreement State, subject to the jurisdiction of that State, who has been exempted from the licensing requirements of that State, to the extent permitted under such exemption ;
- to any person authorised to receive such special nuclear material under terms of a specific licence or a general licence or their equivalents issued by the Commission or an Agreement State ; or
- to any person abroad pursuant to an export licence issued under Part 110 ;
- as otherwise authorised by the Commission in writing.

Before transferring special nuclear material to a specific licensee of the Commission or an Agreement State or to a general licensee who is required to register with the Commission or with an Agreement State prior to receipt of the special nuclear material, the licensee transferring the material must verify that the transferee's licence authorises receipt of the type, form, and quantity of special nuclear material to be transferred.

The following methods for such verification are acceptable :

- the transferor may have in his possession, and read, a current copy of the transferee's specific licence or registration certificate ;
- the transferor may have in his possession a written certification by the transferee that he is authorised by licence or registration certificate to receive the type, form, and quantity of special nuclear material to be transferred, specifying the licence or registration certificate number, issuing agency and expiration date ;
- for emergency shipments, the transferor may accept oral certification by the transferee that he is authorised by licence or registration certificate to receive the type, form, and quantity of special nuclear material to be transferred, specifying the licence or registration certificate number, issuing agency and expiration date, provided that the oral certification is confirmed in writing within ten days ;
- the transferor may obtain other sources of information compiled by a reporting service from official records of the Commission or the licensing agency of an Agreement State as to the identity of licensees and the scope and expiration dates of licences and registrations ; or
- when no such methods of verification are readily available or when a transferor desires to verify that information received by one of such methods is correct or up-to-date, the transferor may obtain and record confirmation from the Commission or the licensing agency of an Agreement State that the transferee is licenced to receive the special nuclear material.

Section 70.44 provides, pursuant to Section 184 of the Atomic Energy Act, consent to the creation of any mortgage, pledge, or other lien upon any special nuclear material, not owned by the United States, which is subject to licensing provided that the rights of any creditor so secured be exercised only in compliance with and subject to the same requirements and restrictions as would apply to the licensee and that no creditor so secured may take possession of the special nuclear material prior to either the issuance of a licence by the Commission or the transfer of a licence pursuant to Section 70.36, *supra*.

"Creditor", as used in Section 70.44, includes the trustee under any mortgage, pledge, or lien on special nuclear material made to secure any creditor, any trustee or receiver of the special nuclear material, appointed by a court of competent jurisdiction in any action brought for the benefit of any creditor secured by such mortgage, pledge, or lien ; the term also covers any purchaser of such special nuclear material at sale upon foreclosure of the mortgage, pledge, or lien or upon exercise of any power of sale or any assignee of such a purchaser.

Section 70.51 provides material balance, inventory and records requirements. Each licensee is required to keep records showing the receipt, inventory (including location), disposal, acquisition, and transfer of all special nuclear material in his possession regardless of its origin or method of acquisition.

Section 70.54 of Part 70 provides for submission of material transfer reports by licensees. Those requirements are set out in 10 CFR Part 74.

3. Transfers of Source Material

The Atomic Energy Act of 1954, as amended, provides the statutory basis for the regulation of the transfer of source material by the Nuclear Regulatory Commission. Source material is defined in Section 11(z) of the Act [42 USC Section 2014(z)], as :

— uranium, thorium, or any other material which is determined by the Commission pursuant to the provisions of Section 61 to be source material ; or
— ores containing one or more of the foregoing materials, in such concentration as the Commission may by regulation determine from time to time.

Section 61 of the Act provides that the Commission may determine that material other than that defined in Section 11 is source material if the Commission finds that such material is essential to the production of special nuclear material and that the determination that such material is source material is in the interest of the common defence and security. The President must have expressly assented in writing to the determination.

Neither the Atomic Energy Commission nor the Nuclear Regulatory Commission have used this provision to expand on the statutory definition of source material.

Section 62 of the Act provides for the licensing of source material. Specifically, it provides that a person must receive a general or specific licence from the NRC before that person may :

"transfer or receive in interstate commerce, transfer, deliver, receive possession of or title to, or import into or export from the United States any source material after removal from its place of deposit in nature...".

Section 63 of the Act provides the general criteria for the issuance of licences for the domestic distribution of source material. The Commission can only issue a licence to qualified applicants for one of the four reasons specified in the Section. The categories are broad and essentially permit a person to obtain a licence for any valid and lawful purpose.

The Regulations governing the licensing of source material can be found in 10 CFR Part 40. The regulations provide detailed criteria for the issuance of licences to, among other things, transfer source material. The regulations with respect to transfer of licensed material are scattered throughout Part 40.

The Act and Part 40 provide for two types of licences, general and specific. There are two main categories of general licences in Part 40. Section 40.22 provides that certain persons, such as commercial firms, educational institutions, or local governments, can use and transfer not more than 15 lb of source material at any one time for purposes related to the functions of the institution, agency, or firm. Persons authorised to possess, use, or transfer source material under this licence may not receive more than a total of 150 lb of source material in one year. Section 40.25 provides a general licence to persons using certain industrial products and devices manufactured pursuant to a specific licence issued under Section 40.34.

There are no restrictions in the general licence issued pursuant to Section 40.22 with respect to the transfer of material except as provided in that Section. On the other hand, the general licence provisions of Section 40.25 contain a number of restrictions with respect to transfer of source material. The Section 40.25 licensee must establish controls to ensure that depleted uranium is not delivered or transferred to an unauthorised recipient. Any transfers by the general licensee must comply with the provisions of Section 40.51. See *infra* for a discussion of Section 40.51. A general licensee who transfers material must report to the NRC, within thirty days of the transfer, the name and address of the transferee. In addition, the transferor must supply the transferee with a form to register the transferee's use of the device with the NRC or the appropriate Agreement State agency and a copy of the regulations pertaining to general source material licensees.

Part 40 also provides a general licence to own source material similar to that in Part 70 for special nuclear material.

For the issuance of a specific licence, essentially, Part 40 requires that the applicant demonstrate that the intended use of the material is permitted by the Act ; that the applicant is qualified to use the material for the purpose intended ; and that the issuance of the licence will not be inimical to the public health and safety or the common defence and security.

In addition to the general requirements, the regulations specify more detailed requirements for certain types of source material utilisation. For example, an applicant that wants to produce uranium hexafluoride must provide the Commission with detailed information regarding the proposed facility's effect on the environment (10 CFR Section 40.32). Similarly, applicants planning to manufacture products that contain depleted uranium must submit enough information on the manufacturing process to demonstrate that the depleted uranium to be used in the product will not result in excessive radiation exposures (10 CFR Section 40.34).

In the case of an applicant planning to incorporate source material in manufactured goods, Section 40.35 details certain conditions of the specific licence granted pursuant to Section 40.34. A number of the conditions are related to the transfer of source material within the manufactured product. The regulations require the licensee to label each unit containing source material to identify the manufacturer or initial transferor of the unit [10 CFR Section 40.35(b)(1)]. Each transfer to a person operating under a general licence issued pursuant to Section 40.25 must be reported to the NRC within thirty days after the end of the calendar quarter in which the transfer occurred. The report must contain the transferee's name, address, point of contact within the transferee's organisation, type and model number of the device, and the quantity of source material contained in the device [10 CFR Section 40.35(e)]. For those transferees subject to Agreement State regulation, the Section 40.34 licensee must report the information specified in Section 40.35(e)(1) to the appropriate Agreement State agency.

The transfer of source material is specifically regulated by Section 40.51. Subsection (a) prohibits the transfer of source material except as provided by that Section. Subsection (b) generally permits the transfer of source material by a licensee to the Department of Energy, an Agreement State agency which regulates the use of source material pursuant to Section 274 of the Atomic Energy Act, to persons exempt under the Act and the regulations to the extent of the exemption, to persons exempt under comparable provisions of an Agreement State, to any person authorised by a general or specific licence from the NRC or an Agreement State to receive the source material to the extent of the authority in the licence, or as otherwise authorised by the NRC. In summary, the ability of a licensee to transfer material depends upon the restrictions, if any, in the transferor's and transferee's licences.

A transferor of source material is required to verify that the specific licence or general licence issued under Section 40.25 authorises the prospective transferee to receive the type, form, and quantity of the source material [10 CFR Section 40.51(c)]. Subsection (d) provides five methods of verifying the prospective transferee's authorisation. The transferor may have a copy of the licence or the form submitted pursuant to Section 40.25. The transferor may obtain a written certification from the prospective transferee stating that the prospective transferee is authorised to receive the source material. In addition, the prospective transferee's certification must contain the registration number, the issuing agency, and the expiration date of the registration. An oral certification is possible for emergency shipments to be followed by written certification within ten days of the oral certification. The regulation does not define "emergency situation"; nor does it specify the criteria used in determining the existence of an emergency situation. The transferor can bypass the prospective transferee by obtaining the pertinent information from a reporting service that compiles information from the records of the NRC or appropriate Agreement State agency; or the transferor can go directly to the NRC or to the Agreement State for confirmation. Once the transferor has obtained confirmation, the transferor may ship the source material in accordance with the regulations and the licence.

In summary, the NRC regulates the transfer of source material through licences issued pursuant to Section 62 of the Atomic Energy Act. Prohibitions against transfers are not based on detailed regulatory requirements but rather on the authority of a prospective transferee of source material to receive the material.

4. Transfers of By-Product Material (Radioisotopes)

Section 81 of the Atomic Energy Act of 1954, as amended, prohibits the transfer or receipt in interstate commerce of by-product material, defined, in Section 11e of that Act, as any radioactive material (except special nuclear material) yielded in or made radioactive by exposure to the radiation incident to the process of producing or utilising special nuclear material[20]. The Commission is authorised by Section 81 to issue general or specific licences to applicants seeking to use by-product material for research and development, medical therapy, industrial or agricultural uses, or such other useful applications as may be developed. Section 81 also authorises the Commission to establish classes of by-product material and to exempt certain classes or quantities of by-product materials or kinds of uses or users from the requirement for a licence when it makes a finding that such exemption will not constitute an unreasonable risk to the common defence and security and to the health and safety of the public.

Part 30 of the NRC regulations provides "Rules of General Applicability to Domestic Licensing of By-product Material". Section 30.13 exempts from the regulations in Parts 30-35 and the requirements for a licence set forth in Section 81 of the Atomic Energy Act common and contract carriers, freight forwarders, warehousemen and the United States Postal Service to the extent that they transport or store by-product material in the regular course of carriage for another or storage incident thereto.

Sections 30.15 through 30.20 (NRC Regulations) contain exemptions from the requirement for a licence for receipt and transfer, among other things, of certain concentrations of by-product material and specified by-product material in timepieces, hands and dials; lock illuminators, balances of precision, automobile shift quadrants, marine compasses, thermostat dials and pointers, election tubes, ionizing radiation measuring instruments, spark gap irradiators, resins for use in oil wells, certain quantities of self-luminous products, and gas and aerosol fire detectors. However, these exemptions do not authorise the manufacture or initial transfer for sale or distribution of such products. Persons wishing to manufacture or initially transfer such products must hold a specific licence issued pursuant to Part 32.

Section 30.41 contains provisions relating to transfer of by-product material similar to those for transfer of source material described above.

General licences for by-product material are provided in Part 31. They include general licences for specified by-product material in certain measuring, gauging or controlling devices, static eliminators, ion generating tubes, luminous safety devices for use in aircraft, calibration or reference sources, and prepackaged units for in vitro clinical or laboratory testing (Sections 31.3, 31.5-31.11). Part 31 also provides a general licence to own by-product material, similar to those in Part 70 for special nuclear material and Part 40 for source material. As with exempt products, the general licences do not allow manufacture or initial transfer by the general licensee. General licensees are subject to specified Parts and Sections of the Commission's regulations.

As noted above, 10 CFR Part 32 prescribes requirements for the issuance of specific licences to persons who manufacture or initially transfer exempt concentrations and items containing by-product material and generally licensed items containing by-product material. Part 33 provides for issuance of specific licences of broad scope for possession, use and transfer of by-product material.

5. Standards for Protection Against Radiation

The NRC regulations (10 CFR Part 20), Standards for Protection Against Radiation, are applicable to *all* NRC licensees. Of importance to this study is Section 20.205, which prescribes procedures for picking up, receiving and opening packages containing radioactive material.

A licensee who expects to receive a package of radioactive material in excess of Type A quantities (IAEA classification — see under V below) must make arrangements to receive the package, or if the licensee expects to pick up the package at the carrier's terminal, to make arrangements to be notified at the time of arrival. In the latter case, the licensee must pick up the package expeditiously.

Licensees receiving packages of radioactive material must, with some exceptions, monitor the external surfaces of the packages for contamination caused by leakage, as soon as practicable after receipt. If the contamination is above certain levels, the licensee must notify the carrier and the NRC immediately. Licensees receiving a package containing quantities of radioactive material in excess of Type A quantities, other than those transported by exclusive use vehicle, must also monitor the external radiation levels of the package, and, if higher than a specified amount, immediately notify the NRC.

IV. PHYSICAL PROTECTION OF NUCLEAR MATERIAL

Part 73 of NRC regulations (10 CFR Part 73) prescribes requirements for the establishment and maintenance of a physical protection system which will have capabilities for the protection of special nuclear material at fixed sites and in transit and of plants in which special nuclear material is used. The design basis threats, referenced in Part 73 to be used to design safeguards systems are radiological sabotage and theft or diversion of formula quantities of strategic special nuclear material.

Part 73 prescribes requirements for the physical protection of special nuclear material in transportation by any person who is licensed pursuant to the regulations in Part 70 and Part 110 who imports, exports, transports, delivers to a carrier for transport in a single shipment, or takes delivery of a single shipment free on board (FOB) where it is delivered to a carrier, formula quantities of strategic special nuclear material, special nuclear material of moderate strategic significance or special nuclear material of low strategic significance.

Part 73 also applies to shipments by air of special nuclear material in quantities exceeding either 20 grams or 20 curies, whichever is less, of plutonium or uranium 233, or 350 grams of uranium 235 (contained in uranium enriched to 20 per cent or more in the U-235 isotope); and to shipment of irradiated reactor fuel in quantities that in a single shipment both exceed 100 grams in net weight of irradiated fuel (exclusive of cladding or other structural or packaging material) and have a total radiation dose in excess of 100 rems per hour at a distance of three feet from any accessible surface without intervening shielding.

Each licensee who, among others, is authorised to transport or deliver to a carrier for transportation pursuant to Part 70 formula quantities of strategic special nuclear material; takes delivery of formula quantities of strategic special nuclear material free on board the point at which it is delivered to a carrier for transportation; or imports or exports formula quantities of strategic special nuclear material, must establish and maintain or make arrangements for a physical protection system which will have as its objective to provide high assurance that activities involving special nuclear material are not inimical to the common defence and security, and do not constitute an unreasonable risk to the public health and safety. The physical protection system must be designed to protect against the design basis threats of theft or diversion of strategic special nuclear material and radiological sabotage.

Licensees must ensure that the following "Safeguards Information"[21] is protected in transit (Section 73.21) :

- the composite transportation physical security plan ;
- schedules and itineraries for specific shipments. (Routes and quantities for shipments of spent fuel are not witheld from public disclosure. Schedules for spent fuel shipments may be released ten days after the last shipment of a current series) ;
- details of vehicle immobilisation features, intrusion alarm devices, and communication systems ;
- arrangements with and capabilities of local police response forces, and locations of safe havens ;
- details regarding limitation of radio-telephone communications ;
- procedures for response to safeguards emergencies.

Section 73.24 prohibits shipment of special nuclear material in passenger aircraft in excess of either 20 grams or 20 curies, whichever is less, of plutonium or uranium 233, or 350 grams of uranium 235 (contained in uranium enriched to 20 per cent or more in the U-235 isotope).

Further, unless otherwise approved by the Commission, no licensee may make shipments of special nuclear material in which individual shipments are less than a formula quantity, but the total quantity in shipments in transit at the same time could equal or exceed a formula quantity, unless specified conditions are met.

Section 73.25 sets out performance capabilities for physical protection of strategic special nuclear material in transit.

Licensees are required to restrict access to and activity in the vicinity of transports[22] and strategic special nuclear material. To achieve this capability the physical protection system must minimise the vulnerability of the strategic special nuclear material by preplanning itineraries for the movement of strategic special nuclear material ; periodically updating knowlege of route conditions for the movement of strategic special nuclear material ; maintaining knowledge of the status and position of the strategic special nuclear material en route ; and determining and communicating alternative itineraries en route as conditions warrant.

The physical protection system must also be able to detect and delay any unauthorised attempt to gain access or introduce unauthorised materials by stealth or force into the vicinity of transports and strategic special nuclear material by use of both controlled access areas to isolate strategic special nuclear material and transports to assure that unauthorised persons shall not have direct access to, and unauthorised materials shall not be introduced into the vicinity of the transports and strategic special nuclear material, and by access detection sub-systems and procedures to detect, assess and communicate any unauthorised penetration (or attempts) of a controlled access area by persons, vehicles or materials.

The system must also have the capability to detect attempts to gain unauthorised access or introduce unauthorised materials into the vicinity of transports by deceit, using access authorisation controls and procedures to provide current authorisation schedules and access criteria for persons, materials and vehicles ; and access controls and procedures to verify the identity of persons, materials and vehicles, to assess such identity against current authorisation schedules and access criteria before permitting access, and to initiate response measures to deny unauthorised entries.

The physical protection system must be able to prevent or delay unauthorised entry or introduction of unauthorised materials into, and unauthorised removal of, strategic special nuclear material from transports. To achieve this capability the physical protection system must detect attempts to gain unauthorised entry or introduce unauthorised materials into transports by deceit ; and to gain unauthorised entry or introduce unauthorised material into transports by stealth or force, by use of transport features to delay access to strategic special nuclear material sufficient to permit the detection and response system to function, inspection and detection procedures, and surveillance systems and procedures to detect, assess and communicate any unauthorised presence of persons or materials and any unauthorised attempt to penetrate the transport.

Prevention of unauthorised removal of strategic special nuclear material from transports by deceit is required as is detection of attempts to remove strategic special nuclear material from transports by stealth or force.

The licensee must be able to respond to safeguards contingencies and emergencies and to engage and impede adversary forces until local law enforcement forces arrive by having : a security organisation composed of trained and qualified personnel, including armed escorts, to execute response functions ; assessment procedures to assess the nature and extent of security related incidents ; a predetermined plan to respond to safeguards contingency events ; equipment and procedures to enable rapid and effective responses to security-related incidents ; and equipment, vehicle design features, and procedures to protect security organisation personnel in their performance of assessment and response-related functions.

The licensee must transmit detection, assessment and other response related information by using :

- communications equipment and procedures to rapidly and accurately transmit security information among armed escorts ;
- equipment and procedures for two-way communications between the escort commander and the movement control centre to rapidly and accurately transmit assessment information and requests for assistance by local law enforcement forces, and to co-ordinate such assistance ; and

— communications equipment and procedures for the armed escorts and the movement control centre personnel to notify local law enforcement forces of the need for assistance.

Liaison must be established with local law enforcement authorities to arrange for assistance en route.

The licensee must assure that a single adversary action cannot destroy the capability of armed escorts to notify the local law enforcement forces of the need for assistance.

Section 73.26 requires specific transportation systems features as follows :

— shipments must be scheduled to avoid regular patterns and preplanned to avoid areas of natural disaster or civil disorders, such as strikes or riots and be planned in order to avoid storage times in excess of 24 hours and to assure that deliveries occur at a time when the receiver at the final delivery point is present to accept the shipment ;
— arrangements must be made with law enforcement authorities along the route of shipments for their response to an emergency or a call for assistance ;
— security arrangements for each shipment must be approved by the Commission prior to shipment. In addition, information on the following must be provided :
  - shipper, consignee, carriers, transfer points, modes of shipment,
  - point where escorts will relinquish responsibility or will accept responsibility for the shipment,
  - arrangements made for transfer of shipment security, and
  - security arrangements at the point where escorts accept responsiblity for an import shipment.

Hand-to-hand receipts must be completed at origin and destination and at all points enroute where there is a transfer of custody.

For import shipments, the importer must make arrangements to assure that the material will be protected in transit as follows :

— an individual designated by the licensee or his agent, or as specified by a contract of carriage, must confirm the container count and examine locks and/or seals for evidence of tampering, at the first place in the United States at which the shipment is discharged from the arriving carrier ;
— the shipment must be protected at all times within the geographical limits of the United States as provided in Part 73.

A licensee who exports a formula quantity of strategic special nuclear material must comply with the pertinent requirements of Part 73 up to the first point where the shipment is taken off the means of transport outside the United States.

The licensee or his agent must establish a transportation security organisation, including personnel or guards, and a movement control centre manned and equipped to monitor and control shipments, to communicate with local law enforcement authorities, and to respond to safeguards contingencies. Armed escort and armed response force personnel armament must include handguns, shotguns, and semi-automatic rifles.

The licensee (or his agent) must instruct every armed escort and all armed response personnel to prevent or impede acts of radiological sabotage or theft of strategic special material by using sufficient force to counter the force directed at him, including the use of deadly force when armed escorts or armed response personnel have a reasonable belief that it is necessary in self-defence or in the defence of others.

In the case of domestic shipments of strategic special nuclear material, the material must be placed in a protected area at transfer points if transfer is not immediate from one transport to another. Where a protected area is not available, a controlled access area must be established for the shipment. The transport may serve as a controlled access area[23].

Access to protected areas, controlled access areas, transports, escort vehicles, aircraft, rail cars, and containers where strategic special nuclear material is located must be limited to individuals who have been properly identified and have been authorised access to these areas.

Strategic special nuclear material must be shipped in containers that are protected by tamper-indicating seals. The containers must also be locked if they are not in another locked container or transport. The outermost container or transport must also be protected by tamper-indicating seals.

1. Shipment by Road

If a shipment is being made by road, a detailed route plan must be prepared which shows the route to be taken, the refuelling and rest stops, and the call-in times to the movement control centre. All shipments must be made on primary highways with minimum use of secondary roads. All shipments must be made without intermediate stops except for refuelling, rest or emergency stops.

Cargo compartments of the trucks or trailers must be locked and protected by tamper-indicating seals.

The shipment must be made in either :

— a specially designed cargo vehicle truck or trailer that reduces the vulnerability to theft with two separate escort vehicles accompanying the cargo vehicle and a total of seven armed escorts with at least two in the cargo vehicle ; or

— an armoured car cargo vehicle accompanied by three separate escort vehicles and seven armed escorts, with at least two in the cargo vehicle.

All escort vehicles must be bullet-resisting.

The licensee must assure that no unauthorised persons or materials are on the cargo vehicle before strategic special nuclear material is loaded, or on the escort vehicles, immediately before the trip begins.

Cargo and escort vehicles must maintain continuous intraconvoy two-way communication and have radio-telephones capable of communicating with the movement control centre. Calls to the movement control centre must be made at least every half-hour to convey the status and position of the shipment. In the event no call is received in accordance with these requirements, the licensee or his agent must immediately notify the law enforcement authorities and the appropriate Commission Regional Office.

At refuelling, rest, or emergency stops, at least seven armed escorts or other armed personnel must be available to protect the shipment and at least three armed escorts or other armed personnel maintain continuous visual surveillance of the cargo compartment.

2. Shipment by Air

Section 73.26(j) requires that all shipments on commercial cargo aircraft be accompanied by two armed escorts able to converse in a common language with the captain of the aircraft.

Transfers of these shipments must be minimised. Shipments of strategic special nuclear material shall be scheduled so that that material is loaded last and unloaded first.

At scheduled stops, at least seven armed escorts or other armed personnel must be available to protect the shipment and at least three armed escorts or other armed personnel maintain continuous visual surveillance of the cargo compartment.

Export shipments must be accompanied by two armed escorts from the last terminal in the United States until the shipment is unloaded at a foreign terminal and primary responsibility for physical protection is assumed by agents of the consignee. While on foreign soil, the escorts may surrender their weapons to legally constituted local authorities. After leaving the last terminal in the United States, the shipment must be scheduled with no intermediate stops.

Import shipments must be accompanied by two armed escorts at all times within the geographical limits of the United States. These escorts must provide physical protection for the shipment until relieved by verified agents of the United States consignee.

Procedures must be established to assure that no unauthorised persons or material are on the aircraft before strategic special nuclear material is loaded on board.

Arrangements must be made at all domestic airports to assure that the seven required armed escorts or other armed personnel are available and that the required security measures will be taken upon landing.

Arrangements must be made at the foreign terminal at which the shipment is to be unloaded to assure that security measures will be taken on arrival.

3. Shipment by Rail

Section 73.36(k) requires that a rail shipment be escorted by seven armed escorts in the shipment car or an escort car next to the shipment car of the train. Escorts must detrain at stops when practicable and when time permits to maintain the shipment cars under continuous visual surveillance and to check car or container locks and seals. Only containers weighing 5 000 lbs (2 270 kg) or more may be shipped on open rail cars.

A voice communication capability between the escorts and the movement control centre shall be maintained. A redundant means of continuous communication shall be available. Calls to the movement control centre shall be made at least every half-hour to convey the status and position of the shipment. In the event no call is received in accordance with these requirements, the licensee or his agent must immediately notify the law enforcement authorities and the appropriate Commission Regional Office and initiate the contingency plan.

4. Shipment by Sea

Section 73.26(1) of Part 73 requires shipments by sea to be made on container-ships. Strategic special nuclear material containers must be loaded into exclusive use cargo containers conforming to American National Standards Institute (ANSI) Standard MH5.1 "Basic Requirements for Cargo Containers (1971) or International Standards Organisation (ISO) 1496, "General Cargo Containers" (1978). Locks and seals must be inspected by the escorts whenever access is possible.

All shipments must be accompanied by two armed escorts who shall be able to converse in a common language with the captain of the ship.

Minimum domestic ports of call shall be scheduled and there shall be no scheduled transfer to other vessels after the shipment leaves the last port in the United States.

At all ports of call the escorts must ensure that the shipment is not removed. At least two armed escorts or other armed personnel must maintain continuous visual surveillance of the cargo area where the container is stored up to the time the ship departs.

An export shipment must be accompanied by two armed escorts from the last port in the United States until the shipment is unloaded at a foreign terminal and prime responsibility for physical protection is assumed by agents of the consignee. While on foreign soil, the escorts may surrender their weapons to legally constituted local authorities.

Import shipments must be accompanied by two armed escorts at all times within the geographical limits of the United States. These escorts shall provide physical protection for the shipment until relieved by agents of the consignee.

Ship-to-shore communications shall be available, and a ship-to-shore contact must be made every six hours to relay position information, and the status of the shipment. Arrangements must be made at the foreign terminals at which the shipment is to be unloaded to assure that security measures will be taken upon arrival.

***

Section 73.27 provides ***notification*** requirements for shipments of formula quantities of strategic special nuclear material. Shippers (licensees) must immediately notify the consignee by telephone, telegraph, or teletype, of the time of departure of the shipment, and notify or confirm with the consignee the method of transportation, including the names of carriers, and the estimated time of arrival of the shipment at its destination.

Each licensee who receives a shipment of formula quantities of strategic special nuclear material must immediately notify by telephone and telegraph or teletype, the person who delivered the material to a carrier for transport and the appropriate Commission Regional Office of receipt of the material.

Each licensee who makes arrangements for physical protection of a shipment of formula quantities of strategic special nuclear material must immediately conduct a trace investigation of any shipment that is lost or unaccounted for after the estimated arrival time and file a report with the Commission.

***

Section 73.37 sets out the requirements for physical protection of ***irradiated reactor fuel in transit.*** A licensee who transports, or delivers to a carrier for transport, in a single shipment, a quantity of irradiated reactor fuel in excess of 100 grams in net weight of irradiated fuel, exclusive of cladding or other structural or packaging material, which has a total external radiation dose rate in excess of 100 rems per hour at a distance of 3 feet from any accessible surface without intervening shielding must establish and maintain, or make arrangements for, and assure the proper implementation of, a physical protection system for shipments of such material to minimise the possibilities for radiological sabotage of such shipments, especially within heavily populated areas; and facilitate the location and recovery of spent fuel shipments that may have come under the control of unauthorised persons.

To achieve these objectives, the physical protection system must provide for early detection and assessment of attempts to gain unauthorised access to, or control over, spent fuel shipments; provide for notification to the appropriate response forces of any spent fuel shipment sabotage attempts; and impede attempts at radiological sabotage of spent fuel shipments within heavily populated areas, or attempts to illicitly move such shipments into heavily populated areas, until response forces arrive.

To this effect, the physical protection system must, among other things, provide for notification of the Commission in advance of each shipment and include procedures for coping with circumstances that threaten deliberate damage to a spent fuel shipment and with other safeguards emergencies. It must also include arrangements with local law enforcement agencies along the routes of road and rail shipments, and at United States ports where vessels carrying spent fuel shipments are docked, for their response to an emergency or a call for assistance. Finally, it must provide for advance approval by the NRC of the routes used for road and rail shipments of spent fuel, and of any United States ports where vessels carrying spent fuel shipments are scheduled to stop, and ensure that at least one escort maintains visual surveillance of the shipment during periods when the shipment vehicle is stopped, or the shipment vessel is docked.

For shipments by ***road***, the physical protection system for any portion of a spent fuel shipment by road must provide that a transport vehicle within a heavily populated area is occupied by at least two individuals, one of whom serves as escort, and escorted by an armed member of the local law enforcement agency in a mobile unit of such agency; or led by a separate vehicle occupied by at least one armed escort.

A transport vehicle carrying spent fuel not within any heavily populated area must be occupied by at least one driver and one other individual who serves as escort; or occupied by a driver and escorted by a separate vehicle occupied by at least two escorts; or escorted as required for a heavily populated area.

Escorts must have the capability of communicating with the communications centre, local law enforcement agencies, and one another, through the use of a citizens band radio available in the transport vehicle and in each escort vehicle; a radio-telephone or other NRC-approved equivalent means of two-way voice communications available in the transport vehicle or in an escort vehicle committed to travel the entire route; and citizens band radio and informal local law enforcement agency radio communications in any local law enforcement agency mobile units used for escort purposes.

The transport must be equipped with NRC-approved features that permit immobilisation of the cab or cargo-carrying portion of the vehicle.

The transport vehicle driver be familiar with, and be capable of implementing, transport vehicle immobilisation, communications, and other security procedures.

For shipments by ***rail***, in addition, the physical protection system for any portion of a spent fuel shipment must provide that a shipment car within a heavily populated area be accompanied by two armed escorts (who may be members of a local law enforcement agency), at least one of whom is stationed at a location on the train that will permit observation of the shipment car while in motion. A shipment car not within any heavily populated area must be accompanied by at least one escort stationed at a location on the train that will permit observation of the shipment car while in motion; and escorts must have the capability of communicating with the communications centre and local law enforcement agencies through the use of a radio-telephone or other NRC-approved equivalent means of two-way voice communications, which shall be available on the train.

The physical protection system for any portion of a spent fuel shipment by ***sea*** must provide that:

- the shipment vessel, while docked at a United States port within a heavily populated area, is protected by two armed escorts stationed on board the shipment vessel, or stationed on the dock at a location that will permit observation of the vessel; or by a member of a local law enforcement agency, equipped with a normal radio communication system who is stationed on board the vessel, or on the dock at a location that will permit observation of the vessel;
- the vessel, while within United States territorial waters, or while docked at a United States port not within a heavily populated area, be accompanied by an escort, who may be an officer of the vessel's crew, who will assure that the shipment is unloaded only as authorised by the licensee;
- escorts have the capability of communicating with the communications centre and local law enforcement agencies through the use of a radio-telephone, or other NRC-approved equivalent means of two-way voice communications.

Prior to the transport of spent fuel within or through a state, the licensee must notify the Governor or the Governor's designee. The notification must be in writing and be sent to the office of each appropriate Governor or the Governor's designee. The notification must include the following information:

- the name, address, and telephone number of the shipper, carrier and receiver;
- a description of the shipment as specified by the Department of Transportation;
- a listing of the routes to be used within the state;
- a statement that the information is required by NRC regulations to be protected in accordance with NRC requirements.

The licensee must provide the following information to the Governor or his designee on a separate enclosure to the written notification:

- the estimated date and time of departure from the point of origin of the shipment;
- the estimated date and time of entry into the Governor's state;
- in the case of a single shipment whose schedule is not related to the schedule of any subsequent shipment, a statement that schedule information must be protected until at least ten days after the shipment has entered or originated with the state;
- in the case of a shipment in a series of shipments whose schedules are related, a statement that schedule information must be protected until ten days after the last shipment in the series has entered or originated within the state and an estimate of the date on which the last shipment in the series will enter or originate within the state.

The licensee must notify a responsible individual in the office of the Governor or in the office of the Governor's designee of any schedule change that differs by more than six hours from the schedule information previously furnished and inform that individual of the number of hours of advance or delay relative to the written schedule information previously furnished.

State officials, state employees, and other individuals, whether or not licensees of the Commission, who receive the above schedule information must protect that information against unauthorised disclosure.

Reports of unaccounted for shipments, suspected thefts, unlawful diversion, radiological sabotage, or events which significantly threaten or lessen the effectiveness of safeguards are required.

Section 73.72 provides that each licensee who plans to import, export, transport, deliver to a carrier for transport in a single shipment, or take delivery, at the point where it is delivered to a carrier, formula quantities of strategic special nuclear material, or special nuclear material of moderate strategic significance, or irradiated fuel required to be protected in accordance with Section 73.72 must notify the NRC at least ten days before transport of the shipment commences at the shipping facility.

The NRC must also be notified by telephone at least ten days before transport of the shipment commences at the shipping facility that an advance shipping notice has been sent. The NRC must also be informed of any changes to the shipment itinerary prior to the shipment date. Road shipments or transfers with one-way transit times of one hour or less in duration between installations of a licensee are not subject to Section 73.72.

V. PACKAGING AND TRANSPORTATION OF RADIOACTIVE MATERIAL

NRC's regulations on packaging and transportation of radioactive material (10 CFR Part 71) apply to all radioactive material subject to NRC jurisdiction. They cover requirements for packaging, preparation for shipment, transportation of licensed material and procedures and standards for NRC approval of packaging and shipping procedures for fissile material and for other licensed material in excess of a Type A quantity. These regulations are now compatible with those of the International Atomic Energy Agency (IAEA) in Safety Series No. 6 and thus with those of most major nuclear nations in the world.

Each licensee subject to Part 71 who transports or delivers to a carrier for transport licensed material is required to comply with the appropriate regulations of the United States *Department of Transportation* (DOT), particularly those related to packaging, marking and labelling, placarding, monitoring, accident reporting and shipping papers. This is true even if, technically speaking, the NRC licensee is not subject to DOT jurisdiction (Section 71.5).

If the licensee wishes to ship in a package not generally licensed, he must apply for approval of the package design. This applies for certain previously approved Type B packages (Section 71.13); DOT specification containers (Section 71.14); a package the design of which has been approved in a foreign national competent authority certificate which has been revalidated by the DOT (Section 71.16); a shipment of specified fissile material if shipped as a Fissile Class II package, (Sections 71.18, 71.20) and certain Fissile Class III shipments (Sections 71.22, 71.23).

The package design approval standards are set out in Subpart E of Part 71.

Package and special form tests are set out in Subpart F. Lifting and tie down standards are provided for all packages (Section 71.45) as are external radiation standards (Section 71.47) and both general and specific standards for fissile material packages (Sections 71.55, 71.57, 71.59 and 71.61). Special requirements are imposed on shipments of plutonium (Sections 71.63, 71.88).

Subpart G of Part 71 imposes operating controls and procedures on licensees, while Subpart H contains quality assurance requirements for the design, purchase, fabrication, handling, shipping, maintenance, repair and modification of components of packaging which are important to safety.

VI. ANALYSIS OF THE PRINCIPLES GOVERNING NUCLEAR CO-OPERATION AGREEMENTS

The Atomic Energy Act requires that exports of nuclear facilities and special nuclear material (except some plutonium 238 and other special nuclear material exempted by the Commission) be made pursuant to an agreement for co-operation. Although source material export licences do not, as a matter of law, require an agreement for co-operation, as a matter of fact, the NRC does require that exports of source material for nuclear end uses be made pursuant to such an agreement.

The United States currently has agreements for co-operation with twenty-four States, Taiwan, the European Atomic Energy Community (EURATOM), and the IAEA (see list of agreements in *Annex III*). The *1978 Nuclear Non-Proliferation Act* directed the President to seek to renegotiate existing agreements in order to obtain the additional controls which the law now requires for new agreements. Since the enactment of the NNPA, twelve new or amendments to existing agreements have entered into force.

Nuclear co-operation can take place under a bilateral

agreement for co-operation or, in the case of an IAEA Member State, through the United States-IAEA agreement. All co-operation by the United States with the twelve States which are a part of the European Community is undertaken through the United States-EURATOM agreements or, in the case of direct transfer to Spain and Portugal, under the agreements for co-operation with those countries now in force. Agreements for co-operation, with the exception of EURATOM, essentially meet present Atomic Energy Act (Section 123) requirements. [Adherence to the NPT is not a requirement for such an agreement, but has been encouraged in United States negotiations.] In sum, the requirements of Section 123 are :

- a guarantee that safeguards as set forth in the agreement will be maintained with respect to all nuclear materials and equipment transferred pursuant thereto, and with respect to all special nuclear material used in or produced through the use of such materials and equipment, so long as the material or equipment remains under the jurisdiction or control of the co-operating party, irrespective of the duration of other provisions in the agreement or whether the agreement is terminated or suspended for any reason ;
- in the case of non-nuclear-weapon States, a requirement that IAEA safeguards be maintained with respect to all nuclear material in all peaceful nuclear activities within the territory of such State, under its jurisdiction, or carried out under its control anywhere ;
- except in the case of those agreements arranged pursuant to sub-section 91c of the Atomic Energy Act, a guarantee by the co-operating party that no nuclear material and equipment or sensitive nuclear technology be transferred pursuant to the agreement, and no special nuclear material produced through the use of any nuclear material and equipment or sensitive nuclear technology transferred pursuant to the agreement, will be used for any nuclear explosive device, or for research on or development of any nuclear explosive device, or for any other military purpose ;
- except in the case of those agreements arranged pursuant to sub-section 91c of the Atomic Energy Act and agreements with nuclear-weapon States, a stipulation that the United States shall have the right to require the return of any nuclear material and equipment transferred pursuant thereto and any special nuclear material produced through the use thereof if the co-operating party detonates a nuclear explosive device or terminates or abrogates an agreement providing for IAEA safeguards ;
- a guarantee by the co-operating party that any material or any Restricted Data transferred pursuant to the agreement and, except in the case of agreements arranged pursuant to sub-sections 91c, 144b or 144c (Atomic Energy Act), any production or utilisation facility transferred pursuant to the agreement or any special nuclear material produced through the use of any facility or through the use of any material transferred pursuant to the agreement, will not be transferred to unauthorised persons or beyond the jurisdiction or control of the co-operating party without the consent of the United States ;
- a guarantee by the co-operating party that adequate physical security will be maintained with respect to any nuclear material transferred pursuant to the agreement and with respect to any special nuclear material, used in or produced through the use of any material, production facility, or utilisation facility transferred pursuant to the agreement ;
- except in the case of agreements for co-operation arranged pursuant to sub-sections 91c, 144b or 144c, a guarantee by the co-operating party that no material transferred pursuant to the agreement and no material used in or produced through the use of any material, production facility, or utilisation facility transferred pursuant to the agreement will be reprocessed, enriched or (in the case of plutonium, uranium 233, or uranium enriched to greater than 20 per cent in the isotope 235, or other nuclear material which has been irradiated) otherwise altered in form or content without the prior approval of the United States ;
- except in the case of agreements for co-operation arranged pursuant to sub-sections 91c, 144b, or 144c, a guarantee by the co-operating party that no plutonium, no uranium 233, and no uranium enriched to greater than 20 per cent in the isotope 235, transferred pursuant to the agreement or recovered from any source or special nuclear material so transferred or from any source or special nuclear material used in any production facility or utilisation facility transferred pursuant to the agreement will be stored in any facility that has not been approved in advance by the United States ; and
- except in the case of agreements for co-operation arranged pursuant to sub-sections 91c, 144b or 144c, a guarantee by the co-operating party that any special nuclear material, production facility, or utilisation facility produced or constructed under the jurisdiction of the co-operating party by or through the use of any sensitive nuclear technology transferred pursuant to such agreement for co-operation will be subject to all the requirements specified in Section 123.

The President may exempt a proposed agreement for co-operation (except an agreement arranged pursuant to sub-sections 91c, 144b, or 144c on military co-operation) from any of the foregoing requirements if he determines that inclusion of any such requirement would be seriously prejudicial to the achievement of United States non-proliferation objectives or otherwise jeopardise the common defence and security. However, the President cannot exempt a proposed agreement from any of the requirements that are also criteria for the issuance of export licences under Sections 127 and 128 of the Act.

The United States has a programme to negotiate new agreements for co-operation and to renegotiate existing ones. By statute, this activity is undertaken by the Secretary of State, with the technical assistance and concurrence of the Secretary of Energy and in consultation with the Director of the Arms Control and Disarmament Agency (ACDA).

After a negotiated text is initialed, the proposed agreement together with the views and recommendations of the Secretaries of State and Energy, the NRC, and the Director of ACDA, is submitted to the President. The Director of ACDA also submits an unclassified Nuclear Proliferation Assessment Statement which must analyse the consistency of the agreement with the requirements of the Atomic Energy Act, with specific attention as to whether it is consistent with the criteria in Section 123 and "regarding the adequacy of the safeguards and other control mechanisms and the peaceful use assurances contained in the agreement . . . to ensure that any assistance furnished thereunder will not be used to further any military or nuclear explosive purpose"[24].

After making a determination that the performance of the proposed agreement will promote and not constitute an unreasonable risk to the common defence and security, the President authorises its execution. Normally, the agreement, signed by representatives of the two governments involved, is submitted to Congress together with the presidential approval and determination, the NPAS, and the concerned agencies' views. A thirty-day consultation period between the President and cognisant Congressional committees concerning the consistency of the agreement with the requirements of the Atomic Energy Act is required, followed by a period of sixty days of continuous session during which Congressional hearings must be held[25]. If Congress takes no action to disapprove the agreement by joint resolution during that period, the agreement can then be brought into force.

UNITED STATES

NOTES AND REFERENCES

1. Public Law 83-703; 83rd Congress, 2nd Session, 68 Stat. 919, 42 USC 2011-2284.
2. Sections 102-104.
3. Public Law 93-438, 88 Stat. 1233, 42 USC 5801-5891, Sections 104(a), 201. The NRC is an independent regulatory agency with five Commissioners of whom no more than three may be members of the same political party. They are appointed by the President with the consent of the Senate for a five-year period. The NRC structure consists of several offices, some established by the Energy Reorganization Act and some set up through internal organization decisions.
4. Public Law 95-91, 91 Stat. 565, 42 U.S.C. 7151, Section 301(a).
5. The following laws and regulations govern nuclear trade:
   - Atomic Energy Act of 1954, as amended;
   - Code of Federal Regulations (CFR);
   - Nuclear Non-Proliferation Act of 1978;
   - Export Administration Act;
   - Arms Export Control Act;
   - Comprehensive Anti-Apartheid Act of 1986.
6. However, following the Indian explosion of a nuclear device in 1974, detailed findings were in fact made for nuclear exports, pursuant to procedures required by Executive Order 11902.
7. An extensive discussion of these is found in Bettauer, *The Nuclear Non-Proliferation Act of 1978*, 10 Law and Policy in International Business 1105-80 (1978).
8. A subsequently enacted statute has limited the NRC's export licensing authority over depleted uranium. Depleted uranium incorporated in defence articles or commodities solely to take advantage of high density or pyrophoric characteristics unrelated to radioactivity is now exempt from NRC jurisdiction when subject to the controls of the State Department and the Commerce Department under the Arms Export Control Act or the Export Administration Act. (Section 110 of the International Security and Development Cooperation Act of 1980, Public Law 96-553, 22 USC 2778a).
9. A group of countries supplying nuclear material and equipment, the so-called London Club. For further details see Volume I on international aspects of nuclear trade.
10. The Procedures Established Pursuant to the Nuclear Non-Proliferation Act of 1978 by the Departments of State, Energy and Commerce, as amended on 16th May 1984 (49 Fed. Reg. 20780) do, however, provide (Section 17b) that when a proposed export requires approval for enrichment pursuant to Section 402(a) and the proposed export for enrichment is licensed by the NRC, the Secretary of Energy, with the concurrence of the Secretary of State and having consulted with the Director of the Arms Control and Disarmament Agency (ACDA), the NRC, and the Secretary of Defence, hereby approves such enrichment.
11. Sections 53, 57, 69, 81, 103, 104.
12. The NRC's interpretation of these two statutes in this regard was upheld by the United States Court of Appeals for the District of Columbia Circuit in *National Resources Defence Council* v. *Nuclear Regulatory Commission*, 647 F.2d 1345 (1981).
13. "Parastatal organisation" is defined as a corporation, partnership or entity owned or controlled or subsidised by the Government of South Africa, but not a corporation, partnership or entity which previously received start-up assistance from the South African Industrial Development Corporation but which is now privately owned.
14. When the Atomic Energy Commission was abolished by the Energy Reorganization Act of 1974, *supra.* note 3, no attempt was made by the Congress to amend the Atomic Energy Act or by other statute to designate which agency got the authority of the Atomic Energy Commission in the various Sections of the Atomic Energy Act. A helpful, but not authoritative, guide is found in the reports of the cognisant Congressional committees on the Energy Reorganization Act. See Senate Report No. 93-980, 93rd Congress, 2d Session, pp. 82-85 and H. Rep. Report No. 93-707, 93d Congress, 2d Session, pp. 25-27.
15. Section 274 of the Atomic Energy Act authorises the NRC to enter into agreement with the Governor of any State to discontinue the Commission's regulatory authority with respect to by-product materials, source materials and special nuclear materials in quantities not sufficient to form a critical mass, and for the State to regulate such materials within the State for the protection of public health and safety from radiation hazards. These States are known as "Agreement States". States which have not entered into an agreement with the NRC, or its predecessor, the Atomic Energy Commission, are known as "Non-Agreement States".
16. A formula quantity is defined as strategic special nuclear material in any combination in a quantity of 5 000 grams or more computed by the formula, grams=(grams contained U-235)+ 2.5 (grams U-233+ grams plutonium). 10 CFR Section 70.4(y).
17. "Strategic special nuclear material" means uranium 235 (contained in uranium enriched to 20 per cent or more in the U-235 isotope), uranium 233, or plutonium. 10 CFR Section 70.4(x).
18. The applicable pertinent regulations are those in 10 CFR Part 20, Standards for Protection Against Radiation, Part 71, Part 73, and Part 74.
19. When used in domestic legislation and regulations, "safeguards" means "physical protection", unlike its meaning when used in international documents.
20. Section 11e (2) also defines by-product material to include the tailings or wastes produced by the extraction or concentration of uranium or thorium from any ore processed primarily for its source material content. Licensing and regulation of such "by-product material" is beyond the scope of this study.
21. "Safeguards Information" is defined as information not otherwise classified as National Security Information or Restricted Data which specifically identifies a licensee's or applicant's detailed security measures for the physical protection of special nuclear material, or security measures for the physical protection and location of certain

plant equipment vital to the safety of production or utilisation facilities.

22. "Transport" although not defined, means a vehicle of any kind, including a truck, car, boat or airplane.

23. All transfers must be protected by at least seven armed escorts or other armed personnel, at least five of whom shall be available to protect the shipment and at least three of the five must keep the strategic special nuclear material under continuous surveillance while it is at a transfer point. The two remaining armed personnel must take up positions at a remote monitoring location. Each of the seven armed escorts or other armed personnel must be capable of maintaining communication with each other. The commander must be able to communicate with personnel at the remote location and with local law enforcement agencies for emergency assistance. The commander must call the remote location at least every 30 minutes to report the status of the shipment. If the calls are not received within the prescribed time, the personnel in the remote location must request assistance from the law enforcement authorities, notify the shipment movement control centre and initiate the appropriate contingency plans. Armed escorts or other armed personnel must observe the opening of the cargo compartment of the incoming transport and ensure that the shipment is complete by checking locks and seals. A shipment loaded onto or transferred to another transport must be checked to assure complete loading or transfer. Continuous visual surveillance of the cargo compartment must be maintained up to the time the transport departs from the terminal. The escorts must observe the transport until it has departed and notify the licensee or his agent of the latest status immediately thereafter.

A numbered picture badge identification procedure must be used to identify all individuals who will have custody of a shipment. The identification procedure must require that the individual who has possession of strategic special nuclear material shall have, in advance, identification picture badges of all individuals who are to assume custody for the shipment. The shipment may be released only when the individual who has possession of strategic special nuclear material has assured positive identification of all of the persons assuming custody for the shipment by comparing the copies of the identification badges that have been received in advance to the identification badges carried by the individuals who will assume custody of the shipment.

24. 42 USC 2153.

25. The procedure for Congressional review of agreements for co-operation was changed by Section 301 of the Export Administration Amendments Act of 1985, Public Law 99-64.

LIST OF ACRONYMS

ACDA	Arms Control and Disarmament Agency
DOE	Department of Energy
DOT	Department of Transportation
NNPA	Nuclear Non-Proliferation Act
NPAS	Nuclear Proliferation Assessment Statement
NRC	Nuclear Regulatory Commission
SNEC	Interagency Sub-group on Nuclear Export Co-ordination

Annex I

EXTRACTS FROM NUCLEAR REFERRAL LIST IN COMMODITY CONTROL LIST AS AT 1ST JANUARY 1987*

....

Reason for control. The "Reason for Control" paragraph for each Export Control Commodity Number (ECCN) specifies the statutory basis under which that commodity is controlled. Reasons for control include:

National security
Short supply (resource assessment)
Foreign policy
Nuclear non-proliferation
Crime control (foreign policy)

....

ECCN 1075A Spin-forming and flow-forming machines specially designed or adapted for use with numerical or computer controls and specially designed components therefor.

Validated licence required: Country Groups QSTVWYZ (see Annex II)

ECCN 1091A Numerical control units, numerically controlled machine tools, dimensional inspection machines, direct numerical control systems, specially designed sub-assemblies, and "specially designed software". (See section 376.11 for special information to include on the validated license application and re-export request.)

Validated licence required: Country Groups QSTVWYZ)

....

List of Commodities Controlled by ECCN 1091A

(a) Units for numerically controlling simultaneously co-ordinated (contouring and continuous path) movement of machine tools and dimensional inspection machines in two or more axes, except those having all of the following characteristics:

(i) No more than two contouring interpolating (any mathematical function including linear and circular) axes can be simultaneously co-ordinated. Units may have:

(1) One or more additional axes for which rate of movement is not co-ordinated, varied or modulated with that of another axis;

(2) One additional set of two contouring axes provided a separate feed rate number, standard or optional, does not control more than any two contouring axes; or

(3) Two contouring axes switchable out of any number of axes;

(ii) Minimum programmable increment equal to or greater than 0.001 mm (0.00004 in.);

(iii) Interfaces limited as follows:

(1) No integral interface designed to meet ANSI/IEEE standard 488-1978, IEC publication 625-1, or any equivalent standard; and

(2) No more than two interfaces meeting EIA standard RS-232-C, or any equivalent standard;

(iv) On-line (real-time) modification of the tool path, feed rate and spindle data limited to the following:

(1) Cutter diameter compensation normal to the centerline path;

(2) Automatic acceleration and deceleration for starting, cornering and stopping;

* Commodity Control List (15 CFR Ch. III, Part 399). The commodities on that list (Supplement No. 1 to Part 300.1) with "nuclear non-proliferation" included in the "Reason for Control" paragraph of the applicable Export Control Commodity Number (ECCN) have been identified as those that could be of significance for nuclear explosive purposes. These commodities are entitled the Nuclear Referral List. The extracts here concern items controlled for reasons of nuclear non-proliferation.

(3) Axis transducer compensation including lead screw pitch compensation (measurements on one axis may not compensate another axis);

(4) Constant surface speed with or without limits;

(5) Spindle growth compensation;

(6) Manual feed rate and spindle speed override;

(7) Fixed and repetitive cycles (does not include automatic cut vector generation);

(8) Tool and fixture offset;

(9) Part program tape editing, excluding source program language and centerline location data (CLDATA);

(10) Tool length compensation;

(11) Part program storage;

(12) Variable pitch threading;

(13) Inch/metric conversion;

(14) Feed rate override based on spark voltage for electrical discharge machines;

(v) Word size equal to or less than 16 bits [excluding parity bit(s)];

(vi) "Software"/"firmware", including "software"/"firmware" of any programmable unit or device furnished, shall not exceed control unit functions as provided in (i) to (v) above, and is restricted as follows:

(1) Only the following application programs can be furnished, which shall be executable without further compilation, assembly, interpretation, or processing, other than control unit parameter initialisation, and memory storage loading, and each shall be supplied as an entity rather than in modular form:

(a) An operating programme to allow the unit to perform its normal functions;

(b) One or more diagnostic programs to verify control or machine performance and permit localisation of hardware malfunctions;

(c) A translator program with which the end-user can program the control-to-machine interface;

(2) Program documentation for application programs shall not contain the following:

(a) Listing of program instructions (except that necessary for diagnostics for routine hardware maintenance);

(b) Description of program organisation or function beyond that required for program use and for maintenance of hardware with which these programs operate;

(c) Flow charts, logic diagrams or the algorithms employed (*except* those necessary for use of diagnostics for routine hardware maintenance);

(d) Any reference to specific memory storage locations (except those necessary for diagnostics for routine hardware maintenance);

(e) Any other information about the design or function of the "software" that would assist in the analysis or modification of all or part of the "software";

....

(b) Machine tools and dimensional inspection machines that, according to the manufacturer's technical specifications, can be equipped with numerical control units covered by sub-item (a) above, except:

i) Borings mills, milling machines, and machining centers have all of the following characteristics:

(1) Not more than three axes capable of simultaneously co-ordinated contouring motion, i.e. the total number of linear plus rotary contouring axes cannot exceed three. A secondary parallel contouring axis, e.g. W axis on horizontal boring mills, is not counted in the total of three contouring axes.

A secondary rotary table, the centerline of which is parallel to the primary rotary table is also not counted in the total of three contouring axes. Machines may have non-contouring parallel or non-contouring non-parallel rotary axes in addition to the three axes capable of simultaneously co-ordinated contouring motion. Machines having the capability of being simultaneously co-ordinated in more than three axes are not excluded from control even if the numerical control unit attached to the machine limits it to three simultaneously co-ordinated contouring axes. For example, a machine with a control unit switchable between any three out of four contouring axes is not excluded from control;

(2) Maximum slide travel in any axis equal to or less than 3 000 mm (120 in.);

(3) Spindle drive motor power equal to or less than 35 kw (47 hp);

(4) Single working spindle (the machine may have multiple tool heads or turrets as standard or optional, but only one working spindle may be operative at a time). A spindle capable of driving a multiple drill head is considered as a single spindle;

(5) Axial and radial axis motion measured at the spindle axis in one revolution of the spindle equal to or greater than $D \times 2 \times 10^{-5}$mm TIR (peak-to-peak) where D is the spindle diameter in mm;

(6) An incremental positioning accuracy equal to or greater (coarser) than ± 0.002 mm in any 200 mm of travel (± 0.00008 in in any 8.0 in of travel);

(7) Overall positioning accuracy in any axis equal to or greater (coarser) than:

(a) 1 ± 0.01 mm (0.0004 in) for machines with total length of axis travel equal to or less than 300 mm (12.0 in);

(b) ± [0.01+(0.0025/300 × (L-300)] mm (with L expressed in mm) [0.0004 ± (0.0001/12 × (L-12)] in (with L expressed in inches) for machines with a total length axis travel, L, greater than 300 mm (12 in) and equal to or less than 3 300 mm (130.0 in);

(c) ± 0.035 mm (0.0014 in) for machines with a total length of axis travel greater than 3 300 mm (130.0 in);

. . . .

(ii) Machine tools [other than boring mills, milling machines and machining centers described in *(i)* above] and dimensional inspection machines, having all of the following characteristics:

(1) Radial axis motion measured at the spindle axis equal to or greater than 0.0008 mm (0.00003 in) TIR (peak-to-peak) in one revolution of the spindle (for lathes, turning machines, contour grinding machines, etc.);

(2) Meeting the requirements of *(i)*(1), *(i)*(6) and *(i)*(7) above;

(For high precision turning machinery, see also ECCN 1370A.)

(c) "Direct numerical control systems" (DNC) consisting of a dedicated stored program computer acting as a host computer and controlling, on-line or off-line, one or more numerically controlled machine tools or inspection machines, as defined in sub-item *(b)* above, related "software", and interface and communication equipment for data transfer between the host computer memory, the interpolation functions, and the numerically controlled machine tools;

(d) Specially designed sub-assemblies and "software" that, according to the manufacturer's technical specifications, can upgrade the capabilities of numerical control units and machine tools so that they would become controlled by sub-items *(a), (b)* or *(c)* above.

. . . .

ECCN 1093A Components and specially designed parts for machine tools and dimensional inspection machines described by ECCN 1091A.

Validated licence required: Country Groups QSTVWYZ

. . . .

List of Components and Specially Designed Parts for Machine Tools and Dimensional Inspection Machines Described by ECCN 1091A that are Controlled by this ECCN 1093A

(a) Spindle assemblies, consisting of spindles and bearings as a minimal assembly, except those assemblies with axial and radial axis motion measured along the spindle axis in one revolution of the spindle equal to or greater (coarser) than the following:

(1) 0.0008 mm (0.00003 in) TIR (peal-to-peak) for lathes and turning machines; or

(2) $D \times 2 \times 10^{-5}$ mm TIR (peak-to-peak) where D is the spindle diameter in millimeters for milling machines, boring mills, jig grinders, and machinery centers;

(b) Lead screws, including ball nut screws, except those having all of the following characteristics:

(1) Accuracy equal to or greater (coarser) than 0.004 mm/300 mm (0.00016 in/ft);

(2) Overall accuracy equal to or greater (coarser) than $(0.0025 + 5 \times 10^{-6} \times L)$ mm, where L is the effective length of the screw in millimeters and $(0.0001 + 5 \times 10^{-6} \times L)$ in. where L is the effective length of the screw in inches; and

(3) Concentricity of the center line of the journal bearing surface and the center line of the major diameter of the screw equal to or greater (coarser) than 0.005 mm(0.0002 in) TIR (peak-to-peak) at a distance of 3 times the diameter of the screw or less from the journal bearing surface;

(c) Linear and rotary position feedback units including inductive type devices, graduated scales, and laser systems, except:

(1) Linear types having an accuracy equal to or greater (coarser) than $(0.0004 + 13 \times 10^{-6} \times L)$ mm, for L equal to or less than 100 mm and $(0.0015 \pm 2 \times 10^{-6} \times L)$ mm, for L greater than 100 mm, where L is the effective length of the linear measurement in millimeters and $(0.000016 + 13 \times 10^{-6} \times L)$ in for L equal to or less than 4.0 in and $(0.00006 + 2 \times 10^{-6} \times L)$ in where L is the effective length of the linear measurement in inches; and

(2) Rotary types having an accuracy equal to or greater (coarser) than 2 seconds of arc;

(d) Linear induction motors used as drives for slides, having all of the following characteristics:

(1) Stroke greater than 200 mm;

(2) Nominal force rating greater than 45 N; and

(3) Minimum controlled incremental movement less than 0.001 mm; and

(e) Specially designed parts and accessories therefor.

ECCN 4094B Mandrels and bellows forming dies.
Validated licence required: Country Groups QSTVWYZ and Canada

. . . .

List of Mandrels and Bellows Forming Dies Controlled by ECCN 4094B

(a) Mandrels or forming dies, two piece cylindrical having a single indented circumferential convolution bisected by the two halves and having the following dimensions:

(1) 3 in to 16 in outside diameter;

(2) 0.5 in or more in length; and

(3) Single convolution depth more than 2 mm.

. . . .

ECCN 1110A Equipment for the production of liquid fluorine, and specially designed components therefor

. . . .

List of Gas Liquefying Equipment Controlled by ECCN 1110A

. . . .

(b) Equipment for the production of liquid fluorine; and

(c) Specially designed parts and accessories therefor.

ECCN 2120A Cryogenic equipment.
Validated licence required: Country Groups QSTVWYZ

. . . .

ECCN 4127B Pipe valves, having all of the characteristics listed in paragraphs *(a)*, *(b)* and *(c)* of the list below; and parts, n.e.s.
Validated licence required: Country Groups QSTVWYZ

. . . .

List of Pipe Valves Controlled by ECCN 4127B

Pipe valves having all of the following characteristics:

(a) A pipe size connection of 8 inches or more inside diameter;

(b) All flow contact surfaces made of or lined with alloys of 10 per cent or more nickel and/or chromium;

(c) Rated at 1 500 psi or more; and

(d) Parts, n.e.s.

. . . .

ECCN 4128B Pipes, valves, fittings, heat exchangers, or magnetic, electrostatic or other collectors made of graphite or coated in graphite, yttrium or yttrium compounds resistant to the heat and corrosion of uranium vapor.
Validated licence required: Country Groups QSTVWYZ

. . . .

ECCN 1131A Pumps (except vacuum pumps listed under Entry 1129A) having any of the characteristics in paragraphs *(a)* and *(b)* of the list below, and specially designed parts and accessories therefor.

. . . .

List of Pumps Controlled by ECCN 1131A

Pumps having any of the following characteristics:

(a) Pumps designed to move molten metals by electromagnetic forces; or

(b) Pumps having all flow contact surfaces made of 90 per cent or more tantalum, titanium, or zirconium, either separately or combined, except when such surfaces are made of materials containing more than 97 per cent and less than 99.7 per cent titanium; and

(c) Specially designed parts and accessories therefor.

. . . .

ECCN 3131A Valves, 0.5 cm or greater in diameter, with bellows seal, wholly made of or lined with aluminium, nickel or alloy containing 60 per cent or more nickel, either manually or automatically operated; and specially designed parts and accessories therefor.

Validated licence required: Country Groups QSTVWYZ and Canada

. . . .

ECCN 1205A Electromechanical, semi-conductor, and radioactive devices for the direct conversion of chemical, solar, or nuclear energy to electrical energy.

Validated licence required: Country Groups QSTVWYZ

. . . .

List of Electromechanical, Semi-Conductor, and Radioactive Devices Controlled by ECCN 1205A

. . . .

(c) Power sources based on radioactive materials systems other than nuclear reactors, except:

(1) Those having an output power of less than 0.5 Watt and a total weight (force) of more than 890 N (90.7 kg, 200 lb);

or

(2) Those specially designed and developed for medical use within the human body.

. . . .

ECCN 1206A Electric arc devices for generating a flow of ionized gas in which the arc column is constricted (except devices wherein the flow of gas is for isolation purposes only and devices of less than 100 kW for cutting, welding, melting, plating or spraying); equipment incorporating such devices; specially designed components, accessories and control or test equipment.

Validated licence required: Country Groups QSTVWYZ

. . . .

ECCN 3261A Neutron generator system, including tubes, designed for operation without an external vacuum system, and utilizing electrostatic acceleration to induce a tritium-deuterium nuclear reaction; and specially designed parts therefor.

Validated licence required: Country Groups QSTVWYZ

. . . .

ECCN 4261B Particle accelerators having all of the specifications described in the List below.

. . . .

List of Specifications for Particle Accelerators Controlled by ECCN 4216B

(a) Peak boom power exceeding 500 MW;

(b) Output energy exceeding 500 kV; and

(c) An output beam intensity exceeding 2 000 amperes with a pulse width of 0.2 microseconds or less; and

(d) Specially designed parts and accessories therefor.

. . . .

ECCN 1312A Isostatic presses; specially designed dies and molds (except those used in isostatic presses operating at ambient temperatures), components, accessories and controls therefor; and "specially designed software" therefor.

Validated licence required: Country Groups QSTVWYZ

. . . .

List of Equipment Controlled by ECCN 1312A Isostatic Presses, as follows:

....

(b) Having a controlled thermal environment within the closed cavity and possessing a chamber cavity with an inside diameter of 127 mm (5 in) or more.

....

ECCN 3336A Plants specially designed for the production of uranium hexafluoride (UF_6) and specially designed or prepared equipment (including UF_6 purification equipment), and specially designed parts and accessories therefor.

Validated licence required: Country Groups QSTVWYZ and Canada

....

ECCN 4337B Compressors and blowers especially designed or prepared to be corrosion resistant to hydrogen sulfide, and having all of the characteristics as described in this entry.

Validated licence required: Country Groups QSTVWYZ

....

Definitive List of Characteristics Describing Compressors and Blowers Controlled by Entry No 4337B

(a) Capable of sustaining a pressure in hydrogen sulfide in excess of 15 atmospheres;

(b) Having an intake-to-discharge pressure ratio between 0.3 and 3.0; and

(c) Having a capacity equal to or equivalent to or requiring at least 500 hp.

ECCN 4360B Centrifugal balancing machines, fixed or portable, horizontal or vertical having all of the characteristics described in this entry.

Validated licence required: Country Groups QSTVWYZ and Canada

....

Definitive List of Centrifugal Balancing Machine Characteristics Controlled by ECCN 4360B

(a) Suitable for balancing flexible rotors having a diameter of from 3 inches to 16 inches, and a length of 24 inches or more; and

(b) Mass capability of from 2 to 50 lbs; and

(c) Capable of balancing to a residual imbalance of 09.001 in-lb/lb per plane or greater; and

(d) Capable of balancing in three or more planes.

ECCN 1362A Vibration test equipment.

Validated licence required: Country Groups QSTVWYZ

....

Definitive List of Vibration Test Equipment as Controlled by ECCN 1362A

(a) Vibration test equipment using digital control techniques and specially designed ancillary equipment and software therefor, except:

(1) Individual exciters (thrusters) with a maximum thrust of less than 100 kN (22 500 lb);

(2) Analog equipment;

(3) Mechanical and pneumatic exciters (thrusters);

(4) Vibrometers;

(5) Digital ancillary equipment not covered by ECCN Nos. 1529A, 1513A, 1565A or 1568A;

(b) High intensity acoustic test equipment capable of producing an overall sound pressure level of 140 dB or greater referenced to 2×10^{-5} N/m^2, or with a rated output of 4 kW or greater and specially designed ancillary equipment and software therefor, except:

(1) Analog equipment;

(2) Digital ancillary equipment not covered by ECCN Nos. 1529A, 1531A, 1565A or 1568A;

(c) Ground vibration (including modal survey) test equipment that uses digital control techniques and specially designed ancillary equipment and software therefor, except:

(1) Analog equipment;

(2) Digital ancillary equipment not covered by ECCN Nos. 1529A, 1531A, 1565A or 1568A.

ECCN 3362A Power generating and/or propulsion equipment specially designed for use with military nuclear reactors. (This ECCN does not modify Office of Munitions Control coverage, as indicated in Category VI, Part e, of the US Munitions List. See Supp. No. 2 to Part 370.)

Validated licence required: Country Groups QSTVWYZ and Canada

. . . .

ECCN 3363A Electrolytic cells for the production of flourine with a production capabity greater than 250 grams of flourine per hour; and specially designed parts and accessories thereof.

Validated licence required: Country Groups QSTVWYZ and Canada

. . . .

ECCN 4363B Nuclear reactor and nuclear power plant related equipment.

Validated licence required: Country Groups QSTVWYZ

. . . .

List of Commodities Controlled by ECCN 4363B

(a) Reactor and power plant simulators, models or mock-ups;

(b) Process control systems intended for use with nuclear reactors;

(c) Generators, turbine-generator sets, steam turbines, heat exchangers, and heat exchanger type condensers designed or intended for use in a nuclear reactor; and

(d) Commodities, parts and accessories specially designed or prepared for use with nuclear plants (e.g., snubbers, airlocks, reactor inspection equipment) except items licensed by the NRC pursuant to 10 CFR Part 110.

ECCN 1370A Machine tools for generating optical quality surfaces, specially designed components and accessories therefor.

Validated licence required: Country Groups QSTVWYZ

. . . .

Definitive List of Commodities Controlled by ECCN 1307A

(a) Turning machines using a single point cutting tool and having all of the following characteristics:

(1) Slide positioning accuracy less (finer) than 0.0005 mm per 300 mm of travel, TIR (peak-to-peak);

(2) Slide positioning repeatability less (finer) than 0.00025 mm per 300 mm of travel, TIR (peak-to-peak);

(3) Spindle runout (radial and axial) less than 0.0004 mm TIR (peak-to-peak);

(4) Angular deviation of the slide movement (yaw, pitch and roll) less (finer) than 2 seconds of arc (peak-to-peak) over full travel;

(5) Slide perpendicularity less than 0.001 mm per 300 mm of travel, TIR (peak-to-peak);

(b) Fly cutting machines having both of the following characteristics:

(1) Spindle run-out (radial and axial) less than 0.0004 mm TIR (peak-to-peak);

(2) Angular deviation of slide movement (yaw, pitch and roll) less (finer) than 2 seconds of arc (peak-to-peak) over full travel;

(c) Specially designed components, as follows:

(1) Spindle assemblies consisting of spindles and bearings as a minimal assembly, except those assemblies with axial and radial axis motion measured along the spindle axis in one revolution of the spindle equal to or greater (coarser) than 0.0008 mm TIR (peak-to-peak);

(2) Linear induction motors used as drives for slides, having all of the following characteristics:

(i) Stroke greater than 200 mm;

(ii) Nominal force rating greater than 45 N; and

(iii) Minimum controlled incremental movement less than 0.001 mm; or

(*d*) Specially designed accessories, i.e., single point diamond cutting tool inserts having all of the following characteristics:

(1) Flawless and chipfree cutting edge when magnified 400 times in any direction;

(2) Cutting radius between 0.1 and 5 mm; and

(3) Cutting radius out-of-roundness less than 0.002 mm TIR (peak-to-peak)

. . . .

ECCN 1502A Communication, detection or tracking equipment of a kind using ultraviolet radiation, infrared radiation or ultrasonic waves, and specially designed components therefor.

Validated licence required: Country Groups QSTVWYZ

. . . .

List of Equipment controlled by ECCN 1502A

Communication, detection or tracking equipment of a kind using ultraviolet radiation, infrared radiation or ultrasonic waves, and specially designed components, except:

(*a*) Ultrasonic devices that operate in contact with a controlled material to be inspected, or that are used for industrial cleaning, sorting or materials handling, industrial and civilian intrusion alarm, traffic and industrial movement control and counting systems, medical applications, emulsification, homogenization, or simple educational or entertainment devices;

(*b*) Underwater ultrasonic communications equipment, designed for operation with amplitude modulation and having a communications range of 500 m or less (Sea State 1), a carrier frequency of 40 to 60 kHz and a carrier power supplied to the transducer of 1 W or less;

(*c*) Industrial equipment employing cells not described in ECCN 1548;

(*d*) Industrial and civilian intrusion alarm, traffic and industrial movement control and counting systems;

(*e*) Medical equipment;

(*f*) Industrial equipment used for inspection, sorting or analysis of the properties of materials;

(*g*) Simple educational or entertainment devices that employ photo cells;

(*h*) Flame detectors for industrial furnaces;

(*i*) Equipment designed for measuring radiated power or energy for laboratory, agricultural or industrial purposes using a single detector cell with no scanning of the detector and single detector cell assemblies or probes specially designed therefor, having a response time constant exceeding 1 microsecond;

(*j*) Infrared geodetic equipment, provided that equipment uses a lighting source other than a laser and is manually operated, or uses a lighting source (other than a laser or a light-emitting diode) remote from the measuring equipment; and specialized parts therefor;

(*k*) Equipment for non-contact temperature measurement for laboratory or industrial purposes utilizing a single detector cell with no scanning of the detector;

(*l*) Instruments capable of measuring radiated power or energy having a response time constant exceeding 10 milliseconds; and

(*m*) Infrared or ultraviolet sensing devices, not otherwise controlled for export by Supp. No. 2 to Part 370 of the Export Administration Regulations, controlled for export by ECCN 1555 of the Commodity Control List.

ECCN 1522A Lasers and laser systems including equipment containing them.

Validated licence required: Country Groups QSTVWYZ

. . . .

List of Lasers and Laser Systems Controlled by ECCN 1522A

(*a*) Lasers and specially designed components therefor, including amplification stages, except the following when not specially designed for equipment covered by sub-paragraph (b) below:

(*i*) Argon, krypton, and non-tunable dye lasers with both of the following characteristics:

(1) An output wavelength in the range from 0.2 to 0.8 micrometer;

(2) A pulsed output not exceeding 0.5 Joules per pulse and an average or continuous wave maximum rated single- or multi-mode output power not exceeding 20 watts;

(*ii*) Helium-cadmium, nitrogen and multigas lasers not otherwise specified in this ECCN with both of the following characteristics:

(1) An output wavelength shorter than 0.8 micrometer; and

(2) A pulsed output not exceeding 0.5 Joules per pulse and an average or continuous wave maximum rated single- or multi-mode output power not exceeding 120 watts;

(iii) Helium-neon lasers with an output wavelength shorter than 0.8 micrometer;

(iv) Ruby-lasers with both of the following characteristics:

(1) An output wavelength shorter than 0.8 micrometer; and

(2) An energy output not exceeding 20 Joules per pulse;

(v) CO_2, CO or CO/CO_2 lasers having either or both of the following characteristics:

(1) An output wavelength in the range of 9 to 11 micrometers, and a pulsed output not exceeding 2.0 Joules per pulse and a maximum rated average single- or multi-mode output power not exceeding 1 200 watts or a continuous wave maximum rated single- or multi-mode output power not exceeding 2 500 watts;

(2) An output wavelength in the range of 5 to 7 micrometers and having a continuous wave maximum rated single- or multi-mode output power not exceeding 50 watts;

(vi) Nd: YAG lasers having an output wavelength of 1.06 micrometers with either of the following characteristics:

(1) A pulsed output not exceeding 0.5 Joules per pulse and maximum rated average single- or multi-mode output power not exceeding 10 watts or a continuous wave maximum rated single- or multi-mode output power not exceeding 50 watts; or

(2) A pulsed output not exceeding 10 Joules per pulse with a pulse width not less than 50 microseconds and maximum rated average single- or multi-mode output power not exceeding 50 watts;

(vii) Nd: Glass lasers with both of the following characteristics:

(1) An output wavelength of 1.06 micrometers; and

(2) A pulsed output not exceeding 2 Joules per pulse;

(viii) Tunable CW dye lasers, with both of the following characteristics:

(1) An output wavelength shorter than 0.8 micrometer; and

(2) An output not exceeding an average or continuous wave maximum rated single- or multi-mode output power of 1 watt;

(ix) Tunable pulsed laser (for argon and krypton lasers, see sub-paragraph *(a)*(1) of this ECCN, including dye and N_2, with all of the following characteristics:

(1) An output wavelength shorter than 0.8 micrometer;

(2) A pulse duration not exceeding 100 nanoseconds; and a peak power output not exceeding 1 MW;

(x) Single-element semiconductor lasers with a wavelength shorter than 1 microsecond designed for, and used in, equipment as defined under sub-paragraphs *(b)*(xiii) and (xiv) of this ECCN;

(b) Laser systems or equipment incorporating lasers, and specially designed components therefor, except the systems and equipment listed below incorporating lasers excluded from export controls under sub-paragraph *(a)* above:

(i) Specially designed for industrial and civilian intrusion detection and alarm systems;

(ii) Specially designed for medical applications;

(iii) Equipment for educational and laboratory purposes;

(iv) Specially designed for traffic and industrial movement control and counting systems;

(v) Specially designed for detection of environmental pollution;

(vi) Optical spectrometers and densitometers;

(vii) Equipment containing continuous wave helium-neon gas lasers [but see sub-paragraph *(c)* of this ECCN];

(viii) Textile-cutting and textile bonding equipment;

(ix) Paper cutting equipment;

(x) Equipment containing lasers for drilling diamond dies for the wire drawing industry;

(xi) Electronic scanning equipment with auxiliary electronic screening unit specially designed for printing processes, including such equipment when used for the production of color separations;

(xii) Laser-radar (lidar) equipment specially designed for surveying or meteorological observations;

(xiii) Consumer-type reproduceers for video or audio discs, employing non-erasable media;

(xiv) Price scanners (point of sale);

(xv) Systems designed for surveying purposes, provided that there is no capability of measuring range;

(xvi) Equipment specially designed for the marking of components;

(xvii) Specially designed gravure (printing plate) manufacturing equipment;

(c) Laser measuring systems that maintain over the full scale a resolution equal to or less (finer) than 0.0001 mm and an accuracy equal to or less (finer) than 1.0 ppm for a 48-hour period over a temperature range of $\pm$ 10 °C around a standard temperature and at a standard pressure (standard temperature and pressure as indicated in IEC Publication No. 160).

. . . .

ECCN 1529A Electronic measuring, calibrating counting, testing and/or time interval measuring equipment, whether or not incorporating frequency standards.

Validated licence required: Country Groups QSTVWYZ

. . . .

List of Equipment Controlled by ECCN 1529A

. . . .

(g) Transient recorders, utilizing analog-to-digital conversion techniques, capable of storing transients by sequentially sampling single input signals at successive intervals of less than 50 nanoseconds.

. . . .

ECCN 4530B UF_6 Mass spectrometers.

Validated licence required: Country Groups QSTVWYZ and Canada

. . . .

List of Spectrometers Controlled by ECCN 4530B

(a) Mass spectrometers, magnetic or quadrupole:

(1) Instruments having all of the following characteristics:

(i) Unit resolution greater than mass 320; and

(ii) Electron-bombardment ionization source; and

(2) Having any of the following characteristics:

(i) Molecular beam ion sources;

(ii) Ion source chambers constructed of or lined with nichrome or monel, or nickel plated;

(iii) A collector system suitable for simultaneous collection of two or more isotopic species; or

(b) Sources for mass spectrometers:

(1) Molecular beam source; or

(2) Ion source chambers constructed of or lined with nichrome or monel, or nickel plated; or

(3) Sources for mass spectrometers designed especially for use with UF_6.

. . . .

ECCN 1532A Precision linear and angular measuring systems as follows, and specially designed components therefor.

Validated licence required: Country Groups QSTVWYZ

. . . .

List of Precision Linear and Angular Measuring Systems,
and Specially Designed Components and Software therefor
Controlled by ECCN 1532A

(a) Contact-type systems and linear voltage differential transformers (LDVT) therefor, of the following descriptions:

(1) Systems having all of the following characteristics:

(i) Range equal to or less than 5 mm;

(ii) Linearity equal to or less than 0.1 per cent;

(iii) Drift equal to or less than 0.1 per cent per day at standard ambient test room temperatures ±1 °C;

(2) Linear voltage differential transformers with no compensation networks and having either of the following characteristics:

(i) Range equal to or less than 5 mm;

(ii) Linearity equal to or less than 0.2 per cent

(linearity measurements are made in the static mode);

(b) Linear measuring machines, *except optical comparators*, with two or more axes having both of the following characteristics:

(1) Range in any axis greater than 200 mm;

(2) Accuracy (including any compensation) less (finer) than 0.0008 mm per any 300 mm segment of travel;

(c) Angular measuring systems having an accuracy equal to or less than 1 second of arc, except optical instruments, such as autocollimators, using collimated light to detect angular displacements of a mirror;

(d) Non-contact type systems having either of the following characteristics:

(1) Effective probe measurement diameter less than 0.5 mm and drift less than 0.5 per cent per day at standard ambient test room temperatures ± °C;

(2) Linearity less than 0.3 per cent and drift less than 0.5 per cent per day at standard ambient test room temperatures ± 1 °C.

. . . .

ECCN 1534A Flatbed microdensitometers (except cathode-ray types) having any of the characteristics in the List below, and specially designed components therefor.

Validated licence required: Country Groups QSTVWYZ

. . . .

List of Flatbed Microdensitometers Controlled by ECCN 1534A

Flatbed microdensitometers, except cathode-ray types, specially designed parts, components and assemblies therefor, having any of the following characteristics:

(a) A recording or scanning rate exceeding 5 000 data points per second;

(b) A figure of merit better (less) than 0.1, defined as the product of the density resolution (expressed in density units) and the spatial resolution (expressed in micrometers);

(c) An optical density range greater than 0 to 4.

(Density resolution, expressed in density units, is measured over the optical density range of the instrument.)

ECCN 1541A Cathode-ray tubes.

Validated licence required: Country Groups QSTVWYZ

. . . .

List of Cathode-Ray Tubes Controlled by ECCN 1514A

Cathode-ray-tubes having any of the following characteristics:

. . . .

(b) With travelling wave or distribution deflection structure using delay lines, or incorporating other techniques to minimize mismatch of fast phenomena signals to the deflection structure; or

(c) Incorporating microchannel plate electron multipliers; and

(d) Specially designed parts and accessories therefor.

. . . .

ECCN 1542A Cold cathode tubes and switches.

. . . .

List of Cold Cathode Tubes and Switches Controlled by ECCN 1542A

(a) Triggered spark-gaps, having an anode delay time of 15 microseconds or less and rated for a peak current of 3 000 A or more; specially designed parts therefor, and equipment incorporating such devices;

(b) Cold cathode tubes, whether gas-filled or not, operating in a manner similar to a spark gap, containing three or more electrodes and having all of the following characteristics:

(1) Rated for an anode peak voltage of 2 500 V or more;

(2) Rated for peak currents of 100 A or more;

(3) An anode delay time of 10 microseconds or less; and

(4) An envelope diameter of less than 25.4 mm (1 inch).

ECCN 1549A Photomultiplier tubes.

Validated licence required: Country Groups QSTVWYZ

....

List of Photomultiplier Tubes Controlled by ECCN 1549A

Photomultiplier tubes of the following description:

(a) Those for which the maximum sensitivity occurs at wavelengths shorter than 300 nanometers;

Note: Photomultiplier tubes specially designed for use in spectrophotometry having a peak sensitivity at a wavelength shorter than 300 nanometers are not covered by this sub-paragraph.

(For photosensitive components, see ECCN 1548A.)

(b) Having an anode pulse rise time of less than 1 nanosecond; or

(c) Containing microchannel plate electron multipliers; and

(d) Specially designed parts and accessories therefor.

....

ECCN 1553A Flash discharge type X-ray systems (including tubes) and specially designed parts and accessories therefor.

Validated licence required: Country Groups QSTVWYZ

....

List of X-ray Systems Controlled by ECCN 1553A

Flash discharge type X-ray systems (including tubes) and specially designed parts and accessories therefor, having all of the following characteristics:

(a) Peak power greater than 500 MW;

(b) Output voltage greater than 500 kV; and

(c) Pulse width less than 0.2 microsecond.

ECCN 1555A Electron tubes and specially designed components therefor. Control for ECCN 1555A.

Validated licence required: Country Groups QSTVWYZ

....

List of Electron Tubes Controlled by ECCN 1555A

Electron tubes, as follows and specially designed components therefor:

(a) Electron tubes for image conversion or intensification, incorporating:

(1) Fiber-optic face-plates covered by ECCN 1556A*(a)*;

(2) Microchannel plate electron multipliers; or

(3) Gallium arsenide or other epitaxially grown semi-conductor photocathodes covered by ECCN 1556A*(c)*;

(b) Electron tubes for television/video cameras:

(1) Incorporating fiber-optic face-plates covered by ECCN 1556A*(a)*;

(2) Incorporating microchannel-plate electron multiplier; or

(3) Coupled with electron tubes covered by paragraph *(a)* of this ECCN;

(c) Ruggedized electron tubes for television/video cameras having a maximum length-to-bulb diameter ratio of 5:1 or less.

....

ECCN 1559A Hydrogen/hydrogen isotope thyratrons of ceramic-metal construction having any of the characteristics in the List below, and accessories therefor.

Validated licence required: Country Groups QSTVWYZ

....

List of Equipment Controlled by ECCN 1559A

Hydrogen/hydrogen isotope thyratrons of ceramic-metal construction having any of the characteristics, and accessories therefor:

(a) A peak pulse power output exceeding 20 MW;

(b) A peak anode voltage greater than 25 kV;

(c) A peak current rating greater than 1.5 kA.

....

ECCN 1565A Electronic computers, "related equipment", equipment or systems containing electronic computers; and specially designed components and accessories for these electronic computers and "related equipment".

....

Nuclear Non-Proliferation Controls:

The following equipment is subject to nuclear non-proliferation controls and requires a validated licence for Country Groups QSTVWYZ and, in the case of *(a)*(1) through (4) below, for Canada:

(a) Electronic computers intended for ultimate consignees engaged directly or indirectly in any of the following activities:

(1) Designing, developing or fabricating nuclear weapons or nuclear explosive devices; or devising, carrying out, or evaluating nuclear weapons tests or nuclear explosions;

(2) Designing, assisting in the design of, constructing, fabricating or operating facilities for the chemical processing of irradiated special nuclear material, for the production of heavy water, for the separation of isotopes of any source or special nuclear material, or specially designed for the fabrication of nuclear reactor fuel containing plutonium;

(3) Designing, assisting in the design of constructing, fabricating or furnishing equipment or components specially designed, modified or adapted for use in such facilities; or

(4) Training personnel in any of the above activities; and

(b) Advanced electronic digital computers with a processing data rate of 20 million bits per second or more (including digital differential analyzers) except:

(1) Electronic computers that do not exceed a total processing data rate of 1 000 million bits per second are not subject to nuclear non-proliferation controls for destinations listed in Supp. Nos. 2 or 8 to Part 373 of the Export Administration Regulations unless the activities cited in *(a)* above are involved; or

(2) Electronic computers that do not exceed a total processing data rate of 250 million bits per second are not subject to nuclear non-proliferation controls for destinations listed in Supp. No. 3 to Part 373 of the Export Administration Regulations unless the activities cited in *(a)* above are involved.

....

List of Electronic Computers and Related Equipment Controlled by ECCN 1565A

(a) "Analog computers" and "related equipment" therefor, designed or modified for use in airborne vehicles, missiles, or space vehicles and rated for continuous operation at temperatures from below 228 K (− 45 °C) to above 328 K (+ 55 °C);

(b) Equipment or systems containing "analog computers" controlled by paragraph *(a)*;

(c) "Analog computers" and "related equipment" therefor, other than those controlled by paragraph *(a)*, except those that neither:

(1) Are capable of containing more than 20 summers, integrators, multipliers or function generators; nor

(2) Have facilities for readily varying the interconnections of such components;

(d) "Hybrid computers" and "related equipment" therefor, with all the following characteristics:

(1) The analog section is controlled by paragraph *(c)*;

(2) The digital section has an internal fixed or alterable storage of more than 2 048 bit; and

(3) Facilities are included for processing numerical data from the analog section in the digital section or vice versa;

(e) "Digital computers" or controlled "analog computers" containing equipment for interconnecting 'analog computers" with "digital computers";

(f) "Digital computers" and "related equipment" therefor, with any of the following characteristics:

(1) Designed or modified for use in airborne missiles, or space vehicles and rated for continuous operation at temperatures from below 228 K (– 45 °C) to above 328 K (+ 55 °C);

(2) Designed or modified to limit electromagnetic radiation to levels much less than those required by government civil interference specifications;

(3) Designed as ruggedized or radiation hardened equipment and capable of meeting military specifications for ruggedized or radiation hardened equipment; or

(4) Modified for military use;

(g) Equipment or systems containing "digital computers" controlled by paragraph *(f)*;

(h) "Digital computers" and "related equipment" therefor, other than those controlled by paragraph *(e)* or *(f)*, even when "embedded" in, "incorporated" in, or "associated" with equipment of systems:

....

(1) Including "digital computers" and "related equipment", as follows:

....

(A) "Signal processing";

(B) "Image enhancement";

(C) "Local area networks";

....

(D) "Multi-data-stream processing";

....

(E) Combined recognition, understanding and interpretation of image, continuous (connected) speech or connected word text other than "signal processing" or "image enhancement" described in sub-paragraph *(h)*(1)*(i)*(A) or (B);

(F) "Real time processing" of sensor data"

(1) Concerning events occurring outside the "computer using facility"; and

(2) Provided by equipment controlled by ECCNs 1501, 1502, 1510 or 1518;

....

(G) Microprocessor or microcomputer development systems;

....

(H) "Fault tolerance";

....

(I) [Reserved];

(J) "User-accessible microprogrammability";

....

(K) "Data (message) switching";

(L) "Stored program controlled circuit switching"; or

(M) "Wide area networks";

(ii) Having the following characteristics:

(A) Size, weight, power consumption and reliability or other characteristics (e.g., bubble memory), that allow easy application in mobile tactical military systems; and

(B) Ruggedized above the level required for a normal commercial (office) environment, but not necessarily up to levels specified in paragraph *(f)*;

(2) Except:

(i) "Digital computers" or "related equipment" therefor, provided that:

(A) They are "embedded" in other equipment or systems;

(B) They are not the "prinicpal element" of the other equipment or systems in which they are "embedded";

(C) The other equipment or systems are not described by other ECCNs of the Commodity Control List identified by the code letter "A", nor covered by the International Traffic in Arms Regulations, by 10 CFR 110 or by 10 CFR 810;

(D) The "total processing data rate" of any one "embedded" "digital computer" does not exceed 28 million bit per second;

(E) The sum of the "total processing data rate" of each "embedded" "digital computer" does not exceed 50 million bit per second; and

(F) The "embedded" "digital computers" or "related equipment" therefor do not include:

(1) Equipment or systems controlled by ECCN 1519*(c)* or by ECCN 1567; or

(2) Equipment described in sub-paragraph *(h)*(1)*(i)*(A) to (M), other than for:

(i) "Signal processing" or "image enhancement" when lacking "user-accessible programmability" and when "embedded" in medical imaging equipment; or

(ii) "Local area networks" implemented by using integral interfaces designed to meet ANSI/IEEE Std 488-1978 or IEC Publication 625-1;

. . . .

(ii) "Digital computers" or "related equipment" therefor, provided that:

(A) They are "incorporated" in other equipment or systems;

(B) They are not the "principal element" of the other equipment or systems in which they are "incorporated";

(C) The other equipment or systems are not controlled by other ECCNs of the Commodity Control List identified by the code letter "A", nor covered by the International Traffic in Arms Regulations, by 10 CFR or by 10 CFR 810;

(D) The "total processing data rate" of any one "incorporated" "digital computer" does not exceed 5 million bit per second;

(E) The "total internal storage available to the user" does not exceed 4.9 million bit; and

(F) The "incorporated" "digital computers" or "related equipment" therefor do not include:

(1) Controlled "related equipment";

(2) Equipment or systems controlled by ECCN 1519*(c)* or by ECCN 1567;

(3) Equipment described in sub-paragraph *(h)*(1)*(ii)*; or

(4) Equipment described in sub-paragraph *(h)*(1)*(i)*(A) to (M), other than for:

(i) "Signal processing" or "image enhancement" when lacking "user-accessible programmability" and when "embedded" in medical imaging equipment; or

(ii) "Local area networks" implemented by using integral interfaces designed to meet ANSI/IEEE Std 488-1978 or IEC Publication 625-1;

. . . .

(iii) [Reserved];

(iv) "Digital computers" other than those described in sub-paragraph *(h)*(1), shipped as complete systems and having all the following characteristics:

(A) Designed and announced by the manufacturer for identifiable civil use;

(B) Not specially designed for any equipment controlled by any other ECCN of the Commodity Control List identified by the code letter "A", by the International Traffic in Arms Regulations, by 10 CFR 110 or by 10 CFR 810;

(C) "Total processing data rate" not exceeding 2 million bit per second;

(D) "Total internal storage available to the user" not exceeding 1.1 million bit; and

(E) Not including any of the following:

(1) A central processing unit implemented with more than one microprocessor or microcomputer microcircuit;

....

(2) A microprocessor microcomputer microcircuit with:

(i) A principal operand (data) word length of more than 8 bit; or

(ii) A typical 'speed'-power dissipation product of less than:

(A) 2 microjoules for microprocessor microcircuits; or

(B) 1.2 microjoules for microcomputer microcircuits;

....

(3) Analog-to-digital or digital-to-analog converter microcircuits:

(i) Exceeding the limits of ECCN 1568*(k)*; and

(ii) Not for direct driven video monitors for normal commercial television;

(4) Controlled "related equipment"; or

(5) Equipment controlled by ECCN 1519*(c)* or by ECCN 1567;

(v) Peripheral equipment, as follows, that may contain "embedded" microprocessor microcircuits but lacks "user-accessible programmability":

(A) Card punches and readers;

(B) Paper tape punches and readers;

(C) Manually-operated keyboards and teletype devices;

(D) Manually-operated graphic tablets not having more than 1024 resolvable points along any axis;

(E) Impact printers;

(F) Non-impact printers, not controlled by ECCN 1572*(b)* or *(c)*, that do not exceed:

(1) 2 000 lines per minute; or

(2) 300 characters per second;

(G) Plotting equipment, not controlled by ECCN 1572*(b)* or *(c)*, producing a physical record by ink, photographic, thermal, or electrostatic techniques, that has:

(1) A linear accuracy worse than or equal to ± 0.004 per cent; and

(2) An active plotting area less than or equal to 1 700 mm (66.9 inch) by 1 300 mm (51.2 inch);

(H) Digitizing equipment, generating rectilinear coordinate data by manual or semi-automatic tracing of physical records, that has:

(1) A linear accuracy worse than or equal to ± 0.004 per cent; and

(2) An active digitizing area less than or equal to 1 700 mm (66.9 inch) by 1 300 mm (51.2 inch);

(I) [Reserved];

(J) Optical mark recognition (OMR) equipment;

(K) Optical character recognition (OCR) equipment that:

(1) does not contain "signal processing" or "image enhancement" equipment; and

(2) Is only for:

(i) Stylized OCR characters;

(ii) Other internationally standardized stylized character fonts; or

(iii) Other characters limited to non-stylized or hand printed numerics and up to 10 hand printed alphabetic or other characters;

(L) Cathode-ray tube displays for which circuitry and character-generation devices, external to the tube, limit the capabilities to:

(1) Alpha-numeric characters in fixed formats;

(2) Graphs composed only of the same basic elements as used for alpha-numeric character composition; or

(3) Graphic displays for which the sequence of symbols and basic elements of symbols are fixed;

(M) Cathode-ray tube graphic displays, not containing cathode-ray tubes controlled by ECCN 1541, limited as follows:

(1) The "maximum bit transfer rate" from the electronic computer to the display does not exceed 9 600 bit per second;

....

(2) Not more than 1 024 resolvable elements along any axis; and

(3) Not more than 16 shades of gray or color;

(N) Cathode-ray tube graphic displays, not containing cathode-ray tubes controlled by ECCN 1541, provided that they are:

(1) Part of industrial or medical equipment; and

(2) Not specially designed for use with electronic computers;

(O) Graphic displays specially designed for signature or security checking having an active display area not exceeding 150 sq cm (23.25 sq inch);

(P) Other displays, provided that:

(1) Circuitry and character-generation devices, external to the display device (e.g., panel, tube) and the construction of the display device limit the capability to:

(i) Alpha-numeric characters in fixed formats;

(ii) Graphs composed only of the same basic elements as used for alpha-numeric character composition; or

(iii) Graphic displays for which the sequence of symbols and basic elements of symbols are fixed; and

(2) They are limited to:

(i) A capability for displaying no more than 3 levels (off, intermediate, and full on); and

(ii) A minimum character height of not less than:

(A) 5.5 mm (0.22 inch) if the area is 1 200 sq cm (186 sq inch) or less; or

(B) 20 mm (0.79 inch) if the area is more than 1 200 sq cm (186 sq inch); and

(3) They do not have as an integral part of the display device:

(i) Circuitry; or

(ii) Non-mechanical character-generation devices;

(Q) Light gun devices or other manual graphic input devices that are:

(1) Part of uncontrolled displays; and

(2) Limited to 1 024 resolvable elements along any axis;

(R) Disk drives for non-rigid magnetic media (floppy disks) not exceeding:

(1) A "gross capacity" of 17 million bit;

(2) A "maximum bit transfer rate" of 0.52 million bit per second; or

(3) An "access rate" of 6 accesses per second;

(S) Cassette/cartridge tape drives or magnetic tape drives not exceeding:

(1) A "maximum bit packing density" of 63 bit per mm (1 600 bit per inch) per track;

(2) A "maximum bit transfer rate" of 1.28 million bit per second; or

(3) A maximum tape read/write speed of 254 cm (100 inch) per second; or

(T) Cassette/cartridge tape drives not exceeding:

(1) a "maximum bit packing density" of 107 bit per mm (2 700 bit per inch) per track; or

(2) A "maximum bit transfer rate" of 0.128 million bit per second;

(vi) Input/output interface or control units, as follows, that may contain "embedded" microprocessor microcircuits but lack "user-accessible programmability":

(A) Designed for use with peripheral equipment free from control under sub-paragraph *(h)*(2)*(v)* above; or

(B) Designed for use with digital recording or reproducing equipment specially designed to use magnetic card, tag, label or bank check recording media, free from control according to ECCN 1572*(a)(ii)*;

....

ECCN 1567A Stored program controlled communication switching equipment or systems and technology therefor; and specially designed components therefor for the use of these equipment or systems.

Validated licence required: Country Groups QSTVWYZ

....

List of Stored Program Controlled Communication Switching Equipment or Systems, and Specially Designed Components therefor for the use of these Equipment or Systems Controlled by ECCN 1567A

(a) Communication equipment or systems for "data (message) switching", including those for "local area network" or for "wide area network";

(b) Communication equipment or systems for "stored program controlled circuit switching"; except:

[Equipment described in sub-paragraphs (1), (2) and (3) below is not controlled by this ECCN 1567A, but it may be controlled by ECCN 1565A.]

(1) Key telephone systems that:

(i) Do not provide direct dial access to a group of shared exchange lines or "trunk circuits";

(ii) Are not designed to be upgraded to "private automatic branch exchanges (PABXs)";

(2) "Stored program controlled telegraph circuit switching" equipment or systems that:

(i) Are designed for civil end-use; and

(ii) Provide only the services as defined in CCITT Recommendation F.60 to 79 (Volume II — Fascicle II.4, VII Plenary Assembly, 10-21 November 1980), i.e., the telegraph service whereby subscribers, as defined in CCITT Recommendation X.1 classes 1 and 2 can communicate directly and temporarily between themselves using start-stop telegraph equipment operating:

(A) At 300 baud or less; and

(B) With the international telegraph alphabets No. 2 or 5;

(3) "Stored program controlled telephone circuit switching" equipment or systems, provided that:

(i) The equipment or systems are designed for fixed civil use as "space division analog exchanges" or "time division analog exchanges" which fulfill the definition of "private automatic branch exchanges (PABXs)";

(ii) The equipment or systems do not contain "digital computers" or "related equipment" controlled by:

(A) ECCN 1565*(f)*;

(B) ECCN 1565*(h)*(1)*(i)*(A) to (K) or (M); or

(C) ECCN 1565*(h)*(1)*(ii)*;

(iii) "Communication channels" or "terminal devices" used for administrative and control purposes:

(A) Are fully dedicated to these purposes; and

(B) Do not exceed a "total data signalling rate" of 9 600 bit per second;

(iv) Voice channels are limited to 3.100 Hz as defined in CCITT Recommendation G.151;

(v) The PABXs do not have "trunk circuit"-to-subscriber line ratios that exceed:

(A) 35 per cent for PABXs with fewer than 100 subscriber lines; or

(B) 20 per cent for PABXs with 100 or more subscriber lines;

(vi) The PABXs do not have the following features:

(A) Multi-level call preemption, including overriding or seizing of busy subscriber lines, "trunk circuits" or switches; or

(B) "Common channel signalling";

....

ECCN 1568A Equipment as defined in the List below.
Validated licence required: Country Groups QSTVWYZ

....

List of Equipment Controlled by ECCN 1568A

(b) Synchros and resolvers (and special instruments rated to have the same characteristics as synchros and resolvers in (1) and (2) below, such as Microsyns, Synchro-Tels and Inductosyns), possessing any of the following characteristics:

(1) A rated electrical error of 7 minutes of arc or less or of 0.2 per cent or less of maximum output voltage;

(2) A rated dynamic accuracy for receiver types of 1 ^{o} or less, except that for units of size 30 (3 inches (76.2 mm) in diameter) or larger a rated dynamic accuracy of less than 1 ^{o};

(3) Multi-speed from single shaft types; or

(4) Designed for gimbal mounting;

(c) Amplifiers, electronic or magnetic, specially designed for use with resolvers, of the following description:

(1) Isolation types having a variation of gain constant (linearity of gain) of 0.2 per cent or bett;

(2) Summing types having a variation of gain constant (linearity of gain) or an accuracy of summation of 0.2 per cent or better; or

(3) Employing solid state Hall effect;

(d) Induction potentiometers (including function generators and linear synchros), linear and non-linear, possessing any of the following characteristics:

(1) A rated conformity of 0.25 per cent or less, or of 13 minutes of arc or less;

(2) Employing solid state Hall effect; or

(3) Designed for gimbal mounting;

....

(f) Servo-motors (gear-head or plain) of the following description:

(1) Designed to operate from power sources of more than 300 Hz, except those designed to operate from power sources of over 300 Hz up to and not exceeding 400 Hz with a temperature range of from − 55 ^{o}C to + 125 ^{o}C;

(2) Designed to have a torque-to-inertia ratio of 50 000 radians per second^{2} or greater; or

(3) Incorporating special features to secure internal dampling;

(g) Precision potentiometers, except potentiometers using only switched elements (for the purpose of this paragraph, a precision potentiometer means one having a rated conformity better than 0.25 per cent for a linear potentiometer; or 1 per cent for a non-linear potentiometer), and special instruments rated to have the same characteristics as potentiometers in (1) and (2) below, such as Vernistats, of the following description:

(1) Linear potentiometers having a constant resolution and a rated linearity of better than 0.05 per cent absolute;

(2) Non-linear potentiometers having a variable resolution and a rated conformity of:

(i) 1 per cent or less when the resolution is inferior to that obtained with a linear potentiometer of the same type and of the same track length; or

(ii) 0.5 per cent or less when the resolution is better than or equal to that obtained with a linear potentiometer of the same type and of the same track length; or

(3) Designed for gimbal mounting;

. . . .

(j) Synchronous motors, of the following description:

(1) of size 20 [2 in (50.8 mm) in diameter] and smaller and having synchronous speeds in excess of 3600 rpm;

(2) Designed to operate from power sources of more than 400 Hz;

(k) Analog-to-digital and digital-to-analog converters other than digital voltmeters or counters (see ECCN 1529A), of the following description:

(1) Electrical input type analog-to-digital converters having any of the following characteristics:

(i) A conversion rate of more than 200 000 complete conversions per second at rated accuracy;

(ii) An accuracy in excess of 1 part in more than 10 000 of full scale over the specified operating temperature range;

(iii) A figure of merit of 1×10^8 or more (derived from the number of complete conversions per second divided by the accuracy);

(2) Electrical input type digital-to-analog converters having any of the following characteristics:

(i) A maximum "settling time" of less than 3 microseconds for voltage output devices and less than 250 nanoseconds for current output devices;

(ii) An accuracy in excess of 1 part in more than 10 000 of full scale over the specified operating temperature range;

(iii) A figure of merit greater than 2×10^9 for voltage output converters or $1\text{x}10^{10}$ for current output converters (the figure of merit is defined as the reciprocal of the product of the maximum settling time in seconds and the accuracy);

(3) Solid-state synchro-to-digital or digital-to-synchro converters and resolver-to-digital or digital-to-resolver converter (including multipole resolvers) having a resolution of better than ± 1 part in 5 000 per full synchro revolution for single speed synchro systems or ± 1 part in 40 000 for dual speed systems;

(4) Mechanical input types (including but not limited to shaft-position encoders and linear displacement encoders, but excluding complex servo-follower systems), of the following description:

(i) Rotary types having an accuracy of better than ± 1 part in 40 000 of full scale; or

(ii) Linear displacement types having a resolution better than ± 5 micrometers;

. . . .

(m) Specially designed components and test equipment (including adapters, couplers, etc.) for the above.

. . . .

ECCN 4596B Inverters, converters, frequency changers, and generators having a multiphase electrical power output within the range of 600 to 2 000 hertz.
Validated licence required: Country Groups QSTVWYZ

. . . .

ECCN 1570A Thermoelectric materials and devices.
Validated licence required: Country Groups QSTVWYZ

. . . .

List of Thermoelectric Materials and Devices Controlled by ECCN 1570A

(a) Thermoelectric materials with a maximum product of the figure of merit (Z) and the temperature (T in $^{\circ}$K) in excess of 0.75;

. . . .

(d) Other power generating devices, and specially designed components therefor, that generate in excess of 22 W per kg (10 W per pound) or of 17.70 kW per cubic meter (500 W per cubic foot) of the devices' basic thermoelectric components.

. . . .

ECCN 1584A Cathode-ray oscilloscopes and specially designed components therefor, including associated plug-in units, external amplifiers, pre-amplifiers and sampling devices, as listed in this entry.
Validated licence required: Country Groups QSTVWYZ

. . . .

List of Characteristics of Cathode-ray Oscilloscopes and Specialized Parts therefor Controlled by ECCN 1584A

(a) An amplifier or system bandwidth greater than 250 MHz (defined as the band of frequencies over which the deflection on the cathode-ray tube does not fall below 70.7 per cent of that at maximum point measured with a constant input voltage to the amplifier);

(b) A horizontal sweep faster than 1 nanosecond per cm with an accuracy (linearity) better than 2 per cent;

(c) Containing or designed for use with cathode-ray tubes controlled by ECCN 1541A*(c)*;

(d) Ruggedized to meet a military specification;

(e) Rated for operation over an ambient temperature range of from below − 25 °C to + 55 °C;

(f) Using sampling techniques for the analysis of recurring phenomena that increase the effective bandwidth of an oscilloscope or time-domain reflectometer to a frequency greater than 4 GHz; or

(g) Digital oscilloscopes with sequential sampling of the input signal at an interval of less than 50 nanoseconds.

. . . .

ECCN 1585A Photographic equipment.
Validated licence required: Country Groups QSTVWYZ

. . . .

List of Photographic Equipment Controlled by ECCN 1585A

. . . .

(b) High speed cameras, and specially designed parts and accessories therefor, in which the film does not move, and which are capable of recording at rates exceeding 1 000 000 frames per second for the full framing heights of standard 35 cm wide photographic film, or at proportionately higher rates for lesser frame heights, or at proportionately lower rates for greater frame heights;

(c) Cameras incorporating electron tubes defined in ECCN 1555*(a)*;

(d) Streak cameras having writing speeds of 10 mm/microsecond and above, and specially designed parts and accessories therefor;

(e) Camera shutters with speeds of 50 nanoseconds or less per operation, and specialized parts and accessories therefor;

(f) Film, of the following description:

(1) Having a intensity dynamic range of 1 000 000:1 or more; or

(2) having a speed of ASA 10 000 (or its equivalent) or better;

. . . .

(g) High speed plates having an intensity dynamic range of 1 000 000:1 or more.

ECCN 4585B Photographic equipment
Validated licence required: Country Groups QSTVWYZ

. . . .

List of Photographic Equipment controlled by ECCN 4585B

(a) Streak cameras capable of recording events which are initiated by, or synchronized with, the camera mechanism (i.e., discontinuous access type), having a design capability for writing speeds of 8 mm per microsecond and above and a time resolution of 100 nanoseconds or less, and parts and accessories, n.e.s.;

. . . .

ECCN 5585C Photographic equipment.

Validated licence required: Country Groups QSTVWYZ, Afghanistan and the People's Republic of China

. . . .

List of Photographic Equipment Controlled by ECCN 5585C

(a) Other high-speed continuous writing, rotating drum cameras capable of recording at rates in excess of 2 000 frames per second, and parts and accessories, n.e.s.;

. . . .

ECCN 4592B Equipment for measuring pressures to 100 Torr or less having corrosion-resistant sensing elements of nickel, nickel alloys, phosphor bronze, stainless steel, or aluminium.

Validated licence required: Country Groups QSTVWYZ

. . . .

ECCN 3604A Zirconium metal; alloys containing more than 50 per cent zirconium by weight; compounds in which the ratio of hafnium content to zirconium content is less than one part to five hundred parts by weight; manufactures wholly thereof; and waste and scrap; except zirconium metal and alloy in shipments of 5 kilograms or less; and zirconium in the form of foil or strip having a thickness not exceeding 0.025 mm (0.00095 in) and specially fabricated and intended for use in photo flash bulbs, in shipments of 200 kilograms or less.

. . . .

ECCN 3605A Nickel powder and porous nickel metal.

Validated licence required: Country Groups QSTVWYZ

. . . .

List of Nickel Powder and Porous Nickel Metal Controlled by ECCN 3605A

(a) Powder with a nickel content of 99 per cent or more, and a particle size of less than 100 micrometers; and

(b) Porous metal material with a mean pore size of 25 micrometers or less, and a nickel purity content of 99 per cent or more, except single porous nickel metal sheets not exceeding $930m^2$ (144 square inches) in size, intended for use in batteries for civil applications.

[Paragraph *(b)* above refers to porous nickel metal manufactured from nickel powder defined in paragraph *(a)* above which has been compacted and sintered to form a metal material with five pores interconnected throughout the structure.]

. . . .

ECCN 3607A Lithium.

Validated licence required: Country Groups QSTVWYZ

. . . .

List of Forms of Lithium Controlled by ECCN 3607A

(a) Metal, hydrides, or alloys containing lithium enriched in the 6 isotope to a concentration higher than the one existing in nature (7.5 per cent on an atom percentage basis);

(b) Any other materials containing lithium enriched in the 6 isotope (including compounds, mixtures, and concentrates), except lithium enriched in the 6 isotope incorporated in thermoluminescent dosimeters.

. . . .

ECCN 3608A Hafnium of the following description: metal, and alloys and compounds of hafnium containing more than 60 per cent hafnium by weight, and manufactures thereof, except shipments of the above having a hafnium content of 1 kilogram or less.

Validated licence required: Country Groups QSTVWYZ

. . . .

ECCN 3609A Beryllium.

Validated licence required: Country Groups QSTVWYZ

. . . .

List of forms of Beryllium Controlled by ECCN 3609A

Metal, alloys containing more than 50 per cent of beryllium by weight, compounds containing beryllium, manufactures thereof, and waste and scrap, except metal windows for X-ray machines; oxide shapes in fabricated or semi-fabricated forms specially designed for electronic component parts or as substrates for electronic circuits; shipments of 500 grams or less of beryllium having a purity of 99 per cent or less, or 100 grams or less of beryllium having a purity of greater than 99 per cent, provided that shipments exclude single crystals: and shipments of 5 kilograms or less of beryllium contained in compounds with a purity of less than 99 per cent.

ECCN 4635B Pressure tube, pipe, and fittings therefor, of 8 inches or more inside diameter, having a wall thickness of 8 per cent or more of the inside diameter and made of stainless steel, copper-nickel alloy, or other alloy steel containing 10 per cent or more nickel and/or chromium.

Validated licence required: Country Groups QSTVWYZ

. . . .

ECCN 4638B Calcium containing both less than one tenth per cent (0.01) by weight of impurities other than magnesium and less than 10 parts per million of boron.

Validated licence required: Country Groups QSTVWYZ

. . . .

ECCN 4654B Magnesium containing both less than one fiftieth per cent (0.0002) by weight of impurities other than calcium and less than 10 parts per million of boron.

Validated licence required: Country Groups QSTVWYZ

. . . .

ECCN 4674B Specialized packings made of phosphor bronze mesh designed for use in vacuum distillation towers, suitable for use in separating heavy from light water.

Validated licence required: Country Groups QSTVWYZ

. . . .

ECCN 4675B Cylindrical tubing, raw, semifabricated, or finished forms, made of aluminium alloy (7 000 series) or maraging steel or high-strength titanium alloys (e.g., Ti-6 Al-4 V, etc.).

Validated licence required: Country Groups QSTVWYZ and Canada

. . . .

List of Characteristics of Cylindrical Tubing Controlled by ECCN 4675B

(a) Wall thickness of 0.5 inch, or less;

(b) Diameter of 3 inches or more.

ECCN 4676B Cylindrical rings, or single convolution bellows, made of high-strength steels.

Validated licence required: Country Groups QSTVWYZ and Canada

. . . .

List of Characteristics of Cylindrical Rings of Single Convolution Bellows, Made of High-Strength Steels Controlled by ECCN 4676B

(a) Tensile strength of greater than or equal to 150 000 psi;

(b) Wall thickness of 3 millimeters of less;

(c) Diameter of 3 inches or more.

ECCN 4677B Cylindrical discs, in raw, semifabricated, or finished form.

Validated licence required: Country Groups QSTVWYZ

....

List of Characteristics of Cylindrical Discs, in Raw, Semifabricated, or Finished Form Controlled by ECCN 4677B

(a) Having a 0.5 to 2 inch peripheral lip;

(b) Having a diameter of 3 inches or more;

(c) Made of maraging steel or aluminium alloy (7 000 series).

ECCN 4678B Corrosion resistant sensing elements of nickel, nickel alloys, phosphor bronze, stainless steel, or aluminium specially designed for use with equipment which measures pressures to 100 Torr or less.

Validated licence required: Country Groups QSTVWYZ and Canada

....

ECCN 4698B Depleted uranium (any uranium containing less than 0.711 per cent of the isotope (U-235), the following only: shipments of more than 1 000 kilograms in the form of shielding contained in X-ray units, radiographic exposure or teletherapy devices, radioactive thermoelectric generators, or packaging for the transportation of radioactive materials.

Validated licence required: Country Groups QSTVWYZ and Canada

....

ECCN 3709A Beryllium oxide ceramic and refractory tubes, pipes, crucibles, and other shapes in semi-fabricated or fabricated form, except forms specially designed for electronic component parts or as substrates for electronic circuits.

Validated licence required: Country Groups QSTVWYZ

....

ECCN 3711A Chlorine trifluoride, except shipments of 5 kilograms or less.

Validated licence required: Country Groups QSTVWYZ

....

ECCN 1715A Boron, as described in this entry.

Validated licence required: Country Groups QSTVWYZ

....

List of Boron Controlled by ECCN 1715A

(a) Boron element, boron compounds and mixtures in which the boron 10 isotope comprises more than 20 per cent of the total boron content;

(b) Boron element (metal) all forms; and

(c) Boron compounds, mixtures and composites containing 5 per cent or more of boron, except pharmaceutical specialities packaged for retail sale, as follows:

(1) Non-ceramic boron-mitrogen compounds (e.g., borozanes, borozines and boropyrazoyls);

(2) Boron hydrides (e.g. boranes), except sodium boron hydride, potassium boron hydride, monoborane, diborane and triborane;

(3) Organoboron compounds, including metallo-organoboron compounds.

ECCN 4720B Radioisotopes, cyclotron-produced or naturally occurring, except those having an atomic number 3 through 83, and compounds and preparations thereof.

Validated licence required: Country Groups QSTVWYZ

....

ECCN 1763 "Fibrous and filamentary materials" that may be used in composite structures or laminates, and such composite, structures and laminates.

Validated licence required: Country Groups QSTVWYZ

. . . .

List of Materials Controlled by ECCN 1763A

(a) "Fibrous and filamentary materials" having both of the following characteristics:

(1) "Specific modulus" greater than 3.18×10^6m (1.25×10^8in);

(2) "Specific tensile strength" greater than 7.62×10^4m (3×10^6in);

(b) "Fibrous and filamentary materials" having both of the following characteristics:

(1) "Specific modulus" greater than 2.54×10^6m (1×10^8in);

(2) Melting or sublimation point higher than 1 922 K (1 649 °C) (3 000 °F) in an inert environment, except:

(i) Carbon fibers having a "specific modulus" less than 5.08×10^6m (2×10^8in) and a "specific tensile strength" less than 2.54×10^4m (1×10^6in);

(ii) Multi-phase polycrystalline alumina fibers having a "specific modulus" less than 3.56×10^6m (1.4×10^8in);

(c) Resin-impregnated fibers (pre-pregs) and metal-coated fibers (pre-forms) made with materials covered by paragraphs *(a)* or *(b)* above;

(d) Composite structures, laminates and manufactures thereof made either with an organic matrix or a metal matrix utilizing materials covered by paragraphs *(a)* or *(b)* above.

Annex II

COUNTRY GROUPS LISTED FOR EXPORT CONTROL PURPOSES AT 1ST JANUARY 1987*

Supplement No. 1 — Country Groups

For export control purposes foreign countries are separated into seven country groups designated by the symbols "Q", "S", "T", "V", "W", "Y", and "Z". Listed below are the countries included in each country group. Canada is not included in any country group and will be referred to by name throughout the Export Administration Regulations.

COUNTRY GROUP Q

Romania

COUNTRY GROUP S

Libya

COUNTRY GROUP T

North America

Northern Area:

- Greenland
- Miquelon and St. Pierre Islands

Southern Area:

- Mexico (including Cozumel and Revilla Gigedo Islands)

Central America

- Belize
- Costa Rica
- El Salvador
- Guatemala
- Honduras (including Bahia and Swan Islands)
- Nicaragua
- Panama

Bermuda and Caribbean Area:

- Bahamas
- Barbados
- Bermuda
- Dominican Republic
- French West Indies
- Haiti (including Gonave and Tortuga Islands)
- Jamaica
- Leeward and Windward Islands
- Netherlands Antilles
- Trinidad and Tobago

South America

Northern Area:

- Colombia
- French Guiana (including Inini)
- Guyana
- Surinam
- Venezuela

Western Area:

- Bolivia
- Chile
- Ecuador (including the Galapagos Islands)
- Peru

Eastern Area:

- Argentina
- Brazil
- Falkland Islands (Islas Malvinas)
- Paraguay
- Uruguay

* 15 CFR Ch. III, Part 370

UNITED STATES

COUNTRY GROUP V

All countries not included in any other country group (except Canada).

COUNTRY GROUP W

Hungary
Poland

COUNTRY GROUP Y

Albania
Bulgaria
Czechoslovakia
Estonia
German Democratic Republic (including East Berlin)
Laos
Latvia
Lithuania
Mongolian People's Republic
Union of Soviet Socialist Republics

COUNTRY GROUP Z

North Korea
Vietnam
Cambodia
Cuba

Annex III

LIST OF AGREEMENTS FOR PEACEFUL NUCLEAR CO-OPERATION CONCLUDED BY THE UNITED STATES

Agreement	Date signed	Effective date	Termination date
Argentina	25th June 1969	25th July 1969	24th July 1999
Australia	5th July 1979[1]	16th January 1981	15th January 2011
Austria	11th July 1969	24th January 1970	-
amendment	14th June 1974	8th October 1974	23rd January 2014
Bangladesh	17th September 1981	24th June 1982	23rd June 1992
Brazil	17th July 1972	20th September 1972	19th September 2002
Canada	15th June 1955	21st July 1955	-
amendment	26th June 1956	4th March 1957	-
amendment	11th June 1960	14th July 1960	-
amendment	25th May 1962	12th July 1962	-
amendment	23rd April 1980	9th July 1980	1st January 2000
China, People's Republic of	23rd July 1985	30th December 1985	29th December 2015
Colombia	8th January 1981	7th September 1983	6th September 2013
Egypt	29th June 1981	29th December 1981	28th December 2021
European Atomic Energy Community (EURATOM)	29th May and 18th June 1958	27th August 1958	-
Additional Agreement	11th June 1960[2]	25th July 1960	-
amendment	21st and 22nd May 1962	9th July 1962	-
amendment	22nd and 27th August 1963	15th October 1963	31st December 1995
amendment	20th September 1972	28th February 1973	-
Finland	8th April 1970[3]	7th July 1970	6th July 2000
India	8th August 1963	25th October 1963	24th October 1993
waiver of certain obligations	30th November 1982	30th November 1982	-
Indonesia	30th June 1980	30th December 1981	29th December 1991
International Atomic Energy Agency (IAEA)	11th May 1959	7th August 1959	-
amendment	12th February 1974	31st May 1974	6th August 2014
amendment	14th January 1980	6th May 1980	-
Japan	26th February 1968	10th July 1968	-
amendment	24th February 1972	26th April 1972	-
amendment	28th March 1973	21st December 1973	9th July 2003
Korea	24th November 1972	19th March 1973	-
amendment	15th May 1974	26th June 1974	18th March 2014
Morocco	30th May 1980	16th May 1981	15th May 2001
Norway	12th January 1984	2nd July 1984	1st July 2014
Peru	26th June 1980	15th April 1982	14th April 2002
Philippines	13th June 1968	19th July 1968	18th July 1998
Portugal	16th May 1974	26th June 1974	25th June 2014
South Africa	8th July 1957	22nd August 1957	-
amendment	12th June 1962	23rd August 1962	-
amendment	17th July 1967	17th August 1967	-
amendment	22nd May 1974	28th June 1974	21st August 2007
Spain	20th March 1974	28th June 1974	27th June 2014
Sweden	19th December 1983	11th April 1984	10th April 2014
Switzerland	30th December 1965	8th August 1966	7th August 1996
amendment	2nd November 1973	29th January 1974	-
Taiwan	4th April 1972	22nd June 1972	-
amendment	15th March 1974	14th June 1974	21st June 2014
Thailand	14th May 1974	27th June 1974	26th June 2014

1. An agreement on the application of this Agreement was signed with Australia on 2nd August 1985.
2. The Agreement incorporates by reference certain provisions of the expired "Joint Programme" Agreement, signed 8th November 1958.
3. A new Agreement with Finland was signed on 2nd May 1985.

SOME OTHER NEA LEGAL PUBLICATIONS

QUELQUES AUTRES PUBLICATIONS JURIDIQUES DE L'AEN

NEA Statute

Free on request

Nuclear Law Bulletin

(Annual Subscription – two issues and supplements)

ISSN 0304-341-X

Index of the forty five issues of the Nuclear Law Bulletin (included in subscription)

£17.60 US$33.00

Licensing Systems and Inspection of Nuclear Installations (1986)

ISBN 92-64-12776-3

£12.00 US$24.00

Long-term Management of Radioactive Waste – *Legal, Administrative and Financial Aspects (1984)*

ISBN 92-64-12622-8

£7.00 US$14.00

Nuclear Legislation, Analytical Study:
Regulatory and Institutional Framework for Nuclear Activities
Vol. I (1983)
Austria, Belgium, Canada, Denmark, France, Federal Republic of Germany, Greece, Iceland, Ireland, Italy, Japan, Luxembourg, Netherlands

ISBN 92-64-12534-5

£12.50 US$25.00

Vol. II (1984)

New Zealand, Norway, Portugal, Spain, Sweden, Switzerland, Turkey, United Kingdom, United States

ISBN 92-64-12602-3

£15.00 US$30.00

Nuclear Third Party Liability and Insurance – *Status and Prospects* (Proceedings of the Munich Symposium, 1984)

Statuts de l'AEN

Gratuit sur demande

Bulletin de Droit Nucléaire

(Abonnement annuel – deux numéros et suppléments)

ISSN 0304-3428

Index des quarante cinq premiers numéros du Bulletin de Droit Nucléaire (compris dans l'abonnement)

F150,00 DM65.00

Régime d'autorisation et d'inspection des installations nucléaires (1986)

ISBN 92-64-22776-8

F120,00 DM53

Gestion à long terme des déchets radioactifs – *Aspects juridiques, administratifs et financiers (1984)*

ISBN 92-64-22622-2

F70,00 DM31.00

Législations nucléaires, étude analytique :
Réglementation générale et cadre institutionnel des activités nucléaires
Vol. I (1983)
Autriche, Belgique, Canada, Danemark, France, République fédérale d'Allemagne, Grèce, Islande, Irlande, Italie, Japon, Luxembourg, Pays-Bas

ISBN 92-64-22534-X

F125,00 DM56.00

Vol. II (1984)

Nouvelle-Zélande, Norvège, Portugal, Espagne, Suède, Suisse, Turquie, Royaume-Uni, États-Unis

ISBN 92-64-22602-8

F150,00 DM67.00

La responsabilité civile nucléaire et l'assurance – *Bilans et perspectives* (Compte rendu du Symposium de Munich, 1984)

ISBN 92-64-02665-7

£18.00 US$36.00 F180,00 DM80.00

WHERE TO OBTAIN OECD PUBLICATIONS
OÙ OBTENIR LES PUBLICATIONS DE L'OCDE

ARGENTINA - ARGENTINE
Carlos Hirsch S.R.L.,
Florida 165, 4° Piso,
(Galeria Guemes) 1333 Buenos Aires
Tel. 33.1787.2391 y 30.7122

AUSTRALIA - AUSTRALIE
D.A. Book (Aust.) Pty. Ltd.
11-13 Station Street (P.O. Box 163)
Mitcham, Vic. 3132 Tel. (03) 873 4411

AUSTRIA - AUTRICHE
OECD Publications and Information Centre,
4 Simrockstrasse,
5300 Bonn (Germany) Tel. (0228) 21.60.45
Gerold & Co., Graben 31, Wien 1 Tel. 52.22.35

BELGIUM - BELGIQUE
Jean de Lannoy,
Avenue du Roi 202
B-1060 Bruxelles Tel. (02) 538.51.69

CANADA
Renouf Publishing Company Ltd/
Éditions Renouf Ltée,
1294 Algoma Road, Ottawa, Ont. K1B 3W8
Tel: (613) 741-4333
Toll Free/Sans Frais:
Ontario, Quebec, Maritimes:
1-800-267-1805
Western Canada, Newfoundland:
1-800-267-1826
Stores/Magasins:
61 rue Sparks St., Ottawa, Ont. K1P 5A6
Tel: (613) 238-8985
211 rue Yonge St., Toronto, Ont. M5B 1M4
Tel: (416) 363-3171
Federal Publications Inc.,
301-303 King St. W.,
Toronto, Ont. M5V 1J5
Tel. (416)581-1552
Les Éditions la Liberté inc.,
3020 Chemin Sainte-Foy,
Sainte-Foy, P.Q. GIX 3V6,
Tel. (418)658-3763

DENMARK - DANEMARK
Munksgaard Export and Subscription Service
35, Nørre Søgade, DK-1370 København K
Tel. +45.1.12.85.70

FINLAND - FINLANDE
Akateeminen Kirjakauppa,
Keskuskatu 1, 00100 Helsinki 10 Tel. 0.12141

FRANCE
OCDE/OECD
Mail Orders/Commandes par correspondance :
2, rue André-Pascal,
75775 Paris Cedex 16
Tel. (1) 45.24.82.00
Bookshop/Librairie : 33, rue Octave-Feuillet
75016 Paris
Tel. (1) 45.24.81.67 or/ou (1) 45.24.81.81
Librairie de l'Université,
12*a*, rue Nazareth,
13602 Aix-en-Provence Tel. 42.26.18.08

GERMANY - ALLEMAGNE
OECD Publications and Information Centre,
4 Simrockstrasse,
5300 Bonn Tel. (0228) 21.60.45

GREECE - GRÈCE
Librairie Kauffmann,
28, rue du Stade, 105 64 Athens Tel. 322.21.60

HONG KONG
Government Information Services,
Publications (Sales) Office,
Information Services Department
No. 1, Battery Path, Central

ICELAND - ISLANDE
Snæbjörn Jónsson & Co., h.f.,
Hafnarstræti 4 & 9,
P.O.B. 1131 – Reykjavik
Tel. 13133/14281/11936

INDIA - INDE
Oxford Book and Stationery Co.,
Scindia House, New Delhi 110001
Tel. 331.5896/5308
17 Park St., Calcutta 700016 Tel. 240832

INDONESIA - INDONÉSIE
Pdii-Lipi, P.O. Box 3065/JKT.Jakarta
Tel. 583467

IRELAND - IRLANDE
TDC Publishers - Library Suppliers,
12 North Frederick Street, Dublin 1
Tel. 744835-749677

ITALY - ITALIE
Libreria Commissionaria Sansoni,
Via Lamarmora 45, 50121 Firenze
Tel. 579751/584468
Via Bartolini 29, 20155 Milano Tel. 365083
La diffusione delle pubblicazioni OCSE viene assicurata dalle principali librerie ed anche da :
Editrice e Libreria Herder,
Piazza Montecitorio 120, 00186 Roma
Tel. 6794628
Libreria Hœpli,
Via Hœpli 5, 20121 Milano Tel. 865446
Libreria Scientifica
Dott. Lucio de Biasio "Aeiou"
Via Meravigli 16, 20123 Milano Tel. 807679

JAPAN - JAPON
OECD Publications and Information Centre,
Landic Akasaka Bldg., 2-3-4 Akasaka,
Minato-ku, Tokyo 107 Tel. 586.2016

KOREA - CORÉE
Kyobo Book Centre Co. Ltd.
P.O.Box: Kwang Hwa Moon 1658,
Seoul Tel. (REP) 730.78.91

LEBANON - LIBAN
Documenta Scientifica/Redico,
Edison Building, Bliss St.,
P.O.B. 5641, Beirut Tel. 354429-344425

MALAYSIA/SINGAPORE - MALAISIE/SINGAPOUR
University of Malaya Co-operative Bookshop Ltd.,
7 Lrg 51A/227A, Petaling Jaya
Malaysia Tel. 7565000/7565425
Information Publications Pte Ltd
Pei-Fu Industrial Building,
24 New Industrial Road No. 02-06
Singapore 1953 Tel. 2831786, 2831798

NETHERLANDS - PAYS-BAS
SDU Uitgeverij
Christoffel Plantijnstraat 2
Postbus 20014
2500 EA's-Gravenhage Tel. 070-789911
Voor bestellingen: Tel. 070-789880

NEW ZEALAND - NOUVELLE-ZÉLANDE
Government Printing Office Bookshops:
Auckland: Retail Bookshop, 25 Rutland Stseet,
Mail Orders, 85 Beach Road
Private Bag C.P.O.
Hamilton: Retail: Ward Street,
Mail Orders, P.O. Box 857
Wellington: Retail, Mulgrave Street, (Head Office)
Cubacade World Trade Centre,
Mail Orders, Private Bag
Christchurch: Retail, 159 Hereford Street,
Mail Orders, Private Bag
Dunedin: Retail, Princes Street,
Mail Orders, P.O. Box 1104

NORWAY - NORVÈGE
Narvesen Info Center – NIC,
Bertrand Narvesens vei 2,
P.O.B. 6125 Etterstad, 0602 Oslo 6
Tel. (02) 67.83.10, (02) 68.40.20

PAKISTAN
Mirza Book Agency
65 Shahrah Quaid-E-Azam, Lahore 3 Tel. 66839

PHILIPPINES
I.J. Sagun Enterprises, Inc.
P.O. Box 4322 CPO Manila
Tel. 695-1946, 922-9495

PORTUGAL
Livraria Portugal,
Rua do Carmo 70-74,
1117 Lisboa Codex Tel. 360582/3

SINGAPORE/MALAYSIA - SINGAPOUR/MALAISIE
See "Malaysia/Singapor". Voir «Malaisie/Singapour»

SPAIN - ESPAGNE
Mundi-Prensa Libros, S.A.,
Castelló 37, Apartado 1223, Madrid-28001
Tel. 431.33.99
Libreria Bosch, Ronda Universidad 11,
Barcelona 7 Tel. 317.53.08/317.53.58

SWEDEN - SUÈDE
AB CE Fritzes Kungl. Hovbokhandel,
Box 16356, S 103 27 STH,
Regeringsgatan 12,
DS Stockholm Tel. (08) 23.89.00
Subscription Agency/Abonnements:
Wennergren-Williams AB,
Box 30004, S104 25 Stockholm Tel. (08)54.12.00

SWITZERLAND - SUISSE
OECD Publications and Information Centre,
4 Simrockstrasse,
5300 Bonn (Germany) Tel. (0228) 21.60.45
Librairie Payot,
6 rue Grenus, 1211 Genève 11
Tel. (022) 31.89.50
United Nations Bookshop/Librairie des Nations-Unies
Palais des Nations,
1211 – Geneva 10
Tel. 022-34-60-11 (ext. 48 72)

TAIWAN - FORMOSE
Good Faith Worldwide Int'l Co., Ltd.
9th floor, No. 118, Sec.2
Chung Hsiao E. Road
Taipei Tel. 391.7396/391.7397

THAILAND - THAILANDE
Suksit Siam Co., Ltd., 1715 Rama IV Rd.,
Samyam Bangkok 5 Tel. 2511630
INDEX Book Promotion & Service Ltd.
59/6 Soi Lang Suan, Ploenchit Road
Patjumamwan, Bangkok 10500
Tel. 250-1919, 252-1066

TURKEY - TURQUIE
Kültur Yayinlari Is-Türk Ltd. Sti.
Atatürk Bulvari No: 191/Kat. 21
Kavaklidere/Ankara Tel. 25.07.60
Dolmabahce Cad. No: 29
Besiktas/Istanbul Tel. 160.71.88

UNITED KINGDOM - ROYAUME-UNI
H.M. Stationery Office,
Postal orders only: (01)211-5656
P.O.B. 276, London SW8 5DT
Telephone orders: (01) 622.3316, or
Personal callers:
49 High Holborn, London WC1V 6HB
Branches at: Belfast, Birmingham,
Bristol, Edinburgh, Manchester

UNITED STATES - ÉTATS-UNIS
OECD Publications and Information Centre,
2001 L Street, N.W., Suite 700,
Washington, D.C. 20036 - 4095
Tel. (202) 785.6323

VENEZUELA
Libreria del Este,
Avda F. Miranda 52, Aptdo. 60337,
Edificio Galipan, Caracas 106
Tel. 951.17.05/951.23.07/951.12.97

YUGOSLAVIA - YOUGOSLAVIE
Jugoslovenska Knjiga, Knez Mihajlova 2,
P.O.B. 36, Beograd Tel. 621.992

Orders and inquiries from countries where Distributors have not yet been appointed should be sent to:
OECD, Publications Service, 2, rue André-Pascal, 75775 PARIS CEDEX 16.

Les commandes provenant de pays où l'OCDE n'a pas encore désigné de distributeur doivent être adressées à :
OCDE, Service des Publications. 2, rue André-Pascal, 75775 PARIS CEDEX 16.

71784-07-1988

OECD PUBLICATIONS, 2, rue André-Pascal, 75775 PARIS CEDEX 16 - No. 44175 1988
PRINTED IN FRANCE
(66 88 07 1) ISBN 92-64-13121-3